Early Modern
autobiography

Early Modern
autobiography

Theories, Genres, Practices

Ronald Bedford,
Lloyd Davis, &
Philippa Kelly, Editors

The University of Michigan Press   *Ann Arbor*

A CIP catalog record for this book is available from the British Library.

Library of Congress Cataloging-in-Publication Data

Early modern autobiography : theories, genres, practices / Ronald
Bedford, Lloyd Davis, and Philippa Kelly, editors.
            p.   cm.
ISBN-13: 978-0-472-09928-3 (cloth : alk. paper)
ISBN-10: 0-472-09928-0 (cloth : alk. paper)
ISBN-13: 978-0-472-06928-6 (pbk. : alk. paper)
ISBN-10: 0-472-06928-4 (pbk. : alk. paper)   1. Autobiography.
I. Bedford, Ronald, 1959-   II. Davis, Lloyd, 1959–2005   III. Kelly, Philippa.
CT25.E27   2006
920—dc22   2006001570

*T*his volume is dedicated to the memory of Lloyd Davis, who died of a brain tumor on 7 August 2005, aged 46. We will miss him more than we can say.

Acknowledgments

✳

This volume of essays emerged from "The Theory and Practice of Early Modern Autobiography," a colloquium held at the Humanities Research Centre in Canberra, Australia, in December 2002. Our thanks to the Humanities Research Centre for its welcome and for the use of its wonderful conference facility. Special thanks are also due to the Australian Research Council for the generous ARC Large grant awarded to us at the end of 1998 and to our universities—the University of New England, the University of Queensland, and the University of New South Wales—for helping in all sorts of ways to facilitate our activities. And, of course, neither the colloquium, nor the book could have eventuated at all were it not for our speakers and authors, with all of whom it has been an honor to work. Chris Collins and Chris Hebert of the University of Michigan Press have assisted us with quiet efficiency, and for this we are most appreciative. Our thanks to Anna Bemrose and the MAC Store in Berkeley, California for their valuable assistance, and to the Frick Collection, the Kunsthistorisches Museum, and the British Library for use of their images. Finally, we are grateful for the enabling power of a friendship that has lasted between the three of us for many years now. Through it we have learned to be more curious, more critical, and more generous in our scholarly endeavors than we might have been alone, while its delights and consolations have helped enrich our lives.

Contents

✱

Introduction

Philippa Kelly, Lloyd Davis, and Ronald Bedford

> There is no description so hard, nor so profitable, as is the
> description of a man's own life. Yet must a man handsomely
> trimme-up, yea and dispose and range himselfe, to appeare on the
> Theatre of this World. Now I continually tricke up my selfe; for I
> uncessantly describe my selfe.
>
> (Montaigne, "Of Exercise or Practice," Montaigne's Essays,
> trans. John Florio, 3 vols. London: Dent, 1965, vol. 2, 49–61 p. 59.)

*W*hat are the moments that successfully "describe my selfe"? Are
they the stylized moments of self-revelation—those in which, as Montaigne puts it, one "trimmes" oneself with an eye to public appearance—or the myriad of modest repetitive actions that fall outside the
realm of careful disposition? This question goes to the heart of current
debate about literature and autobiography. It addresses the contentious issues of what is meant by early modern English autobiography; what is meant, essentially and socially, by the notion of "selfhood,"[1] how autobiography was written, and whose writings can be
deemed appropriately self-representational. Many scholars are now
skeptical of finding the key to expressions of selfhood in the list of
hugely worked-over plays and occasional writings that have been
marked as literary treasures, but this skepticism should be tempered
by an acknowledgment of the highly structured society in which carefully "trimmed-up" writings were taken as the template for many more
harried, and perhaps necessarily less contemplative, people—people
who did not have the luxury of time and means afforded to scholars
such as Montaigne—to use as guides for living their lives.

The collection *Early Modern Autobiography* does not set up an exclu-
sive focus on the literature of the sixteenth and seventeenth centuries.
Beginning as early as the fifteenth century, it brings together
researchers from a number of disciplines—literary studies, women's

studies, history, and politics—in order to examine the practice of auto-biographical writing and self-representation. In drawing this histori-cal arc, the volume rejects a critical tradition that insists on the six-teenth century as a discrete thrust forward in self-understanding; it develops new readings of significant autobiographical works while also suggesting the importance of many texts and contexts that have rarely been analyzed in detail. These moves enable us to explore devel-opments across a range of life-writing genres, reflecting on, and chal-lenging, many prevailing notions about what it means to write autobi-ographically and about the development of self-representation. The collection recognizes the continuities and changes between modes of autobiographical authorship, as well as acknowledging the relation-ships among different autobiographical forms and genres.

Throughout its three sections, the collection is premised on the belief that early modern writing displays a constant interplay between two poles: the grand ideals of selfhood (immortality, stability, pres-ence), and the everyday terrain of passing observations, travels, daily records, household expenditures, pleasures, and the like. Moreover, the incessant pressure of spiritual beliefs on secular life means that access to "real" selves is granted not through one pole (the spiritual) or the other (the secular and everyday) but rather through a complex per-sonal, spiritual, and social interweaving of these perspectives. To take what now seems a somewhat amusing example, excess consumption of plums may merit the recording of both physical and moral intemper-ance, as the clergyman Samuel Ward suggests in his diary entry for 18 June 1596.

> also think how intemperate thow was in eating so many plums before supper, and think how thow mightest have prevented ytt if thow hadst gone out of the orchard when thow mett Mr. Newhouse, and learn to avoid even the occasions of sin . . . (Ward and Rogers 113)

More than a gastronomic oversight, a stomachache can signal the weakness of the flesh and the sin of greed. Ward's scruples remind us that approaching autobiographical writing from the sixteenth and sev-enteenth centuries means understanding "selfhood" as a fascinating composite, shifting between the spiritual and the mundane, the stage script and the scrap of paper, the pressure of "immortal longings" and the secular concerns of everyday endurance. *Early Modern Autobiogra-phy* aims to convey the density of such experiences, describing the autobiographical "I" as a nexus of spiritual and secular understandings that inflected the most ordinary activities and experiences.

This complex melding of self-experience speaks also to the canonical heritage of works from the late medieval and early modern periods—including, for example, Chaucer, Montaigne, Shakespeare, Browne, and Milton. These writers' finely crafted puns, wordplay, and philosophical speculations might at first glance appear commensurate with a division between the elegant robes of display (rhetorical and philosophical) and the unvarnished realities of everyday life. Such a distinction between surface and truth is more in keeping, however, with the cultural formations of modernity than with those of the late medieval and early modern periods. The "real" self was not displaced by the intricate formulations of language to be found in poems, plays and narratives: far from it. These kinds of rhetorical "show"—such as Shakespeare telling the time, "When I do count the clock that tells the time / And see the brave day sunk in hideous night" (Sonnet 12), or a John Ford character invited to look in a mirror, "If you would see a beauty more exact / Than art can counterfeit or nature frame, / Look in your glass, and there behold your own" (Ford 1.2.205–7)—served to bring identity into perspective. They functioned as ornate, accepted forms of personal and social speculation in a society that rarely encouraged such suppositions within commonplace daily circumstances. And in more workaday writings—running diaries, household records and the like—moments of self-speculation often emerge seemingly out of nowhere, indicating not so much an idiosyncratic moment of perception as a deeply ingrained awareness of the individual as a part of a greater schema: "This weeke the Lord was good to mee and mine," observes Ralph Josselin, as is his habit when in receipt of good fortune, "in our peace, plenty, continuance of our health, and in restoring us to it in some measures, in food, raiment, in all outward mercyes, in inward peace, in preservacon from grosse sins . . ." (24). Such observations betray an instinctive acknowledgment of what Basil Willey once called the "simultaneously available" worlds between which people could move quite naturally (42). Philip Henry affords another example when Roger Puleston, who was under his charge at Oxford, "assaulted me in wrath, whereby my unruly passions being stir'd I strook againe and hurt his face, against the command of our Lord Jesus, which requires the turning of the other cheek" (18). The biblical precept represents the cheek as an overarching spiritual emblem, so that, while the diary note records a bad-tempered incident, it also strives to make penance before God. What such structuring does—whether the unreflective diary entry against day and month and year or the organization of a life in relation to, perhaps in subservience to, a larger moral "plot"—is to confirm and acquiesce in a sense of the fundamental importance of spiritual order and structure and the ordinariness, the un-uniqueness, of every individual. Everyone marks time to the clock and calendar; everyone processes, with varying degrees of success or dignity, toward death and divine judgment, and everyone is constantly reminded that, while temporal sensations pass and eternity is what remains, the most ordinary temporal experiences can affect one's standing in the eyes of a constantly vigilant Maker.

It is necessary, therefore, that we read these texts in ways that are cognizant of their times, understanding that formality of style does not necessarily mean impersonality, and, moreover, that impersonality does not mean lack of personhood. We need also to read in terms of the huge differences in communication modes and practices between then and now. News and information were conveyed at a very different tempo, which affected the reception and representation of life-changing events. A striking example is afforded by Elias Ashmole, who makes the retrospective diary notation: "*Dec. 5.* My dear wife fell suddenly sicke about evening, and died. . . ." The next entry, on 14 December, marks Ashmole's journey toward Cheshire, where he lived with his wife. An entry for 16 December remarks, "Arriving at Lichfield, I first heard of my wife's death" (Ashmole 18). In his comments on the event, Ashmole soberly praises his wife's goodness and humility, also finding an opportunity to mention his own virtues. Given the number of deaths constantly befalling families and acquaintances (indeed, throughout the course of his diary Ashmole enthusiastically monitors each minute detail of his own health and treatments), a spouse's demise, no matter how unfortunate, is never beyond one's expectation. The sense of detachment that pervades his diary note is granted not only by this condition but also by the fact that he finds out about her death a full eleven days after its occurrence. Given that time lag, how should he record the immediacy of an event that is over before he can experience it? In assessing Ashmole's diary as "self-writing," then, judgments cannot be usefully applied without an understanding of the contextual boundaries of a historical life.

In any age, autobiographical writing is generally triggered by an event, or an experience, that provokes self-reflection, and the events and experiences are as diverse as the circumstances in which each writer lives. Thomas Whythorne is moved to self-scrutiny by his birthday: "considering with myself that I was now above thirty years of age and growing toward the age of forty, at the which years begins the first part of the old man's age, I took occasion to write thereof this sonnet following . . ." The ensuing sonnet follows a conventional "ages of man" format.

> The force of youth is well nigh past,
> Where heat and strength of late took place,
> And now is coming in all haste
> The cold, weak age for to deface
>   The show of youth . . .
>
>   (115)

As he approaches his sixth climacteric, or seven-year span in the nine that were understood to be a person's expected allowance, the reflection of time's scythe appears to have prompted Whythorne to speculate about himself and his place in the world, in which his over-whelming consciousness is of an ever-advancing, never-returning "progress" through successive individual moments of decay and loss. It is a familiar topos from the period, but, as many of the essays included here show, a wide range of situations and events could prompt people to explore their lives and identities in writing. Isabella Whitney is provoked to write poems about London as a relief from her immersion within the overdetermined roles of maidservant and prospective wife, allowing her tentatively to adopt the typically mas-culine position of social critic. Thomas Hoccleve's autobiographical *Complaint* is inspired by a moment of extreme cultural dislocation: finding himself dislodged from his public office and persona through a mental breakdown, Hoccleve discovers that these roles no longer exist: "For3eten I was, al oute of mynde, a wey, / As he that deed was from hertis cherte." Christopher Love, the author of over fifty tracts against Cromwell, tries to beat back the sense of a newly conferred identity as he awaits death in prison. Proclaiming himself innocent, he aims to restore his reputation by repeatedly asking the "Reader to take notice" of his detailed description of his trial. Conversion narratives, like William Langland's, mark a point if not of epiphany then certainly of turning or departure for the self: it is time, in Langland's view, to "bigynne a tyme / That alle tymes of my tyme to profit shal turne." Other autobiographical texts, like Anne Clifford's, stage and record complicated legal battles for claiming rightful inheritance and there-after the management of property and estate.

While these triggers to self-representation were as varied as the circumstances in which people found themselves, our collection finds striking points of confluence in the social and hierarchical structures within which they were understood and expressed. In all of the instances of life writing we provide, individual experiences are defined by a strong sense of social expectation and obligation. Such definition is rarely (as it is today) in the service of revealing one's own, or another's, psychology or of setting out to explore one's unique individuality; indeed, the texts in question are often underwritten by a patchwork of formalized spiritual and secular commonplaces that remark on the *un*-uniqueness of the individual's sensation or experience. But in appreciating what such social understandings *mean* to the subject who observes them and who feels, however obliquely, their coalescing or competing pressures, we can glean some comprehension of the "auto"—its limits and the sensibilities with which it is loaded— in the early modern sense of *autobiography*. And such broader considerations thus frame all of the following questions. Who is this person? What motivates her or him to set pen to paper? Who constitutes the intended readership? What can this document tell us about how the subject conceived of, and expressed, a sense of personhood?

Lloyd Davis begins the book's opening section with a discussion of contemporary debates about the kinds of critical perspectives that have been applied to the study of autobiography as a genre—for example, Schlegel's skepticism, Sturrock's insistence on the autobiographer's will to unify the narrative subject, Eakin's plea for pluralism in the description of autobiography as a composite of many stories. Such debates involve, among other things, questions of canonicity and genre, as well as a recognition of the impact of ways of reading on the understanding of autobiographical texts. In this way, many of the issues in the study of autobiography enable us to question critical and cultural values, expectations, and constraints.

The majority of chapters in our collection focus on specific texts and authors. When read in concert, however, the essays integrate analysis of various texts with critical reflection on relevant cultural and historical contexts and on the theory and practice of life writing and its effects and purposes. This comprehensive approach enables us to address issues concerning the nature and function(s) of autobiographical writing that are raised in the specific details of each text. In "Specifying the Subject in Early Modern Autobiography," the second essay in part 1, Conal Condren instances writers such as Montaigne, Hobbes, and Locke to describe the highly social nature of early modern self-construction, as well as its impact on autobiographical categories and codes. Condren suggests that in the very act of analyzing autobiography, contemporary scholars are tempted to insinuate modern sensibilities into the figurative play that marks early modern texts. In these terms, autobiographical theory might more usefully represent the imposition of perceptual categories than any of the writers' intentions or dispositions.

Perceptual categories are also the subject of Ronald Bedford's essay, "On Being a Person: Elizabethan Acting and the Art of Self-Representation." Bedford asks the question: if early modern audiences saw actors onstage as offering recognizable versions of themselves—however exaggerated—what might such recognition tell us about early modern notions of identity and selfhood? Ideas about, and vocabulary to describe, personhood and its relationship to acting or other forms of representation in the early modern period were largely derived from various theories of *mimesis*, from God's multiple personhood, from debates about Christ's real or symbolic presence in the Eucharist, and from the concept of *theatrum mundi*. Like his counterparts in the theater of life, the actor received a part that was his to imitate or "play." Despite elaborate debates about the nature and functions of this display, the actor's job is generally understood by modern theater critics as that of impersonating the character "to the life," and Bedford discusses the implications of this formulation for our understanding of theatrical records and their relationship to self-representation. For example, whose sense of "to the life" is meant here—our post-Stanislavsky, postmodern sense or one that is immanent to early modern culture?

In "Dialogues of Self-Reflection: Early Modern Mirrors," Philippa Kelly continues this investigation into modes and theories of display. In the early modern period, the complex realm of individuality was importantly linked to images of reflection that were developed from a burgeoning industry in glass mirror making. Kelly suggests that, while it is tempting to regard the mirror as a Burkhardtian emblem of premodern self-consciousness, this view does not exhaust all aspects of the debate about who or what the self was. Social self-production was certainly served by the mirror; yet the issues of what such self-production involved, and what it aimed for, remain contentious. Kelly explores mirrors and their social meanings and, more specifically, the capacity of mirrors in language to help shape certain concepts and practices of self-representation.

Part 2 of the collection, "Life Genres," applies the critical issues raised in the preceding section to a wide range of late medieval and early modern life writing. It begins with "Thomas Hoccleve's Selves Apart," Anne M. Scott's analysis of various approaches to Hoccleve as an autobiographical poet. Some critical perspectives have tended to privilege the generic effects of irony and trope, while others turn to Hoccleve's self-writing as a revelatory form of self-expression. Scott draws on this variety of critical responses to suggest that Hoccleve's poetry—stylized, figurative, and highly conscious of the social connotations of "individuality"—can serve both kinds of critical approach. She posits, for example, *The Regement of Princes* as a political statement and a careful act of social self-positioning. And in discussing Hoccleve's period of insanity she addresses medieval attitudes toward mental "wandringes," which were considered acts of moral and social aberration, reducing man to the status of beast. Yet it is within and through Hoccleve's awareness of his own social self-positioning that he speaks to the subject of autobiography, and it is how, many centuries later, readers strive to define and understand it.

Peter Goodall's essay, "The Author in the Study: Self-Representation as Reader and Writer in the Medieval and Early Modern Periods," relates medieval ideas of "writing" a self to developments in autobiographical topoi in the sixteenth century. Goodall examines a shift in understanding of the relationship between the acts of reading a book and addressing the self. Saint Augustine is in Goodall's view the seminal figure here, but there are other major medieval authors, such as Petrarch, who self-consciously scrutinize the writing and reading of the self. This tendency to self-scrutiny gains cultural and material impetus in the emergence of the study in the fifteenth and sixteenth centuries as a physical place where, for the first time, secular people could read, write, and introspect in relative peace. In tracing this development, at once architectural, literary and personal, Goodall makes something of an ironic preparation for Dosia Reichardt's essay on another kind of secluded place for writing in seventeenth-century England. In "The Constitution of Narrative Identity in Seventeenth-Century Prison Writing," Reichardt discusses the various motivations for writing one's story in prison, not the least of which is the wish to construct a narrative identity by rewriting the verdict that led to incarceration. It may appear somewhat odd that prisons seemed, if not to welcome these accounts, at least to allow for them, since the wealthy and literate were permitted to bring in an unlimited supply of pen and paper. The availability of writing materials suggests that self-writing may have been allowed as a form of tolerated rebellion within an environment where not only inmates, but also their jailers, were often all too aware of the veracity of pleas of innocence.

The essays contributed by Goodall and Reichardt demonstrate that modes of autobiographical representation are sharply influenced by the physical locations in which self-writing can occur. In "Selves in Strange Lands: Autobiography and Exile in the Mid–Seventeenth Century," Helen Wilcox develops this viewpoint by examining the profound physical and psychological associations of exile for early modern people. Noting that the verb "to exile" had by the early sixteenth century come to mean "to ruin or devastate," Wilcox contends that "the experience of exile can signify constancy and integrity and lead to a surprising 'blossom' of unknown yet positive potential." The English Revolution made exile a prevalent condition for many seventeenth-century English people, and Wilcox explores the relationship between these conditions and the flourishing of life writing in the period.

Belinda Tiffen, in "The Visual Autobiographic: Van Dyck's Portrait of Sir John Suckling," notes that critical readings of Suckling's verse have often assumed a strongly autobiographical element in his writing. The few known facts of Suckling's life—such as his disastrous participation in the Bishops' Wars—seem to present an appealing complement to his literary self-presentation as the cavalier par excellence: witty, urbane, and elegant but politically and artistically disengaged from serious matters. At first viewing, Van Dyck's famous portrait of Suckling may seem to echo in paint the self-image (as elegant indifferent) that the poet created of himself in his verse. Yet a closer reading of the portrait reveals both an encoded political comment and a concern with literary seriousness that is unexpected from the figure Suckling presented in his best-known verse. There is enough evidence of Van Dyck's career in England to suggest that his portraits were often directed by his sitters: Suckling may have chosen this portrait as an autobiographical undertone that paradoxically challenges the self-image he fostered in other contexts.

Part 2 of the collection concludes with R. S. White's essay, "Where Is Shakespeare's Autobiography?" which speculates on what happens when people from later periods seek to "write" an early modern autobiography. White begins by suggesting that Shakespeare's omission of an autobiography has proven apposite because scholars have been trying to write his biography ever since he died. Their more or less successful efforts suggest that autobiography and "authorized" biography confront similar dilemmas of self-representation, including memorial and authorial vagaries. These problems are particularly potent in the area of Shakespearean biography. White considers four different biographical records of Shakespeare's life: the "soul biographies" of Dowden, Boas, and Barber; the unashamedly fictional (Burgess, *Shakespeare in Love*); the "documentary" (Schoenbaum, Honigmann); and the iconoclastic (Duncan-Jones). He contends that these different modes pose different challenges to what it means to record a life: first, in the claim to objective analysis implicit in the task of "biography"; second, in the fragments of Shakespeare's life gleaned from his texts under the heading "autobiographical"; and, third, in the authors' obvious need to fill in Shakespeare's famous blank spaces with their own autobiographically oriented perspectives. By drawing on these challenges, White proposes a composite (auto)biographical mode whereby a "life through works" might make use of Shakespeare's plays as primary documents. In this way, the absence of Shakespeare's autobiography provides an occasion to rethink the limits of autobiographical discourse and the strategies of self-representation through which early modern identity can be portrayed in its own time and for later periods.

Whereas the essays in the second section of the volume share a preoccupation with the representational modes through which lives can be portrayed—modes that manipulate public and private spaces, for example, or strenuously juggle perceptual possibilities in the act of self-reflection—the essays in part 3, "Self Practices," examine texts produced for a more workaday purpose (Fulton, Wright); for a more workaday context (Howard); or, as we shall see with the marginalia described by Semler and Mitchell, with an eye to a "running commentary" that provides an overarching, informal mode of dialogue on texts produced for the public record. The pressure of finance defines the strategies through which the authors in this section perceive and depict their lives, building an "I" that self-consciously sees itself as a part of, and a development from, its surroundings. But, while all the authors share a lens that is provided by the worlds of work, survival, and social interaction, they display widely varying conceptions of what such a lens might do or mean.

The section begins with Helen Fulton's "Autobiography and the Discourse of Urban Subjectivity: The Paston Letters." Of the Paston letters, Fulton asks: who is the epistolary self? The letters can be read autobiographically, as the record of a gentry family based in London and Norfolk, yet they also construct subjects of numerous discourses, particularly that of urban materialism. The growing economic power of towns and cities in the late fifteenth and early sixteenth centuries shaped new kinds of subjects, in literary texts as well as in other kinds of writing. Whereas the characters of courtly lyric and romance were broadly categorized according to social standing and moral worth, the individuals of urban writing required the more finely tuned classifications of status, occupation, and material display that marked urban society out from the older, land-based feudalism. In the same way, the identity of the author was redefined in an urban context, constructing an autobiographical self described in terms of the city. Fulton examines the Paston Letters from the point of view of self-construction, self-allegorization, and the expression of an identifiably urban subjectivity. She argues that the letters are "autobiographical" in the sense that they convey an authentic account of subjectivity in the context of medieval and early modern views of selfhood (both Christian and feudal) and the urbanized location in which the letters were generated.

The impact of urban contexts on early modern identity and self-representation is, in a different and more self-conscious way, the subject of Jean E. Howard's essay, "Textualizing an Urban Life: The Case of Isabella Whitney." As Amy Erickson and Martha Howell have shown, last wills and testaments were notable among the documents over which women exercised some control in the early modern period. In their bequests, women sometimes disposed of land, goods, and movables and often bequeathed to kinswomen and friends items with sentimental or emotional value. These documents also provide evidence—highly mediated to be sure—of the lives of their makers. In her essay, Howard considers the poetry of Isabella Whitney, especially her witty and acerbic *Will and Testament*, to the city of London, as a form of life writing through which the writer fashioned a self in print. Though the "facts" of her life are obscure, in her verse Whitney constructs a complex subject position between the coordinates of woman, servant, writer, jilted lover, and urban dweller. Of particular interest is the way she fashions a self in relation to the cityscape, incorporating the complexity of cultural and economic realities that characterize England's capital city. In writing her poetic will, and in making London the executor and beneficiary of her largesse, Whitney uses her pen to narrate a life imagined in terms of the peculiar rigors and freedoms available to an impecunious, but talented, woman of the metropolis.

The analysis of the material circumstances of gender and social context in Fulton's and Howard's essays complements the analysis of Anne Clifford's financial records and obligations provided by Nancy E.

Wright in "Accounting for a Life: The Household Accounts of Lady Anne Clifford." Wright contends that Clifford's diaries carefully build her identity in terms of possible legal challenges to her right to own property and land. Nevertheless Clifford's diaries, letters, and *Life of Me* have often been read as if they were transparent documents in the life of a woman whose consuming passion was to fulfil the duties of her office as heiress in general and landowner, as her female ancestors had done. In order to appreciate Clifford's complex understanding of the duties of the landowner's office, however, we need to evaluate various other writings that record her life. Her estate and household accounts provide an alternative means of reading the records that she collected and produced. Before and during Clifford's lifetime, it was customary for landowners to supervise closely their income and expenditures. Her estate and household record not only her commitment to accumulating the archival records that would substantiate her claim to the Clifford lands but also to accounting for the profits of those lands. The financial records—particularly Clifford's *Books of Household Expenses*, which contain entries and marginal comments in her own hand—provide a means of understanding the many registers and forms in which "a self" and "a life" can be recorded in writing.

In her essay on Clifford, Wright suggests that we might look to margins as a significant textual space in which early modern selfhood is inscribed. Liam E. Semler develops this perception in "Designs on the Self: Inigo Jones, Marginal Writing, and Renaissance Self-Assembly." As we now know him, Inigo Jones is a literary production. In fact, England's first Renaissance neoclassical architect was, Semler suggests, born of marginal annotation. Although Jones wrote almost nothing for print, he was a relentless writer of a particular sort: very few of the books from his personal library escape his marginal annotation, and it is in the privacy of his marginalia that Jones formulates a specific public future for himself. In a script that self-consciously progresses from secretary to gentlemanly italic, and in the margins of works by great Italian writers on art, Jones engages in a strenuous and goal-oriented program of self-education. The marginal notes reveal Jones overwriting a past self that is incoherent and inadequate compared to the lofty office of architect that he is determined to embody. His marginalia are crucial to both plotting out this desired office and bridging the gap between his current self and the publicly authoritative self he intends to become. He graphically embodies the office of architect (adopting its knowledges and behaviors), inserting himself into its generic responsibilities, obligations, and privileges. Having modeled the paradigm in his margins, he inhabits it mentally and socially and then concretizes this office within the existing English office of surveyor, which must expand to accommodate these new dimensions. The figure we now call Inigo Jones is an astonishingly successful example of self-assemblage via the power of books, reading, and, more particularly, directed marginal annotation.

Annotations can also inscribe a self-narrative that complements and sometimes corrects the body proper of an autobiographical text. Adrian Mitchell, in "William Dampier's Unaccepted Life," explores this kind of tension between juxtaposed strains of life writing. The draft copy of Dampier's *New Voyage Round the World* (eventually published in 1697) incorporates a series of running annotations in the author's own hand. What the manuscript provides is evidence of incremental layers of composition. Dampier's annotations are, interestingly, made heavily in the first person—in effect an incipient autobiography largely repressed in the published version of the *Voyage*. This commentary forms something of an intermittent, companion autobiographical narrative to the account of Dampier's travels in the manuscript and published versions of the *Voyage*; it also acts as a virtual apologia for the buccaneering life that is celebrated in the published version. One way to read Dampier's suppressed "life" might be as rogue (auto)biography, which underwrites the buccaneer adventure. Dampier presents himself in this commentary as an informed, and often challengingly opinionated, participating witness rather than the simple prototype of the new scientific traveler. The running marginal annotations to the draft for the *Voyage* are much more specific about events and personalities, more precise about such matters as slavery, and more technical about the ethos of privateering than the narrative itself. Why the liveliness of Dampier's life is suppressed in print is open to question. It is possible that he was aiming for respectability or that his publisher, Knapton, pressed for changes to, and suppression of, the public record of a controversial personal life.

As Semler's and Mitchell's essays suggest, autobiographical texts often orchestrate ongoing dialogues among an author's different roles and personae. Such dialogues can also be interestingly established between various versions of a particular professional identity. Wilfrid Prest concludes part 3 with "Legal Autobiography in Early Modern England," which examines this phenomenon. Prest discusses various examples of autobiographical writing by English common lawyers of the sixteenth to the eighteenth centuries, from John Savile through James Whitelocke to Roger North and William Blackstone. The chapter makes special reference to the themes of vocational and personal identity: how does a particular professional world establish the terms by which its practitioners might understand their personal and professional lives? Despite a considerable burgeoning of legal-historical studies since the 1970s, the law courts, together with the litigants and practitioners who used them more intensively than ever before or since in English history, remain largely neglected. While the memoirs of common lawyers and law students can be analyzed to illuminate the working conditions, mind-set, and private and domestic lives of the English bar through the seventeenth century, they can also be read as cultural artifacts in their own right. Beginning with an overview of late-sixteenth- and seventeenth-century legal autobiography, Prest moves on to consider William Blackstone's unusual self-life, which in some respects represents a revival of what had once been a flourishing subgenre of early modern life writing.

What is the meaning of a life? In terms of present-day preoccupations with unique existential being, this question is the prerogative—and its exploration the challenge—of every individual (to the extent that it has become somewhat ludicrous, anticipating everywhere grand moments of personal crisis or epiphany). For people in early modern England, however, the question of life's meaning was quite different, both in its manifestation and in the conclusions it provoked. Whereas today such meaning—and the reasons to describe it—involve conjectures about the psychology of oneself or one's associates, early modern society was structured around a network of beliefs pertaining to the events of the temporal realm and their impact on the other eternal realm that superseded it. This did not mean that temporal events did not matter. On the contrary, Lady Clifford's acquisition of her lands, Isabella Whitney's response to London, Blackstone's legal diary, or Hoccleve's distress about losing his worldly status, for example, mattered intensely. These events mattered not simply in themselves but *because* they contributed to the sum of a life, acting always, and sometimes inscrutably, as the measure of participation in an ongoing history of entitlement to a part in a greater life to come. Self-description, therefore, referred to understandings of oneself *within* a wider frame, and more often than not individuality was marked less by how one stood *out* than by how effectively one fitted *in*.

    We began this introduction by considering a "selfe" from long ago, a "selfe" that its bearer, Montaigne, acknowledges not always to be carefully "disposed and ranged." Montaigne's "selfe," and those of the many early modern subjects depicted in this collection, bear witness to the relationship—not always fully apparent nor the same in every act of contemplation—between the mundane and the monumental, the routine and the exemplary, the material and the eternal. Their depiction also reflects the special preoccupations of the contributors to this volume, which grant purpose and focus to historical analysis, determining not just *what* we observe but how, and why, we choose subjects for discussion. The contributors to *Early Modern Autobiography* have a variety of aptitudes, interests, and critical frameworks, each one carefully calibrated in the act of contemplating the subject(s) we depict. And we use our understandings to provide illustrative contexts for appreciating the pressures people felt, the ambitions they entertained, and the meaning of such pressures and ambitions for the ways in which they reflected on, and talked about, themselves. Authorial apologetics, memoirs, epistolary collections, theatrical performances, diaries, marginalia, prison narratives, household account books and legal notebooks, these are the diverse and unpredictable modes and voices to which we listen. And in listening to these voices, as critics and as readers, we must attend also to ourselves: our task is not only to observe "who" these people were but how they are mediated through the prism of historical perspectives.

NOTES

1. Idealist, essentialist positions on subjectivity have jostled in recent decades with the various historicist and cultural materialist positions—the critiques of humanist "Renaissance" models offered by Dollimore, Goldberg, Neely, Greenblatt, or Gramsci—which connote the subject as a flexibly fashioned, or determined, cultural construct. Idealist and essentialist positions, deriving from a posited Renaissance model of individualized freedom and human autonomy and its *locus*, especially in texts such as Pico's *Oration on the Dignity of Man*, would include most notably Jacob Burkhardt, *The Civilization of the Renaissance in Italy*, trans. S. C. G. Middlemore, 2 vols. (New York: Harper and Row, 1958), esp. pt. 2, "The Development of the Individual"; and Ernst Cassirer's introduction to *The Renaissance Philosophy of Man*, ed. Ernst Cassirer, Paul Oskar Kristeller, and John Herman Randall Jr. (Chicago: University of Chicago Press, 1948), 16–20. Historicist critiques of "essentialist humanism" are illustrated inter alia in Stephen Greenblatt, *Renaissance Self-Fashioning: From More to Shakespeare* (Chicago: University of Chicago Press, 1981); Coppélia Kahn, *Man's Estate: Masculine Identity in Shakespeare* (Berkeley: University of California Press, 1981); Jonathan Goldberg, "The Politics of Renaissance Literature: A Review Essay," *English Literary History* 49 (1982): 514–42; Jonathan Dollimore, *Radical Tragedy: Religion, Ideology, and Power in the Drama of Shakespeare and His Contemporaries* (Chicago: University of Chicago Press, 1984); Antonio Gramsci, *Selections from Cultural Writings*, ed. David Forgacs and Geoffrey Nowell-Smith (Cambridge MA: Harvard Uni-

versity Press, 1985), q. 17, para.1; and Carol Thomas Neely, "Constructing the Subject: Feminist Practice and the New Renaissance Discourses," *English Literary Renaissance* 18 (1988): 5–18.

WORKS CITED

Ashmole, Elias. *Elias Ashmole (1617–1692): His Autobiographical and Historical Notes, His Correspondences, and Other Contemporary Sources Relating to His Life and Work.* Ed. C. H. Josten. Oxford: Clarendon, 1966.

Burgess, Anthony. *Nothing like the Sun: A Story of Shakespeare's Love Life.* London: Heinemann, 1972.

Burkhardt, Jacob. *The Civilization of the Renaissance in Italy.* 2 vols. Trans. S. C. G. Middlemore. New York: Harper and Row, 1958, especially Part 2, "The Development of the Individual."

Cassirer's, Ernst. Introduction to *The Renaissance Philosophy of Man.* Ed. Ernst Cassirer, Paul Oskar Kristeller, and John Herman Randall Jr. Chicago: U of Chicago P, 1948. 16–20.

Dollimore, Jonathan. *Radical Tragedy: Religion, Ideology and Power in the Drama of Shakespeare and his Contemporaries.* Chicago: U of Chicago P, 1984.

Ford, John. *'Tis Pity She's a Whore.* Ed. Derek Roper. London: Methuen, 1975.

Goldberg, Jonathan. "The Politics of Renaissance Literature: A Review Essay." *English Literary History* 49 (1982). 514–42.

Gramsci, Antonio. *Selections from Cultural Writings.* Ed. David Forgacs and Geoffrey Nowell-Smith. Cambridge, Mass.: Harvard UP, 1985. Q.17, para. 1.

Greenblatt, Stephen. *Renaissance Self-Fashioning: From More to Shakespeare.* Chicago: U of Chicago P, 1981.

Henry, Matthew. *An Account of the Life and Death of Mr. Philip Henry, Minister of the Gospel at Broad-Oak, Near Whitchurch, in Shropshire.* London: Salop, 1765.

Honigmann, E. A. J. *Myriad-Minded Shakespeare.* Basingstoke: Macmillan, 1989.

Josselin, Ralph. *The Diary of Ralph Josselin, 1616–1683.* Ed. Alan Macfarlane. London: Oxford UP for the British Academy, 1976.

Kahn, Coppélia. *Man's Estate: Masculine Identity in Shakespeare.* Berkeley: U of California P, 1981.

Montaigne, Michel de. *Essays.* Trans. John Florio. 3 vols. London: Everyman, 1966.

Neely, Carol Thomas. "Constructing the Subject: Faminist Practice and the New Renaissance Discourses." *English Literary Renaissance* 18 (1988). 5–18.

Schoenbaum, Samuel. *Shakespeare's Lives.* New ed. Oxford: Clarendon, 1991.

Shakespeare, William. *The Riverside Shakespeare.* Ed. G. Blakemore Evans. Boston: Houghton Mifflin, 1974.

Ward, Samuel, and Richard Rogers. *Two Elizabethan Puritan Diaries by Richard Rogers and Samuel Ward.* Ed. M. M. Knappen. Gloucester, MA: Peter Smith, 1966.

Whythorne, Thomas. *The Autobiography of Thomas Whythorne.* Ed. James M. Osborne. London: Clarendon, 1961.

Willey, Basil. *The Seventeenth Century Background.* New York: Columbia UP, 1958.

PART I

Self Theories

✻

Chapter 1

Critical Debates and Early Modern Autobiography

Lloyd Davis

Writing one hundred years ago, the German scholar George Misch reiterated three positive conceptions of autobiography that prevailed in the late eighteenth century when the term first appeared in German and English sources: it held a documentary value for presenting information about people and the world, it revealed important details about people's daily lives, and it offered amusement and instruction (Misch 1.1). Misch's summary captures the major ideas about autobiographical writing that had developed from the classical to the neoclassical period and remained influential into the modern era. As on many issues, Dr. Johnson's opinions are representative and informative: he, too, emphasized autobiography's great didactic value for readers, a position that many mid-twentieth-century critics continued to endorse (see Folkenflik, Introduction 8; cf. Morris 8; Olney vii). The lasting appeal and significance of autobiographical writing were seen by some to exemplify human resilience and triumph. Misch approvingly notes the beliefs of Herder and Goethe, who commended the development of autobiography as part of "the great process of the liberation of human personality" (1.2).

As might be expected, not all Enlightenment figures respond to autobiographical writing with the same enthusiasm. Writing in 1798, Friederich Schlegel condemned it; if nothing else, his position shows that autobiography has often provoked conflicting critical responses.

> Pure autobiographies are written either by neurotics who are fascinated by their own ego, as in Rousseau's case; or by authors of a

robust artistic or adventuresome self-love, Benvenuto Cellini; or by born historians who regard themselves only as material for historic art; or by women who also coquette with posterity; or by pedantic minds who want to bring even the most minute things in order before they die and cannot let themselves leave the world without commentaries. [They] can also be regarded as mere *plaidoyers* [legal pleadings] before the public. Another great group among the autobiographers is formed by the autopseusts [the self-deceivers]. (qtd. Folkenflik, Introduction 3)

There is more to Schlegel's position than a satirical bent against the self-absorption of some writers. The polemical tone can best be read as clearing the way for the celebration of authentic identity and character in the dramatic and poetic work that Schlegel and his brother Augustus promoted, particularly in Shakespeare, whose appeal for them was both universal and profoundly Germanic (Habicht 7). As Augustus puts it, not in indulgent life writing but in the depths of Shakespearean character are the truths of human nature and identity to be found: "a man acts so because he is so. And what each man is, that Shakespeare reveals to us most immediately" (Schlegel 362). At the same time, it is notable that Schlegel's attack on autobiography does not undermine the importance of the didactic and personal values affirmed by proponents of the genre. His point is not that those values are lacking or unimportant but that they are presented excessively and indulgently in self-referential works. Hence it seems that by the beginning of the nineteenth century both admirers and critics regarded the importance of autobiography as its capacity to relate individual personality and conduct to social events and circumstances and then to offer guidance and understanding about these relationships to a contemporary reading public.

Schlegel's skepticism about autobiography stands out amid much critical discussion. Just as the majority of autobiographies are "success stories" of one sort or another (Folkenflik, "Self" 224), so most commentators prize autobiographical writing as ethically and stylistically significant, though not always emphasizing its direct didactic advantage. Endorsement is offered from all kinds of critical and ideological positions. Whether it "celebrates the autonomous individual and the universalizing life story" (Smith and Watson, *Reading* 3), or "serves a larger purpose of valorizing the lives of ordinary, often marginalized subjects" (Smith and Watson, *Reading* 161), autobiography is consistently conceived of as in some way edifying. What Schlegel's disapproval does illuminate, however, is the potential for critical conflict over how that edification might be constructed and received and hence the different modes and media involved in writing and reading it. Smith and Watson distinguish two broadly oppositional critical and ideological perspectives, one of which esteems canonical texts and humanist interpretation and the other of which questions the influential cultural and personal models offered by canonical texts. This second perspective maintains the importance of projecting what were "formerly unspeakable stories" into public discourse in print as well as electronic and digital media (cf. Smith and Watson, *Getting* 15). While both of these positions might be informed by a shared regard for the value of autobiography, they manifest themselves through debates that range across a wide range of critical contexts concerning what kinds of texts best illustrate the virtues of life writing.

The tone used in 1993 by John Sturrock to underscore a proper scholarly focus on canonical texts measures the critical heat that can develop around the nature and value of various kinds of autobiographical representation. Sturrock contends that works such as the *Confessions*, the *Discourse on Method*, or Newman's *Apologia pro Vita Sua* are generically and culturally central because of "their quality" and not as a result of "the coercive impulses of the canon-makers" (19). This notion of quality is interestingly hybrid; it synthesizes what could be called *life value*, the ethical determination with which dilemmas are confronted and goals achieved, with *textual value*, the clarity and earnestness with which those events are represented. Perhaps more importantly in this context, a term such as *quality* also conceals its critical premise—it elides the complicated long-term cultural and generic practices through which certain texts are reproduced as culturally central, inscribing the insight of a handful of exceptional individuals. A corollary of this move is that social-historical factors related to the texts and their ongoing reception are excluded from the interpretive framework. In this approach, regardless of the era in which it was written, each autobiography becomes available for a close formal reading that produces expertly partial interpretations.

The debate over what should comprise the autobiographical canon and its subsidiary questions—how canonical value should be defined, which texts are culturally valuable, and why—does not have to be as oppositional as Sturrock would have it. Recently, Paul John Eakin has tried to move the debate away from restrictively oppositional terms (terms that Smith and Watson, as well as Sturrock, appear to assume) by noting that "there are many stories of self to tell, and more than one self to tell them" (Eakin i). Unfortunately, conceding multiplicity cannot in itself always resolve critical differences. Where some commentators suggest that "autobiography wills the unity of its subject" (Sturrock 5), others affirm that life writing represents the subject in history and culture and actually calls into question an emphasis on individuality or autonomous selfhood. Still others propose audience positioning as the key effect of life writing, shifting critical focus to the genre's "public interpretive uses, as part of a general and perpetual conversation about life possibilities" (Bruner 41; I return to this point later in the chapter). The debates resemble those undertaken in many other fields of literary and cultural studies—raising questions of canonicity and genre (and their implications for cultural politics and history) and of subjection and subjectivity in their metaphysical, gendered, classed, racial, and ethnic dimensions. In short, many of the issues in autobiography studies have significant interpretive and critical implications, placing under scrutiny, in Regenia Gagnier's words, "the systems of values, expectations, and constraints that come into play when one represents oneself to others in the concrete circumstances of daily life" (3). Repeatedly, it is specific ways of valuing those systems and circumstances and the ways of representing them that are being approved or questioned in critical and theoretical debates in autobiography studies.

An examination of these debates provides an important step in trying to develop and practice interpretations of autobiographical writing in all historical periods and social settings. My particular interest here lies in considering how changing and contending critical conceptions of autobiography and self-representation might assist us in understanding early modern modes of life writing. Autobiography tends to be conceived in terms that suggest some kind of faithful identity, as in Misch's influential conception of "the description (*graphia*) of an individual human life (*bios*) by the individual himself (*auto*)" (1.5). The revisionary French critic Philippe Lejeune proposes a related idea of self-authenticity: "Retrospective prose narration written by a real person concerning his own existence, where the focus is his individual life, in particular the story of his personality" (Lejeune 5).[1] Given these definitions and their dependence on quite specific notions of selfhood, individuality, and personality, how might we best try to deal with early modern works that may neither adhere to nor react against such notions but instead conceive and practice self-representation in quite different historical, cultural, and textual terms?

The challenge of talking about these ideas is often acknowledged in early modern studies. In part it arises from the problem of trying *not* to stereotype sixteenth- and seventeenth-century self-fashioning. Even some of the most insightful and important writers on selfhood can scarcely avoid doing so, especially if they are mainly concentrating on describing later forms and issues for identity, choosing to present early modern texts as influential "prequels." It is always difficult to focus on two or more different periods; the demands of explaining one tend to limit the way the other is represented. Practically, it can be tempting to generalize about sixteenth- and seventeenth-century experience for the sake of contrasting modernity, a step that medievalists sometimes discern in early modern studies (cf. Aers). An illustrative case can be considered in Charles Taylor's widely cited *Sources of the Self.* It is, in fact, on account of the importance of Taylor's work that his handling of early modern life writing is representative and consequential. Taylor argues for the necessity of conceiving and acting on self-identity as always "oriented in moral space" (28), "in a space of concerns" for oneself and others (51). Only through doing so, he contends, is it possible to respond to and work through a modern sense of identity's lack of meaning or direction. The relevance of Taylor's position to autobiographical studies is suggested by Janet Varner Gunn's view that "the real question of the autobiographical self . . . becomes *where do I belong*? not, who am I? The question of the self's identity becomes a question of the self's location in a world" (23). The chief critical gain from this spatial conception of autobiographical selfhood, especially when granted an ethical orientation, is that it subordinates reliance on a sense of intrinsic identity to an emphasis on the settings in which the self participates. The focus here is necessarily on the subject's exchanges and interactions with others.

This kind of shift in perspective necessarily means that a "thick" contextual grasp is all the more important. Without detailed reflection on social, cultural, and historical factors—the scrutiny that all the essays in this collection attempt in their analysis of autobiographical discourse—people's orientations and encounters within early modern moral space can only be generally described. How does Taylor handle this consideration? In setting up his analysis of the complexity of moral space in a contemporary world, Taylor draws a typical contrast with the earlier period: "For someone in Luther's age, the issue of the basic moral frame orienting one's action could *only* be put in universal terms. Nothing else made sense" (28). The observation has rhetorical impact, yet the Reformation surely represents a series of events and changes in which religious and moral universals were being searchingly revised if not overthrown. The impacts on self-orientation, meaning, and action are difficult to overestimate. Taylor's assertion is effective in terms of a larger historical narrative, but even if we were to grant the point at a general level, the Reformation has to be seen as a set of debates and actions through which "universal terms" were being disputed and relativized.

The difficulties that surround Taylor's remark illuminate a key issue for autobiography studies in the context of particular periods, none more so than the early modern. Understandings of ethical identity cannot be separated from a complex, often contradictory and discontinuous social history. Yet any analysis of identity in "transhistorical" terms—and all readings of autobiographical texts are to some degree transhistorical—runs a risk of blurring local and particular details of self-experience in the attempt to construct a wider narrative about selfhood. A narrative so developed may remain suggestive for historically focused studies and include particular cases that illustrate important concepts and practices. For example, Taylor's critique of Descartes and Locke is extremely pertinent in recognizing shifts in seventeenth-century conceptions of self-identity. He underscores the "violence" Cartesianism does "to our ordinary, embodied way of experiencing" (146), through instigating "an inwardness of self-sufficiency" (158). He also critically assesses "Locke's aspiration to a disengaged subject of rational control" (49), wherein self-consciousness, in which, Locke claims, "alone consists personal identity" (Locke 67), is set up as a morally neutral process, without any "mode of self-concern" (Taylor 49). Much of the individualist cultural and ideological program that developed through the seventeenth century and beyond is intimated in these observations. What makes them critically effective is their textual and contextual relevance. In contrast, Taylor's broader argument and the comparisons through which it is in part formulated can risk homogenizing historical and cultural details, especially for periods that have not fostered or inculcated those forms of ethical directionlessness symptomatic of modernity.

A similar set of effects can arise in comparative sociological studies. The persuasiveness of a larger argument is offset by the elision of period-specific concerns. Though the analysis is worded very carefully, sociologist Anthony Giddens makes a number of wide-ranging observations about premodern contexts in his important study of modernity and identity: "Whether in situations of work, leisure or the family, an individual usually lived within a set of milieux of a comparable type—a phenomenon strongly reinforced by the dominance of the local community. . . . The settings of modern social life are much more diverse and segmented" (83). This single strand of Giddens's larger argument maintains that a strongly grounded social system had the effect of stabilizing self-conception: "In most pre-modern contexts, the fragmentation of experience was not a prime source of anxiety. Trust relations were localised and formed through personal ties" (189). Of course, the meaning and practice of "personal ties" in the early modern period cannot be simply intuited, given the complex relationships between public and private domains that are explored elsewhere in this collection (such as Conal Condren's discussion in chap. 2 of the changing personae of office and Nancy E. Wright's analysis in chap.13 of the tensions within Anne Clifford's personal, familial, social, legal and administrative maneuvers). Further, the annual movement of people in service, the impact of land enclosure and the population drift toward cities, and the increasingly multifaceted modes of urban, gendered, and exiled identity—which in different ways Helen Wilcox (chap. 8), Helen Fulton (chap. 11), and Jean E. Howard (chap. 12) each analyze in their chapters on early modern sub-jectivity—all combined to subject local milieus and trust relations to ongoing change and disruption. Indeed, Giddens concedes that "Sub-mission to traditional authorities, no matter how deep, did not remove uncertainty from day-to-day life in traditional cultures" (195). Many early modern scholars would add to this proviso that assuming "deep" submission is itself contentious: cultural history and poetics are both expanding the archival sources through which early modern social and power relations can be studied and elaborating increasingly sophisti-cated models of how those relations operated. Such developments bear directly on the ways in which identity and self-representation can be conceived in autobiographical texts from the period.

Hence, in their complex analysis of ethical and sociological prac-tices of identity, Taylor and Giddens provide double-edged under-standings of Renaissance life writing. The larger kinds of conceptual insights they offer regarding the social-historical trajectory of identity and self-representation must be complemented by historical scrutiny that carefully weighs received views of personal and social relations within the early modern period and in relation to ensuing eras. More-over, the terms of critical discussion about these topics have to be used cautiously: *selves*, *lives*, *relationships*, and *society* all have continuing significance in both everyday and specialized discourses. There is always a risk of anachronistic slippage or a confusion of meaning in the movement between colloquial and disciplinary usage. Many of the writers whose essays are collected here do consider, as a deliberate first step, not so much whether but in what ways it is possible to talk about selves, identities, and so on without confusing early modern, modern, and postmodern senses of these terms. This caution, which shadows all historically oriented research and analysis, should ultimately not be regarded as inhibiting. The recurrence of key concepts in autobiography studies intimates their continued importance for authors, readers, and critics. If we do not assume that early modern terms such as *self* or *identity* equate immediately to later usages (the meanings of which are also variable and dependent on context), then the conceptual dialogue across different periods can be regarded as productive and informative. Such terms inscribe "recurrences which would not efface the singularity or the idiom of each text" (Derrida 84), while also disclosing processes of continuity, discontinuity, and change in understandings of selfhood and self-representation. The continuous debate about self-representation within and across periods remains one of the intriguing features that motivate the study and analysis of autobiographical writing. Perhaps it comes closest to illuminating the paradoxical discursive condition that Derrida proposes, "of an autobiography whose signature is entrusted to the other" (51). For, given its particular interest in how self-representation will be received, an autobiographical work addresses more keenly than those of many other genres the unknown others, its readers, and must wait on them to assign meaning and value to the self or selves who are its author(s) and subject(s).

In a recent essay, Debora Shuger addresses a number of these concerns by contesting insinuations of psychological depth or interpellated false consciousness in early modern life writers.[2] Her aim is to question the applicability of post-Renaissance cultural and psychological theory to interpreting the earlier texts. The complications in making connections and adapting explanatory models from modern disciplines to premodern texts and contexts are again at issue. Initially, some of the main features of Shuger's position can be observed by comparing her argument with that made by Stephen Greenblatt in his well-known essay, "Psychoanalysis and Renaissance Culture." Here Greenblatt sought, by reasserting a chronological relationship, to rethink the influence of psychoanalytic notions of identity on interpreting early modern culture and texts: "psychoanalysis is the historical outcome of certain Renaissance strategies" (224). He implies that psychoanalytical readings effect a narrowing of early modern conceptions of identity from a range of social relations to psychic experience.

Such readings are inevitably incomplete, though the historical connection that he asserts between early modern and modern notions of identity grants them a degree of insight into the workings of these texts and the figures they represent. In contrast, Shuger challenges the utter relevance of psychoanalytic interpretation to seventeenth-century life writings. The latter "seem particularly resistant," she argues, "to even vaguely Freudian analyses . . . [and] on the rare occasions when these texts avert to what we could consider 'private' matters, the intimate revelations turn out to be 'public' signifiers. . . . These texts do not explore the subconscious underpinnings of identity" ("Life-Writing" 63–64). Instead, she proposes that analytical models deriving from seventeenth-century discussions of selfhood offer a more appropriate interpretive basis for responding to the texts. She maintains that Locke's "identification of self-hood with the conscious subject of moral judgment (rather than the subconscious subject of psychological analysis) approximates that [which is] implicit in most seventeenth-century life-writings" (64). If the period's politically and religiously oriented life writings disclose internalized versions of public moral frameworks, then, Shuger argues, attempts at deep analysis of individual subjectivity adopt an interpretive framework that effaces or eschews important ethical concerns. Her essay warrants close attention, for it illustrates a number of key critical practices and complications in studying Renaissance life writing.

What is appealing and informative about Shuger's approach is the attempt to apply early modern modes of thinking about the self to the analysis of autobiographical writing. There are, however, some potential limits to the way in which it is handled. First, by locating Locke's position as a crucial reference point for authors, Shuger effaces much of the contemporary controversy around the philosopher's implicit argument that there was no substantive self: "What was disturbing to readers of Locke," Felicity Nussbaum explains, "was the possibility that the self may be *only* consciousness, discontinuous in time and identity" (41). In light of the mixed contemporary reaction to Locke's thesis—the kind of response that we would expect a paradigm-shifting philosophical work to elicit—it is appropriate to interpret autobiographical texts less as adhering or conforming entirely to prevailing "philosophical and religious discourses of the self" than as negotiating, or responding to, the contradictory perspectives about selfhood that these discourses juxtapose (cf. Nussbaum 57). The point is not that seventeenth-century debate over Locke's theories means that psychoanalytic readings of autobiographical works suddenly become appro-

priate; rather, neither Locke's ideas nor those of any other author can
be instated as a single paradigm that is reproduced unequivocally (or
approximately) by autobiographical works.

A second issue that problematizes a historicist approach to autobiographical writing derives less from earlier debate over contextual and
intertextual material than from subsequent responses that might complicate the significance of that material. An endorsement of Lockean
ethics as culturally characteristic can restrict the way in which later
critiques—the sort that Taylor makes, for example, as cited earlier—
can help to reconsider the reception of Locke's position, its connection
to life writing in the period, and the range of issues that autobiographical texts are addressing. In this case, Taylor's questions about the
moral value of Locke's thesis complicate its relation to models of selfhood that other authors might have sought to represent. Taylor's
assessment could be regarded as continuing the conflicting responses
to Locke's work that, as Nussbaum notes, arose at the time of and after
its publication. In methodological terms, his critique also reminds us
that no one context or intertext, notwithstanding historical prominence, can immediately determine interpretation. Such a text, action,
or set of conditions is subject to as wide a range of response as are the
autobiographical works it supposedly informs. Authors in its time and
later readers will react to its influence, and to the surrounding social
dialogue, in diverse and possibly unpredictable ways.

Perceptions and conceptions of an earlier period and society are
inevitably partial—not all features or circumstances can be incorpo-
rated into a single historical interpretation. Analysis is informed by
some principle or effect of selection. In autobiographical studies selectivity often comes into play in terms of the kinds of personae, events,
and life stories on which a critic focuses. Interpretive patterns are sub-
stantially affected by these choices, as are the kinds of conclusions
about life writing that can be drawn. What might appear as a general
feature of life writing could be specific to the subgenre that is being
investigated. In her recent essay, Shuger's focus is on two specific
kinds of autobiographical text—devotional and public-political—and
her examples are written mostly by men. These types of texts are
important forms of life writing in the period, but they are, of course,
not the only kind. They do not constitute "early modern autobiography." Different types of life writing from the period—as analyzed
across the chapters in parts 2 and 3 of this collection—introduce a varied, complicated range of motives, ethics, subject positions, and questions of desire and identity. The urge to settle the genre around a cer-

tain group of autobiographical texts, in short, to constitute a canon, can add critical force and significance to interpretation; but it should be acknowledged (if not resisted) in the interest of recognizing the diversity of early modern lives and life writings.

Effects of canonization and generic limits can also be observed in Michael Mascuch's recent study of a specific mode of autobiography, which he explicitly differentiates "from other possible forms of autobiographical and personal self-identity" (7). Like Shuger, Mascuch focuses on devotional works and spiritual diaries; yet it is unclear why, apart from his argument's trajectory toward an "individualist self," this one mode of life writing assumes substantial presence while others are relegated to "possible forms." Mascuch traces "the stirrings of a personal voice and an individual self-identity," from its beginnings in the mid–seventeenth century, when the "concept of personality is still latent, and altogether pious. But a tendency to place the person before the piety had begun to emerge" (96). The process continues into the eighteenth century, where a particular individualist ethos assumes sharper definition. Shuger's and Mascuch's analyses of these extremely well known kinds of autobiography are fair critical choices, yet, as Jerome Bruner notes, "conventional autobiographical genres, of course, reflect idealized cultural patterns" (41). Such idealization can of course extend for many years after the texts are written and published, as the canon of autobiographical works persists, influencing later authors, readers, and critics. A recognition of the diverse genres of life writing that proliferate in the early modern period can alter and perhaps challenge these patterns; thus also it can influence our overall sense of what early modern autobiographies represent. For they can produce, or reproduce, not only seemingly complete or conventional models of identity but also the kinds of "rapidly interspersed identity fragments" that Sidonie Smith and Julia Watson suggest are a feature of postmodern autobiography (*Getting* 21). In our period, as Nussbaum observes, the "fragmentary nature of the texts is often ignored by modern critics in the interests of defining a cohesive genre" (22) and, we might add, a cohesive sense of self. Once again, critical protocols can be seen to play a direct and potentially restrictive role in shaping the understanding of what constitutes Renaissance life writing.

While critical concepts and the way they are applied affect the horizon of interpretive possibilities for autobiographical texts, there is invariably much debate about the significance of those same concepts: not only which theory or concept, but which version of which theory or concept. In this situation, it proves risky to proscribe in advance any

critical approach to early modern writing. Shuger doubts the usefulness of psychoanalytically based interpretations, but the terms she
uses—*Freudian, the subconscious, psychological analysis*—recall earlier
types of analytic criticism, whose aim was to arrive at singular truths
of identity, ones that predictably invert explicit conduct or confirm a
pathological pattern. More recent analytical approaches are not
invested in the same ideal of "the metaphysical self" that, in Shuger's
terms misrepresents the fundamental nature of early modern selfhood.
Instead, they try to understand processes that are now regarded by
many critics as crucial to the ways in which autobiographical works
operate, including intersubjectivity (Folkenflik, "Self" 234), the tensions between "relational and autonomous modes of identity" (Eakin
181), and the weaving into selfhood of public discourses and routines.
Through such interpretive models, autobiography can be conceived as
a textual practice in which "women and men, privately and publicly,
experiment with interdiscourses and the corresponding subject positions to broach the uncertainties of identity. . . . Such texts may work
simultaneously for and against the ideologies of identity which prevail" (Nussbaum 37). These critical approaches, informed by post-
structural forms of psychoanalytic theory, seem well placed to respond
to the early modern mixture of personal and public frameworks for
conceiving and representing identity. Their notions of subjectivity are
not grounded on a separate sphere of inwardness, as Shuger implies.
Rather, in demystifying the idealized coherent self of autobiographical
tradition, they might open out or recover "social fabrication[s] of
identity" (Greenblatt 223) and the "variety of categories of the person
or conceptions of the self" available in the early modern period (Burke
28). Attempting this complex critical task involves shuttling between
contemporary normalized conceptions of these matters and earlier
ones, which appear both radically different and incipiently modern,
though the latter effect may well stem from a sort of distorting hindsight; in Edward Burns's words, "Shakespeare and his contemporaries
are not somehow 'deconstructing' this notion of the individual, but we
may have to in order to make sense of much of the texts, as they operate outside it" (158). The essays in this collection are mindful that in
reading late medieval and early modern life writing this kind of conceptual time travel inevitably comes into play: it is critically useful and
historically risky.

An important route to accessing the variety of self-conceptions in
the early modern period has proved to be through a range of feminist
critiques of traditional autobiographical discourse. Domna Stanton

recognizes the possibility of a radically different subject for women's autobiography, one marked by its "fundamental alterity and non-presence" (15), while Shari Benstock critically unravels the premises of the autobiographical conception "that there is such a thing as the 'self' and that it is 'knowable.' This coming-to-knowledge of the self constitutes both the desire that initiates the autobiographical act and the goal toward which autobiography directs itself" (11). When juxtaposed, these viewpoints raise possibilities for conceptualizing and writing about the collective, relational, and nonteleological types of identity that we often find in early modern self-representations. They encourage critics to open out options for meaning that are not confined to a discursive model of "the unique, individuated narrating subject" (Smith and Watson, *Reading* 67), nor oriented toward revealing a figure that Sturrock labels the "autobiographical hero" of individuation and singularization (289–91). Instead, they encourage a sense that autobiographical works constantly engage with the shifting and developing roles and identities played by their authors and their readers. Bruner's theory of autobiographical process as publicly negotiable, a "conversation of lives" (43) carried on between authors and readers, whose utterances and responses inform each other, provides a sharper sense of the social and ethical dialogue through which early modern identity is experienced and represented among its first writers and readers.

As a brief, closing illustration of this mode of autobiographical discourse and the various ways of responding to it, we can turn to the relatively well known *Itinerary Written by Fynes Moryson, Gent. Containing His Ten Yeeres Travell thorow Twelve Dominions*, published in 1617, over twenty years after Moryson's trip took place. One moment that is particularly striking is when Moryson interrupts his travel journal to recount the way he learned of his father's death.

Whilst I liued at *Prage*, and one night had set vp very late drinking at a feast, early in the morning the Sunne beames glancing on my face, as I lay in bed, I dreamed that a shadow passing by, told me that my father was dead, at which awaking all in a sweat, and affected with this dreame, I rose and wrote the day and houre, and all circumstances thereof in a paper booke, which Booke with many other things I put into a barrel, and sent it from *Prage* to *Stode*, thence to be conuaied into *England*. And now being at *Nurnberg*, a Merchant of a noble family, well acquainted with me and my friends, arriued there, who told me that my Father died some two moneths past, I list not write any lies, but that which I write is as true as strange. When I returned into *England* some foure yeeres after, I would not open the barrel I sent from *Prage*, nor looke on the paper Booke in which I had written this dreame, till I had called my sisters and some friends to be witnesses, where my selfe and they were astonished to see my written dreame answere the very day of my Fathers death. (19)

As its title suggests, the greater part of the *Itinerary* methodically maps Moryson's trip, paying great attention to costs of food, lodging, and transport and to describing town plans and monuments. The passage just quoted is very different, though it, too, contains references to various cities that Moryson visits and the practicalities of communication, all of which grant a kind of practical, linear structure to his narrative. The linearity of events is disrupted by the uncanny bodily, moral, personal and familial space that he enters through his drunken dream and fearful writing. Through his autobiographical writing, Moryson drafts various "scenes of witness" onto each other: the dream itself; the painstaking transcription of it into a book and the putting of the book into a barrel; the advent, two months later, of the merchant whose narrative confirms the dream; and the subsequent checking of the details of his father's death to determine their parity with the dreamed events sealed within the barrel. It is the imagination of the traveler himself, as he looks back on his encounters (both somnambulant and waking), that enables him to weave them into a network of narratives that speak to, and through, each other to reveal something of his fears, his connection to his family, and his prescience—to reveal, in short, the conditions through which he experiences "himself." And these conditions help us to conceive of the strange mirroring of identity that early modern autobiography often represents. Reading and analyzing the words of those who lived and wrote long ago, we recognize selves, those of others and perhaps our own as well, differently.

NOTES

1. Lejeune's later viewpoint should also be noted: "Telling the truth about the self, constituting the self as complete subject—it is a fantasy" (131).

2. Shuger's work is also discussed in detail in Philippa Kelly's essay in chapter 4. In her discussion of the iconography of the mirror, Kelly cites Shuger's "The 'I' of the Beholder: Renaissance Mirrors and the Reflexive Mind," *Renaissance Culture and the Everyday*, ed. Patricia Fumerton and Simon Hunt (Philadelphia: U of Pennsylvania P, 1999), 19–36.

WORKS CITED

Aers, David. "A Whisper in the Ear of Early Modernists, or Reflections on Literary Critics Writing the History of the Subject." *Culture and History, 1350–1600: Essays on English Communities, Identities, and Writing.* Ed. David Aers. New York: Harvester Wheatsheaf, 1992. 177–202.

Benstock, Shari. "Authorizing the Autobiographical." *The Private Self: Theory and Practice of Women's Autobiographical Writings.* Ed. Shari Benstock. London: Routledge, 1998. 10–33.

Bruner, Jerome. "The Autobiographical Process." *The Culture of Autobiography: Constructions of Self-Representation.* Ed. Robert Folkenflik. Stanford: Stanford UP, 1993. 38–56.

Burke, Peter. "Representations of the Self from Petrarch to Descartes." *Rewriting the Self: Histories from the Renaissance to the Present.* Ed. Roy Porter. London: Routledge, 1997. 17–28.

Burns, Edward. *Character: Acting and Being on the Pre-modern Stage.* New York: St. Martin's, 1991.

Derrida, Jacques. *The Ear of the Other: Otobiography, Transference, Translation.* Ed. Christie McDonald. Trans. Peggy Kamuf. Lincoln: U of Nebraska P, 1988.

Eakin, Paul John. *How Our Lives Become Stories: Making Selves.* Ithaca: Cornell UP, 1999.

Folkenflik, Robert. Introduction: The Institution of Autobiography. *The Culture of Autobiography: Constructions of Self-Representation.* Ed. Robert Folkenflik. Stanford: Stanford UP, 1993. 1–20.

———. "The Self as Other." *The Culture of Autobiography: Constructions of Self-Representation.* Ed. Robert Folkenflik. Stanford: Stanford UP, 1993. 215–34.

Gagnier, Regenia. *Subjectivities: A History of Self-Representation in Britain, 1832–1920.* New York: Oxford UP, 1991.

Giddens, Anthony. *Modernity and Self-Identity: Self and Society in the Late Modern Age.* Stanford: Stanford UP, 1991.

Greenblatt, Stephen. "Psychoanalysis and Renaissance Culture." *Literary Theory/Renaissance Texts.* Ed. Patricia Parker and David Quint. Baltimore: Johns Hopkins UP, 1986. 210–24.

Gunn, Janet Varner. *Autobiography: Toward a Poetics of Experience.* Philadelphia: U of Pennsylvania P, 1982.

Habicht, Werner. *Shakespeare and the German Imagination.* Hertford: ISA, 1994. International Shakespeare Association Occasional Paper No. 5.

Lejeune, Philippe. *On Autobiography.* Trans. Katherine Leary. Minneapolis: U of Minnesota P, 1989.

Locke, John. *An Essay Concerning Human Understanding. The Empiricists.* Garden City: Anchor, 1974. 7–133.

Mascuch, Michael. *Origins of the Individualist Self: Autobiography and Self-Identity in England, 1591–1791.* Cambridge: Polity, 1997.

Misch, George. *A History of Autobiography in Antiquity.* 2 vols. 1907; Westport: Greenwood, 1973.

Morris, John N. *Versions of the Self.* New York: Basic, 1966.

Moryson, Fynes. *An Itinerary Written by Fynes Moryson, Gent. Containing His Ten Yeeres Travell thorow Twelve Dominions.* London, 1617.

Nussbaum, Felicity A. *The Autobiographical Subject: Gender and Ideology in Eighteenth-Century England.* Baltimore: Johns Hopkins UP, 1989.

Olney, James. *Metaphors of Self: The Meaning of Autobiography.* Princeton: Princeton UP, 1972.

Schlegel, Augustus William. *A Course of Lectures on Dramatic Arts and Literature.* Trans. John Black. London: Henry G. Bohn, 1846.

Shuger, Debora. "The 'I' of the Beholder: Renaissance Mirrors and the Reflexive Mind." *Renaissance Culture and the Everyday.* Ed. Patricia Fumerton and Simon Hunt. Philadelphia: U of Pennsylvania P, 1999. 19–36.

———. "Life-Writing in Seventeenth-Century England." *Representations of the Self from the Renaissance to Romanticism.* Ed. Patrick Coleman, Jayne Lewis, and Jill Kowalik. Cambridge: Cambridge UP, 2000. 63–78.

Smith, Sidonie, and Julia Watson, eds. *Getting a Life: Everyday Uses of Autobiography.* Minneapolis: U of Minnesota P, 1996.

———. *Reading Autobiography: A Guide for Interpreting Life Narratives.* Minneapolis: U of Minnesota P, 2001.

Stanton, Domna C. "Autogynography: Is the Subject Different?" *The Female Autograph: Theory and Practice of Autobiography from the Tenth to the Twentieth Century.* Ed. Domna C. Stanton. Chicago: U of Chicago P, 1987. 3–20.

Sturrock, John. *The Language of Autobiography: Studies in the First Person Singular.* Cambridge: Cambridge UP, 1993.

Taylor, Charles. *Sources of the Self: The Making of the Modern Identity.* Cambridge: Harvard UP, 1989.

Watson, Julia. "Toward an Anti-metaphysics of Autobiography." *The Culture of Autobiography: Constructions of Self-Representation.* Ed. Robert Folkenflik. Stanford: Stanford UP, 1993. 57–79.

Chapter 2

Specifying the Subject in
Early Modern Autobiography

Conal Condren

*F*or anyone dealing with the medieval or early modern world, and for anyone swayed by caveats against anachronism and mythmaking, the notion of autobiography needs handling with unusual care. The word *autobiography* is one of those that, as Nietzsche put it, makes us see the world afresh, offering a reclassification of what is to hand. It was a neologism invented to encapsulate clear forms of reflexive narrative from the late eighteenth century onward and is now readily seen as a distinct genre of writing. Yet how far its range can be extended backward and what is actually gained by doing so are altogether more tricky issues. The notion of autobiography is certainly suggestive of a whole, if fleeting, set of discursive practices found in letters, diaries, confessions, poems, and treatises, but to realign them through a later classification may be to lose important points of discrimination and invent what was not there: it can be to elide conceptual modeling with description, a fundamentally nugatory historiographical conflation. For this reason alone, it may be safer to rely on the adjectival *autobiographical*, acting only as a predicate for an existing classification such as diurnal or diary, rather than on the abstract noun that, once reified, can intimate a genre or even a conceptual realm beyond the words people used about themselves and their worlds. Such conceptual realms are apt to be euphemisms for the projection of our own localized priorities.

More specifically, the *auto* in *autobiography* may be problematic. It designates a reflexive agent, and it may be relatively harmless enough to use a word such as *self* or *individual* as an abridgment of this. If so, however, it is clearly incumbent on us to give the term some content. Seeing the world through post-Kantian glasses, however, there is always the danger of reading more into a word such as *self* than is historically tenable. So it is easy either to trade in empty abstractions or to invest agency with all the modernizing expectations of universalized moral autonomy, an understanding of which might take the narrative form of an autobiography charting some development toward a curious condition called "selfhood." Leaving all philosophical difficulties aside, I can think of few if any modern autobiographies that are of autonomous agents per se: they are characteristically of philosophers, actors, businesspeople, soldiers, and politicians, and each kind of autobiography carries its own conventions of disclosure. The modesty topos requires that actors are always lucky, sales figures need businesspeople to be decisive, and fragile reputations require generals and politicians to be right, albeit misunderstood. The record needs putting straight. Indeed, I begin to suspect two related things, that the essentialized autonomous "self" is largely an invention of those who wish to attack it and that the (correct) posited alternative, "selves" as socially constructed and reciprocally related identities, is less the discovery of postmodernism than of the wheel, squared off for easy use.

In a world in which what we might call autobiographies were not principally constructed for the printing press but, from Augustine's *Confessions* to Baxter's *Reliquiae*, were part of a manuscript culture, we do need to ask what the *auto* (if we can use the term) in *autobiography* was, and by what mechanisms it is characteristically distorted, often to create or inject modern selves into the premodern past.

My suggestion is first that human social and moral identity, as opposed to material identity, was presented and presumably conceived not in terms of selves or individuals but personae, what Samuel Pufendorf called *entia moralia* appropriate to given offices (1.1.3–5). The notion of an office was broad and extensive, being expressed through a whole family of quasi synonyms: *calling, vocation, sphere, end, room, trade,* and even *work*. I need hypothesize here nothing more than the general presupposition that the moral world was overwhelmingly articulated as comprised of offices and these, however specified, exhausted proper conduct. There was, in fact, no authentic residual voice for which we can search and which would have been the subject of autobiographical writing. The conduct of a persona was predicated in terms of responsibilities and duties with their correlative enabling liberties or rights. Conversely, improper conduct assumed a physical being incapable of occupying a given office, an official persona who was held to be going beyond a sphere of activity, or one that neglected office. Hence the sense of office carried with it a highly ramified vocabulary of moral critique and defense, which was important to deploy and display whether one was writing privately, for a family or a potential dynasty, or in an overtly public capacity. As will become apparent, an impervious barrier identifying what is now called a public sphere is itself a distorting imposition on a past in which a vocabulary of office was moved fairly freely between public and private and in which private might signify anything but the authentic.

Two additionally entailed features of an official conspectus of the world are worth noting in the context of autobiography. First, offices took on meaning only in patterns of reciprocity with those personae in adjacent offices (such as priest and lawyer) and with those considered under the auspices of one's own, such as parents and children. As John Pym remarked, only God does not exist in "mutual dependence and relationship" (131). For this reason alone, the recent rediscovery that human lives need to be narrated in patterns of intersubjectivity suggests how little a world of offices has been understood. In the medieval and early modern worlds, no one seemed to think otherwise. Second, claims on office were expressions of a faith in ethical and social continuity. The most obvious example of this was the doctrine of the king's (indeed, any ruler's) two bodies, a fiction elaborated to express continuity of office despite the death of the officeholder. As medieval legal theorists maintained, the form of a ship was not destroyed in having its planking replaced (Kantorowicz 294). The result was a sufficiently sophisticated understanding of changing identity over time to provide the preconditions for what we style autobiography.

I am concerned here, then, not with any hypothetical inner or essential being as such, or with the quite inappropriate search for some mythic autonomy, but with the language through which almost any identity was cast or what most plausibly statements about moral and social identity seem to have presupposed. And I want to illustrate the ubiquity of the rhetorics of office with two polar examples that are suggestive of what we call autobiography, that is, writing about oneself either as a philosopher or as a soul. The one was outer, malleable, and accessible; the other was internal and seen as essential and inscrutable but certainly not morally autonomous. In some respects, other personae might for the purposes of my discussion have done as well: the priest, the poet, the parent, or the ruler. But those I have chosen additionally provide some mechanism to help explain the later projection of modern individuality as a site for autobiography and the corresponding quest for a self as agent or outcome of discourse. And the example I shall outline of writing as a philosopher shows why, despite all the dangers, there can occasionally be good reason to cast back the word *autobiography* to embrace a discursive practice.

Since antiquity, philosophy had not simply been a matter of propositions but had involved the presentation of a persona appropriate to doctrines expressed: there were patterns of life to show forth truth. It is for this reason alone that ad hominem argument was so common from Lucian onward. It was simply the obverse of the promotion of the decorous persona: a destruction of the doctrine through its presenter. Thomas Hobbes can be used to make the point clearly enough, for he was the most commonly attacked philosopher of seventeenth-century England. Few who criticized his work did not also assert or insinuate that his character and life were images of the doctrinal outrage upon decency that his printed words committed. He became the image of the libertine atheist, often with no clear distinction being made between the alleged implications of his arguments and his conduct. It was, for example, this public image that kept Hobbes out of the Royal Society. The necessity for a communal persona appropriate to its activities and unthreatening to religious orthodoxy was recognized to be crucial to its survival. Had it elected Hobbes, despite his having the most impeccable of natural philosophic credentials, The Society would have been tainted by association. Attacks on Hobbes could have been surrogates for attacks on it, just as they could be substitutes for attacking an atheistic and libertine royal court. There is, then, something a trifle disingenuous in John Aubrey's explanation that Hobbes was barred merely because of a few personal animosities. This may initially have been so, but, as the Society prospered vicariously and Hobbes's image degenerated, Aubrey's argument loses conviction (Malcolm 330–35).

It is in this context of the politics of the persona that both Aubrey's famous "Life" and Hobbes's own verse *Vita* must be seen. The two are closely connected and can be treated in tandem. Aubrey himself encouraged Hobbes to write his own life, which he finished some seven years before he died in 1679. The two men had been close friends since childhood, when they studied in Malmesbury under the same gifted schoolmaster, Robert Latimer. Each seems to have had a remarkable capacity for making and keeping friends. Aubrey's "Life" of Hobbes is a loving epitaph, "the last Office to my honoured Friend," written to complement and flesh out Hobbes's formal Latin (Aubrey 83). But it is more than reminiscence. The "Life" is implicitly a refutation of the ad

hominem attacks on Hobbes's doctrine, a point borne out by Aubrey's
own reflections on the enterprise (83–86). Aubrey does not defend the
writings but the author's conduct and character; he offers a narrative
display of the philosophical persona (226–38). All this is considered
irrelevant now to the disconcerting doctrines on the page. Who
attacks Lacan or Althusser because one went mad and the other committed murder? We have so narrowed the notion of philosophy to
propositions of a certain sort that neither the "Life" nor the *Vita* is considered philosophically relevant.

Hobbes's *Vita* is a narrative poem in alternating hexameters and
pentameters, with the latter being divided into antithetical parts. It
was a demanding rhyme scheme that had been used by Ovid, as
Hobbes notes in his preface. It announced a command over antiquity
and a scholarly dexterity appropriate to Hobbes's philosophical persona. The work in due sequence recounts the notable features of
Hobbes's place of birth, his early education, his employment, and the
growth of his interests, and it attributes an order to those things he
learned. It deals with the doctrines he developed in the context of his
travels and intellectual engagements with figures such as Mersenne
and the sustaining importance of the patronage of the Cavendish family. It covers the upheaval of the civil wars and the writing and reception of his works. The narrative ends, appropriate to its elegiac character, by claiming, "Nam mea vita meis non est incongrua scriptis"
(14). The English translation loses the litotes but makes the point
emphatically enough: "My Life and Writings speak one Congruous
Sense" (18). It was directed to a print world audience and was a defense
of the epicurean, who knew that the greatest pleasure lay in knowledge
and not physical satisfaction, and of the maligned but discriminating
scholar, who was ever concerned with the responsibilities of etiologi-
cal enquiry. Details in Aubrey's "Life" make the same point more
vividly. He quotes a short, quintessentially epicurean poem by Hobbes
that ends, "Thinke not the man a Fool tho he be old, / Who loves in
Body fair, a fairer mind" (237). In a reminiscence that recalls Hobbes's
own striking image of the human mind as a perpetually working
spaniel amid a field, Aubrey remarks that Hobbes's own mind was
never still, and in its working lay his true delight. For fitness, he
played tennis until seventy-five years of age; he was abstemious and
got drunk only on occasion but made sure he vomited when he did. He
sang loudly and badly (in considerate seclusion) for the sake of his
lungs. It is to be noted also how in the *Vita* the past is streamlined to
give it a sense congruous with doctrine. Aubrey records the question-

able cause of Hobbes's premature birth: "His mother fell in labour with him upon the fright of the Invasion of the Spaniards" (227). But Hobbes went further. His birth became an expression of what would be a central explanatory concept for him, "Ut paretet geminos, meque metumque simul" (18). And to provide a sort of conceptual circularity to the journey of his life, Hobbes concludes that now, in his eighty-fourth year, approaching death "prompts me not to fear" (14). Similarly, Hobbes's vehement criticisms of the universities are given a justification in a firsthand experience, which should be read with skepticism. University education was not necessarily as narrow, stultifyingly old-fashioned, and dangerous as Hobbes notoriously asserted in *Leviathan,* but in recounting that as a fact of his life he prefigures and buttresses later doctrines. Constructed life and doctrine appear to concord, and as a result it is difficult not to use the abstract noun and simply call this one of the earliest of philosophical autobiographies. It is curious that R. G. Collingwood's *Autobiography* similarly distorts his experience at Oxford in a way that supports the later development of crucial doctrines (Collingwood 15–28, 53–54).

If the vocabulary of office was as pervasive as I have suggested, we can expect it to have shaped any sense that people had of an inner being. This prospect initially takes us far from the protean and highly contested office of philosopher. When people wrote of an innermost identity, they wrote of the soul and the conscience with which it was sometimes synonymous. But conscience could also function as a synecdoche, the agent of the soul's operation and a faculty of knowing what was right before and for God. Following one's conscience was a moral imperative that might be acknowledged even by those believing one's conscience to be mistaken. This position already indicates to what extent the hypothesized inner being was described and shaped through the vocabulary of office. Sermonizers such as Donne and Taylor depicted the soul in terms of subordination to God, enabling them to specify conduct in the vocabulary of duty central to the rhetorics of office. Writers such as Montaigne, Charon, and Cornwallis, in dealing with the inner "self," resorted, though by no means exclusively, to the mainstream vocabulary of office. This inner essence of moral probity might be a judge in an inner court, bringing the external world to account, a whole inner republic, or a military command (Clark 66–67). I have suggested that the offices of soul and philosopher may be seen as polar contrasts, but this analytic separation did not stop writers from using the lubricant of the vocabulary of office to bring them both together. The soul could be construed as an inner philosopher. Or, indeed, more commonly, it could occupy the internalized office of the ruler.

It is tempting in Montaigne's case, in particular, to construe his *Essays* as an arduous discovery of individuality and selfhood. After all, he makes it clear that he is the subject of his own writings, and there is much in them that is broadly autobiographical or revealing of biographical detail. But these very aspects of his work are potentially misleading. Much, in fact, pivots on the interplay between the responsibilities of the active and contemplative lives and the persona appropriate to each broad sense of office (Montaigne 174–83, 766–84). And it is characteristic of Montaigne that he used self-reference to destabilize any clear-cut distinction between them. He employed a baffling array of metaphors for soul and inner being, seeming at times to elide spiritual and material identity (Clark 67–70). Moreover, he deliberately problematizes agency when dealing with the texts that populate the inner sanctum of his study and with imagining his own writings as texts taken to the outer world, where they might await readings as tortuous as his own of long-dead writers (cf. Cave). One result is to raise the issue of who or what is really in charge, of who, as he wrote of his relationship with his cat, is playing with whom (331). The textual features that facilitate the insertion of a modern self into his work arise, at least in part, from the interplay of differing official expectations of an active and contemplative life. As the philosopher's duties could be construed in terms of either ideal, there is ample opportunity in the *Essays* to play with official expectations of philosopher and ruler in dealing with the soul-like self.

The reliance on the vocabulary of office to express the conscience or the soul can be seen in other, more straightforward ways. Charles I referred to conscience, quite conventionally, as a "vicegerent"; God was the king of consciences (Charles 98). This sort of use of the language of office, though metaphorically clear enough, was accompanied by elaborate and sophisticated theories of inference. John Cotta, for example, writing in a way immediately reminiscent of Montaigne and reflecting both on the diagnosis of ills and on witchcraft, wrote that the unknown (embracing God, the spirit world, and the causes of physical symptoms) had perforce to be hypothesized by its consequences, causes conjectured from effects. In doing so, however, it was inevitable that the language of description drawn from a world of effects would give only an approximation to the unknown invisible causes as they really were (Cotta 21, 2, 7). The model informing this skeptical understanding of inference was provided by what David Parnham refers to as an apophatic notion of God that had been explored so uncompromisingly by Duns Scotus in the thirteenth century and remained a theologically predominant notion at least until Spinoza (Parnham 67–70). God knowable by effects is unlimited and all-powerful, and this places him beyond the capacities of human description. As Sir Thomas Browne remarked in the *Religio Medici,* "we too narrowly define the power of God, restraining it to our capacities. I hold that God can do all things; how he should work contradictions I do not understand, yet dare not therefore deny" (74).

It is to be expected, then, that with people living in a world pervaded by assumptions of office in social relationships the vocabulary of social office should indeed be enlisted to help shape the hypothetical conjectures of the soul. When this shaping took on a narrative form around the writer's soul, we have something that we might well call autobiographical. For example, James I, who spent much time and energy glossing his understanding of his office of ruler, his duty being taken as coextensive with his conscience, penned highly self-critical reflections and injunctions to himself as a means of monitoring his conduct in office, diarized snippets lacking only the addition of narrative form to suggest autobiographical activity (Sharpe 163–67).

In *The Tribunal of Conscience* (1627), Henry Mason, however, provides a clear and methodical case that gives a clue to the rationale behind what we now might reclassify as autobiography. The soul, he argues, can only perform properly before God, fulfilling its office of subordination to his will, if it persistently examines itself. Know thyself meant know thy soul (Mason 4–10). The knowing conscience would seem to be the means of doing this, except that Mason uses *conscience* and *soul* as synonyms (2). This extreme reflexivity is not easy to realize and requires constant practice. Again, as Browne would later put it, the "inward opticks and the crysteline of thy soul" is the most difficult sort of sight (331). So, Mason argues, it is vital each day to think back through sins and errors and write down the practice as a means of correction and improvement and for memory's sake. In the process of doing so, it is important to keep in mind the vocation, calling, or condition in which one acts, for different offices have characteristic vices and virtues (Mason 37–42). Know the past that we may understand the present and do better in the future. In setting down these exercises of reflexive soul and persona improvement, Mason provides hypothetical illustrations, and the result looks like the template for an autobiographical entry in a diary—one into which large quantities of Samuel Pepys might easily fit (Mason 53). Today I went to the tavern, had too much ale, and was rude to my neighbor. I must mend my ways.

The significance of such practices helps explain something else characteristic of those bodies of early modern writings that seem suggestive of later autobiography: the slippery, indeterminate distinctions between confessions, diaries, characters, letters, poems, collections of state papers such as Lord Clarendon's (later to be written up as *The History of the Great Rebellion*), familial accounting by potential dynasts for their families, and, finally, autobiography. The most intimate were at most overlapping idioms of soul improvement, the rest office examination, justification, and reinforcement. Margaret Cavendish rushed breathlessly between related personae in a persistently defensive fashion: dutiful daughter, loving wife, loyal subject, and philosopher. In this way, also, as Wilfrid Prest shows in chapter 16 of this collection, more narrow familial accounts by successful seventeenth-century lawyers assumed the persona of the gentleman in ore; they were almost proleptic ancestors appropriate to noble houses. In the following century, there was a shift of persona to that of the professional lawyer. All of these may be in some sense autobiographical, but in looking for the "genuine" autobiography, and so tidying up the distinction between it and adjacent styles of writing, we might help create the phenomenon we purport only to be clarifying.

Browne's *Religio Medici*, originally a ruminative manuscript for his own instruction, is a case in point. Browne's was a wide-ranging mind and his imagery of self-description diverse, but what we see in the work is the erratically autobiographical interplay of two personae, the Christian soul and its own examination in counterpoint to the somewhat eclectic and mystical conception of the natural philosopher and physician. It is a detailed description of a compound character. His life, he remarks, is less a narrative than a poem or fable (Browne 190). Browne is a man with a profession, driven by the nature of that office to inquire skeptically for causes from visible effects and inquire in a way at odds with the duties of the Christian soul that in various ways he attempts to understand. In this interplay of personae, of *entia moralia*, lies Browne's fideism—the early modern version of the Averroist doctrine of the two truths that so easily accommodated the potential clash of spheres of responsibility. Elsewhere he specifically remarks of diaries that they should be accounts of God's dealings with us (262). And, indeed, this is a feature of many early modern diaries: Goro Dati's, with its fastidious sense of behavior appropriate to the sense of office in which he sees himself, soul before God, a Florentine businessman and in both cases writing out of an awareness of dynastic office to instruct and inform the immediate and projected family; Brilliana Harley's, with its steel-like, dutiful ethos befitting wife, mother, aristocrat, pious soul, and military commander; and even Samuel Pepys's, with its erratic guilt over his greed, lust, and mendacity.

This sort of pattern will be familiar to those who have read early modern diaries and autobiographical memoirs right up until Franklin's autobiography, conceived initially, it seems, for the instruction of his son (Franklin 5). The early stages, written in 1771, are punctuated by the noting of errors, moral failings to be avoided. The work was interrupted, and when he returned to it around 1784 the significance of citizenly and scientific achievement and the sense of new personae fit for the new republic obscure what might have been a diminished sense of the sinning soul. The autobiography is looking more modern. We are in the world of the neologism.

But exaggeration here is easy, especially if we begin with the almost necessarily anachronizing concern with origins. For origins are, after all, phenomena predicated in terms of later identities. The search for origins might be unproblematic if we are dealing with phenomena governed by necessarily teleological processes of the sort to be found in botany, zoology, or meteorology. It is yet to be shown that such naturalistic teleologies are appropriate to the structure of social and moral time; if these are dealt with historically, the search for origins may, *ab initio*, be distorting. It is a problem that bedevils the trajectory toward that most unstable of concepts, "individualism," in Michael Mascuch's recent study, *The Origins of the Individualist Self.* To repeat, the very act of clarifying a category by seeing it as an origin of something else may effectively be an imposition. This, as I have suggested, might help create the sense of immediacy that comes (much as he predicted) from Montaigne—the richness of his figurative play creates an indeterminacy into which it is easy to slide the modern world. Conversely, the ambivalences and anxieties that we may attribute to the medieval and early modern may be a function of the categories we take to the evidence and confuse with it.

So, with these hermeneutic problems in mind, I would like to ask not what are the origins of modern autobiography but by what mechanisms do we create a sense of origin in the early modern world? How do we put the self and the individual, with all their connotations of moral agency and standing, into a modal world of personae?

Two mechanisms are directly relevant to the examples of the autobiographical that I have chosen. In the cases of the philosopher and soul, the persona is easily replaced with the individual or self, thus injecting modernizing presuppositions into the narratives to be redescribed. In this way, arguments and statements about the nature and potentialities of the philosophical persona lose their crucial modality. To take a simple instance from Hobbes, he is infamous for saying in *Leviathan* that metaphors are an abuse of language and so are improper (25–26). Even in this most intemperate moment, which is often taken to be the whole of his doctrine, it is quite clear that the context is an argument about philosophy, its responsibilities and abuse. In his more considered statements, this modal limitation becomes explicit. Metaphors are definitionally equivocal, to invoke Donald Davidson's controversial argument (245–64). They are more functions of use, unrestricted to any clear meaning, and therefore should be eschewed by philosophers, whose intellectual office and duty are to generate coherent causative accounts of the world. Others, such as the poet, have every business using them. What is at issue, then, is not metaphor per se but the demarcations of intellectual office. To take an altogether grander example: Pico della Mirandola is famous now, but only since Burckhardt, for his seminal doctrine about the protean nature of man. The individual is in a sense self-fashioning; man can be what he will. It is this doctrine that ushers notions of the Burckhardtian Renaissance as the origins of modern individuality.[1] The result is still there in all the textbooks and demands autobiography as a narrative proof.

Yet as William G. Craven painstakingly showed some years ago, Pico's argument is an oratorical performance about the potency and responsibilities of the philosopher: a rhetorical promotion exercise for a platonically redefined intellectual office. "Man" is throughout a self-conscious metaphor for the philosopher. That a metaphorical and hyperbolic piece of epideictic rhetoric has routinely been mistaken for a global claim about human individuality offers, I suppose, some support for Hobbes's "Davidsonian" theory of metaphor.

The second key mechanism in this context has been, as Katharine Eisaman Maus put it, to secularize the soul. We live in a secular age, and the past becomes more immediately recognizable if we effectively replace soul talk with self talk (Maus 27–28). The matter does not have to be taken very far to see how thoroughly distorting and mythmaking it becomes. Consider Stanley Fish's view of the troubled inner world of George Herbert: a self struggling to become itself and retreating at the scale of the enterprise. It is sheer 1960s angst (cf. Malcolmson 213–14).

It is, in conclusion, perhaps worth repeating here what I have suggested elsewhere: if one looks at the use of the word *self* in the early
modern world, it functions as a simple anaphoric pronoun; shorthand
for an identity, it might be any identity, already assumed. It does not
function as an abstract noun encoding any necessary moral individualistic or ontic status, something of which a biography can be written.
Moreover, overwhelmingly the identities assumed are official ones,
both in a negative and a positive sense. That is, self occurs either in
referring back to a persona or, more intriguingly, to suggest an
absence of any sense of official identity, responsibility, and bounded
duty—hence, terms such as *selfish*, *self-willed*, and *self-conceit*. The
more autonomous the agent seems, the more in fact it is being delegit-
imized. Thus, "self-fashioning" is perhaps the least appropriate of
expressions to use of the early modern sense of contingent moral identity and may be the last thing we should be looking for and finding, by
dint of redescription, in early modern autobiography (Condren
115–18).

Notwithstanding this caveat, I think it would be arguable to maintain that what in many ways marks the post-Reformation world is a
fragmentation and proliferation of claims to office, a point intuited by
Stephen Greenblatt's argument about autonomy and self-fashioning as
features of the Renaissance. What I have called the pervasiveness of
the vocabulary of office was effectively an inflation of moral claims
through office, and this gradually required alternative ways of understanding social and moral identity. We are the legatees of what eventually challenged a world of offices; clearly, to understand that change
the last thing we need to do is project our sensibilities back into it. And
in precisely this larger conspectus the autobiography, the signature of
self-awareness, is something of a Greek gift.

Autobiography may and often does evidence an awareness of contingent malleable selves; yet, as that is hardly a modern discovery, it
may encourage the projection of the noun rather than the more cau-
tious adverb. It was, after all John Locke who put *self* on the philosophical map to make just this point about the temporal fragility of
personal identity. His point was taken further by David Hume, and
Locke's arguments were parodied mercilessly by the Scriblerians and
Laurence Sterne, most notably in *Tristram Shandy*, appropriately, for
the time in which it was written, a spurious autobiography that never
quite starts but somehow presides over a millennium of narrative
reflections on personae. It even offers invitations to invent things for
ourselves and read them into the text.

NOTES

1. In chapter 4 of this volume, "Dialogues of Self-Reflection: Early Modern Mirrors," Philippa Kelly also discusses expressions of selfhood in early modern culture. Kelly cites the mirror as a complex social emblem that expressed both a sense of individual autonomy and a strongly ingrained sense of "self" as mediated by social function.

WORKS CITED

Aubrey, John. *Brief Lives.* Ed. Oliver Lawson Dick. 1680; Harmondsworth: Penguin, 1949.

Browne, Sir Thomas. *Religio Medici (1643) and Christian Morals (1716).* Ed. Henry Gardiner. London: Pickering, 1845.

Cave, Terrence. "Problems of Reading in the *Essais.*" *Montaigne: Essays in Memory of Richard Sayce.* Ed. I. D. McFarlane and Ian Maclean. Oxford: Clarendon, 1982. 132–66.

Charles I [attrib.]. *Eikon Basilike.* London, 1649.

Clark, Carol. "Talking about Souls: Montaigne on Human Psychology." *Montaigne: Essays in Memory of Richard Sayce.* Ed. I. D. McFarlane and Ian Maclean. Oxford: Clarendon, 1982. 57–76.

Collingwood, R. G. *An Autobiography.* 1939; Oxford: Clarendon, 1967.

Condren, Conal. "Historicism and the Problem of Renaissance Self-Fashioning." *The Touch of the Real: Essays in Early Modern Culture.* Ed. Philippa Kelly. Perth: U of Western Australia P, 2002. 105–24.

Cotta, John. *The Infallible, True, and Assured Witch.* London, 1624.

Craven, William G. *Giovanni Pico Della Mirandola, Symbol of His Age: Modern Interpretations of a Renaissance Philosopher.* Geneva: Librairie Droz, 1981.

Davidson, Donald. "What Metaphors Mean." *Inquiries into Truth and Interpretation.* Oxford: Clarendon, 1986. 245–64.

Fish, Stanley. *Self-Consuming Artifacts.* Berkeley: U of California P, 1972.

Franklin, Benjamin. *Autobiography.* Ed. W. Macdonald. 1817; London: Dent, 1968.

Greenblatt, Stephen. *Renaissance Self-Fashioning: From More to Shakespeare.* Chicago: U of Chicago P, 1980.

Hobbes, Thomas. *Leviathan.* Ed. Richard Tuck. 1651; Cambridge: Cambridge UP, 1991.

———.*Thomae Hobbesii Malmsesburiensis Vita (1679) and The Life of Mr. Thomas Hobbes of Malmesbury (1680).* Exeter: Rota Press, 1979.

Kantorowicz, Ernst. *The King's Two Bodies: A Study in Medieval Political Theology.* Princeton: Princeton UP, 1957.

Malcolm, Noel. "Hobbes and the Royal Society." *Aspects of Hobbes.* Oxford: Clarendon, 2002. 317–35.

Malcolmson, Christina. *Heart-Work: George Herbert and the Protestant Ethic.* Stanford: Stanford UP, 1999.

Mascuch, Michael. *The Origins of the Individualist Self: Autobiography and Self-Identity in England, 1591–1791.* Cambridge: Polity, 1997.

Mason, Henry. *The Tribunal of Conscience.* London: 1627.

Maus, Katharine Eisaman. *Inwardness and Theater in the English Renaissance.* Chicago: U of Chicago P, 1995.

Montaigne, Michel de. *The Complete Essays of Montaigne.* Trans. Donald M. Frame. 1580–88; Stanford: Stanford UP, 1992.

Parnham, David. *Sir Henry Vane, Theologian: A Study in Seventeenth-Century Religious and Political Discourse.* London: Associated U Presses, 1997.

Pufendorf, Samuel. *De jure naturae et gentium libri octo.* Trans. C. H. Oldfather and W. A. Oldfather. 1672; Oxford: Clarendon, 1943.

Pym, John. *The Speech or Declaration of John Pym* [1641]. *The Struggle for Sovereignty: Seventeenth-Century English Political Tracts.* Ed. Joyce Malcolm. Indianapolis: Liberty Fund, 1999. 1: 130–44.

Sharpe, Kevin. *Remapping Early Modern England: The Culture of Seventeenth-Century Politics.* Cambridge: Cambridge UP, 2000.

Chapter 3

On Being a Person
Elizabethan Acting & the
Art of Self-Representation

Ronald Bedford

*I*n pursuit of what it might mean to be a person in early modern England—and hence to understand how such personhood might be discursively expressed in autobiographical forms—I begin with the suggestion that a member of an audience in an Elizabethan or Jacobean playhouse might have reacted as I can remember doing when, as a teenager obsessed with the idea of being a doctor, I emerged from a Surbiton cinema showing *Not as a Stranger* (1955), for hours afterward rolling my shoulders like Robert Mitchum and convinced that I was wearing a surgeon's gown and not a duffle coat. I refer to the mimesis that occurs not when the dramatist or poet holds a mirror up to nature but when an audience member or reader is moved to imitate what is represented.

There may be no documented examples from Renaissance playgoing of the sort that accompanied *The Beggar's Opera*—teenaged Macheaths hanged for highway robbery—or of the alleged rise in adolescent suicide following Baz Luhrmann's *Romeo + Juliet*, but it is hard to imagine that the defiant swaggerers or the passionate heroes of the theater had no would-be imitators among audiences. But what evidence there is tends to be partial, in the sense that it comes from dramatists hopeful of stirring spectators. This is Thomas Heywood.

> What English blood, seeing the person of any bold Englishman presented, and doth not hug this fame, and hunnye at his valour, pursuing him in his enterprise with his best wishes, and as being wrapt in contemplation, offers to him in his heart all prosperous perfor-

mance, as if the personator were the man personated? So bewitching a thing is lively and well-spirited action that it hath power to
new-mould the hearts of the spectators, and fashion them to the
shape of any noble and notable attempt. What coward, to see his
countrymen valiant, would not be ashamed of his own cowardice?
(*Apology* 251)

Heywood here is not, unfortunately, describing observed audience
reaction but is offering a moral and patriotic defense of playmaking:
his argument is familiar not from the recorded experience of playgoers
but from apologists of poesis like Sir Philip Sidney, who urge readers
to imitate the ideal actions depicted by poets. Nor is Heywood appealing to "the hearts of the spectators" as individuals but to each as a type
of a true English audience member.

Speaking of the "bewitching" power of theater to "fashion" spectators and their actions, Heywood encourages and even demands a reciprocal act of display and performance by those spectators in the public
world outside the theater. With respect to the question of audience
response, he does not assign to the audience a neutral position from
which to appraise the performance but assumes the spectator position
to be one equally as structured and social as the position of the characters onstage.

So how did Elizabethan and Jacobean audiences experience that
sort of mimesis? And if early modern audiences saw actors onstage as
offering recognizable versions of themselves—however exaggerated—a further, more general question is, what might such recognition tell us about early modern notions of identity and selfhood? In our
own individualistic society, our sense of what selfhood means has very
much to do with notions of self-examination, self-excavation, and
"original" self-expression, such that (paradoxically) even a modern-
day actor may be conceived of as expressing his or her "unique" self
through a role.

For the swaggering young man pretending to be a surgeon, the self
has temporarily and willingly borrowed another identity. But let us
imagine an early modern professional actor, Richard Burbage perhaps,
playing a Coriolanus who is being forced against his will to act a part.
Coriolanus's protest, "You have put me now to such a part which never
/ I shall discharge to th' life" (3.2.105–6), has a highly self-reflexive
resonance (like Macbeth's "poor player" soliloquy and many other
Renaissance playhouse speeches). For both the character in the play
world *and* the actor, in their very different ways the issue of person-

ation, the playing of a part "to th' life," is one of political, economic, and individual success or failure and is at bottom a question of convincing dissimulation or, as Coriolanus's mother calls it in a resonantly Elizabethan word, "policy" (3.2.49). The juxtaposition of interiority and exteriority implied in Coriolanus's reluctance to perform before the plebeians would most naturally be interpreted by modern sensibilities as indicative of a conflict between internal, authentically self-defining drives and ambitions and a politically expedient but inauthentic and thus hypocritical surface. Yet it is highly likely that Coriolanus's protests—"Why do you wish me milder? Would you have me / False to my nature? Rather say I play / The man I am" (3.2.13–15) or "Must I with my base tongue give to my noble heart / A lie that it must bear?" (3.2.100–1)—would be interpreted by Jacobean audiences not as an existential dilemma but as a conflict of roles or of projected selves. Coriolanus's speech seeks only to express the limits of his power to conduct himself according to the compositional requirements of his mother and Cominius: he feels unable to "mountebank" and "cog" in the marketplace, not so much because his interior integrity will be compromised as because such a display flatly contradicts his understanding of his script (his "nature") as an aristocratic warrior-hero, a posture fast becoming outdated in the newly organized republican world of Rome. It is suggested here that those same explicitly performative anxieties governed the lives of early modern audiences too, and in ways that conferred on early modern theatergoing a sense of the especially close relationship between the acted or represented and the real. But to know what it meant to "personate," and therefore to act, it will be necessary to explore a little what it meant to be a person in such a society.

In distinguishing between modern and early modern ideas of a "person," some general points regarding the intellectual and semantic background of pre-Enlightenment notions of personhood may be briefly noted: that, for instance, early modern conceptions of, and vocabulary to describe, personhood and its relation to acting or other forms of representation derived not from Lockean, Freudian, or Lacanian psychologies but, first, from the long-standing theories of mimesis in Western cultures and their European Renaissance variations; second, from a vigorous, widespread, and familiar debate on the nature of the Trinity and the multiple personhood of God (a complex of issues drummed into every catechist from childhood); third, from an equally vigorous and widespread debate between Catholics and reformed churches about whether Christ's presence in the Eucharist is real or symbolic, defining a fundamental divide on what may be understood by representation; and fourth, from the familiar and frequently rehearsed metaphor of the theater of the world, in which men and women and the parts, or persons, they play are conceived of in the same relation to ultimate "reality" as stage or symbolic performance is to social, temporal, and circumstantial "reality." For practicing actors, playwrights, and theater managers, of course, this metaphor was real enough, and the motif of the globe of the world's theater adorned the King's Men's most famous playhouse.

Much has been written (and more left unwritten for lack of evidence) about Elizabethan acting, and most discussion, up to and including recent decades, has centered on the business of acting itself and how it was done. Some few critics have concentrated specifically on the Elizabethan audience's response to theater and the illusion of playing and have made suggestions about the division between, or identity of, actor and character in an Elizabethan viewer's mind (Barroll; Gras). For the most part, Elizabethans were not theater critics or arts journalists, and hence there is little extant contemporary comment on or description of actual performances. This has left the play texts themselves as the primary evidence of how the representation (and, by implication, the playing) of dramatic "characters" was conceived in any particular instance. One claim that has been made—a claim that reached its most strenuous form in late Victorian Shakespearean criticism—is that Shakespeare's dramatic practice was distinctively evolved to produce highly individualized and psychologically complex characters, as evidenced by the sorts of parts he wrote for actors. Despite a certain logical circularity in this view, it is very difficult to argue otherwise; indeed, Andrew Gurr's survey of acting concludes that "Shakespeare's company . . . appear to have been the outstanding company of the age in their naturalism" (Gurr 111–12; cf. Hattaway 72–79; Thomson 114ff.; Leggatt 76–105). An associated claim is that this interest, somewhat peculiar to Shakespeare, may in part have been a response to the particular talents of Richard Burbage, for many years the most notable actor in Shakespeare's company and an actor specifically praised for his "lively" or lifelike acting. But a countersuggestion is also possible, which is that the contemporary claims for Burbage's "lifelike" and "natural" playing could argue less for the expression of an inwardness familiar to us four centuries later and more for a conformity with the familiar (to early modern audiences) compositional effects that went to make up sixteenth- and seventeenth-century notions of identity and premised the act of "playing" itself.

Burbage's career and the impression he made on audiences have been more richly documented than those of most actors, and he was praised especially for his personal "invisibility," his technique of personation. What he seems to have projected as an actor was what Gurr identifies as "the Elizabethan norm": natural acting, "counterfeiting" nature and playing a part "to the life" or with "lively action," lifelike presentation, it is argued, being the artistic aim of the best theater companies (98, 110). Again a circularity of argument may be suspected here, but the questions that beg to be asked are: whose natural and lifelike behavior do these claims assert is being reproduced? Is it our own sense of what is to us lifelike and natural or what may have been perceived as natural and lifelike to a member of Elizabethan London society? And how can—or why should—we assume that the effects thus reproduced would be identical?

Perhaps the most frequently quoted remark about Burbage's acting, by Richard Flecknoe, was in fact made quite late in the seventeenth century.

> He was a delightful Proteus, so wholly transforming himself into his part, and putting off himself with his cloaths as he never (not so much as in the Tyring-house) assumed himself again until the play was done. (*Short Discourse* sig.G4r)

Yet Burbage should not be mistaken for an early method actor. Although he would have blacked up and worn a woolly wig to play Othello (as in the depiction of Aaron the Moor in Henry Peacham's sketch of a 1595 staging of *Titus Andronicus* by Shakespeare's company, reproduced in the *Norton Shakespeare* [3291]), it is very unlikely that he intended by transforming himself into his part what we would call "impersonation" of the kind that, for example, prompted Laurence Olivier (though certainly no method actor either) to learn to walk as he imagined a black person would and to do vocal exercises to drop his voice an octave before playing Othello. Contemporary comments on Elizabethan acting tend to indicate that a rather different set of criteria is at work, one that could sharpen our understanding of what lifelike playing might mean. The most frequent and stable relationship between the part—or the character—and the actor in early modern thinking seems to be one in which the character is reified, is an object created *not* by a player (whose actual low status and disabling lack of social esteem has to be ignored by the audience) but by the dramatist, as if he were a father and the author of his (or her) life. For example, Thomas Heywood's 1633 Prologue to Marlowe's *The Jew of Malta* asserts, "by the best of Poets [Marlowe] in that age / The Jew of Malta had being and was made" (343). It is the job of the actor to imitate this preexisting figure, and he is judged on his ability to "personate" ("like Proteus for shapes, and Roscius for a tongue") those compositional effects that identify the Jew—or Titus, or Othello, or Hamlet. *Personate* clearly meant "to imitate," and there are many examples of such contemporary usage (Gras 1.29–30), most often meaning to imitate the poet/dramatist's created persona or character, in the sense of striving most truly to represent the role.

While the notion of acting as an imitative art is strong, it is also acknowledged, however, that the dramatic character, who is already a reflection of a fictive or historical person, makes the actor a mirror image of a reflection. His imitation tends toward an instructively mirroring function rather than an imitation dedicated to the representation of *personality* or *subjectivity* in the way that we understand those terms. Consequently, the idea of an *actor* creating a character is a very subordinate one. The player is seen as receiving a role rather than constructing one, as though the dramatic character were the ghost of a deceased person whose "proper" traits the actor must re-present. This seems very far from the more modern notion of the actor "creating" the part by becoming himself a new and unique Barabas, or Bussy d'Ambois, and very different from our response, say, to "Gielgud's Hamlet" or "Mel Gibson's Hamlet." The difference may be accounted for in several ways: by contrasting the status of Elizabethan actors with the iconic star status conferred on them by our own society; by noting that (outside of Brechtian epic theater at least) we no longer regard an emblematic and instructive conception of representation as a primary mimetic mode; or by suggesting that our own understanding of how subjectivity can or should be represented may not coincide with theirs.

Yet this kind of perception of emblematically conferred personhood, so notably characteristic of early modern theater practice, appears—paradoxically perhaps—inconsistent with the documentary record of direct accounts (rather than subsequent prologues or tributes) of performance by contemporary spectators, in which plots are understood as if history, characters as if real persons.[1] John Manningham—famously and exceptionally—responds like a theater historian to a performance of *Twelfth Night* at the Inns of Court, but of the direct accounts of performance that survive almost none shows a specific consciousness of the actors or even of theatrical performance. Burbage, the best-known actor, is not mentioned in direct performance accounts (though he is in other contexts of course). Rather, the accounts always stress the inalienable world of the drama and speak of the illusory theatrical world of characters and events as if they were real. No doubt exactly what is meant by *real* here is again problematic: but *real* can very adequately mean "in conformity with experience or with the observable world," and in that sense the observable world of Elizabethan London and the experience of its citizens may well have been that their individual selves were for the most part publicly and emblematically represented rather than privately and subjectively conceived and that the performance of a character onstage conformed closely enough to the conditions of social performance operating in real life and hence could indeed be described as "natural," "lifelike," and "real." When the fictive nature of the theater is unavoidably emphasized, as when a disaster occurred at a performance, the boundaries between the real and the represented become interestingly blurred. There were, for instance, cases of fatal stabbings during a performance, but the most familiar example of this kind is found in the documents of the burning of the Globe, where the curious thing is the way not only the actors (Burbage, Hemming, Condell) are seen as present but the historical characters represented in the performance are too: the fire regarded "neither Cardinalls might / nor yet the rugged face of Henry the eight." And the real fire is called "the doleful tragedie / That late was playd at the globe." (The text of the ballad is reproduced in *The Norton Shakespeare*, "Documents" 3339–40.) This sort of perspective could be regarded as either oddly ingenuous or sophisticatedly metatheatrical, but it is probably neither: it simply reflects the common play on the familiar stage-world, world-stage analogy that, as Erasmus, Montaigne and a host of others indicate, lies at the heart of early modern theatrical theology (Erasmus 104; Montaigne 1.296–97).

The apparent contradiction between spectator awareness of the constructed and artificial nature of theater and simultaneous awareness of its mirrored "reality," where that reality is also accepted or understood as constructed and socially performed, suggests, of course, the elements of a long-standing debate about the nature and possibilities of mimetic art. In the specific context of the sixteenth and early seventeenth centuries in England, it may be glossed socially as well as theologically by observing the many ways in which members of that society, at all levels, both perceived and represented themselves as

prototypes of social, moral, and intellectual construction—and potentially instruction. The sense that every individual's part has been
assigned to him or her, and that there is a preexisting costume and
script for its performance, is one that pervades almost every early
modern articulation of "selfhood." From a multitude of possible
instances, John Maynard's collection of lute songs and the poems by
Sir John Davies, *The XII Wonders of the World* (London, 1611), may
serve as an illustration. Sir John Davies had several years earlier presented his twelve "light and trifling" character poems ("The Courtier,"
"The Soldier," "The Physician," "The Country Gentleman," "The
Wife," etc.) to the new lord treasurer, Thomas Sackville, first earl of
Dorset, as items to entertain his lordship's guests. The "poesies" were
painted on wooden roundels or trenchers with a cartoon of the figure
speaking: when the cheese or fruit on the plain side was eaten, the
guest would turn the platter over and read the verse to the amused
company. Though each character, speaking in the first person, strives
for individuality and idiosyncrasy, nevertheless each is finally and
firmly defined—like the poet or the lord treasurer or the guests themselves—within "my calling," "my occupation," "my trade," "my sex," or
"my marriage." Maynard's musical settings and their subsequent
social performance add further dimensions and currency to notions of
occupation or station so familiar in Jacobean England. Individuals are
in the world only as others see them, and the actor's success lies in how
he is seen by the viewer. Just as the courtier's success is judged by how
"true to the life" he is as a courtier (Davies's courtier has not yet
learned how "To sell poor suitors smoke, nor where I hate to smile"), a
widow's success by how far she conforms to the social expectations of
widowhood, and the success (as it were) of the dying man by how truly
one can see God in his visage, so, too, the actor is judged by how "true
to the life"—the life as experienced outside the theater—he is. The
Elizabethan and Jacobean fascination with playgoing and the experience people sought from the theater seem to have been intimately
bound up with the factors governing what it meant to perform "to th'
life," what it meant to be oneself in the drama and oneself again outside
the theater. That is, the basic touchstones of *true* and *life* in these contexts appear—possibly disturbingly—to have rather different
inflections for this earlier period than they do for our own.

Just how "real" dramatic characters might be, and what social interactions between onstage and offstage "selves" might follow, is fasci-
natingly illustrated by the well-known anecdote related to Manningham by Mr. Touse and recorded in his diary on 13 March 1601.

Upon a tyme when Burbidge played Rich⌈ard⌉ 3, there was a Citi-
zen grewe soe farr in liking with him, that before shee went from
the play shee appointed him to come that night unto hir by the name
of Rich⌈ard⌉ the 3. Shakespeare, overhearing their conclusion, went
before, was intertained, and at his game ere Burbidge came. Then
message being brought that Richard the 3ᵈ was at the dore, Shakespeare caused returne to be made that William the Conqueror was
before Rich⌈ard⌉ the 3. Shakespeare's name William.

While the story may be no more than a male sexual rivalry joke, the
woman's notion of sleeping with Richard III is a fantasy made the
more intriguing by the way Shakespeare and Burbage, in the anecdote,
slip in and out of personation. In referring to himself as William the
Conqueror, antecedent and superior to Richard III, the Shakespeare of
the story asserts his right to sleep with the woman who wants to sleep
with his creation, the king who is not a person but a robe that can be
put on by anyone. At the same time (and the joke depends on it), there
is the underlying assumption of authenticity: it was a *Richard* she
wanted to sleep with, and it is *William* the conqueror with whom she
is sleeping, that is, William Shakespeare, not a dramatic creation or a
historical figure but a real person. All this can readily be teased out of
the anecdote—though what cannot be teased out is also of interest.
Did the woman in this male-enacted bed trick know, for instance, that
it was the author of Burbage's stage persona who had presented himself and not the actor? Was she happy that this was so when she found
out? We cannot know, but we can at least surmise the extent to which
this Mermaid Tavern saloon-bar story might align itself with real
social assumptions about the power—in this case sexual—that may
literally be "invested" in roles, robes, offices, and *personae*, or masks.
But in addition I think the anecdote, in the manner in which it ducks
and weaves between the ludic and the authentic, can generate the easy
to ask but difficult to answer question of how it is that we—in twenty-
first-century Western society—have come by our special ideal of personal authenticity.

As for Shakespearean characters, many of them are highly emblematic, even (as with Hamlet perhaps) emblematic of their own metatheatricality. Yet this very same metatheatricality may also be seen, by
both playwrights and audiences, as a means of testing the parameters
of emblematic selfhood and its representation—of insinuating, or
revealing, an interiority accessible only through disclosure or confession figured as "outside" the official performance—the device, whether

explicit or implicit, of the play within the play. This paradox of, or the conceptual tension between, a view of individuality as socially, functionally, and emblematically defined and in which the type is the individual (and vice versa), juxtaposed with, or against, an emerging sense of selfhood as a uniquely subjective interiority, could be seen as a characteristic tension not only of Elizabethan and Jacobean theater (and specifically Shakespeare's) but of the daily experience of social and personal life in early modern England.

The connection between the verb *to personate* and theater was, of course, a matter of common etymological knowledge in a culture educated in Latin, *personate* deriving, like the word *person* itself and all its cognates, from the Latin *persona*, meaning precisely "a mask (used by a player); a person or character acted (*dramatis persona*), one who plays or performs any part, a character" (*Oxford English Dictionary*). If personation was what actors did on stage, it was also what people did in real life in the sense of portraying, fulfilling, or representing their office, function, or capacity. A "person" was a character sustained or assumed both in a drama and in actual life, a part played, and "personation" was what persons did "naturally" in presenting themselves for public scrutiny. Thus, the term *naturalism* may need to be applied with more caution to the mingled social and theatrical performativity of life in early modern England, for not only did early modern sensibilities juxtapose "art" (the artificial) and "nature" (the natural)—a topic of familiar commentary and negotiation in the period—but, as we have seen, early modern subjects show symptoms of a willingness to run together the "acted" and the "real" in a way that suggests that acting, performance, and the playing of parts was a normal, if also contradictory, dimension of social experience and exchange. Hence the constant claims for the competing veracity of art and nature.

And there could be good reasons for puzzlement. Personation (later "impersonation") was also what some people did in real life to counterfeit another person, usually for purposes of fraud or deception: Robert Cawdrey's *A Table Alphabeticall of English Wordes* (1604) defines *personate* simply as "to counterfeit anothers person." The *OED* quarries Sir William Brereton's lexicon in *Travels in Holland* for "The Countess of Oxford personated the Queen and deceived the child," but sixteenth-century Europe had long been fascinated by the celebrated trial in France of the impostor who for years had successfully impersonated Martin Guerre, deceiving a whole community, an extended family, and even "passing" with Martin Guerre's wife (see Zemon Davis). Vulnerability to imposture, being deceived by one's neighbor or tricksters assuming accents or flaunting the sumptuary laws, or having one's own identity or paternity stolen or mimicked are all fears characteristically—even obsessively—expressed on and offstage in Elizabethan discourse (see Woodbridge). The other side, and hence cause, of those fears of disintegration is the imperative of a sense of order, of the roles, offices, and functions to be enacted and the inviolable social distinctions to be observed that set bounds to the performing space of every individual. And the pressure point of this anxiety lies precisely in the very externality, the explicitly compositional nature, of early modern selfhood and its opposition in the emerging—and potentially disruptive—sense of the interiority of the individual and the uniqueness of the human person. The evidence from theatrical representation and reception would seem to indicate that notions of selfhood in the period are characterized by a movement and countermovement in which the typically emblematic and public images of selfhood are contested by internalized gestures toward more modern-day notions of personhood and that the tension between them can be anarchic (Gloucester's "I am myself alone"), poignant (Lear's "Who is it can tell me who I am?—Lear's shadow") or both poignant and witty (Rosalind's "Well, in her person I say I will not have you," capped by Orlando's "Then in mine own person I die" [*AYLI*, 4.1.79–80]).

The two kinds of discourse exist—as in a sense they always do—side by side. Reflection on the notion of personhood is one of those occasions when, to paraphrase Bernard Williams, we need to say *both* that there is significant historical variation between an idea or concept as used by two different groups (ourselves and early modern people) *and* that these are in some sense variant forms of the same concept (Williams 7–9). When Hamlet famously seeks to distinguish between what is "within" and what is only "show" and wonders how he can be denoted "truly" (1.2.76–87), we might ask whether he is making an existential or a social point. The vast amount of commentary on the play outside of the seventeenth century has no trouble answering that question, but in the context of the rigidly hierarchical and functionally stratified social structures of early modern life it was evidently not easy to distinguish the show from what was within, nor, presumably, was it meant to be easy or even necessarily desirable. Hamlet does not deny that his "inky cloak" and his melancholic behavior denote him truly; he only claims that they are "not alone" in doing so because they happen to chime with his interior feelings. He is not, like a modern self-analyst, repudiating the external as somehow unhappily wedded to the interior while unable to express it; rather, he suggests the limits of the explicit, the composite, in any act of personation. The "actions that a man might play" and the costuming that accompanied them (in this case, the gestures of mourning and black garments) were designed, and understood as, an expressive social semiotics that, unembarrassed by modern notions of a mandatory subjectivity, also allowed "that within which passeth show" to remain within if so desired (an option Hamlet subsequently in the play makes great use of, of course). And, significantly, the metaphorical language that Hamlet uses to describe this traffic between outward expressiveness and inward authenticity is that of theatrical performance, the adoption of the "trappings and the suits," the playing of a part, and the discharging of it "to th' life." In Shakespeare's plays in particular, we may feel the strain of personation, as his characters take shape by openly acknowledging the difficulties pertaining both to their status as actors and to their explicitly compositional forms.

Further, the relation between theatrical role-playing and personal role-playing in terms of the *orbis theatrum mundi* would seem to be that one is played before one's peers, but in the other performing space the only spectator is a being called God, "from whom no secrets are hid" (*Book of Common Prayer*), a metaphysical and spiritual arena, with its radical confusion of actor-character divisions and the utter transparency of its personations, which, as in the play *Hamlet*, can become itself the subject of intense dramatic exploration.

NOTES

1. This is according to Henk Gras, who analyzes almost all the available responses to performance.

WORKS CITED

Barroll, J. Leeds. *Artificial Persons: The Formation of Character in the Tragedies of Shakespeare.* Columbia: U of South Carolina P, 1974.

Brereton, Sir William. *Travels in Holland.* London, 1636.

Cawdrey, Robert. *A Table Alphabeticall of English Wordes.* London, 1604.

Erasmus, Desiderius. *The Praise of Folly* (1509). Trans. Betty Radice. Harmondsworth: Penguin, 1978.

Flecknoe, Richard. *A Short Discourse of the English Stage.* London, 1664.

Gras, Henk. *Studies in Elizabethan Response to Theatre.* 2 vols. Frankfurt: Peter Lang, 1993.

Gurr, Andrew. *The Shakespearean Stage, 1574–1642.* 2nd ed. Cambridge: Cambridge UP, 1980.

Hattaway, Michael. *Elizabethan Popular Theatre: Plays in Performance.* London: Routledge and Kegan Paul, 1982.

Heywood, Thomas. *Apology for Actors* (1612). Rpt. in *The Elizabethan Stage.* Ed. E. K. Chambers. 4 vols. Oxford: Clarendon, 1923. 4: 250–54.

———. Prologue to *The Jew of Malta* (1633). *Christopher Marlowe: The Complete Plays.* Ed. J. B. Steane. London: Penguin, 1986. 343–44.

Leggatt, Alexander. *Jacobean Public Theatre.* London: Routledge, 1992.

Manningham, John. *The Diary of John Manningham of the Middle Temple, 1602–03.* Ed. Robert Parker Sorlein. Hanover, NH: UP of New England, 1976.

Marlowe, Christopher. *Christopher Marlow: The Complete Plays.* Ed. J. B. Steane. London: Penguin, 1986.

Maynard, John. *The XII Wonders of the World: Set and Composed by . . . John Maynard.* London, 1611. Poems by Sir John Davies.

Montaigne, Michel de. *Essays.* Trans. John Florio. 3 vols. London: Everyman, 1965.

Shakespeare, William. *The Norton Shakespeare.* Gen. ed. Stephen Greenblatt. New York: Norton, 1997.

Thomson, Peter. *Shakespeare's Theatre.* 2nd ed. London: Routledge, 1992.

Williams, Bernard. "Why Philosophy Needs History." *London Review of Books* 17 October 2002: 7–9.

Woodbridge, Linda. "Impostors, Monsters, and Spies: What Rogue Literature Can Tell Us About Early Modern Subjectivity." *Early Modern Literary Studies*, special issue 9 (January 2002): 1–11. http://purl.oclc.org/emls/si-09/woodimpo.htm

Zemon Davis, Natalie. *The Return of Martin Guerre.* Harvard: Harvard UP, 1983.

Chapter 4

Dialogues of Self-Reflection
Early Modern Mirrors

Philippa Kelly

*I*n many texts and contexts during the sixteenth and seventeenth centuries, the complex realm of individuality was importantly linked to
images of mirroring, whose impact developed in part from a burgeoning industry in glass mirror making. While it is tempting to regard the
mirror as a Burckhardtian emblem of premodern self-consciousness,
this view does not exhaust all aspects of the debate about who, or what,
"the self" was. Social self-production was certainly served by the mirror, yet the issues of what such self-production involved, and what it
aimed for, remain contentious. The focus of this chapter is on mirrors
and their social meanings and, more specifically, on the capacity of
mirrors in *language* to help shape certain concepts and practices of self-
representation and life writing.

The connections among mirrors, autobiography, and self-representation are marked by an abundance of artistic tropes. While mirrors
were not absent from literature before the sixteenth and seventeenth
centuries, they proliferated during that period, and attempts to his-
toricize and record them have inspired exhaustive studies such as Herbert Grabes's *The Mutable Glass*. Yet, while poetry and drama, such as
the 1606 play *Wily Begvilde*, declared the "looking glasse" to be a place
"indeed / Wherein a man a History may read," mirrors did not consistently feature as part of vernacular discourse about the self: replete
with multiple meanings, they ornamented the language of artistic
endeavor and occasional tracts and papers as conspicuously as the
large, framed artifacts themselves enriched an upper-class family

home. Large mirrors were very difficult to make and expensive to produce, unlike the common household item we recognize today. Reflection and mirroring, tropes of the self par excellence for many modern literary and cinematic works, did not have the same pervasive contemporary cultural basis.

Somewhat paradoxically, there are two points that both limit and elevate the mirror as a figure for early modern selfhood. First, very few everyday journals and housekeeping records describe even brief physical encounters with the mirror; the sparse references in diaries are highly metaphorical in tone, as in Richard Rogers's "endeavour to see one year thus passed, that it may be a glass to me hereafter . . ." (96). Yet, given the upper- and upper-middle-class demographic of "ordinary" diaries and records, it is safe to assume that most "autobiographical" writers—Rogers, Margaret Hoby, Grace Mildmay, John Worthington, and Elias Ashmole, to name just a few—had access to looking glasses in which they could check their appearance at will. The fact that they never wrote about these glasses contests the notion that—despite the mirror's obvious importance to the practice of philosophical and spiritual contemplation, not to mention the abundance within advice literature of references to inward and outward reflection[1]—the simple act of observing one's physical reflection served as an everyday psychological touchstone.[2] Second, just as a mirror of sizable proportions was a luxury item, so its literary traces are largely confined to art and philosophical contemplation in the canonical works of writers such as Shakespeare, Donne, Milton, Browne, Descartes, and others. If we put these two points together, we may wonder what the relevance of mirrors to the subject of "autobiography" might be. Can an analysis of the mirror tell us anything more than that canonical writers preferred to use it as a trope? And in its capacity as trope, did it indeed serve generally shared notions of selfhood in the period? Or does it now function, perhaps, as an artifact to which critics, looking back to the early modern period, attach unwieldy and anachronistic literary pretexts?

Most journals and diaries of the period were begun as straightforward records, not as inward-looking excavations replete with the conceptual machinery of mirrors and other speculative devices. I contend, however, that the mirror and its literary contexts provide a useful way into the study of autobiography in sixteenth- and seventeenth-century England. They can be seen, for example, as highly stylized, accepted forms of personal and social speculation in a society that rarely encouraged such perspectives within commonplace household circumstances. The act of looking at a mirror implies the act of looking *at* and perhaps *into* oneself, practices which, though they may be very familiar to us today, were for many people of that period exceptional experiences rather than the norm. The argument is not that people in the sixteenth and seventeenth centuries did not look at themselves but rather that they had very different notions of what this meant and different ways of doing it. Similarly, the argument is not that seemingly un-self-reflexive writing—that is, much of the writing that falls outside of canonical self-representation—failed to reveal considerations about selfhood but that such considerations often lacked the declarative element that we find in many canonically valued texts. In the wake of new historicism and cultural materialism, scholars are unwilling to see the early modern period as available to us exclusively through canonical texts; but we are also unwilling to dismiss these texts as irrelevant to the lives and thoughts of many ordinary men and women who heard, read, and discussed them, or perhaps saw them performed, and whose own written reflections, if they indeed occurred, are less explicitly "self-representational."

The question of mirrors, then—who owned them, who wrote about them, what they "meant"—marks a point of beginning for an inquiry into modes of self-representation. The canonical texts and images in which mirrors abound offer a place to stage philosophical problems and considerations about selfhood and its representation in the early modern period. The complicated, highly stylized trope of mirroring can be used to amplify many of the debates that describe and display aspects of selfhood in early modern life.

Making Mirrors

Glass mirrors date back to the third century A.D. in Egypt, Gaul, Asia Minor, and Germany. These mirrors were very small, one to three inches in diameter, and the quality of reflection was not good. For many centuries, then, metal mirrors of steel, silver, and gold were preferred until a technique was found for producing long, flat, thin glass and artisans devised a means of spreading hot metal onto glass without causing breakage (Melchior-Bonnet 112–13). The term *mirror* referred to metal mirrors as well as "water mirrors," crystal mirrors and mirrors of glass, while *looking glass* or, less commonly, *seeing glass,* designated mirrors made of a glass compound (Grabes 70–74). At the end of the twelfth century, looking glasses were revived, adopted first in Germany and Italy and gradually reaching England (Grabes 71). A mixture of antimony and lead was heated two or three times. Molten resin was poured into the mixture, which was blown by means of a pipe into a spherical bowl with a hole in it. The bowl was shaken so that the mixture would spread around the inner wall, and the leftover liquid was drained out of the opening. The bowl was then left to stand until the amalgam had cooled and hardened, when it was cut in half to make two convex mirrors. Such mirrors provided a novel way of distorting the face.[3]

In sixteenth-century Venice, the production of glass mirrors became an important industry, and techniques for making mirrors were significantly refined. The round bowls used as molds for convex mirrors were replaced by the middle of the century with glass cylinders that could be leveled out to make flat mirrors. The reverse side of a mirror was covered with an amalgam of tin and mercury, in the production of which a sheet of tinfoil was set on a table. On top of the foil, the glassmakers poured pure mercury, and over that they placed a sheet of paper. Before it hardened, the glass, cut and flattened from the cylindrical mold, was lowered onto the paper. The artificers subsequently removed the piece of paper so that the glass would touch the surface of the mercury. They weighted the glass down to allow the excess mercury to seep out, leaving a thin layer that would bind itself to the tin, forming a backing. A month later a piece of metal was attached to this backing, and the resulting glass mirror gave a very good reflection (cf. Popova).

Because they pushed the technology of the day to its limits, large glass mirrors were very difficult to make, and thus they were neither cheap nor readily accessible (Popova 186–87; Grabes 70–93; Melchior-Bonnet 30). In mid-seventeenth-century Venice, a silver-framed looking glass, 115 by 65 cm, cost eight thousand pounds, while a Raphael painting cost three thousand (Melchior-Bonnet 30).[4] On the continent, at least, the acquisition of large mirrors was linked to a person's lifestyle and craving for aristocratic connections rather than to the availability of personal resources (Melchior-Bonnet 29). And if John Aubrey's description of Francis Bacon's house at Gorhambry is anything to go by, the looking glass was a mark of grandeur (and, indeed, an enhancement of grandeur) in England as well.

The upper part of the uppermost dore on the east side, had inserted into it a large looking-glasse, with which the stranger was very gratefully deceived, for (after he had been entertained a pretty while, with the prospects of the ponds, walks, and countrey, which this dore faced) when you were about to returne into the roome, one would have sworn *primo intuitu*, that he had beheld another Prospect through the howse: for, as soon as the stranger was landed on the balconie, the conserge that shewed the howse would shutt the dore to putt this fallacy on him with the Looking-glasse. (195)

Mirrors were frequently used in courtesans' toiletry and were important both in crafting a toilette and as artifacts that helped to define the intimacy of a dressing room (Santore; Pennell 555; Melchior-Bonnet 28). Small, mass-produced glass mirrors were also available in sixteenth-century Venice, making their way to England by the middle of the century. While these were not hugely expensive, their use was mainly for urbanites and those working at court, and mirrors the size of a powder compact were worn decoratively at the waist by women and in the cap by men (Grabes 71; Melchior-Bonnet 23).

In considering the availability of mirrors outside urban and court circles, it is helpful to examine regional inventories such as that afforded by the parish of the market town of Darlington. Only two of the testators—both among the wealthier members of the town—bequeathed looking glasses. The looking glass left by Mary Throckmorton must have been of a reasonable size, given that it was valued, along with sundry small items, at six shillings (Atkinson 172); another, left by Mary Lascelles, was valued at only one shilling and sixpence (152). A set of twelve small glasses left by Anthony Dennis was valued at less than two shillings (112). Given that a bed was valued at between two and six shillings (154, 172), a mare and foal with saddle and bridle cost four shillings (121), a set of linen sheets could fetch between five and thirteen shillings (148, 172), and five bushels of wheat and rye were valued at sixteen shillings (164), these looking glasses and small glass mirrors were not beyond the means of country people.[5] Notwithstanding the affordability of small mirrors, they do not appear to have been considered particularly necessary or desirable.

Among the more elevated classes, however, the small "seeing glass" was professionally useful, as service in court circles depended heavily on personal grooming. Castiglione's conduct manual, *The Book of the Courtier*, which was widely read in court circles throughout Europe and in England, offered praise for the courtier who showed "a meticulous regard for . . . personal appearance" (68). But Castiglione also added a caution in view of the growing fascination with this newly industrialized means of reflection, criticizing those rather excessive individuals who carried "a mirror in the fold of [their] cap[s] and a

comb in [their] sleeve[s] . . . walking through the streets always followed by a page with a brush and sponge" (68). Mirrors, then, were
capable of revealing an unseemly concern with one's social persona.

Because the system of patronage and coterie culture at work in the
upper classes effectively nurtured poets, dramatists, and visual artists,
the circulation of the small glass among such people can offer a plausible explanation for the burgeoning interest in the mirror as a literary
motif of self-scrutiny. But what exactly was *meant* by *self-scrutiny* or,
indeed, *self-expression?* The subtle social issues that press this question
can be approached by examining the multiple ways in which mirror
motifs gesture toward worldly conduct, spiritual issues, the cosmos,
and, indeed, the shape staring back at the beholder from an often shadowy, opaque glass.[6]

The Mirror and the Speaking Subject

Reveling in his self-conceit, Shakespeare's poet of Sonnet 62 peers into
the looking glass, stopping short at the image of "myself indeed, /
Beaten and chapped with tanned antiquity."[7] His looking glass reveals
the unsettling disparity between the face he imagines he has and the
face he owns. He ruefully recalls the alacrity with which he first
approached the mirror, expecting there to individuate himself from
other, less worthy lovers:

> Methinks no face so gracious is as mine,
> No shape so true, no truth of such account,
> And for my self mine own worth do define
> As I all other in all worths surmount.

In his glass, he sees reflected not his superior worth but his ordinariness, his own mortality, and a foolhardiness that links him "indivisi-
bly" to a "tanned antiquity" of other lovers. The poet's trip to the mirror is thus a salutary one. No longer spry and self-loving, in a
quasi-neoplatonic gesture he soberly offers to replace his own image
altogether with that of the lover he had hoped to woo.

Or so it seems. Something quite complicated happens, however, in
this ritual gesture of temperance in which the poet assembles an intricate set of counterimages that challenge the conceit of self-reflection.
First, it is not his physical reflection that strikes the poet—it is the
"sin" of "self-love" that engrosses him, possessing "all mine eye, / And
all my soul, and all my every part." His reflection in the mirror is thus
more moral than corporeal. Second, in availing the poet of a private

moment of spiritual chastisement, the mirror effectively becomes a form of spiritual soliloquy, a way of talking with God. Through these images of reflection, the mirror takes on the task of spiritual instruction. Somewhat perversely, however, while the poet modestly recoils at the foolish vanity he sees reflected, it is nonetheless the mirror that permits him to gloat: through the conceit of reflection, he argues for his possession of two of the most important Aristotelian virtues, humility and magnanimity. In one refracted image, the sonnet itself thus effectively becomes a convex mirror, simultaneously collapsing the poet's words into a history of *vanitas* while also parading his merits.

Shakespeare's complicated system of reflections in Sonnet 62 evokes a speaking self that does all sorts of things in front of the mirror. It preens, self-castigates, peeps modestly from behind self-deprecating images, and even offers to absent itself altogether. The rhetoric of reflection articulates various spiritual and worldly attributes within the givens and obscurities of the spoken word. But is the poet's self a rhetorical one and, if so, to what extent? Does the trope of reflection work to display an individuated self or to mediate it as a social function? The pioneering work of Stephen Greenblatt laid the ground for two subsequent decades of critics, who have speculated on autobiographical self-representation in the early modern period.[8] This debate finds an intersection in recent arguments developed by Deborah Shuger and Sabine Melchior-Bonnet.

Deborah Shuger argues that mirrors in early modern English artistic practice—writings, paintings, woodcuts, and the like—describe not a reflexive self-consciousness that might be seen to herald the birth of modern subjectivity but in fact the reverse (21). She suggests that, while representations of mirrors reflected many things, they almost never revealed, or even purported to display, an individuated self (22). They were instruments of correction; platonically angled, upward-tilted mirrors intended to reflect paradigms of virtue; remembrances of mortality; and cruel reminders that sins such as vanity must be punished. (They functioned, indeed, as all of the symbols toward which Shakespeare gestures in Sonnet 62.) On this basis, Shuger argues convincingly that the early modern mirror was not a Burckhardtian exemplar of the birth of an individuated self but the mark of a culture that did not yet have a place, or a vocabulary, for the kind of "I" with which we are now so familiar.

Shuger's thesis is borne out by various visual and verbal artifacts of the period, which counterpoise different kinds of mirrors—physical

and spiritually perceptual—to different effect. The impassioned Giovanni in John Ford's *'Tis Pity She's a Whore* (1633) assures us that the
truth of the glass can surpass both nature and counterfeit.

> If you would see a beauty more exact
> Than art can counterfeit or nature frame,
> Look in your glass, and there behold your own . . .
>   (1.2.205–7)

While Ford's glass can penetrate beyond the countenance to mirror
one's intentions, Thomas Watson, in Sonnet 45 of his sequence *Tears
of Fancy*, postulates rather that the "heart" of an adoring beholder dis-
tills the subject's spirit in a reflection more accurate than any cold
glass: "With steadfast eyes she gazed on my heart. / Wherein she saw
the picture of her beauty . . ." (157). Ben Jonson uses the mirror of
moral reflection to expose "the time's deformity / Anatomised in every
nerve, and sinew, / With constant courage, and contempt of
fear"(*Every Man Out*, "After the Second Sounding," ll.120–22). The
passage alludes to a conventional association between the glass and
anatomy, the exposure of organs that reflected secret truths.

In this sense, mirrors—whether physical or inwardly perceptual—
do not reveal an individuated self so much as a social self. Mirrors offer
a means of self-correction and self-abasement in the eyes of God or,
perhaps, a picture of folly. Leonardo da Vinci cites the glass mirror as
a figurative tool, instructing the painter to "keep his mind as clear as
the surface of a mirror, which assumes colours as various as those of
the different objects" (Vezzosi 136). The mirror can be seen as a touchstone of clarity more real than "reality" itself.[9]

If early modern mirrors offer a multifaceted means of stylized display, it is important to note that their images, while instructive, are
very often not simply or singularly so. What we see in the mirror is
familiar and unsettling, reassuringly symbolic as well as cosmologi-
cally unstable. In Milton's *Paradise Lost*, for example, Eve comes upon
a "smooth lake" and stoops down to see a "shape within the wat'ry
gleam / Bending to look on me." Starting in bewilderment, she finds
that "it started back" (4.457–69), suggesting less the self-loving nar-
cissist than a child enchanted by a new companion whose movements
are in tune with her own. For Philip Sidney, reflections can distort the
truth in the same moment as they purport to reveal it: if a writer's
feigning "made David as in a glass see his own filthiness" (228), yet at
times poetry's feigning needs to be countered by the "unflattering
glass of reason" (212–15). In "The Good Morrow," Donne writes of

the act of reflection that reveals the face of another, the capacity of this face to reveal the heart, and the image of a sphere through which these two reflected selves display the unity of the cosmos.

> My face in thine eye, thine in mine appears,
> And true plain hearts do in the faces rest;
> Where can we find two better hemispheres,
> Without sharp North, without declining West?
>
> (ll.89–90)

Donne's hemispheres—the reflective gazes exchanged between two lovers—represent the "reality" that emerges from their union, while also alluding to the convex physical shape of the eye. If the eye is itself a convex mirror, then the question is left gaping from Donne's poem: does the eye distort a "real" physical world or is this physical world itself merely the *creation* of the eye, subject to the twists and tricks of perception?

Artful Individuation: Mirrors and Movement

In these diverse contexts, artistic mirrors serve a highly social and gestural function. Shuger concludes that while people four centuries ago would not have hesitated to use an available mirror to remove spinach from their teeth, the mirror as trope has a special function. Rather than a preemptive sign of our own contemporary, postindustrial individuality, she sees it as in fact the opposite, designating a self that lacks "reflexivity, self-consciousness, and individuation, and that hence differs fundamentally from what we usually think of as the modern self" (35). Shuger's early modern subject is not uninterested in the relationship between the reflected self and the cosmos: far from it, the subject uses the mirror as a highly emblematic means of exploring the boundaries and complexities of this relationship. But Shuger sees the mirror motif itself as profoundly medieval in representing a being that "is not identical to oneself but *like* it—a significantly similar other prior to about 1660." It reflects "those whom one will or does resemble" rather than oneself (37).

In context with Shuger's compelling argument, it is useful to consider Melchior-Bonnet's book-length study, *The Mirror: A History*. Like Shuger, Melchior-Bonnet argues for the mirror's symbolic representation of selfhood. Though the early modern mirror was "a tool of precision and control in the teaching and enforcement of civility," it was "not yet an instrument of individual rights even if it allowed the possibility of a solitary interaction with the self. The feeling of self-hood that the mirror awakened was a conflictual one of modesty or shame, consciousness of the body and of one's appearance under the watchful eye of another" (139–40). While Shuger places special emphasis on the emblematic capacities of the mirror, Melchior-Bonnet stresses its capacity for fracture and internal distance. Whereas its medieval function was in keeping with a universe that was "closed, circular, and susceptible to being deciphered," the early modern period no longer assumed "a structured universe by which one could rise from an inferior sphere to a superior one." Once used as a reflection of God's perfection in man's imperfect being, the mirror now "imposes distance and separation within a formerly closed system" (Melchior-Bonnet 119).

In terms of this topos, the man who sees himself in God sees a reflection of God's power, so that resemblance is apprehended not in symbolic forms but in sensory ones. In discovering the physical, sensory reflection of God in his own image, man enters "a new experience of subjectivity." Thus, painters such as Van Eyck use the mirror image to suggest their *own* presence in a painting—and the painter, by portraying "himself in the form of a miniscule silhouette in the divine eye-mirror, precisely at the vanishing-point of the painting," signifies the infinite. The invisible is made present within the visible. In this way "the mirror . . . lends itself to self-examination and interior dialogue. The eye-mirror of the humanist presents a new way of looking at the world, but it continues to situate itself at the core of a system of correspondences and analogies akin to the medieval mirror" (Melchior-Bonnet 126–27).[10] In *Self-Portrait in a Convex Mirror*, Parmigianino represents himself in a convex mirror on a specially prepared convex panel. Distorted by the panel, the face has a hint of caricature, turned slightly to the side, the eyes hooded and world-weary, the cheeks full and somewhat pompous-looking in a young person. The hands, distorted also by the convex panel, are enormous, and the tapered fingers drape quietly in front of his body. This distortion mirrors the salient features of the artist as he sees himself—his perception of himself as disenchanted with the world; as inward and contemplative, his face refusing to meet our gaze head-on; and as a man whose hands, the instruments of his art, find themselves oddly disproportionate not just to the room in which the painter is seated but to the canvas itself. Parmigianino's canvas, with its convex mirror, draws us into his privately skeptical realm even while it tempts us out toward the light depicted in the far left-hand corner.

In using the mirror to negotiate the meaning of early modern self-hood, the different emphases proposed by Shuger and Melchior-Bon-net enable a fascinating convergence of the physical and the iconic, the emblematic and the instructive. The mirror roots the seeing self in the realm of premodern nonreflexivity while gesturing toward those spaces and hidden depths within the self for which there is, in the period, as yet no commonly understood vocabulary. As an artistic function, the mirror offers not just a flat, stable reflection of, for instance, mortality or *vanitas* but something else: in a conflation of refracted images, it invites (and facilitates through its variety of emblematic associations) a sense of movement, shifting from a physical function to a compound of often contradictory speculations. Real as well as figurative, then, the mirror's physical function spins the act of reflection into a series of epistemological uncertainties and anxieties, so that it becomes in itself a trope of transition. Within the language of mirrors are embedded multiple reverberations, echoes, twists and con-tortions, and physiological and cosmological speculations. It is for this reason, too, perhaps, that many of the mirrors represented visually and verbally are convex; conveying more than one individuated image, they reflect a range of speculations about the place of the "I" in a world marked by enormous changes in cartography, the shape of the earth, and the shape of the universe itself (Gillies). And in "reflecting" the radical instability of the "I," the mirror posits the *specular* as the means of social speculation.

Outside the Frame? Mirrors in Tracts and Journals

So far, our discussion has posited literary artifacts and paintings as highly stylized contexts for the representation of a mirrored self—a self dealing in images that are emblematic and in some fashion instruc-tive but which is also epistemologically speculative. Ideals of good conduct and unflattering admonishments of frail humanity—these are the hallmarks of the mirror, while in juxtaposing closure with internal distance and separation their transitional element suggests intense speculation about the nature and manifestation of selfhood. But what of the texts outside such artistically imaginative and fictional contexts, the journals, essays, and tracts that make up the bulk of early modern written artifacts? Do they offer alternative concepts for the form and function of reflection or are their images equally resonant with emblematic significance?

The musician Thomas Whythorne's life narrative offers a straightforwardly functional example, comparing mirrors with portraiture. Visiting in London the artist who painted several portraits of him, Whythorne notices about the painter's house

> many pictures, as well of those that were much elder than I, as of some such that were of my years, yea, and much younger than I was. The which caused me to think that as some young folks, for that they having a pleasure to behold their beauties and favours, caused their picture to be made, so those that were older than I, although they had no such cause for beauty and favours' sake as many young folk have, did cause their pictures or counterfeits to be painted from time to time to see how time doth alter them.
>
> But now, peradventure, you would say that they may see themselves when they will in a looking-glass. To the which I do say that the glass showeth but the disposition of the face for the time present, and not as it was in time past. Also it showeth the face the contrary way, that is to say, that which seemeth to be the right side of the face is the left side in deed; and so likewise that which seemeth to be the left side is the right. And also the perfection of the face that is seen in a glass doth remain in the memory of the beholder little longer than he is of beholding the same. For so soon as he looketh off from the glass he forgetteth the disposition and grace of his face. (115)

In Whythorne's view, the mirror is a mark of mutability because it offers no capacity for historical reflection. It is simply a temporal reflection of a face whose aspect is all too fleeting, progressively marked by life's vicissitudes. A portrait, on the other hand, offers the opportunity to imprint one's face permanently on the world, so that in looking at a canvas one can contemplate one's history. The mirror's limitations are compounded by its distortion of left and right and by the fact that having looked in a mirror one forgets immediately the shape of one's face, so that the reflection itself is not really worth having.

The mirror can be fairly unambiguous not only in the literal terms described by Whythorne but also in its emblematic signification. In the context of that dominant English Renaissance preoccupation with the provision of good counsel to kings, for example, Bishop Joseph Hall writes to Mr. Newton, tutor to the prince:

> How happy a service shall you do to this whole world of ours, if you shall still settle in that princely mind a true apprehension of himself . . . break those false glasses that would present him a face not his

own: to applaud plain truth, and bend his brows upon excessive praises! (1.137–38)

And in his more "private" meditations he further ornaments his thinking with the emblem of reflection, not so much of himself as of the self-authenticating world around him.

> It is good for a man not always to keep his eyes at home, but sometimes to look abroad at his neighbours, and to compare his own condition with the worse estate of others. If we do not sometimes make these, not proud, but thankful comparisons, and look upon ourselves, not with direct beams, but by reflection upon others, we shall never be sensible enough of our own mercies. (1.627)

An anonymously authored tract, "The Sicke Man's Comfort," positions the mirror as a conventional means of self-improvement in the eyes of God.

> When we have laid all this [our sins] to the sicke man's charge, and in the Law as in a Mirrour wee have set before his eyes to behold his judgement and sentence of condemnation: when we perceive him wounded and pearced to the heart with sorowe, we must them laye to his wound some asswaging medicine, and do as Masons do when they hewe their stone; first they give grete blowes with their hammer, and make gret peaces fall off, and then they poolish it over with a plaine, that the strokes are no more seen: so must we do, after we have handled the sick patient roughly, and thrust him downe to hel by the rigorous threats of the lawes: we must comfort him, and fetche him againe by the sweete amiable promises of the Gospel, to the end that the sowplenes of this oyle may asswage the nipping sharpnes of the law. (61)[11]

The mirror motif pleads an understanding of God's judgment and the law. In the end, it is God who recognizes the truth of which man himself can see merely the reflection; and it is only God who can unify the broken body in embracing the soul. (We will see another connection to this speech later in the account of Walter Devereaux's death scene.)

A more complicated, speculative assessment of the mirror is offered by Montaigne, who imbues it with his characteristic skepticism. "My looking glasse doth not amaze me," he claims as he looks into his glass, noting a degeneration in "my face and eyes" so severe that "I often move my friends to pitty, ere I feele the cause of it." "[E]ven in my youth," he continues, it hath divers times befaln me, so to put-on a dusky looke, a wan colour, a troubled behaviour and of ill presage, without any great accident; so that the Physitions perceiving no inward cause to answer this outward alteration, ascribed the same to the secret minde or some concealed passion, which inwardly gnawed and consumed me. They were deceived: were my body directly by me, as is my minde, we should march a little more at our ease.... I am of the opinion, that this her temperature hath often raised my body from his fallings: he is often suppressed, whereas she, if not lasciviously wanton, at least in quiet and reposed estate. I had a quartan ague which held me foure or five months, and had altogether disvisaged and altered my countenance, yet my mind held ever out, not onely peaceably but pleasantly . . . ("Of Experience" 3.369–70)

Montaigne sees his reflected face as an unruly member that runs out of sync with his mind. If his face could only be governed in the disciplined way that his mind is, it would not have a scurvy hue; but faces, he suggests, may not match the rude health of souls. Hence, while he acknowledges the flatness of reflection—the sense that an image means something, that one's complexion can signify a physical or emotional state—Montaigne is also intrigued by the possibility of shifting asymmetries. The self that gazes back at him is skeptical, signifying a whole range of things and nothing entirely and, indeed, questioning the consonance between mind and body that was later to be crystallized as Cartesian dualism.

While Montaigne accepts that his glass displays an asymmetry between body and soul, many writers struggle to resolve this asymmetry. The engrossments of a glass, they suggest, may render a subject incapable of self-censure, necessitating another kind of glass to conjoin subjective perception with reality. This point is made by both Sir Francis Bacon and Sir Thomas Elyot. Bacon writes that

observing our faults in others is sometimes improper for our case; but the best receipt (best, I say, to work, and best to take) is the admonition of a friend. It is a strange thing to behold what gross errors and extreme absurdities many (especially of the greater sort) do commit, for want of a friend to tell them of them, to the great damage both of their fame and fortune: for, as St. James saith, they are as men, that look sometimes into a glass, and presently forget their own shape and favour. (Bacon 304)

Here Bacon offers two kinds of glass. One, the physical image in the mirror, is closed and static, promoting a self-regarding gaze in which, quite ironically, one loses sight of oneself. This physical mirror prompts Bacon to speculate on a second kind of reflection, in which the glass of friendship counters scopic self-involvement. In observing and defining one's passage through the world, a friend can ward off the absurdities of pride and willful blindness. In *The Booke of the Governor,* Sir Thomas Elyot also writes of selves that act as glasses, though his trope of reflection is more conventionally hierarchical (as is, indeed, Bacon's in his essay, "Of Praise" [552–53]). In Elyot's view, the self should be elevated through "the glasse of auctorite" to a level where it may enlighten those of "inferior understandynge." This reflected self is not *simply* superior, however: the act of elevation enables it to "se and also be sene." Its "excellent witte" measures the movement of those beneath its level at the same time as it confirms its own superiority (6).

In both of these instances, static physical images invoke their own limitations while promoting a transitional mode of spiritual speculation. In other words, the "thisness" of the physical mirror provokes speculation on what it cannot reveal in a static sense—aspects of selfhood that can only emerge in transit or, to put it another way, in one's passage through the world. Even then, these aspects may be shadowy and half realized, depending on friendship to impose form and definition. Walter Devereux, second earl of Essex, describes a similar speculation on the capacity of friendship to reflect, and define, aspects of the soul that may elude the physical mirror.

> He that thinkes he hath, or wisheth to have, an excellent face, noe sooner is tould of any spott or uncomelines in his countenaunce then he hyes to shew himself to a glasse, that the glasse may shew againe his true likenes unto him. (ff.101r–125v)

On one level, we might entertain a compellingly familiar image of the earl, like someone today in a restaurant bathroom, anxiously checking his face in the glass to compare corporeal reality with report. But the word *again* is arresting. It suggests that no matter what sores or spots may visit the complexion the mirror will take the observer back to another visage. This could be an act of repetition that restores a familiar unblemished state, or it could be an act of idealization that "restores" an ideal, platonically inflected beauty. There is a strong sense, then, of the mirror as something unfixed, of a multivalent image that encourages, and allows for, *transition*. In revealing the physical spot on the face, the mirror also offers a likeness that is implicitly retrospective or ideal or both. Thus, the earl goes on within the same passage to say that the mirror can accurately reveal *both* the blemish and a state of perfection and that, likewise, a true friend can recall one to a spiritual countenance unblemished by present sin.

> The same curiositye moves me, that desire to have a fayre minde, to shew the true face and state of my minde to my true freind, that he like a true glasse (without injury or flattery) may tell me whether nature or accident have sett soe fowle a blemish in it as my accusers pretend. I am charged that either in affection or opinion, or both, I preferre warr before peace, and soe consequently that all my actions, counsells and endeavours doe tend to keepe the state of England in contynuall warrs, espetially att this tyme when some peace may be had and I only impugne it . . .

Ever the courtier alert to the slightest imperfections in his outward mien, the earl is accustomed to checking his physical appearance in the glass. But in its literary manifestation the mirror holds this physical image in the very moment of transforming it into a series of speculations. The truth-telling capacities of the (literal and figurative) glass are counterpoised with the false images reflected back on the earl by those who assess his body as part of a wider social organism. In this relatively simple passage, Essex thus presents a kaleidoscope of mirrors, countering each perspective with a series of others: the physical mirror in which the subject looks at himself, the truthful gaze of the friend who faithfully mirrors back to him his physical imperfections, the friend's simultaneous capacity to serve as a mirror for his moral self-correction, the reflection of this moral countenance in the speaker's outward mien, and the sullying (and implicitly inaccurate) reflection thrown back at the speaker by the eyes of the world. In enabling the very function of self-scrutiny, these multiple reflections also imply the subjection of any image thus garnered to the vagaries of perception, both private and public.

Essex's mirror motif makes a fascinating comparison with an anonymous description of his father, Walter Devereaux, who had called for a mirror at his deathbed twenty-two years earlier. In this description, the looking glass functions as a nexus for the first earl's literal and metaphoric gaze.

> This daye in the morninge about six of the clocke he called for his looking glasse and, looking in it, he asked of us, why do yow thinck that I looke in the glas? It is not for pride, but I hadd almost for-

gottest my favor and I looke in the glas that I might carie the remembraunce of my countenance with me that I shall apeare with before my Lord Jhesus Christ. (An Account ff.115r–120r)

The mirror indeed "reflects" not the elderly earl's "favour," which he has "almost forgot" anyway, but that same passage from the apostle James's epistle alluded to by Whythorne and Bacon: "Anyone who listens to the word but does not do what it says is like a man who looks at his face in a mirror and, after looking at himself, goes away and immediately forgets what he looks like" (James 1.23–24). And the biblical echo itself evokes a mass of associations. It suggests an image of the first earl prudently composing himself in his final hours to meet his Maker. The biblical precedent implies that the earl is so at one with God's Word that he does not *know* himself apart from this Word. (This is a conventional spiritual trope, as suggested, for example, by Mary Rich, who writes that "thoughts of eternity were so much on my mind, indeed it was no wonder to me that I appeared so much altered . . . for I was so much changed to myself that I hardly knew myself, and could say with that converted person, I am not I" [Palgrave 163].) It is likely that the representation of the earl has been carefully composed by subsequent report, marking out the lines of his spiritual passage toward his Maker. Whatever the source of authorship, the mirror motif provides a complex, reverberative system of unstable reflections for the earl. Compounding the literal Word of God with a vigilant sense of worldly *sprezzatura*, he perfectly mirrors the biblical figure who gives over his self to God and is content to see himself only through reflection, and in comporting himself under his final duress in a manner ideally suited to a man about to meet his Maker he maintains the grace of the ideal courtier.

Aside from the multiple levels of mirroring offered by its biblical connotations, the passage has a deeper relation to self-fashioning in an existential sense. In the very act of peering into a glass, the dying man suggests a self that he does not know. Its favor is "almost forgot," as he gives way entirely to the eternal, collapsing the corporeal into the immortal being. A further point of interest is provided by the way in which both father and son are described in terms of the mirror as a means of self-scrutiny that combines intimacy and display. In this shared trope, they afford their own generational form of "mirroring." For both earls, mirrors provoke speculation, challenging the reality of the very physical images they define through the superimposition of an atemporal self-reflection. They suggest the complexity of perspectives from which a self can be known in the early modern world—a world in which the most commonplace event has a possible spiritual reverberation—and the diversity of functions that it therefore serves.

Further significant abstractions on reflection are offered by Descartes and Sir Thomas Browne. For Descartes, while the corporeal is *known* through its reflection in the mind's eye, "things" cannot be confused with their reflections: "physical things, the images of which are formed in my thought and which the senses themselves explore, are much more distinctly known than the unknown me who is outside the scope of the imagination" (27). While the body is anatomically divisible, moreover, the soul (for Descartes, synonymous with the mind) is not, for

> we can understand the body only as divisible whereas, in contrast, we can understand the mind only as indivisible. Nor can we conceive of half a mind, as we can of even the smallest body. Thus their natures are recognized as being not only distinct but even in some sense opposites. (14)

Browne, in his 1642 tract, *Religio Medici*, also uses the mirror motif to identify the relation of body to soul, contending that earthly knowledge is transmitted to the angels through mirroring: "If they have that intuitive knowledge, whereby, as in reflection, they behold the thoughts of one another, I cannot peremptorily deny but they know a great part of ours" (41). Browne goes on to argue for the "inorganic" nature of the soul through a triple negative—"Nor, truly, can I peremptorily deny that the soul . . . [is] inorganical"—suggesting as evidence the fact that the products of bestial acts are not merely beasts but have also "an impression and tincture of reason in as high a measure" (41). "Sense," the property of animals and humans, is organic, but the "soul," belonging to humans alone, is not an organ. The body speaks to both the corporeal sameness and the ineffable difference between man and beast, for "in the brain, which we term the seat of reason, there is not anything of moment more than I can discover in the crany of a beast. . . . Thus we are men, and we know not how . . ."(42). And if "we know not how" we are men, then perhaps, as he contends, we come closest to an understanding of our humanness through the reflection that is "intuitive."

The function of the mirror in the tracts cited here offers little to suggest a marked departure from the kinds of mirrors that appeared in fictional and visual art (the kinds of mirrors exemplified in the "Mirror and the Speaking Subject" section of this chapter). The first-person

discussions of Montaigne, Bacon, Elyot, and Browne, for example, do
not offer a more private engagement with the glass that would mark a
difference from the function of the artistic mirror; rather, mirrors in
these discursive passages emerge as similarly emblematic and instructive, similarly gestural and potentially multifaceted. Whether it be to
suggest mutability or moral instruction, to magnify faults or display
ideals of virtue—or, perhaps, to play on various of these functions—
the mirror appears to be as carefully and pragmatically modeled in
tracts and occasional papers as it is in sonnets, plays, and paintings.
And yet the very multiplicity to which it refers—the metaphysical
shift from world to world—suggests uncertainties that rendered the
early modern world uncertain as well as systematically self-assured.

Looking through Mirrors

In current-day terms it may seem platitudinous to say that the mirror
affords a way of looking at and into oneself. Yet early modern England
affords a remarkable opportunity to exhibit a variety of self-reflexive
perspectives, often within a single, multifaceted trope. In its various
poetic, dramatic, and occasional contexts, the trope of the mirror combines the familiar emblematic marks of medieval selfhood with the
internal distance and separation that gesture toward modern concepts
of individuality. And in its relationship to the subject of autobiography
the mirror raises questions about basic critical categories and distinctions concerning the stylized selves that can pose as "real" and the verbal and pictorial structures that yield them. What is the relationship
between the emblematic "I" and the "I" of journals, tracts, and other
modes of life writing, particularly when the emblematic "I"—the self
represented in Shakespeare's sonnets, for example, in Donne's "The
Good Morrow," or in various discursive tracts and spiritual passages—is very much more intimate than the detached voice found in
many autobiographical texts? Are these intimate, and self-reflexive,
illustrative selves any less real for originating outside the realm of
more prosaic discourse? And, if not, then what does this say about the
nature of autobiographical self-reflection and the mirror's usefulness
to this subject?

In raising such a question, the study of mirrors suggests that the
relation between the real and the rhetorical is paradoxical: whereas
early modern writers may have lacked within the structure and vocabulary of everyday life a means for self-reflection, they were able to gesture toward this means through the complex stylized structures of art-

ful discourse. And central to this access is the trope of the mirror, a trope that could stage self-reflexivity through a variety of perspectives. This paradox resonates with significant moments in the study of "self-representation" in early modern England. Any observation about the real and the rhetorical, or the "normal" and the temporary, should not provide a convenient excuse for rejecting the flatness of many everyday records in favour of carefully fashioned verbal complexities. Instead, my point is that we can use many of the "staged" perspectives set up thus far as a way *into* observations about different forms of language that can reflect on, and depart from, the reified abstractions of rhetoric, allowing us to rethink and explore the terms and conditions of what we see as "autobiographical" information across the early modern period's many different modes of life writing.

NOTES

1. Advice literature abounded with mirrors. Note, for example, Thomas Salter's laborious comparison between the vanities of a "Christall Mirrhor" and the mirror used to "garnishe the inwarde mynde": "In my imagemente there is nothing more meete, especially for yong Maidens, then a Mirrhor, therin to see and beholde how to order their dooyng, I meane not a Christall Mirrhor, made by handie Arte, by whiche Maidens now adaies, dooe onely take delight daiely to tricke and trim their tresses, standying tootyng two howers by the Clocke, looking now on this side, now on that, least any thing should bee lacking needefull to further Pride, not suffering so muche as a hare to hang out of order, no I meane no suche Mirror, but the Mirrhor I meane is made of an other maner of matter, and is of muche more worthe then any Christall Mirrhor, for as the one teacheth how to attire the outwarde bodie, so the other guideth to garnishe the inwarde mynde. . . . The Mirrhor of modestie meete for all Mothers and auncient Matrones to looke in, to decke their yong daughters and maidens myndes by: Made by T. S." (St. Clair and Maasen 5.13–15). Richard Braithwaite also abominates the vanities of ladies' glasses: "What a serious intercourse or sociable dialogue is between an amorous Mistresse and her Looking-glasse! The point or pendant of her feather wags out of a due posture; her Cheeke wants her true tincture; her captious Glasse presents to her quicke eyes one error or other, which drives her into a monstrous distemper. Pride leaves no time for prayer. This is her CLOSET FOR LADIES, where she sits and accommodates her selfe to *Fashion*, which is the period of her content, while purer objects are had in contempt. This is not the way to make Privacy your mindes melody" (6.151). Barnabe Rich uses the mirror as an emblematic tool to examine the cleanliness of his soul: "Yet by this Glasse me thus composed, it is not to view any exterior part of the body, but first to grope the conscience, and then by a diligent observation to survey the interior part of the soule: And as I have not fashioned any smooth resemblance whereby to flatter, so I have not forged any deformities thereby to slander" (4.216).

2. The point is not that the mirror failed to offer a form of introspection but rather that it failed to facilitate this as a part of everyday self-scrutiny.

3. Convex mirrors were not new; classical metal mirrors were all slightly convex.

4. Note that Popova, in her essay, puts the pricing very differently: the mirror at 68,000 lira and the Raphael painting at 3,000 (roughly one twenty-second of the price).

5. Into the late seventeenth century, English inventories list looking glasses as a commonly inventoried possession specific to the gentry and the lower echelons of the upper classes; see Weatherill.

6. Mirrors were often stained and opaque because they were silvered with lead or because of the addition of manganese oxide, which gave a dirty yellow color. Manganese oxide also produced air bubbles (Melchior-Bonnet 13–17).

7. All references to Shakespeare's works are from *The Norton Shakespeare.*

8. Katherine Eisaman Maus begins *Inwardness and Theatre in the English Renaissance* with a brief discussion of recent views about early modern self-hood and what it might constitute (1–34). Some critics, like Maus herself, argue that people of that period were very much preoccupied with individuality, that is, with the connection between public selves and private, interior motivations. Others contend that interiority constitutes a retrospective imposition on the historical subjects of the early modern period; that Shakespeare, in his recognition of interiority, was an anachronistic prophet who looked forward to our own later interests (Barker; Maus 2); and that artists of the time were commonly concerned not with individuation but with reflections of social themes.

9. Elsewhere in his writing, Leonardo used the concept of mirroring more literally, as a means of disguise.

10. Melchior-Bonnet suggests, furthermore, that the mirror "hardly reveals any kind of iconic reality, distorting the 'real' with which it identifies itself. It no longer hides a secret—the secret is henceforth in the mind that perceives and recognizes the resemblance" (131).

11. Elizabeth of Bridgewater writes similarly in her eulogy for her infant daughter that, "though her soul is singing Alelujahs, yet is her sweet body here, seized on by worms, and turned to dust till the great day shall come when all appear united both body and soule, before the judgement of God" (sig.121r).

WORKS CITED

An Account of the Death of Walter Devereux, 1st Earl of Essex, in Dublin, Sept. 1576. BL, Harleian Ms 293, ff.115r–20r.

Anon. *A Pleasant Comedie, Called Wily Begvilde: Spectrum.* London, Clement Knight, 1606. Internet reference: http://www.shef.ac.uk/~tdrg/Texts/60tq79wb.htm

——. *The Sicke Man's Comfort.* London, 1590.

Atkinson, J. A., et al., ed. *Darlington Wills and Inventories, 1600–1625.* New-castle-upon-Tyne: Athenaeum, 1993.

Aubrey, John. *Brief Lives and Other Selected Writings.* Ed. Anthony Powell. New York: Scribner's, 1949.

Bacon, Francis. *Bacon's Essays.* 5th ed. Ed. Richard Whately. London: John W. Parker, 1860.

Barker, Francis. *The Tremulous Private Body: Essays in Subjection.* London: Methuen, 1984.

Braithwaite, Richard. "The English Gentlewoman." *Conduct Literature for Women.* Ed. William St. Clair and Irmgard Maasen. London: Pickering and Chatto, 2000. 97–364.

Browne, Thomas. *Religio Medici, Hydriotaphia, and The Garden of Cyrus.* London: Everyman, 1902.

Castiglione, Baldassare. *The Book of the Courtier.* Trans. Thomas Hoby. Harmondsworth: Penguin, 1967.

Descartes, René. *Meditations and Other Metaphysical Writings.* Trans. Desmond M. Clarke. New York: Penguin, 1998.

Devereux, Walter, Second Earl of Essex. *Apologie: Preface.* PRO, SP 12/269/71, ff.101r–125v. Scribal copy, with marginated heading: "An apologie of the earle of Essex against those who falsely & maliciously taxe him to be thonely hinderer of the peace & quyet of this kingdome, written to Mr Anthony Bacon." 1598.

Donne, John. *John Donne.* Ed. John Carey. Oxford: Clarendon, 1990.

Elizabeth of Bridgewater. Diary. British Library 236.

Elyot, Sir Thomas. *The Boke of the Governour Devised by Sir Thomas Elyot, Knight* (1531). Ed. H. S. Croft. 2 vols. New York: Burt Franklin, 1967.

Ford, John. *'Tis Pity She's a Whore.* Ed. Derek Roper. London: Methuen, 1975.

Gillies, John. *Shakespeare and the Geography of Difference.* Cambridge: Cambridge UP, 1994.

Grabes, Herbert. *The Mutable Glass: Mirror Imaging in Titles and Texts of the Middle Ages and the English Renaissance.* Cambridge: Cambridge UP, 1982.

Greenblatt, Stephen. *Renaissance Self-Fashioning: From More to Shakespeare.* Chicago: U of Chicago P, 1981.

Hall, Joseph. *The Works of the Right Reverend Joseph Hall.* Ed. Philip Wynter. 10 vols. Oxford: Oxford UP, 1863.

Jonson, Ben. *Everyman Out of His Humour: The Complete Plays of Ben Jonson.* Ed. G. A. Wilkes. 4 vols. Oxford: Clarendon, 1981. 1: 275–411.

Maus, Katharine Eisaman. *Inwardness and Theatre in the English Renaissance.* Chicago: U of Chicago P, 1995.

Melchior-Bonnet, Sabine. *The Mirror: A History.* Trans. Katharine H. Jewett. New York: Routledge, 2001.

Milton, John. *Paradise Lost.* New York: Signet, 1982.

Montaigne, Michel de. *Essays of Montaigne.* Trans. John Florio. Ed. W. E. Henley. 3 vols. New York: Everyman, 1967.

Palgrave, Mary. *Saintly Lives: Mary Rich, Countess of Warwick.* London: Dent, 1901.

Pennell, Sara. "Consumption and Consumerism in Early Modern England." *Historical Journal* 42.2 (1999): 555.

Popova, S. N. "Istoria Zerkal [History of Mirrors]." *Voprosy Istorii* 5 (1982): 184–88.

Rich, Barnabe. "'The Excellenciy of Good Women' and 'My Ladies Looking Glasse.'" *Conduct Literature for Women*. Ed. William St. Clair and Irmgard Maasen. London: Pickering and Chatto, 2000. 4: 205–88.

Rogers, Richard. *Two Elizabethan Puritan Diaries by Richard Rogers and Samuel Ward*. Ed. M. M. Knappen. Gloucester, MA: Peter Smith, 1966.

St. Clair, William, and Irmgard Maasen, eds. *Conduct Literature for Women, 1500–1640*. 6 vols. London: Pickering and Chatto, 2000.

Santore, Cathy. "The Tools of Venus." *Renaissance Studies* 11.3 (1997): 179–93.

Shakespeare, William. *The Norton Shakespeare*. Ed. Stephen Greenblatt, Walter Cohen, Jean E. Howard, and Katharine Eisaman Maus. New York: Norton, 1997.

Shuger, Deborah. "The 'I' of the Beholder: Renaissance Mirrors and the Reflexive Mind." *Renaissance Culture and the Everyday*. Ed. Patricia Fumerton and Simon Hunt. Philadelphia: U of Pennsylvania P, 1999. 19–36.

Sidney, Sir Philip. *The Defence of Poesy*. Ed. Katherine Duncan-Jones. Oxford: Clarendon, 1989.

Vezzosi, Alessandro. *Leonardo da Vinci: The Mind of the Renaissance*. New York: Discoveries, 1997.

Watson, Thomas. "Tears of Fancy, or Love Disdained." *Elizabethan Sonnets*. Introd. Sydney Lee. Vol. 1. London: Westminster, 1904.

Weatherill, Lorna. "A Possession of One's Own: Women and Consumer Behaviour in England, 1160–1740." *Journal of British Studies* 25.2 (1986): 131–56.

Whythorne, Thomas. *The Autobiography of Thomas Whythorne*. Ed. James M. Osborn. London: Oxford UP, 1962.

Fig. 4.1. Parmigianino, Francesco Mazzola, gen.
(Kunsthistorisches Museum, Vienna.)

PART II

Life Genres

✳

Chapter 5

Thomas Hoccleve's Selves Apart

Anne M. Scott

*T*homas Hoccleve has long been recognized as the first seriously autobiographical poet in English literature. In his position as clerk of the Privy Seal serving four English monarchs, in the politically turbulent period from 1387 to 1426, Hoccleve was both a professional *scriptor*, whose business was the writing out of documents, and an *auctour*, a poet of authority. The persistent element of autobiography that appears in Hoccleve's poetry has become, for many modern readers, the most challenging aspect of his work. Because the facts about Hoccleve's life are verifiable, his autobiographical statements can be set within historical and literary contexts. Yet we are still left with the critical question as to how the autobiographical interventions relate to the poetry as a whole. Why should the prologue to a mirror for princes, Hoccleve's *Regement of Princes*, become an occasion of self-revelation? Why should an appeal for money, such as *La Male Règle*, be framed as the confession of the poet's misrule in his youth? As Burrow says of the *Complaint and Dialogue*, "It is only too easy to see why a medieval poet might write about 'the sinful madness of mankind'; but why should he choose to write about his own mental breakdown and its aftermath?" ("Autobiographical" 400). Recent critical attention to the purpose and effect of autobiography in Hoccleve's poetry has produced increasingly subtle insights into the work of a poet who was once thought dull and now is recognized to be tantalizingly complex. This essay argues that one particularly striking aspect of this complexity is the intense self-reflection of Hoccleve's *Complaint*, a poem that has many features that identify it as medieval but develops what seems a remarkably modern representation of the self. I offer it as a contribution to the discussion of medieval subjectivity developed more than ten years ago by David Aers in an essay that challenges the notion that medieval literature does not engage in the exploration of the self. The work of Thomas Hoccleve, and his *Complaint* in particular, demonstrates an acute consciousness of the self as subject. (cf. Aers).

Late-nineteenth- and early-twentieth-century scholars such as Furnivall and Bennett approach Hoccleve's work as literally autobiographical, accepting all he has to say at face value and agreeing with him that he is a poor poet. Furnivall sums him up as a "weak, sensitive, look-on-the-worst side kind of man" (Mitchell xxxviii). According to Furnivall, "the chief merit of Hoccleve is that he was the honourer and pupil of Chaucer" (Mitchell xxx). Serious interest in Hoccleve as a poet has developed only in the past thirty years, and two main responses to the autobiographical content are now common. One is to read the autobiography as convention and trope, particularly the trope of poetic modesty and the convention of first-person confession. Greetham sees Hoccleve's autobiographical interventions as ironic and artful excursions into the art of writing. Doob and Thornley see the fictive Hoccleve as an exemplary figure. Kohl, concerned to sift what he calls exemplary character portrayal from "real" autobiography, discusses the "persona" of the fictive Hoccleve, who is written by the "real" author Hoccleve, both of whom are present in the texts.

The other major response follows Burrow, who argues against "a tacit identification of conventionality with fictionality" and questions the belief "that convention and autobiographical truth are in general to be taken as incompatible alternatives" ("Autobiographical" 393). His comment that Hoccleve writes especially well "when he is dealing with the particulars of his own experience" suggests that, in contrast to the studied anonymity of many contemporary poets, Hoccleve intends to reveal information about the historical person, Thomas Hoccleve. In medieval poetry, authorial presence and signature are usually expressed in cryptic, allusive in-jokes for an elite coterie readership (de Looze; Middleton). The past decade has produced important scholarship that accepts Hoccleve's autobiographical details as pertaining to the historical figure about whom much of the information contained in the poetry can be matched by documented fact (Burrow *Thomas Hoccleve*). This scholarship recognizes the complexity of Hoccleve's poetic mode, which responds to conventions of religion, philosophy, and literature within historical situations that impose their own restrictions on the subject matter and voice assumed by the poet.

Strohm, for instance, argues that Hoccleve uses his own predicaments to illuminate general issues related to the new conditions of Lancastrian rule, writing that "in addition to an exciting impression of self-revelation, Hoccleve's insistence on his flawed nature possesses a political dimension" (186). Bryan accepts the literalness of the biographical materials and reassesses them as essential aspects of the *Complaint* and *Petition*, forms that use the author's sometimes obsessive interiority to highlight the public concerns of the audience. Significant themes addressed by modern critics include the relationship of Hoccleve's poetry to Lancastrian image making (Strohm; Pearsall); the significance of madness in texts (Simpson "Madness"; Goldie); the role of poetry of petition, patronage, and religious fervor (Simpson "Nobody's Man"; Scanlon; Bryan); and, most recently, the emergence of bureaucratic poetry (Knapp). These scholars do not deny the autobiographical importance of the writing but reinterpret its function as a feature of Hoccleve's poetry and its effects on poetic "truth."

There is room for considerably more study of the autobiographical impulse in Hoccleve's work, if only to make a synthesis of scholarship already in existence. My principal aim here is to use Hoccleve's account of his own madness and its aftermath as part of an exploration into late medieval conceptions of the self. Hoccleve writes himself through conventions used by other medieval writers of the self—allegory, moral exemplum, *consolatio*, and many more—but in the *Complaint* he turns a sharp inward focus on the restoration of his reason with acute self-awareness. Only when his reason is again functioning properly does he turn outward and, in conventional medieval fashion, attribute his cure to God.

Self-awareness is a concept readily grasped by modern readers, who derive notions of a self that is able to reflect on itself from theories of self-analysis developed by thinkers such as Descartes and Locke in the seventeenth century and Freud and Lacan in the twentieth. Hoccleve has been analyzed according to Lacanian principles by, for instance, Hasler in his article "Hoccleve's Unregimented Body," and his madness has been the subject of modern psychoanalysis, as reported by Medcalf (129–30). Through his poetry, Hoccleve tries to exercise control over a self on which he obsessively focuses. He reviews it, assesses what is happening, and decides on what actions are to be taken, while simultaneously recognizing that he is not in control of the whole person but is, in part, controlled by his insanity.

In spite of the personal nature of his best work, all of Hoccleve's poetry is public, having been commissioned, designed as a petition, or written to attract patronage. Before turning to the *Complaint*, Hoccleve's most widely copied and presumably most popular poem, *The Regement of Princes*, can be considered. This he wrote for Prince Henry during his period as temporary ruler of the kingdom while Henry IV was ill. In writing for the future king, who was partially out of favor with his father—dismissed from his post as temporary ruler when Henry IV recovered in November 1411 before eventually becoming king in 1413—Hoccleve demonstrated a shrewd grasp of politics. The poem, as Derek Pearsall has cogently demonstrated, is calculated to reinforce the prince's self-concept not merely as the ideal monarch but as the one who will consolidate the English nation. Significantly, the poem elevates English as a language worthy of the king and hence the nation. This happens by means of a pointed eulogy of Chaucer as "The firste fyndere of our faire langage," who is said to be equal to Aristotle, Virgil, and Cicero, the greatest philosopher, poet, and rhetorician all rolled into one. Conversely, Hoccleve ironically presents himself, dull and slow-witted, as the best that England now can offer. A humility topos is at work, for Hoccleve is, by implication, presenting himself as Chaucer's successor, a poet schooled in his art by the master and ready to assume the mantle as poet laureate. For a few years, this indeed was the case. Hoccleve became, for a time, a kind of official court poet, "receiving commissions from Henry V or his advisers for a number of political and propagandist poems" (Pearsall 410).

To have held this working position both as poet in the court and working scribe in the office of the Privy Seal, dealing with documentation for petitions and in contact with the day-to-day visitors to and officials of the court, is evidence that Hoccleve was a public person of some moment. Yet soon after 1415 his commissioned poetry came to an end, presumably because he was afflicted with what he called a "wyld infirmytie," which, from the account he gives of himself in his *Complaint*, must have been a bout of insanity. This account reveals the inner workings of Hoccleve's mind, reflecting on itself in such a way as to suggest consciousness of a self that is the Thomas Hoccleve who exists independently of his public office because that office has temporarily ceased to exist.

To the modern reader, the use of terms such as *identity* and *self* are influenced by the terminology of psychology, which has developed an expectation that a person can be aware of the individual self and be aware of what comprises identity. Medieval terminology was different. Caroline Bynum has made a good case for the view that in the twelfth and thirteenth centuries the individual gained identity by virtue of the social group. She points out that the Middle Ages did not have twentieth-century concepts of the "individual" or the "personality." Their word *individuum* (*individualis, singularis*) was a technical term in the study of dialectic; what they thought they were discovering when they turned within was what they called "the soul" (*anima*), the "self" (*seipsum*), or the "inner man" (*homo interior*) (87). The *Middle English Dictionary* (*MED*) records *self* as used mainly adjectivally: "the self same; in the self manner." When used as a noun or pronoun, it has the force of an emphatic reflexive: "Cristes self" means "Christ himself" or it can mean "individually"—"bi þe selfe." The closest I can find to its use as a substantive, "some thynges been good of þesylf," carries the meaning of "intrinsically." Yet when Hoccleve speaks of his recovery from madness, he uses the expression "But now myself to myself haue ensurid (promised) / For no swich wondrynge aftir this to mourne" (Burrow *Complaint* 304–5).

It is an expression of self-reflection, Hoccleve addressing himself with a sophisticated awareness of a self that can be controlled by the same self. There are other moments when Hoccleve uses expressions that suggest his consciousness of a divided self. He says, for instance: "Debat is now noon twixt me and my wit, / Althogh þat ther [see above] were a disseuerance / As for a tyme betwixt me and it" (247–49). To use the word *debat* suggests some inner conflict between his reason (wit) and himself.

The point is often made by critics that a medieval poet who wants to demonstrate inner debate uses allegorical figures. Langland, for instance, in *Piers Plowman*, represents considerable consciousness of the self in his main character, Will, but expresses his spiritual and intellectual development through the medium of allegorical meetings with characters called Thought, Wit, Reason, Conscience, and Imaginatif. The character Will goes through intense self-analysis, and, like Hoccleve, even suggests that he is going mad, but the personal experience of madness as such is not a matter for his consideration. The issues Will faces are those of conscience, he is concerned with his moral probity and spiritual development, and his entire aim is to attain salvation. Hoccleve, less intellectual and scholarly than Langland, is, nonetheless, more concerned with the workings of his mind seen as the organ of his reason and with the interaction between his mind and body. Where Langland's Will discourses with an allegorical character called Wit, Hoccleve speaks of his own intellectual faculty: "my wit." It is crucial to Hoccleve that he is in command of his reason and able to "commune" intelligibly with others. In this sense, he moves beyond the often-accepted paradigm for medieval self-expression.

When Hoccleve writes about a period of insanity, he appears to use the term *self* as an entity on which he can independently reflect. What Hoccleve describes is a dislocation within himself. Part of his technique is to use another term, *persone*, a word that, in the second sense in the *MED* ("an individual's physical being, body; appearance") signifies the outward appearance of someone. The physical quality of the person denotes his vulnerability, the flesh and bones encasement of something individual and deeply significant—the king's person as opposed to his sovereignty. The *MED*'s third sense stresses the unique individuality of the term, which was used frequently with the qualifier *proper*. *Persone* is a crucial term for Hoccleve because it is his outward appearance that governs his acceptance or rejection by his former colleagues and friends. His experience of insanity sends him inward, yet simultaneously it makes him acutely aware that the physical aspect of his individuality constitutes him and makes him vulnerable to the damage others' opinions may cause to his own self. In self-consciously articulating the interrelationship of his mind and body, he anticipates what has been termed a supposedly new and proleptic discourse about human nature: "Modern thought adapted the ancient language of the soul, humours, temperaments and spirits, but it also added a new discourse about human nature, mind and subjectivity" (Smith 57).

Hoccleve's concept of insanity is firmly founded in medieval theories of medicine. His approach to the experience of insanity is to admit that he suffered from a "wylde infirmitee" during which "the substaunce of my memorie / Wente to pleie as for a certain space" (Burrow *Complaint* 50–51). Hoccleve claims to have lost his memory in a sickness he accepts as having been sent by God. Here he is speaking not just about amnesia but about the loss of the most powerful mental faculty perceived in the Middle Ages, that which enables a person to order, *racio* or reason, and *imaginatio*, the faculty that receives images and transfers them for use by the memory. Mary Carruthers has demonstrated convincingly the vital importance of this faculty to the medieval mind: "Training the memory was much more than a matter of providing oneself with the means to compose and converse intelligently when books were not readily to hand, for it was in trained memory that one built character, judgment, citizenship, and piety" (9). It was the memory that was the treasure-house of the mind—indeed, Bartholomeus Anglicanus refers to *memory* and *mind* as interchangeable terms.

> The innere witte is departid aþre by þre regiouns of þe brayn, for in þe brayn beþ þre smale celles. þe formest hatte *ymaginatua*, þerin þingis þat þe vttir witte apprehendiþ withoute beþ i-ordeyned and iput togedres withinne, *vt dicitur Iohannicio I*. þe middil chambre hatte *logica* þerin þe vertu estimatiue is maister. þe þridde and þe laste is *memoratiua, þe vertu of mynde. þat vertu holdiþ and kepiþ in þe tresor of mynde þyngis þat beþ apprehendid and iknowe bi þe ymaginatif and* racio. . . . But *memorativa*, þe vertu of mynde, puttiþ vp in saue warde liknes of þinges and kepiþ hem þat ha beþ nou3t for3ete. þerfore on seide þat mynde is þe cofer or [s]kepet of resoun. (98–99; emphasis added)

For Hoccleve, reliable clerk of the Privy Seal for twenty-seven years and court poet for the previous three, to lose the substance of his memory was to lose the ability to act with prudence, wisdom, and moral virtue, as well as to lose the treasure-store of his accumulated knowledge—a public and terrible affliction. The attribution of the illness to loss of memory is unmistakably medieval in its force. So, too, is its association with melancholy. The *Secreta Secretorum* succinctly expresses the inseparability of body and soul: "Kynde is so grete a fellowe betwen body and Sowle, that the Passyons of body chaungyth the sowle; and the Passions of Sowle, chaungyth the body" (218). Bartholomeus Anglicus describes the influence of such matters as diet, solitude, anxiety, and too much study on those prone to "the thoughtfull maladie" (350). Hoccleve exhibited all the classic symptoms of the melancholic, indulging in lengthy bouts of study and preferring solitude and sadness to company when in the throes of despair (Furnivall, *Regement* 85–112). Burrow pertinently notes that Hoccleve sees himself as having suffered a sickness that affected his mind. He associates it with the attack of "venim," which can be ascribed to the burned or adust melancholic humors that cause *alienatio* or derangement of the mind (*Complaint* lxii). Knapp makes the convincing suggestion that the sickness Hoccleve attributes to a visitation of God is temporary but the tendency toward melancholy is a permanent condition (170–71). Hoccleve was susceptible to mental illness and knew it.

It was a widely held medieval view that the mentally ill person was wholly or in part to blame for this condition. Penelope Doob describes

the social and moral stigma arising from the perception that all sickness, in particular madness, was caused by sin (8). Yet, although Hoccleve calls his sickness a stroke of God, at no point in the *Complaint*
does he suggest that it is caused by sin, whereas in his earlier poem, *La
Male Règle*, this is indeed his approach. He acknowledges that his
friends made pilgrimages to pray for his restoration to health (46–49)
but recounts the symptoms of the sickness and his own attempts to
control it without referring to God for intervention. In this, he seems
to move away from a medieval mode of thinking toward a modern concept of self-determination. *The Complaint* purports to be written after
his cure, but reflection on the experience leads him to re-create in the
poetry the sense of personal fragmentation and physical torment that
his mental anguish induced.

We can deduce some of the external manifestations of Hoccleve's
insanity by considering the reactions of others. He overhears them
commenting on how, in the worst stages of his mania, his legs and feet
were always on the move, his eyes were always straying while he
talked—commonly held symptoms of insanity. Bartholomeus
describes the frenzy of black choler or melancholy in terms echoed by
Hoccleve. The references to animals—"here and there forþe stirte I as
a roo," coupled with looking like a "wilde steer" and having a "bukkish"
brain—are dangerously graphic reminders that madness and bestiality
are not far apart; once man has lost his reason he is no different from
the animals (Aquinas 1a–2ae.vi.2). Such "wild man" behavior is particularly inappropriate in an urban setting (Goldie 33). The wild man of
medieval romance goes apart to the forest; he does not pound the pave-
ments of Westminster to and from the Privy Seal.

The main thrust of the *Complaint* is that inwardly Hoccleve knows
he is cured; yet his former colleagues refuse to accept this. He
describes his fruitless attempts to reassert his identity in terms of his
public office and persona, only to find that they no longer exist:
"For3eten I was, al oute of mynde, awey, / As he þat deed was from
hertis cherte" (80–81). His reaction is to turn inward, using the image
of locking his mouth with a key. In the privacy of his home, physically
withdrawn from a world that is rejecting the person it perceives, he
tries to keep a grip on the self he knows himself to be. Looking into the
mirror, Hoccleve initially expresses an intense desire to conform to
external expectations; the *speculum*, after all, was the medieval term for
a model of how men ought to live. A few lines of unnerving truthfulness describe how he regularly makes a little jump, to try to catch himself out in the mirror in case anything "outher were . . . than it oghte"

(159). If so, he will change his *chere*, his countenance, a divided self trying to make outer and inner the same (161–62). It is a telling picture of
an inner self trying to control an outer self.

It is clear at this point in the poem that Hoccleve still believes his
identity to be given by the public world outside his home as a liveried
servant of the Crown (Green 19). If he ceased to mean anything in this
environment, he was in serious danger of ceasing to have any existence. The strain and stress of the divided spirit are evident—"my
spirites labouriden" (148)—and the physical effects of the artificiality
of trying to conform to outward demands "to peint countenance, chere,
and look" make him shake, sweat, and suffer extremes of temperature,
medieval as well as modern symptoms of psychiatric disorder (149–54).

It is remarkable to find this "mirror scene" in a fifteenth-century
poem. Knapp makes the point explicitly, as I do, that it is "an immediate challenge to any who would still maintain that one cannot expect
to find complex, interiorized representations of subjectivity in
medieval poetry." He goes on to link it with Lacan's perceptions that
the mirror offers "a simultaneous presence of two images of the self
and the consequent fragmentation of that self into both subject and
object of perception" (170). The mirror image of Hoccleve is as uncertain as is his sense of sanity: the person seen there is not clear, as in a
modern mirror, but distorted. Hoccleve is at pains to fashion or construct a self to conform to society's norms, while fiercely defending the
rightness of his own judgments about himself. In the worst moments
of insecurity, he struggles to get his outward appearance into line by
looking in the mirror, yet he goes on to say that others do him an
injustice in assessing him on his outward appearance and actions. As
Knapp shrewdly points out, he uses the terms of manuscript emenda-
tion and portraiture as a metaphor for creating the right kind of persona to be taken for sane: "to peynte contenance / cheere and look"
(170). Like Renaissance portraits, this is a self that must fulfill certain
social requirements.

What seems early modern rather than medieval about this expression is Hoccleve's acute consciousness of himself as a being with a
responsibility to himself as well as to society. Montaigne's claim about
the way authors communicate with the world corresponds to the way
Hoccleve sees himself: "Authors communicate with the world in some
special and peculiar capacity; I am the first to do so with my whole
being, as Michel de Montaigne, not as a grammarian, a poet, or a
lawyer" (Smith 54). Hoccleve conceives of himself as both a clerk to the
Privy Seal and a poet. The identity of *auctour* is one he is anxious to

fulfill, as is evident in the prologues to his long works. Yet the whole-ness of his "whole being" is a matter that also concerns him keenly, and it is in the forefront of *The Complaint*, which itself acts as a prologue to a public work of moral instruction. Without such wholeness, he feels he lacks identity in the court world.

In distress, Hoccleve turns to a book that gives him consolation. Discussing such strained assertions of sanity, Simpson suggests that textual devices ranging from reading a book to participation in a dia-logue about writing are used to create an "extra-textual context for his poetry in which readers will be persuaded that Hoccleve is sane" (see "Madness" 20–26). I want to put a slightly different spin on the poem by suggesting that in describing his processes of reading and thinking Hoccleve demonstrates that he is in control of and using his mental faculties (cf. Burrow "Hoccleve's *Series*"). The poem's closing stages are Hoccleve's account of his reason in action. He reads a book and makes deductions from it, applying them to his own life. He also uses his memory, recalling aphorisms, scriptural quotations, and common wisdom. Hoccleve is restoring reason's balance by recalling material from his stored memory—the process of *cogitatio*. As Mary Carruthers describes it: "The medieval *cogitatio* translates . . . not as our own phrase 'reasoning out' (with its emphasis on logical connection) but as 'mulling over,' a process that depends heavily on free association and one's 'feeling for' a matter" (201).

By locking himself away, Hoccleve is rejecting external stimuli in order to convince himself that his reason has control, irrespective of what his *chere*, his outward appearance, looks like. It is reminiscent of the practice of scholars searching the treasure-house of memory in the process of composition. They would shut out all external stimuli, espe-cially visual ones, and often lie prostrate in order to prompt their rec-ollective eye (Carruthers 201). Hoccleve, too, cuts off external stimuli and, using the image of the mirror, demonstrates symbolically the way he is turning inward to his memory to restore the full use of reason. At this stage, it is the inner man who seems to be the true Hoccleve. Fou-cault writes of the essential truth held and preserved by the madman in society: a truth that the rest of society outlaws by insisting that the madman conform to its systems (xiv). Hoccleve knows full well that he is cured, yet he also understands the mind-set of former colleagues; their judgments are based on preconceptions, not on Hoccleve as he is. He knows that he has to act according to their norms if he is to regain their acceptance.

"If that I not be sen amonge þe prees,
Men deme wole that I myn heed hide
and am werse than I am, it is no lees."
O lorde, so my spirit was restelees.

(191–94)

The poet demonstrates remarkable tenacity of purpose in clinging to
his belief that, in spite of others' judgments, he is truly at one with
himself. Drawing a contrast between the people who make judgments
on what they see with their eyes—Hoccleve's face, expression, and
bearing—and the man who lives intensely in his own mind, he lucidly
weighs his situation, knowing that in the society of his former friends
he has been disempowered: "I demed wel and knew wel eke, / What so
þat euere I shulde answere or seie / They wolden not han holde it
worth a leke" (141–43).

The acute mental torment of this period is expressed in physical
terms: "Not haue I wist hou in my skyn to tourne" (303). Unable to
reestablish himself in his former, official life, he wants to "crepe into
[his] graue" (261). His farewell to life is, significantly, a farewell to
court employment: "I am no lenger of ȝoure liuere. / ȝe haue me putte
oute of ȝoure retenaunce" (271–72).

The act of dying to his former life becomes the turning point of self-
discovery. He recognizes that the people who judge him are themselves in a dark cloud: "A dirke clowde / Hir siȝt obscurid withynne
and wiþoute, / And for al þat were ay in suche a doute" (292–94).

They, not he, are divided from the truth; in recognizing this, he is
one step nearer clearing the division within himself. Division is located
outside the self, in the people making judgments. Once he is convinced
that his mental processes are working properly, he can act as a man
who is whole. In the process of asserting his cure, not only does he
employ his memory and his reason but he is also quite conscious of
what he is doing. Hoccleve insists that he is able to *commune*—"communicate"—with what he terms "homely resoun" (221), consciously
reflecting on his mental processes. Once he recognizes that wholeness
depends on his own control of his reason and not on others' assessments of his appearance and behavior, his physical agony ceases. The
melancholy sickness had possessed him, but now Hoccleve has the
power to "vnpike / Of suche þouȝtful dissese and woo the lok / And
lete hem out þat han me made to sike" (387–89). This is a material view
of inner suffering; what is within must be let out so that the subject can

become whole. It reflects, too, the process of writing the poem, for at the start the poet had "brast out" into verse to release pent-up emotions. The process of composition, as well as of reading, reasoning, and remembering, is part of Hoccleve's awareness and control of both his inner and outer selves.

At the end of the poem the language becomes assured; once Hoccleve has demonstrated that he is whole again, he bids farewell to sorrow in briskly colloquial terms: "Farwel my sorwe! I caste it to the cok" (386). It is as if he no longer needs courtly rhetoric to express himself, nor the endorsement of court connections; he is his own point of reference. Only when he has demonstrated his sanity does he formally thank God, yet his consolation derives not from God's intervention, a reaction we might have expected from a medieval writer, but from faith in his ability to exercise reason. Having reached this quietus, he is ready to turn once again to writing, as he demonstrates in the poem that immediately follows, *The Dialogue*. This text, as Simpson has pointed out, endorses Hoccleve's sanity and restores authority to the poet ("Madness" 23–26).

Much more needs to be written on Hoccleve's sense of identity as an *auctour*. In this essay, I have been concerned principally with the way self-representation emerges through medieval and apparently early modern forms of poetic expression. The form of the poem as a complaint, its conventional opening, which inverts Chaucer's "Whan that Aprille," as noted by many scholars, the reference to Hoccleve reading a book as an authority, the textual echoing of the psalms and the pervasive tone of Boethian lament for instability—all of these features make the poetry distinctively medieval. Yet Hoccleve moves through the medieval conventions, both literary and religious, and writes himself into the poetry in ways that make the self an important consideration in its own right, not only material for salvation. The concept of an interior life is not foreign to medieval writers, but it usually refers to a spiritual life of holiness in opposition to the material life of bodily indulgence. Hoccleve's interior life is not that of the soul searching for God, but of a man who is aware of himself as a consciousness existing within his own body: "Not haue I wist hou in my skyn to tourne" (303). His mind and wit are components of his interior life, on which he is able to reflect: "My wit and I haue ben of suche accord / As we were or the alteracioun / Of it was" (59–61).

While he takes obsessive care to ensure that he conforms physically to the expectations of how a sane man ought to look, he articulates the suffering this effort entails as a fragmenting between inner and outer life. Within he is martyr to the reactions in himself that result from the words and attitudes he meets outside. Mental suffering manifests itself physically: "Sith þat time haue I be sore sete on fire / And lyued in greet turment and martire" (62–63). He is intensely concerned with his role in society and portrays himself as divided between the person who desperately wants to conform and the one who lives an interior life of self-reflection. He fashions a fictive self based on the experiences of a historically attested identity. All of these acts and the recording of them anticipate the fashioning of the self that many scholars claim to be an early modern phenomenon, and point forward to modern perceptions of the self developed by Freud and other psychoanalysts.

If Hoccleve can write with this kind of self-awareness in the early fifteenth century, there are grounds for suggesting that the fashioning of self began well before the sixteenth century, even though the term *fashioning* may not have been used (Greenblatt 2). In "Self-Reflection and the Self," Roger Smith speaks of the early modern period as introducing an innovative discourse about human nature: "This new discourse stressed self-reflection and self-control, it individualized refined social values and it lay the basis for modern subjective sensibility" (57). The all-pervasive autobiographical elements in Hoccleve's work are central to any critical appraisal of his poetry. They are too consistent not to be highly self-conscious, starting in his early poetry and continuing to his last work, a treatise on how to prepare for death. The introspective appraisal of insanity and the painful account of a return to society give a graphic view of a man re-creating himself in the aftermath of a mental breakdown. Yet, although the process of recovery preoccupies the poet, the really interesting factor for a modern reader is not whether Hoccleve can demonstrate that he has regained his sanity. The acts of writing, remembering, and reflecting demonstrate that this has happened. It is that he is able to reflect on himself, whether mad or sane, and record his mental and physical processes with striking verisimilitude. The textual creation of the fictive Hoccleve is also the psychological self-creation of the poet. Hoccleve's *Complaint* is a salutary reminder that to give labels such as medieval, early modern, or modern, is to ignore the constant and organic development of thought and attitude that transcends notions of periodization.

WORKS CITED
Aers, David. "A Whisper in the Ear of Early Modernists, or Reflections on Literary Critics Writing the History of the Subject." *Culture and History,*

1350–1600: Essays on English Communities, Identities, and Writing. Ed. David
    Aers. New York: Harvester Wheatsheaf, 1992. 177–202.

Aquinas, Saint Thomas. *The Summa Theologica*. 2000 (online). Available at
    http://www.newadvent.org/summa/ (accessed 19 February 2003).

Bartholomeus Anglicus. *On the Properties of Things: John Trevisa's Translation
    of Bartholomeus Anglicus'* De proprietatibus rerum. Ed. M. C. Seymour et al.
    Oxford: Clarendon, 1975.

Bryan, Jennifer E. "Hoccleve, the Virgin, and the Politics of Complaint."
    PMLA 117.5 (2002): 1172–87.

Burrow, J. A. "Autobiographical Poetry in the Middle Ages: The Case of
    Thomas Hoccleve." *Proceedings of the British Academy* 68 (1982): 389–412.

———. "Hoccleve's *Series:* Experience and Books." *Fifteenth-Century Studies:
    Recent Essays*. Ed. R. F. Yeager. Hamden: Archon, 1984. 259–74.

———. *Thomas Hoccleve*. Variorum: Aldershot, 1994.

Burrow, J. A., ed. *Thomas Hoccleve's Complaint and Dialogue*. Oxford: Oxford
    UP for Early English Text Society, 1999.

Bynum, Caroline. "Did the Twelfth Century Discover the Individual?" *Jesus
    as Mother: Studies in the Spirituality of the High Middle Ages*. Berkeley: U of
    California P, 1982. 82–109.

Carruthers, Mary J. *The Book of Memory: A Study of Memory in Medieval Cul-
    ture*. Cambridge: Cambridge UP, 1990.

de Looze, Laurence. "Signing Off in the Middle Ages: Medieval Textuality
    and Strategies of Authorial Self-Naming." *Vox Intecta: Orality and Textual-
    ity in the Middle Ages*. Ed. A. N. Doane and Carol Braun Pasternak. Wis-
    consin: U of Wisconsin P, 1991. 162–78.

Doob, P. B. R. *Nebuchadnezzar's Children: Conventions of Madness in Middle
    English Literature*. New Haven: Yale UP, 1974.

Foucault, Michel. *Madness and Civilization: A History of Insanity in the Age of
    Reason*. Trans. Richard Howard. London: Routledge, 1967.

Furnivall, F. J., ed. *The Regement of Princes, A.D. 1411–12, from the Harleian
    MS. 866, and Fourteen of Hoccleve's Minor Poems from the Egerton MS. 615,
    Hoccleve's Works*. Vol. 3. Early English Text Society e.s. 72, 1897.

Goldie, Matthew Boyd. "Psychosomatic Illness and Identity in London,
    1416–1421: Hoccleve's *Complaint and Dialogue with a Friend.*" *Exemplaria*
    11.1 (1999): 23–52.

Green, R. F. *Poets and Princepleasers: Literature and the English Court in the Late
    Middle Ages*. Toronto: U of Toronto P, 1980.

Greenblatt, Stephen. *Renaissance Self-Fashioning from More to Shakespeare*.
    Chicago: U of Chicago P, 1980.

Greetham, D. C. "Self-Referential Artifacts: Hoccleve's Persona as a Literary
    Device." *Modern Philology* 86 (1989): 242–51.

Hasler, Antony. "Hoccleve's Unregimented Body." *Paragraph* 13 (1990):
    165–83.

Knapp, Ethan. *The Bureaucratic Muse: Thomas Hoccleve and the Literature of a
    Late Medieval England*. University Park, PA: Pennsylvania State UP, 2001.

Kohl, S. "More than Virtues and Vices: Self-Analysis in Hoccleve's 'Autobi-
    ographies.'" *Fifteenth Century Studies* 14 (1988): 115–27.

Langland, William. *Piers Plowman: A Parallel-Text Edition of the A, B, C, and Z Versions.* Ed. A. V. C. Schmidt. London: Longman, 1995.

Medcalf, Stephen. "Inner and Outer." *The Later Middle Ages.* Ed. Stephen Medcalf. London: Methuen, 1981. 108–71.

Middleton, Anne. "William Langland's 'Kynde Name': Authorial Signature and Social Identity in Late-Fourteenth-Century England." *Literary Practice and Social Change in Britain, 1380–1530.* Ed. Lee Patterson. Berkeley: U of California P, 1990. 15–82.

Mitchell, Jerome, and A. I. Doyle, eds. *Hoccleve's Works: The Minor Poems.* Ed. F. J. Furnivall and I. Gollanz. Oxford: Oxford UP for Early English Text Society, 1970.

Pearsall, Derek. "Hoccleve's *Regement of Princes:* The Poetics of Royal Self-Representation." *Speculum* 69 (1994): 386–410.

Scanlon, Larry. "The King's Two Voices." *Literary Practice and Social Change in Britain, 1380–1530.* Ed. Lee Patterson. Berkeley: U of California P, 1990. 216–47.

Secreta Secretorum: Three Prose Versions. Early English Text Society, e.s. 74, London, 1898.

Simpson, James. "Madness and Texts: Hoccleve's *Series.*" *Chaucer and Fifteenth-Century Poetry.* Ed. J. Boffey and J. Cowan. London: Centre for Late Antique and Medieval Studies, 1991. 15–29. King's College London Medieval Studies No. 5.

———. "Nobody's Man: Thomas Hoccleve's *Regement of Princes.*" *London and Europe in the Middle Ages.* Ed. Julia Boffey and Pamela King. London: Centre for Medieval and Renaissance Studies, U of London, 1995. 149–80.

Smith, Roger. "Self-Reflection and the Self." *Rewriting the Self: Histories from the Middle Ages to the Present.* Ed. Roy Porter. London: Routledge, 1997. 49–57.

Strohm, Paul. *England's Empty Throne: Usurpation and the Language of Legitimation, 1399–1422.* New Haven: Yale UP, 1998.

Thornley, E. M. "The Middle English Penitential Lyric and Hoccleve's Autobiographical Poetry." *Neuphilologische Mitteilungen* 68 (1967): 295–321.

Chapter 6

The Author in the Study
Self-Representation as Reader & Writer in the
Medieval and Early Modern Periods

Peter Goodall

Debates about the authenticity of an autobiographical self, and what this means, have preoccupied scholars since the days of New Criticism. It has become an axiom that medieval writers use personae and write within such an elaborate and comprehensive system of literary conventions that it is impossible to identify the voice of the real author, even when he or she is speaking as an "I," and impossible to differentiate the voice of the author from that of the narrator or, more broadly, the voice of the author/narrator from the text itself.[1] I will begin with literary descriptions of selfhood from Augustine through Abelard, Dante, Petrarch, and Chaucer. An analysis of medieval selfhood is less a piecing together of a "lived" authenticity as reflected in literary representations than it is a nurturing and development of authenticity through literary representations. As the fifteenth and sixteenth centuries progress, this locus of subjectivity in the written word finds its emblem in the emergence of the private study. The study was the place to which a person could withdraw in order to think, read, and compose heartfelt commitments and judicious responses. To the medieval mind—to which privacy in one's home was a new and increasingly prized state—the study became not just a place where one might experience one's inmost, "authentic" emotions but a symbol of this authenticity itself. The authentic self was thus the literary representation of lived experience as nurtured in the study.

By *study*, I mean the location of reading and writing in a particular, designated space, called variously a study, oratory, library, or simply a chamber. I have written elsewhere about the emergence of the study as an important manifestation of the drive toward private space in the late medieval world. There were a number of changes to the structure of the domestic house in the late Middle Ages, especially in the fifteenth century, that enabled a more extensive provision of private space and rooms intended for sole occupancy. Among the various reasons for this change, the invention of the wall fireplace (found in Italian houses from the fourteenth century), which obviated the need for a high roof in the hall to disperse fire smoke and enabled a second story of rooms to be built above the hall, was of special importance.

Augustine and His Influence

Inevitably, a discussion of the relationship of writing and reading to self-representation in the Middle Ages begins with Augustine's *Confessions*. Yet this great work provides a powerful though ambivalent exemplar of the broader category of autobiography. Throughout the *Confessions*, Augustine writes extensively about his own reading: classical literature and philosophy, scripture, and rhetoric. He records the love of Latin literature that he had from childhood: "I loved Latin literature, not the elementary lessons but those which I studied later under teachers of literature" (33). He was much attracted to the theater and marveled at the paradox that an audience could enjoy the spectacle of sorrow and tragedy. The reading of Cicero "altered my outlook on life" (58). Augustine's comments on the practice and hermeneutics of reading are nearly always interesting. Toward the end of the *Confessions*, there is an extended passage that depicts a long and animated disputation between scholars about the interpretation of the text, "In the beginning God created heaven and earth." The *Confessions* reveals much more than the habitual reading practice of a literate man, however. In adult life, Augustine was a professor of rhetoric, and literary creation—whether in terms of public speaking and teaching or of writing as well as reading—was fundamental to his sense of himself. In another way, reading became crucial to the process of conversion. At the critical moment, Augustine hears a child singing the refrain to a song, *tolle et legge*, "take and read." This is no ordinary piece of soul-searching through the medium of the written word, however. With a writer's feel for the vivid detail, Augustine remarks that he had never heard a childish song with such a refrain before. The book he takes up is no ordinary text either but the Bible—Paul's Epistle to the

Romans—and the reading method is unconventional, opening the book at random like a fortune-teller.

The pleasure that reading gave Augustine was, however, always an ambivalent one. It became more so as he grew older and moved toward the crisis of his conversion. One reason for this is that the literature that enticed him always seemed to bear an oblique and disjunctive relationship to the course of his inner life. As a child, he reveled in the "wanderings" of Aeneas but payed no attention to the erratic ways of his own soul. He was troubled by the very beauty of literary form that attracted him. He had been trained to value "eloquence" more than anything in literature, and so it came as a shock to him when he discovered Cicero's *Hortensius*, and for the first time recognized the primacy of ideas over language: "For I did not use the book as a whetstone to sharpen my tongue. It was not the style of it but the contents that won me over" (59). This came to a head as he began to read the Bible and to consider what special kind of literature this was.

> So I made up my mind to examine the holy Scriptures and see what kind of books they were. I discovered something that was at once beyond the understanding of the proud and hidden from the eyes of children. Its gait was humble, but the heights it reached were sublime . . . [W]hen I first read the Scriptures . . . they seemed quite unworthy of comparison with Cicero, because I had too much conceit to accept their simplicity and not enough insight to penetrate their depths. (60)

Although the *Confessions* continued to be widely read throughout the Middle Ages, Augustine had no followers worthy of the name in this kind of writing. One of the paradoxes of the history of autobiography is that such a brilliant exemplar by such a towering figure should have had no imitators. Georg Misch, the great historian of autobiography, explained this by seeing Augustine as finishing up the classical tradition of autobiography rather than beginning a medieval or modern tradition: "Augustine's work [was] not a beginning but a completion" (17). The only major autobiography to be written in the early Middle Ages is Peter Abelard's *Historia Calamitatum*, usually translated as *The Story of My Misfortunes*, a gripping narrative but short and disconcerting in its paranoia and will to self-justification and focused mainly on the suppression of Abelard's writings and on the events surrounding his relationship with Héloïse. One or two other texts can be mentioned in this context: Guibert of Nogent's *Monodiae*, which is rather more memoir than autobiography, and bits here and there of the writings of Giraldus Cambrensis. It is sometimes also possible for the reader to construct a kind of "serial autobiography" of certain figures by putting together letters, sermons, and occasional autobiographical remarks.

Even when medieval historians such as Charles Homer Haskins and R. W. Southern formulated a "twelfth-century Renaissance," it was defined in markedly different ways from the "individualism" that was the defining characteristic of the Renaissance of the thirteenth and fourteenth centuries. Although Burckhardt does write about political history and works of art, he characterizes the Italian Renaissance first and foremost in terms of the emergence of a certain kind of individual subject. Burckhardt's views have been extensively revised, but there are studies of the twelfth century that respond in the terms he established, for example, Colin Morris's *The Discovery of the Individual, 1050–1200*. Nevertheless, the commonest means of characterizing the twelfth-century Renaissance has been in terms of its intellectual centers and their production, its books, and its literature. It is a "humanist" renaissance only in the sense of a revival of classical learning. Almost a quarter of Haskins's book on the twelfth-century Renaissance is concerned with the translation of Greek and Arabic texts. It is also, compared with Burckhardt's study, a picture of a quiet and impersonal world; there are no figures comparable in dramatic presence to Petrarch or to the Visconti. Whereas Augustine had linked "bookishness," whether as writer or reader, to the emergence of subjectivity, the dominant tendency of the early Middle Ages is to separate them. The strongest religious traditions in this period are communal. Even the large numbers of religious solitaries of one kind or another commonly sought the external validation of a "rule" under which to live. In an essay, "Consciousness of Self and Perceptions of Individuality," published in a collection marking the fiftieth anniversary of the publication of Haskins's book, John F. Benton makes the point that "in the Middle Ages the journey inward was a journey toward self for the sake of God; today it is commonly for the sake of self alone" (285).

Common Medieval Traditions

There are two main traditions of self-representation as reader and writer in the late Middle Ages. The first is an essentially literary tradition that describes and reflects on the process of composing particular works. The second tradition is perhaps better characterized as philosophical rather than literary. It is the Stoic philosophical tradition that links self-understanding with withdrawal from society and with study and writing in particular. Seneca's famous statement *otium sine litteris mors est*, "withdrawal without study [letters] is death," sets the tone for thought and writing in this tradition. Although the first tradition is only occasionally concerned with the physical space in which reading or writing is carried out, the sense of "place" is of the essence in Stoic writings about withdrawal.

The greatest exemplar of literary self-representation in the first tradition is Dante's *Vita Nuova*, composed in the late thirteenth century. As is well known, the text consists of a series of love poems to Beatrice and a commentary in prose that provides a narrative of Dante's relationship with her, explaining the personal and historical circumstances that attended the composition of each poem. The prose commentary also offers a literary analysis, in which Dante discusses the structure and artistry of the poems. In Dante's hands, this is a highly sophisticated method, and it offers many interesting suggestions about the relationship between autobiography and literary self-consciousness.

> On that day when a year was completed since this lady had become a citizen of life eternal, I was sitting in a place where, thinking of her, I was designing an angel on certain panels; and while I was drawing it, I turned my eyes and saw beside me men to whom it was proper to pay respects. . . . When I saw them, I arose, and greeting them, said: "Someone was just now with me, therefore, I was in thought." After they had left, I returned to my work, that is, to designing figures of angels: and while doing that, there came to me the thought of writing words in rhyme as for her anniversary, and to address those who had come to me; and I then wrote this sonnet, which begins: *Into my mind had come*, which has two beginnings. (127)

In this example, we can see how Dante's self-narration and literary creativity interact, offering alternative beginnings to the poem that emerges.

The Stoic tradition of self-representation as writer and reader is well exemplified by Petrarch's *De vita Solitaria*, "The Life of Solitude," composed mainly in 1346 during Petrarch's residence in the Vaucluse. The work is often cited as a transitional work between the Middle Ages and the Renaissance. Although there is a strong influence throughout of Seneca's *Epistolae Moralia*, part 2 draws on copious examples of solitary life from the essentially Christian tradition of asceticism. Petrarch needs solitude, but he does not want to reject humanity; there is little *contemptus mundi* in the text. Petrarch was drawn to the sublime beauty of the Vaucluse, and his book is the first to discuss at length the value of solitary places instead of the much more traditional topic of the active versus the contemplative life. Zeitlin sees the desire for both solitude and society—the latter somehow perfected in the pursuit of the former—as the twin sides of the Renaissance ideal of individualism. At the heart of Petrarch's text is a distinction between life in the populous city, seen as a den of corruption, and life in the countryside, seen as the abode of virtue and self-honesty. Petrarch links solitude particularly to freedom from hypocrisy and self-delusion. Life in the countryside is not, however, a life of indolence but a life of study. For this reason, the occasional companionship of like-minded friends is not precluded. The connection between *otium* and *studium* is fundamental: "Isolation without literature is exile, prison, and torture; supply literature, and it becomes your country, freedom, and delight. 'What is sweeter than lettered ease?' is a well known saying of Cicero" (131).

"Allone, withouten any compaignye"

Chaucer's work abounds in examples drawn from both of these traditions, although there is no evidence that he knew either the *Vita Nuova* or *De Vita Solitaria*. There are many passages of direct or indirect reflection on the writing process by narrators sometimes clearly differentiated from Chaucer himself and sometimes not. Such scenes are found in one way or another in all of the minor poems: in the narrator's reading of the story of Seys and Alcione in Ovid's *Metamorphoses*, prompted by insomnia brought on by eight years of lovesickness, which leads into the dream of the Black Knight and ends with the narrator's resolution to turn the whole experience into the verse of the *Book of the Duchess*; and in the reflections on the relationship between the short life of the experience of love and the long craft of writing about it that open the *Parlement of Foules*. In *Troilus and Criseyde*, the narrator is so obtrusive, commenting on his difficulties with the story, his sources (real and imagined), his strengths and weaknesses and the bearing of the story on his own life, that a whole generation of New Critics on the poem, including some fine ones such as E. Talbot Donaldson, treated the narrator as a kind of fourth character in the story. Reflection on the writing process is present from first to last in the *Canterbury Tales*: from the series of portraits that opens it, including a self-portrait of the "I," one among the pilgrim troupe, who describes the others, to the "Retractions" that ends it, a passage often read in the past as a comment by the "real" Chaucer on his literary career in a moment in which the author drops his characteristic obliqueness. Perhaps the most extraordinary of these literary self-representations occurs in the prologue to the *Man of Law's Tale*. The impressive but pompous sergeant at law compares his own literary skills to Chaucer's and rehearses a substantial list of Chaucer's works, complete with commentary.

In many, if not all, of these cases, there is ambivalence in the self-representation as reader and writer. Chaucer usually speaks ironically of the author's or narrator's status and of the relationship between autobiography and literary self-creation. There is a continual tension between experience and reading as sources of authenticity, between direct experience and the vicarious experience of books, especially "old" books. On the one side, sources are an invaluable guide to self-knowledge, but sometimes the author in "as myn auctor sayde" is fictitious, and the narrator of *Troilus and Criseyde* worries about the inevitable changes in the form of speech that will confuse his meaning and render his meter unmusical.

"Within myn oratur": The Study

There are, too, many study scenes in Chaucer's works. Nicholas's study-bedroom in the *Miller's Tale*, where he dwells "allone withouten any compaignye," is perhaps the earliest and one of the most vividly realized private rooms in English literature. The room becomes a projection in spatial terms of the secretive nature of its inhabitant: plotting ways of spending the night with his landlord's lovely young wife, studying astrology after he had finished with the course in logic of the undergraduate at university. When Pandarus informs Criseyde that Troilus wants to become her lover, Chaucer's most meditative heroine retires alone to her "closet" to consider the proposal. It is there that she writes a letter to Troilus, the first she has ever written in her life. In the *House of Fame*, the scene of literary self-reflection and the study scene are brought together. The Eagle accuses the narrator (with details that echo the real Chaucer's work at the Wool Custom) of the scholar's traditional antisocial behavior.

> For when thy labour doon al ys,
> And hast mad alle thy rekenynges,
> In stede of reste and newe thynges

Thou goost hom to thy hous anoon,
And also domb as any stoon,
Thou sittest at another book
Tyl fully daswed ys thy look.

                    (652–58)

When characterizing himself as narrator, Chaucer tends to speak either as writer/reader or teller/listener in roughly equal terms, but here Chaucer is unmistakably the modern author: in a study, a compulsive reader and, more than that, a silent reader, not like the "mumblers" who were still the dominant type in the late Middle Ages.

During the fifteenth and sixteenth centuries, the study acquired a new importance both as a realized space in the new kinds of private dwellings that emerged and as a site for both introspection and literary creation. By the late fifteenth century, the depiction of studies or study-bedrooms is a common theme in painting. Some of the favorite subjects are Saint Jerome, sometimes in a kind of study-cave and sometimes in a proper study, and Saint Augustine. Petrarch is probably the commonest secular figure in the study painting. The influence of the study scenes occurs in less expected contexts as well. As early as the thirteenth century, Mary was shown in Italian paintings holding a book, a detail that gradually replaced the spindle (inspired by the Apocryphal gospels) of earlier traditions. In later Italian paintings, Mary usually receives the angel in an outdoor space, often a portico leading to a garden. Leonardo's painting of the Annunciation shows the penetration of this tradition into the sixteenth century. But in northern European paintings of the Annunciation in the late fourteenth and fifteenth centuries Mary is almost always shown receiving Gabriel indoors, in a patently bourgeois domestic setting in what looks like the kind of study-bedroom Nicholas inhabits in the *Miller's Tale*. The finest examples of this are, perhaps, Roger van der Weyden's Annunciations of the mid–fifteenth century. In the painting in the Louvre, Gabriel appears to Mary as she occupies a large and comfortable room on her own, dominated by a richly dressed red bed. The bedroom, the *thalamus virginis*, is highly appropriate for this moment, of course, and many of the details of the scene are both naturalistic and symbolic, such as the open window and the fruit and glassware, but the room has that mixed occupational use so common in medieval interiors. It is more than just a room for sleeping. There is a benchlike sofa with cushions, a cupboard, and shelves, and Mary is kneeling before a lectern with a book open in her hand.

The most memorable literary study in English in the period is Robert Henryson's "oratory" in *Troilus and Cresseid*, his continuation of Chaucer's poem, written in the third quarter of the fifteenth century. Henryson begins in his "oratur" but because of the cold shifts to his "chamber," where there is a lighted fire and greater comfort. This chamber, where he continues his reading, seems in kind very like the room where the Virgin receives Gabriel in van der Weyden's painting. In some ways the author's self-dramatization is a conventional piece: for instance, aspects of it recall the narrator's melancholy reading at the beginning of the *Book of the Duchess*. But it is also a moment that leaps out at us across the centuries in its vividness. It may be 1470 in Dunfermline, but Henryson the reader is an all too familiar figure: alone and feeling his age; a bit depressed; drawing near to the fire on a cold night, drink in hand; taking up Chaucer's poem for diversion, wondering what happened to Cressida in the Greek camp and whether "all that Chauceir wrait was trew" (64); and pondering how the story might be continued.

The Room behind the Shop

The final literary example takes us well into the sixteenth century. We can find in Montaigne's life and work a striking coincidence of the factors I have been seeking: an introspective temperament; the creation of a new literary form, the *essai*, to express the autobiographical impulse; and the construction of a particular kind of dwelling in which the reading and writing were done.

After a life at court, Montaigne retired to his chateau near Bordeaux in 1571. There he converted one of the towers to a triple-storied private space: a private chapel at the bottom, a bedchamber over it, and a round study at the top. The particular embodiment of this idea of the study is important, although it is not always clear from Montaigne's writing how consistently the space was differentiated. The presence of the private chapel recalls Henryson's oratory and the presence of the bedchamber recalls Nicholas's room in the hostelry. Montaigne does not seem to have been any more than a dutiful husband, but he also says that he never spent the night in the bedchamber in the tower. There is a similar ambivalence about the study room itself. We know that it contained Montaigne's library of over a thousand books, but he also states in the *Essais* that he had his best ideas when he was riding around his estate. It recalls in some ways Wordsworth's study at Rydal Mount, a favorite place of pilgrimage for early-nineteenth-century visitors to the Lakes. It was an impressive place, although the butler frequently pointed out to visitors that the place where Wordsworth actually did both his thinking and his writing was outside.

The private tower functions less ambiguously as a metaphor for that part of one's life that is truly one's own:

> A man that is able, may have wives, children, goods, and chiefly health, but not so tie himselfe unto them, that his felicitie depend on them. We should reserve a store-house for ourselves, what need soever chance, altogether ours, and wholly free, wherin we may hoard up and establish our true libertie, and principall retreat and solitariness. (254)

In his translation, Florio captures the notion of the place of retreat, where solitude can be found and the individual can express himself most freely and genuinely, but his English translation of the French term *une arrièreboutique* as "store-house" elides the true force of Montaigne's idea. Doubtless such rooms were used for storage, but storage and hoarding are not the key ideas. The force of Montaigne's metaphor for the private self is that it is not only a room but also the room *behind* the shop: the space behind the shopfront from which the public is excluded. And without this room behind the shop there would be no writing, no introspection, no commerce with the self and others, at all.

This discussion has traced the experience of selfhood in the late Middle Ages into the early modern period through reading and writing, functions through which people mediated their experience, realizing it largely in terms of spiritual connotations. The formulation and expression of one's autonomous being required the capacity to read and reflect. And the study, created most immediately in the interests of physical warmth, became a place for repose, a place where one might pause to record thoughts and reflections that might be deemed "autobiographical."

NOTES

1. In a lecture published in the 1960s that is still influential, George Kane warned a generation of scholars of the "autobiographical fallacy" in studies of medieval authors. This critical tendency was sustained from a different direction by the kind of historical work done at the same time by scholars of the school of D. W. Robertson, which enmeshed writers such as Chaucer and Langland, whom previous generations had thought of as free spirits, in a net of prescribed views about religion and literature.

WORKS CITED

Augustine. *Confessions.* Trans. R. S. Pine-Coffin. Harmondsworth: Penguin, 1961.

Benton, John F. "Consciousness of Self and Perceptions of Individuality." *Renaissance and Renewal in the Twelfth Century.* Ed. Robert L. Benson and Giles Constable. Oxford: Clarendon, 1982. 263–95.

Chaucer, Geoffrey. *The Riverside Chaucer.* Ed. Larry D. Benson. 3rd ed. Oxford: Oxford UP, 1988.

Dante Alighieri. *Vita Nuova.* Trans. Dino S. Cervigni and Edward Vasta. Notre Dame: U of Notre Dame P, 1995. Italian text with facing English translation.

Donaldson, E. Talbot. "The Ending of 'Troilus.'" *Speaking of Chaucer.* London: Athlone, 1970. 84–101.

Haskins, Charles Homer. *The Renaissance of the Twelfth Century.* Cambridge: Harvard UP, 1927.

Henryson, Robert. *The Poems.* Ed. Denton Fox. Oxford: Clarendon, 1987.

Kane, George. *The Autobiographical Fallacy in Chaucer and Langland Studies.* London: University College, London, 1965. Chambers Memorial Lecture, delivered 2 March 1965.

Misch, Georg. *A History of Autobiography in Antiquity.* London: Routledge and Kegan Paul, 1950.

Montaigne, Michel de. *Essays.* Trans. John Florio. 3 vols. London: Dent, 1965.

Morris, Colin. *The Discovery of the Individual, 1050–1200.* London: University of Toronto Press, 1972.

Petrarch. *The Life of Solitude.* Trans., with introduction and notes, by Jacob Zeitlin. 1924; Urbana: Hyperion, 1978.

Robertson, D. W. *A Preface to Chaucer: Studies in Medieval Perspectives.* Princeton: Princeton UP, 1962.

Southern, R. W. *The Making of the Middle Ages.* London: Hutchinson, 1953.

Chapter 7

The Constitution of Narrative Identity in Seventeenth-Century Prison Writing

Dosia Reichardt

Although the centrality of the prison experience for readers and writers of the early modern period has been recognized within the last decade or so (principally by Anselment, Marotti, and Potter), the diversity of writings originating from prison cells and their place in the development of an early modern subjectivity has not been thoroughly examined. Petitions, confessions, justifications, poems, meditations, letters, translations, travel narratives, journals, and political and religious manifestos were all produced in prisons in the early and mid–seventeenth century. They testify to a wide repertory of available modes of textual self-presentation and participate in a shift of focus from the psychology of Christianity and the rhetoric of conversion to the emergence of a more deliberate if precarious narrative identity. Moreover, the cultural vitality of these texts challenges the classical idea, derived from Livy and Tacitus, of the necessity of physical and political liberty for creativity. For some social groups—women, millenarian sects, even debtors and merchants from a putative bourgeoisie—prison provided an opportunity to be heard in print for the first time; for others, Cavalier poets in particular, imprisonment inhibited the expression of autonomous selfhood. The tension between the dynamic of a desired reunification with a group identity beyond prison and the impetus toward the expression of individuality and interiority through the use of the lyrical "I" reveals itself in the strategies of dissimulation used by prison writers: allegory, scriptural quotation, and allusion, narratives in which the narrator does not actually participate.

In some writing, this tension leads ironically to the eventual elision of the pronominal subject, which, according to A. C. Spearing, owed much of its being in earlier centuries to the very experience of incarceration: "It is not by chance that the connection between writing and imprisonment in and around the fifteenth century coincides with a striking intensification of the focus on subjectivity in writing" (87).

Spearing notes that much of the canonical and secondary literature of the fifteenth-century period was produced by prisoners who wrote out of their prison experience: Malory, Charles d'Orleans, James I of Scotland, Thomas More, George Ashby, and Thomas Usk. He goes on to argue that this leads to readers' recognition of a distinct poetic personality. This personality features a self defined by the circumstances and contingencies of real life; it represents not a grand abstraction but the real discovery of the individual. More recently, Marotti finds it interesting that so many important Tudor poets and public figures wrote prison poetry, and he provides a list very similar to Spearing's (4). Although he states that prison was a common context for composition, most of the figures on Marotti's list did not produce much more than a single farewell poem. Lois Potter, writing of the Royalists in the Civil War, points out the interest in prison writing among the reading public and also notes the prolific nature of the output: "They seem to have had access to unlimited supplies of pens and paper, and to have been so successful in conveying their work to the outside world that at one point there were rumours of a secret press in the Tower" (135).

The literary productions from the Tower of London, though varied, originated from aristocratic or noble prisoners for whom writing was part of a courtly being, but there also existed a substratum of noncanonical literature that helped to shape the expectations of a burgeoning reading public, especially between 1640 and 1660. As might be expected, the majority of prison literature is in the form of legal petitions and letters, sometimes penned by the lawyer on behalf of the prisoner or by visiting friends. Linked to these is a vast outpouring of vindications, declarations, proposals, appeals, accounts of suffering, and narrations from those imprisoned for debt. Examining these particular works of prose (and sometimes poetry), it is evident that direct experience is mediated by the search for a suitable genre. The form chosen for the life writing of a debtor often indicates the interests and literary aspirations of the prisoner. Popular books that were admired and imitated include Montaigne's and Bacon's essays and Joseph Hall's *Characters of Virtues and Vices* (1608). The informed outlook derived from these models is combined with medieval allegory in *Essayes and*

Characters of a Prison and Prisoners by G. M. of Grayes-Inne, Gent. (1638).
The author seems to expect that his readers will not regard this production as a work of fiction conveying allegorical truth but rather as
an allegorical commentary on a text (such as the Bible) whose literal
level is true. G. M. is also reframing his experiences as part of something larger than himself. In "Autobiography, Allegory, and the Construction of Self," David Herman argues that allegory constitutes an
ingredient of every autobiographical account rather than being a con-
tamination by the imaginary or an intrusion of fiction into fact (351).
G. M.'s fifty-page document, with a large cast of allegorical characters,
provides exhaustive coverage of all aspects of prison life in perhaps
unintentionally comic terms. The Porter is a fury, and Chamberlain
Hardusage sends him sheets fit for a horse. His chamber fellows,
"Thred-beare and Monilesse," relieve him of his cloak, and in the
morning Pot-hearbe the gardener demands payment for a walk outside. Mistresse Mutton-chops, the head cook, greases her fingers with
his silver, "so on all sides the blood of thy purse must be paid out to
maintain such mercilesse blood hounds, and continuall purse-leeches"
(25). G. M.'s prose is enlivened by Latin phrases and literary allusions,
despite his declaration on the first page that he cannot call on the talents of Cicero, Horace, Virgil, or Martial but only on his own unpol-
ished phrases and dull apprehension. His essays are written in the
third person, with familiar appeals and advice to the reader: "If thou
walkest abroad with thy Keeper use him friendly" (27). G. M. fashions
himself not as the prisoner but as an educated if withdrawn author
with whom the reader might be expected to empathize.

The search for a less legalistic and more individual mode of representing what was essentially a collective experience led at least one
debtor to attempt verse. *The Distressed Merchant. And the Prisoners
Comfort in Distresse* (1645) appears to be unique in its format if not its
content. William Bagwell produced nearly a hundred short poems of
meticulously annotated religious verse carefully divided by columns in
a list of contents between those dedicated "To his fellow-prisoners"
and those dedicated "To others, not prisoners." The former advise a
humble and grateful acceptance of the Lord's chastisement yet are
directed perhaps at those friends and acquaintances mentioned in the
dedication, who have "left him to himself in a miserable state and condition" (A3). The latter are admonitory pieces with descriptive titles.
The prefatory material betrays Bagwell's desire to develop a dialogue
with the potential readers he has already identified by reformulating
the identity that authority has forced on him. This strong conscious-

ness of an audience is consistently found in prison writing and was often combined with an attempt to shift the focus of attention toward the future and away from immediate experience. Marmaduke Johnson, though ostensibly producing a historical account, writes about Ludgate in 1659 as an appeal for reform. His experiences as "a late Prisoner there" serve as a warning. He specifies on his frontispiece that his account of the history and conditions of the prison are "Very useful and profitable to all sorts of persons, especially in London, whether Creditors or Debtors."

Rather better known to his contemporaries and posterity are the volumes of James Howell's familiar letters. Howell spent eight years of the 1640s imprisoned in the Fleet. The volumes of letters he produced there form a large body of reflections on contemporary topics but do not represent an authentic correspondence. There are only scanty flashes of self-reflection or references to actual conditions.

> To Sir L.D. in the Tower. Sir, To help the passing away of your weary hours between these disconsolate Walls I have sent you a King of your own name to bear you company. . . . I think dead men of this nature are the fittest companions for such that are buried alive as you and I are. (*Epistolae*)

Or:

> Madam, Since I was hurl'd amongst these walls, I had divers fits of melancholy and such *turbid intervalls* that use to attend close prisoners, who for the most part have no companions, but confus'd troops of wandring cogitations (Letter XXXI, 44); To Sir L. Dives in the Tower . . . I have been fastened to the walls of this prison any time these fifty-five moneths; I have been here long enough to be made the Philosopher's Stone. (Letter XLIII, 55)

Howell's main fear is that he has been "clapp'd up to be forgotten," a concern that publication of the letters serves to address. He writes from the purgatory of an indefinite political confinement, but he was lodged in the most comfortable prison in London and still possessed what condemned prisoners were deprived of: a legal identity.

In contrast, the author of over fifty tracts against Cromwell, Christopher Love, points out that his testimony is not legally valid in his last publication, *A Cleare and Necessary Vindication of the Principles and Practices of Me Christopher Love, since My Tryall before, and Condemnation by, the High Court of Iustice . . . Written by Me Christopher Love, Master of Arts, Minister of Lawrence Iury, London; Penned by Me the*

Eighth of August, Fourteen Days before My Death (1651). The title itself forms a narrative, and the amount of information on the frontispiece clearly aims to fix Love's identity by providing as much information as possible. Love's prose is a desperate attempt to reformulate and rewrite his identity from guilty to "innocent as his child that is not yet three years old." He repeatedly desires the "Reader to take notice" as he gives his own detailed version of the trial and prints the text of the petition that the court rejected. With apparently total recall, he relates and comments on the lengthy testimonies that condemned him. He plans his gallows speech and is humble and quiescent. His arguments are backed by biblical quotations, and the only personal information provided is an aside in which he complains of being kept a close prisoner and only his wife being allowed to visit him. More informative are the journals of George Fox, which cover his many periods in various prisons and provide a model for future Quaker autobiographies. "The Horrors of Doomsdale" describes in graphic detail the sufferings of the Quakers there in 1656 and their ability to ignore them and turn many of their tormentors to their own way of thinking (227). Though crammed with detail, the journals also consistently draw the reader's attention to the performative heroics of Fox but omit his actual words.

> And soe wee was kept in prison & diverse people came farr & nigh to see us: & severall people of account; Itt was ye talke of ye tounde & Country: That never men Aunswered soe as wee did & that ye Judge & Justices was not able to aunswer us one worde in 12. (225)

This indirection recurs throughout the journal; the reader cannot judge Fox's text, only Fox's own estimation of it. Fox, however, is part of a huge upsurge in the prison literature of emerging religious and political radicals, much of it produced by Quakers (and Quaker women especially) but also by men and women of other minorities: Levelers, Ranters, Diggers, Fifth Monarchists, Shakers, and Muggletonians, who were all repeatedly imprisoned. In the prison literature produced by these sects, the incarcerated writer struggles with two contradictory impulses: the impetus to reveal the self in the manner of a confession, and the desire to present a limited version of the self carefully edited to fit a variety of didactic impulses. As a result, straightforward narrative accounts of prison life are rare, although there do exist some that provide a vivid relation of experience. *The Inhumanity of the Kings Prison-Keeper at Oxford* (1643) is a prose relation of a forced march and subsequent six months' incarceration (Chillenden). It describes the daily miseries of captured Puritan soldiers, and of those who attempted to help them, in a fast-paced, unemotive narrative. A list of the officers involved follows the text, leaving the impression that the document was not solely the production of Edmund Chillenden, the first-named author, but is inclusive of the "70 hands" subscribed on the title page.

The ubiquity of prison writings is perhaps best indicated by the production of parodies that mock both their layout and their language. John Taylor, the water poet, includes among his works a pamphlet, *The Praise and Vertue of a Jayle and Jaylers: With the Most Excellent Mysterie, and Necessary Use of All Sorts of Hanging* (1623). Another document, one that does not own to any printer or place of publication, is *The Arraignment, Conviction, and Imprisoning of Christmas: On St Thomas Day Last. And How He Broke out of Prison in the Holidayes and Got Away, Onely Left His Hoary Hair, and Gray Beard, Sticking between Two Iron Bars of a Window . . .* (1645). The personified Christmas is a Cavalier who is less interested in relating his experience than expressing annoyance about the commercial opportunities he has lost since the Puritan ban on Christmas festivities.

In this period, the impulse to write in and of prison stems less from an examination of identity than from a desire to project the writer back into society and to obtain validation for one's conduct, not only from God but from a community of readers. The subject that has been literally "thrown under" (Lat: *subjectum*) emerges via discourse from guilt to innocence, from (feminine) silence to speech, from physical confinement to linguistic exploration. Although enforced leisure and the possibility of imminent physical fragmentation in the form of mutilation or death provide an obvious stimulus to the re-creation of the self as agent, it is the imagined reaction of the absent audience that shapes life writing in prison, so that the dialectic of individual and community becomes an attempt to locate another form of justice. Politically motivated tracts and pamphlets are especially careful to seize control of audience perception by defining themselves *against* tyrants and usurpers. Lilburne and Overton have many such references. The specification of the "other" is, at the same time, recognition that this other represents a skeptical, and indeed disbelieving, part of their readership. Writing for an audience that contains both the hostile and the empathic proves to be something of an inhibition toward the kind of self writing that is anticipated in autobiographical writing. Mid-seventeenth-century prison writers take full advantage of publicizing their plight whenever possible but struggle to find the sort of individuality and originality in their prose or verse that modern readers admire. Although the reading public was expanding, there were also more writers, so the attempt to capture a reader is often focused on the prefatory material, where the layout of the text, sometimes augmented by visual material, promises a uniqueness that the content fails to provide.

Prison life writing inevitably circles around protestations of innocence that depend on the presentation of a stable, predictable self. Evidence of a protean identity, the malleability that often adds interest to a narrative, undermines claims to an unwavering faith or loyalty. Personal change is generally represented as having happened offstage and in a vague past. The before and after experience of the conversion narrative is part of an otherwise shadowy adolescence, almost a form of bourgeois sentimental education. Yet these moments of metamorphosis are often the only personal notes in a life narrative generated in prison, as Hester Biddle's words suggest.

> I spent many years in Oxford, where the carriages of the scholars did trouble me in that day, they were so wild. After the best sort of religion and custom of the nation was I brought up; then the Lord drew me to this city, where I applied my heart both evening and morning and at noon day unto reading and hearing the Common Prayer. . . . Then did the Lord take away my hearing . . . then that faith which I was baptised in did no good. . . . Then did the Lord carry me to a meeting of the people called Quakers. (Salzman 158–59)

Hester is an observer, not a participant, but she writes personally and directly of the effect that the demeanor of the scholars had on her. She does not bother to describe their bad behavior; an account can, however, be found in the *Memoirs* of Sir Christopher Guise (Delany 144–45). The inclusion of a conversion experience (and the example of the apostle Paul, writing from prison, is a potent one) defines the development of the subject as author, since the linear and predictable path of the saved soul has already been embarked on. Though sparing in reference to those details for which autobiographies of our own time are often read, Hester Biddle presents an essential and unified subjectivity and one that resists narrative fragmentation as she herself resists her tormentors. Like many women affiliated with persecuted sects, Hester Biddle uses her religious beliefs within her writings to affirm her identity. As Crawford and Gowing point out: "Religious belief was fundamental to women's sense of themselves as human beings with rights" (245). In taking up the pen, Biddle also takes on a masculine narrative identity. Separatist sects emphasized spiritual gender equality (Otten 49–50), and women writing from prison were able to shift the boundaries of traditional female discourse into realms previously occupied by the church fathers.

In Quaker writings, narrative interest is also generated by the warnings and predictions of what James Holstun terms the rich Utopian futurity of prose during the English Revolution (Holstun 10). Certainty in the writings was countered by an insistence on uncertainty in the immediate physical world that was disturbing to the authorities. Quakers, including George Fox, were often kept in prison when they refused to give undertakings to return to a specific place on release and insisted on preaching where the spirit took them.

Paradoxically, while the need to form a distinct authorial persona in prison is strong, there are many ideological, aesthetic, and rhetorical forces that both underpin and inhibit this development. Many of these pressures are exercised by readers, and they include demands for veracity, immediacy, and conformity to a subject position in which the narrator is both victim and victor. Strong literary models for prison writing were available in Boethius, Saint Augustine, Saint Paul, and Foxe, and the familiarity of writers and readers with texts other than the Bible shaped style and expectations. Many prison narratives, for instance, contain the dual aspect found in Saint Augustine: the aim of achieving the salvation of the "universal reader" and the writer. The *Confessions* could thus act both as a paradigm of the conversion mechanism and a record of the author's own conversion.

Attempts to emulate both the literary style and the religious impact of revered martyrs by early modern prison writers can be misunderstood by contemporary critics. In an attempt to find a "genuine" voice among prison writers, Potter, for instance, describes John Gibson's commonplace book as "a much more personal work than much prison writing I've examined"; yet she quotes his address to Saint Paul, which immediately sets the parameters for his writing (9). However, in the mid–seventeenth century, writers of all social strata worked in an assimilative and imitative way.

It is rare to find prison writing that does not explicitly appeal to a higher authority in the abstract form of truth. The account's truth and impartiality are an advertisement used not only by writers with strong religious and political convictions but also by those in prison for debt. The prison writer invariably stands on a fixed point of immutable truth, from which the memory of the past is constructed and the direction of the future indicated. These claims for truth appear generally in the title matter and provide the prison author with a philosophical quandary. The free mind, or the free soul so often visualized as imprisoned in the body, cannot roam freely in the imagination since it is bound rigidly to an absolute truth. This link between truth and autobiographical writings still exists. Paul John Eakin, in his recent examination of the consequences of breaking the rules of self-narration, examines the cases of two contemporary autobiographies that provoked scandal by varying an externally perceived true history. He explores the basis of these reader expectations and constraints and argues that narrative transgressions signal a failure to display normative models of personhood.

> To link person and story in this way is to hypothesize that the rules for identity narrative function simultaneously as rules for identity. If narrative is indeed an identity content, then the regulation of narrative carries the possibility of the regulation of identity . . . wherever self-narration is practiced, it is done so under certain tacit constraints. (114)

The claims of veracity made by mid-seventeenth-century prison authors indicate that a consciousness of these constraints already existed among writers and readers. Examples are numerous: typical is *Truth Released from Prison, to its Former Libertie; or, a True Discovery, Who Are the Troublers of True Israel* (Claxton). As well as telling the truth, the prison writer is expected to produce and publish while actually in gaol. Writing in 1946, Abramowitz, who claims to have produced the first compendium of prison writings, stresses that he includes literature written *in* prison. He includes the Cavalier poet Lovelace, who is generally supposed to have penned "To Althea, from Prison" while in the London Gatehouse in 1642 and to have polished his poems for the press during another spell in Peterhouse in 1648. Although there is no historical evidence for these claims, they have attained a mythological status. According to one editor, "Lovelace belongs to that illustrious company who in all countries and in all times have produced literature inside prison gates" (Phelps xi). More recently, Nigel Smith refers to Lovelace "writing poetry in prison" (253).

The narrator as victim role is assured in much prison literature if incarceration or execution can be presented as martyrdom, and much prison writing displays a consciousness of the author's future status in the annals of his or her movement. In the seventeenth century, readers did not hesitate to seize the authorial initiative if they felt these elements would be missing. Prison writing, and most notably prison poetry, was not necessarily produced by those in confinement even if it was presented as such. Royalist poets such as Alexander Brome and Charles Cotton wrote prison poems without any personal experience. Legal petitions, especially by women, were often written by lawyers. As a result, the unmediated voices of female authors are rarely heard. Dorothy Traske, for instance, spent over twenty years in prison, but her experience there is narrated by a hostile heresiographer (Crawford and Gowing 93). Prisoners of low social status were unable to get the supplies of pens and paper Potter found among aristocrats in the Tower. (This may have been due to illiteracy or to their being denied the means to write.) Anthony Mellidge, a Quaker, finishes an account of his poor treatment with "And this is written for me being weak my self upon a little straw, from which I have not been many dayes, to the truth whereof I write my name" (1). John Lilburne did not write his own trial transcript, though it is in his voice, but he did validate it later. Impatience is evident among those who feel they can improve on existing narratives. John Taylor produced a six-page pamphlet on the Ranters and included in the title matter, "There is a pamphlet in this kinde, written with too much haste, I know not by whom, with but few truths, which in this are more largely expressed" (Taylor). Similarly, "A Ranter's Creed" is written not by the prisoners but by the magistrate who committed them to gaol (Hubbert). An anonymous G. H. likewise summarizes the beliefs, principles, and prophecies of three Shakers imprisoned in Clerkenwell, declaring himself to be "an earwitness" (G. H.).

Charles I failed to follow his predecessors and wrote no poetry during his periods of confinement, but his voice was appropriated and a number of poems appeared "attributed" to His Majesty. None of these has received any critical attention, though one, "King *Charles's* Lament," is included by Peter Davidson in his anthology of seventeenth-century verse (325). This poem uses the first-person pronoun but is unusual in comparing the troubles of the imprisoned ruler with the freedom of ordinary laborers and does little to promote the iconography of the noble martyr that became so prevalent after 1649. Alexander Brome, whose work was popular in manuscript but unpublished until 1661, uses the ancient topos of the soul's earthly prison so prevalent in prison prose. "A Copie of Verses, Said to Be Composed by His Majestie, upon His First Imprisonment in the Isle of Wight" appeared as an anonymous pamphlet in 1648 and opens defiantly: "Imprison me you Traytor's? must I be / Your fetter'd slave, while you're at liberty" (*Copie*). In directly addressing his political opponents and labeling them as traitors and liars, the speaker in Brome's poem uses the same tone and tactics as the pamphlets of Overton and Lilburne. Thomas Jordan's "The Kingly Complaint: The King Imprison'd at Holmby" is full of contemporary political comment and is to be sung (ironically perhaps) to the tune of "In Faith I Cannot Keep My Sheap" (9). Jordan's poem, as well as others by L'Estrange (Ault 197), Henry Bold's "King Charles I in Prison" (44), and other supposedly "royal" lyrics such as the manuscript poem "The King's Last Farewell to the World" make no attempt to enter into the king's subjectivity but use the prison persona to express support for their cause.[1]

Allied with this borrowing of an imprisoned identity is the consolatory poem directly addressed to a prisoner, who has been silent in his own voice. Sympathy for the duke of Buckingham's murderer, Felton, is expressed in anonymous poems in manuscript;[2] Lady Hester Pulter expresses her sorrow in a lament, "Upon the Imprisonment of His Sacred Majestie That Unparalel'd Prince King Charles the First."[3] Lois Potter mentions a poem found in Cotgrave and Gaywood's *Wits Interpreter* of 1645 as evidence of the public's interest in prison literature, but this poem, in which Julia visits her lover, is full of commonplace conceits of the prison of love and the sanctifying nature of her tearful presence (135).[4] Potter does not mention another poem, "The Prisoner's Song," published in the same volume, compiled by Cotgrave and Gaywood, which illustrates the tendency in prison lyrics to move from the grammatical construction of the subject, from the pronominal "I" of love lyrics, toward the collective "we" and the reintegration of the prisoner within a collective.

> A King lives not a braver life
> Than we merry prisoners do
> Though fools in freedom do conceive
> That we are in want and woe
> When we never doe take care
> For providing of fare
> We have one that doth purvay
> For victuals day by day
> What pray can a King have more
> Than one that doth provide his store?

The Interregnum is especially rich in prison lyrics. Imprisonment provides as much of the Cavaliers' mode as country house retirement or their enduring association with wine, women, and song. It is remarkable how many Caroline poets and dramatists were imprisoned between 1640 and 1660. A nonexhaustive list would include Sir Francis Wortley, who published a number of memorials to the Royalist dead and his *Characters and Elegies* of 1646 from the Tower; William Cartwright, playwright and poet, who was also imprisoned in 1642 and died the following year; Thomas Weaver, who was arrested for treason in 1654 following the publication of his *Songs and Poems of Love and Drollery*, although the judge decided to release the "scholar and man of wit"; William Davenant, who was responsible for the last of the Stuart masques, narrowly escaped execution, and spent 1650–52 in prison, where he finished the last book of *Gondibert;* the prolific pamphleteer and sometime poet Sir Roger L'Estrange, who was sentenced to death in 1644 but allowed to leave Newgate in 1648; Abraham Cowley, who was arrested in connection with a Royalist uprising and prepared his poems for the press in prison in 1656; Sir Richard Fanshawe, who worked on his "Selected Parts of Horace" while imprisoned in Whitehall in 1651; Sir Thomas Urquhart, who translated three books by Rabelais while in prison in 1653; and John Cleveland, a popular satirist, who spent three months in gaol in 1655, where his literary output consisted of a letter to the lord protector. Not all of these men wrote directly of their experience, and, whereas prison narratives are often framed and limited by the conversion experience, most prison lyrics fail to contest the language of Boethian fortitude. "I am no captive I, I find / My soul still free and unconfin'd," writes Thomas Weaver (6). Mildmay Fane concludes his "De Tristibus: To a Cat Bore Me Company in Confinement" with "For I'l conclude no storm of Fortune can / Prevail ore Caesar's barque, an honest Man" (170). Sir Roger L'Estrange, in his much circulated "The Liberty and Requiem of an Imprisoned Royalist," is equally predictable: "Whilst a good Conscience is my bail, / And Innocence my liberty. / Locks, bars, walls, lonenesse, tho together met, / Make me no prisoner, but an Anchoret" (107).

As an expression of interiority and an attempt to construct a literary persona for the external world, prison poetry proves more problematic than prose. The demand for veracity conflicts with the use of conceits and metaphors, the latter regarded as "speaking otherwise" or lying. A consciousness of vulnerability and an unwillingness to speak are summed up in an anonymous epigram, "Upon one, who dy'd in prison":

> Reader, I liv'd, enquire no more,
> Least a spye enter in at doore,

Such are the times a dead-man dare
Nor trust or creditt common ayre:
But dye, and lye entomed here,
By me, I'le whisper in thine eare
Such things as onely dust to dust,
(and without witnesse) may entrust.
                    (Gibson, poem 193)

Poets who wished to assert themselves as prison authors would, in any case, have found the system of transmission and circulation of works less conducive than prose writers. The latter were able to make their names prominent on the frontispieces of their documents and to assert their identities and allegiances, but many unattributed poems circulated in the printed miscellanies and manuscripts of the period. Moreover, self-reference such as "The Oppressed Close Prisoner in Windsor Castle, His Defiance to the Father of Lyes in the Strength of the God of Truth" is diluted in prison lyrics by an aristocratic Stoicism and an adherence to circular theories of history in which the topsy-turvy world of the midcentury would naturally right itself (Feake).

Despite the opportunities to use words as a way to create identity and assert its place in the world outside the prison, the prison writers of the mid–seventeenth century remain for the most part obscure, anonymous, or corporate. The narrative self found in prison writings of the mid–seventeenth century is a fragile construct that uses a variety of literary strategies to avoid revelation. It is often appropriated by and appropriates other voices and is bound by rhetorical and didactic conventions. Frequently it incorporates the voice of an emerging middle class. This voice emerges most forcefully in the prefatory material of prose pamphlets and is most self-consciously created in a subgenre that was soon to replace the aristocratic farewell poem from prison, the gallows speech. This illocutionary act finally reveals that the narrative identity of the prisoner is precipitated not as the truth the author claims but as a fiction constructed in a contractual discourse with the audience.

NOTES

1. BL MS Add. 47111, f.93. See also ff.17, 79, and 83 in the same manuscript for other poems in the king's voice dated 1647.

2. See, for instance, "To F. in the Tower," Bod. MS Rawl. Poet 199, f.62.

3. Lady Hester Pulter, Brotherton MS, Leeds: f.33r.

4. The poem, "Dialogue between a Lover and His Mistress in Prison," is in Cotgrave and Gaywood's *Wits Interpreter, the English Parnassus* (55).

WORKS CITED

Abramowitz, Isidore, ed. *The Great Prisoners: The First Anthology of Literature Written in Prison*. New York: Dutton, 1946.

Anselment, Raymond A. " 'Stone Walls' and 'Ironbars': Richard Lovelace and the Conventions of Seventeenth-Century Prison Literature." *Renaissance and Reformation* 17.1 (1993): 15–34.

Ault, Norman, ed. *Seventeenth Century Lyrics from the Original Texts*. London: Longmans Green, 1950.

Bagwell, William. *The Distressed Merchant: And the Prisoners Comfort in Distresse*. London: 1645.

Bold, Henry. *Poems, Lyrique, Macaronique, Heroique, and C*. London, 1664.

Brome, Alexander. *A Copie of Verses Said to Be Composed by His Majestie, upon His First Imprisonment in the Isle of Wight*. London, 1648.

Chillenden, Edmund. *The Inhumanity of the Kings Prison-Keeper at Oxford; or, a True Relation of the Most Transcendent Cruelties, Cheatings, Cozenings, and Base Dishonest Dealings of William Smith, Provest [sic] Marshall General of the Kings Army, against the Parliament Prisoners under His Custody*. London, 1643.

Claxton Laurence. *Truth Released from Prison to Its Former Libertie; or, a True Discovery, Who Are the Troublers of True Israel*. London, 1660.

Cotgrave, John, and Richard Gaywood. *Wits Interpreter, the English Parnassus; or, a Sure Guide to Those Admirable Accomplishments That Compleate Our English Gentry*. London, 1655.

Crawford, Patricia, and Laura Gowing, eds., *Women's Worlds in Seventeenth-Century England*. London: Routledge, 2000.

Davidson, Peter, ed. *Poetry and Revolution: An Anthology of British and Irish Verse, 1625–1660*. Oxford: Clarendon, 1998.

Delany, Paul. *British Autobiography in the Seventeenth Century*. London: Routledge and Kegan Paul, 1969.

Eakin, Paul John. "Breaking Rules: The Consequences of Self-Narration." *Biography* 24.1 (2001): 113–31.

Fane, Mildmay. *Otia Sacra*. London, 1658.

Feake, Christopher. *The Oppressed Close Prisoner in Windsor-Castle, His Defiance to the Father of Lyes, in the Strength of the God of Truth*. London, 1655.

Fox, George. *The Journal of George Fox*. Ed. Norman Penney. Cambridge: Cambridge UP, 1911.

G. H. *The Declaration of John Robins, the False Prophet, Otherwise Called the Shakers God, and Joshua Beck, and John King, the Two False Disciples, with the Rest of Their Fellow-Creatures Now Prisoners in the New-Prison at Clerkenwell . . .* London, 1651.

Gibson, Colin, ed. *Witts Recreations: Selected from the Finest Fancies of Moderne Muses, 1640*. Aldershot: Scolar, 1990.

G. M. *Essayes and Characters of a Prison and Prisoners by G. M. of Grayes-Inne, Gent*. London, 1638.

Herman, David. "Autobiography, Allegory, and the Construction of Self." *British Journal of Aesthetics* 35.4 (1995): 351.

Holstun, James. *Pamphlet Wars: Prose in the English Revolution*. London: Cass, 1992.

Howell, James. *Epistolæ Ho-Elianæ, Familiar Letters Domestic and Forren, by J. H.* London, 1650.

Hubbert, Thomas. *The Ranter's Creed*. London, 1651.

Johnson, Marmaduke. *Ludgate: What It Is, Not, What It Was; or, a Full and Clear Discovery and Description of . . . That Prison, Also, an Exact Catalogue of the Legacies Now Belonging to the Said Prison, the Names of the Several Donors, and the Persons Appointed to Pay Them . . .* London, 1674.

Jordan, Thomas. *Musick and Poetry Mixed in a Variety of Songs and Poems*. London, 1663.

Marotti, Arthur F. *Manuscript, Print, and the English Renaissance Lyric*. Ithaca: Cornell UP, 1995.

Mellidge Anthony. *Winchester Prison the 21th Day of 1 Month 59 If the Measure of My Sufferings under the Creuel Hands of Unreasonale Men, Be Finished in This Noysome Prison by the Laying Down of My Life*. London, 1659.

Otten, Charlotte F. *English Women's Voices, 1540–1700*. Miami: Florida International UP, 1992.

Phelps, William Lyon, ed. *Lucasta: The Poems of Richard Lovelace, Esquire*. Chicago: Caxton Club, 1921.

Potter, Lois. *Secret Rites and Secret Writing: Royalist Literature, 1641–1660*. Cambridge: Cambridge UP, 1989.

Salzman, Paul, ed. *Early Modern Women's Writing: An Anthology, 1560–1700*. Oxford: Oxford UP, 2000.

Smith, Nigel. *Literature and Revolution in England, 1640–1660*. New Haven: Yale UP, 1994.

Spearing, A. C. "Prison, Writing, Absence: Representing the Subject in the English Poems of Charles D'Orleans." *Modern Language Quarterly* 53.1 (1992): 83–99.

Taylor, John. *Ranters of Both Sexes, Male and Female: Being Thirteen or More, Taken and Imprisoned in the Gate-House at Westminster*. London, 1651.

Weaver, Thomas. *Songs and Poems of Love and Drollery*. London, 1654.

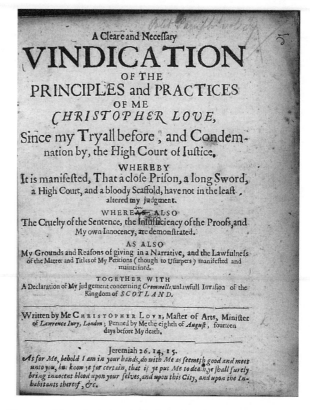

Fig. 7.1. Frontispiece to Christopher Love, "A Cleare and Necessary Vindication" (1651). (By permission of the British Library, halfmark 100e84.)

Chapter 8

Selves in Strange Lands
Autobiography and Exile
in the Mid–Seventeenth Century

Helen Wilcox

To be human, it has often been claimed, is to be fundamentally in a
state of exile. Mortal life is construed as banishment: from God, from
Eden, from the heavenly existence that both precedes and awaits us.[1]
Petrarch, echoing Saint Augustine and Boethius, described the human
condition as being born into exile and thereafter experiencing life as a
perpetual state of estrangement (Petrarch 25; Claassen). The figure of
the "stranger in a strange land" (Exodus 2:22) is indeed an archetype
of biblical narrative, beginning with Adam and Eve making their "solitary way" outside Paradise (Milton 12.649) and continuing with the
"scattered remnant" of the Jews dispersed in Babylon (Isaiah 1:10). But
the wandering exile is equally central to the classical tradition; like
Moses, Ulysses journeys forever through our cultural imagination.
The term *exile* itself, however, is perhaps misleading, since its literal
meaning is "to leap out of"; the etymology seems to imply that exile is
an active or conscious choice, whereas it is more frequently associated
with being *made* to leap, with enforced banishment from the place or
condition we call home. This sense of exclusion is an ancient phenomenon—Euripides wrote in 431 B.C. that "there is no greater sorrow on
earth than the loss of one's native land"—but it is also a bitter current
experience for many groups and individuals in our modern world.[2]
The late Edward Said defined *exile* as "the unhealable rift forced
between a human being and a native place, between the self and its true
home" (173). This comment raises questions about the relationship
between exile and identity—between selves and homes—that will be
explored in the course of this chapter.

The state of exile is not only a persistent symbol and actuality in human experience, but brings with it deep and complex associations. The origins, if not the consequences, of banishment may often be regarded as positive; the exiled individual has generally been forced out for a reason, which is frequently his or her steadfast loyalty to an unpopular principle. As the eleventh-century pope Gregory VII, and Horace before him, claimed, "I have loved justice and hated iniquity, therefore I die in exile."[3] Here the speaker's rejection by society is claimed as a mark of honor, and exile is seen as a condition that tests, and confirms, allegiance to a noble cause. The Jews found themselves in the wilderness on account of their faith, and it was no accident that the same landscape, symbolic of exile, was the location for Christ's resistance of the devil's temptations. The "strange land," the place that is not home, is the setting in which the "Lord's song" can still be sung (Psalms 137:4) and where the song may take on a new beauty and poignancy. The site that signifies rejection can nevertheless be a source of strength and inspiration, recalling the biblical precedent of the rejected stone that ultimately becomes the "cornerstone" (1 Peter 2:6). The exiled condition, being by nature transitory, contains within it the hope of change and eventual renewal. The wilderness is, after all, the place where biblical prophets discover their voices, where nourishment (manna, water) can miraculously be found, and where joy can unexpectedly flourish: "the wilderness and the solitary place shall be glad for them, the desert shall rejoice and blossom as the rose" (Isaiah 35:1).

Exile, then, is a paradoxical condition. It is often the result of cruel rejection, and it has profoundly negative consequences, as witnessed by the fact that the verb *to exile* had by the early sixteenth century come to mean "to ruin or devastate."[4] On the other hand, the experience of exile can signify constancy and integrity and can lead to a surprising "blossom" of unknown yet positive potential. As Susan Stanford Friedman has suggested, the contraries within exile are hinted at in the word *flight*, which expresses the imperative of escaping persecution or danger but also the freedom that comes with soaring in flight (88). The exile must flee but may also fly.

In the mid–seventeenth century, an unusually large number of English men and women found themselves in flight, in both senses, within and beyond their own country as a result of the religious, political, and social changes collectively referred to as the English Revolution.[5] The same period, perhaps not coincidentally, also witnessed a great flourishing of autobiographical writing in many forms and genres, from memoirs and confessions to letters, diaries, and lyric verse.[6] This essay will examine the autobiographical work of a range of mid-seventeenth-century writers in order to suggest the spectrum of kinds of exile experienced in the period and their fascinating relation to the autobiographical process. What are the possible relationships between self and home in the early modern period and how are these articulated? To what extent is exile conducive to self-discovery and creativity? As Michael Seidel has observed, there are strong parallels between the artistic life and the condition of exile, in that writers and exiles both experience "separation as desire, perspective as witness, alienation as new being" (x). He further suggests that exile can provide "imaginative sustenance," though we may wonder if, in fact, the reverse is also true. Does imagination itself give sustenance in an inhospitable wilderness? In the strange limbo of exile, temporarily caught between home and abroad, between past and future, between memory and desire, the autobiographer may be moved to find comfort in writing. Although exile is, from one point of view, a process of removal from society and the effacement of an identity, seen from another angle it can lead to self-sufficiency and provide a powerful impulse in the discovery of selfhood.

My first example of a writing "self" in a "strange land" is Margaret Cavendish, the duchess of Newcastle, one of the group of exiles who spring to mind when thinking of England in the mid–seventeenth century: the Royalists abroad. This type of exile is almost stereotypical; the Royalists found themselves on the losing side in a civil war, forced to abandon their homeland because of their political allegiance and for reasons of personal safety. But when we examine a particular case emerging from the disastrous disruptions of the midcentury we can see how much more complex this apparently archetypal experience could be. Cavendish's secular memoir, "A True Relation of My Birth, Breeding, and Life" (1656), opens with an account of her father, who is said not only to have been "a Gentleman" (an important marker of his daughter's subsequent social identity) but also to have suffered a period of "exile" during the last years of Elizabeth's reign on account of his having killed a man inadvisably in a duel (Cavendish, *Nature's* 368).[7] We are immediately confronted by the idea that the experience of exile can be, as it were, inherited. Though her father was forced to leave his homeland for an entirely different reason, the pattern of his life intriguingly foreshadows Cavendish's own personal narrative. Exile is built into her memoir as a trope of family identity.

As the story of her youth in the Civil War period unfolds, two important aspects of exile emerge. First, it becomes clear that exile can be partly a matter of choice. In 1643, Cavendish (then just twenty years old) was eager to join the queen's entourage. She recalled that

> when the Queen was in *Oxford*, I had a great desire to be one of her Maids of Honour, hearing the Queen had not the same number she was used to have, whereupon I wooed and won my Mother to let me go, for my Mother being fond of all her Children, was desirous to please them, which made her consent to my request: But my Brothers and Sisters seem'd not very well pleas'd, by reason I had never been from home, nor seldome out of their sight; for though they knew I would not behave myself to their, or my own dishonour, yet they thought I might to my disadvantage, being unexperienced in the World . . . (373)

This first stage of Cavendish's account demonstrates that there is such a phenomenon as voluntary exile; she "wooed and won" the chance to leave her mother's house, choosing instead to become part of the court of Queen Henrietta Maria. However, Cavendish observes that the queen, whose household was temporarily located in Oxford in a state of involuntary exile from London as a consequence of the war, is suffering from a lack of "Maids of Honour." The young woman's flight to join the queen's court may thus have come about not only through an element of choice on her own part but also as a response to the (relative) deprivation of the queen's exiled condition and to the distressing circumstances of a country at war with itself, where internal exile breeds its own followers.

Second, it is evident from Cavendish's account of her own experience that exile can be a gradual process rather than the sudden alteration that the basic meaning of the word might lead us to expect. Cavendish's exile is represented as a developing condition, a painful movement farther and farther away from her point of origin. In the passage just quoted, we witness Cavendish leaving her mother, her home, and her anxiously protective siblings (she being the youngest child) and venturing outside her known environment, both geographically and morally. She goes on to note her own anxiety lest she "wander with Ignorance out of the waies of Honour" (374), a revealing metaphor recalling the association of sin with exclusion, equating moral error with "wandering" away from known paths into the wilderness of exile. As the passage proceeds, Cavendish adds progressively to the sense of banishment that followed from her initial eagerness to leave home, writing that

> in truth my bashfulness and fears made me repent my going from home to see the World abroad, and much I did desire to return to my Mother again . . . but my Mother advised me there to stay, although I put her to more charges than if she had kept me at home, and the more, by reason she and my Brothers were sequestred from their Estates, and plundered of all their Goods. . . . But my Mother said, it would be a disgrace for me to return out of the Court so soon after I was placed; so I continued almost two years, untill such time as I was married from thence. (374)

The impression of Cavendish's homelessness in "the World abroad" is particularly intense here since it involves her own mother's rejection of her wish to return home on both social and practical grounds: to leave the court would be "a disgrace," and in any case the Civil War was exiling the rest of her family, too, "sequestred" and "plundered" from their own estate. The young Cavendish is thus not only excluded from her original home but learns of its dispersal; there is no possible return to the security of her mother's house and all that it signified.

In the meantime, Cavendish's new home, the court, was forced into two further stages of exile, "from *Oxford*, and so out of *England*" (373), eventually reestablishing itself in Paris. (This is, of course, a reminder that banishment for one individual—Cavendish—can simultaneously be a homecoming for another—Henrietta Maria, the French queen married to the English king.) We might accurately conclude that Cavendish, on arriving in France with the court, had lost by then most of the contexts and discourses in which identity is normally constructed: her family, her home, her nation, and her own language (she confesses in her memoir that she could not speak French). And yet it was in this situation of displacement, a few years later, that she attempted to scrutinize her self by writing "her own Life" (390). Indeed, the sense of being in "a strange land" was by then even more unsettling, since she and her husband (the marquis of Newcastle, whom she had met during their mutual exile in Paris) had moved on yet again. She wrote that

> after I was married some two or three years, my Lord travell'd out of *France*, from the City of *Paris*, in which City he resided the time he was there, so went into *Holland*, to a Town called *Rotterdam*, in

which place he stayed some six months, from thence he returned to *Brabant*, unto the City of *Antwerpe*, which Citie we past through, when we went into *Holland*, and in that City my Lord settled himself and Family, choosing it for the most pleasantest, and quietest place to retire himself and ruined fortunes in; but after we had remaind sometime therein, we grew extremely necessitated, Tradesmen there being not so rich, as to trust my Lord for so much, or so long, as those in *France*: yet they were so civill, kind and charitable, as to trust him, for as much as they were able; but at last necessity inforced me to return into *England*, to seek for reliefe. (378–79)

The syntax of this narrative as it moves from Paris through Holland to Rotterdam, and through Brabant to Antwerp, is reminiscent of the biblical account of the birth of Jesus ("Joseph also went up from Galilee, out of the city of Nazareth, unto Judaea, unto the City of David, which is called Bethlehem" [Luke 2:4]), importantly reminding the reader of the honorable precedents for being on the move. Indeed, the expression Cavendish uses for the setting of their exiled life—the place where her husband can "retire himself and [his] ruined fortunes in"—suggests further positive overtones. Despite the "ruins," the verb *retire* reminds us of the idea of exile as retreat from danger, evoking the classical tradition of retirement poetry and the pastoral retreat from corruption. However, their life in Antwerp was no idyll, and the "extremely necessitated" Cavendish had no choice but to search for temporary relief from impoverishment by returning to England, the land in which she was by then an outsider and which, therefore, was no longer home.

To what extent does the place of exile, then, itself become "home"? Cavendish gives a hint of an answer in the frontispiece to *Nature's Pictures*, the 1656 volume in which her memoir was published. The engraving (see fig. 8.1) shows Cavendish with about a dozen men and women sitting in a "semy-Circle" in an elegant room with a blazing fire. Is this an image of home? Warmth, conviviality, and company abound, so why is the writer depicted as pensive, even distracted? In the second edition of *Nature's Pictures*, published in 1671, Cavendish offers an explanation. Apart from her husband, all the friends in the picture were actually absent, since she was in exile in 1656; they were simply present in her imagination and drawn to her fireside by her memory and her own creative capacity. In exile, home becomes, as the poet Jenny Bornholdt has put it, a "room in your head," a welcoming place that you "visit often" and where "they always let you in" (8–13).

Two dominant, if contradictory, metaphors for exile thus emerge from Cavendish's autobiographical writing: wandering and seclusion. The first, as we have noted, functions both symbolically and literally as an account of her unsettled experience in the 1640s and 1650s. It may also be said to inform her written style, which is notorious for its rambling eccentricity but which she claimed as a virtue in her poem "The Claspe."[8]

> Give mee the free and Noble Stile
> Which seems uncurb'd, though it be wild
> Though it runs wild about, it cares not where,
> It shows more Courage, then it doth of Feare.
>
> (*Poems* 46)

Cavendish's ideal of an apparently "wild" style, which is actually "noble" on account of its dynamic freedom, epitomizes what she may have seen as the advantages of life in exile: always in motion, "uncurb'd" by the restraints of normal life, fearless in the face of familiar convention. In contrast to this roaming style of living and writing, the other aspect of exile emphasized in Cavendish's metaphors is isolation, both unwanted (exclusion) and actively sought (seclusion). Here, too, her writing worked hand in hand with the experience of exile: her imagination could fill an empty room with company, and her thoughts could turn her mind into a theater, "where my Mind sits as a Spectator" (*CCXI* letter 29, 57). Indeed, this contentedness in enforced absence from family and society became such a habit that in the end she professed to being willing to choose exclusion from society, claiming that

> though I desire to appear at the best advantage, whilest I live in the view of the publick World, yet I could most willingly exclude my self, so as Never to see the face of any creature, but my Lord, as long as I live, inclosing my self like an Anchoret, wearing a Frize-gown, tied with a cord about my waste. (390)

The image of Cavendish as a religious hermit (complete with fashion accessories) hints at the attractiveness of exile for this exuberantly creative woman. There is a striking parallel here between the enforced withdrawal from everyday public life into exile and the willing retreat from society into the anchorite's cell (in her case, in the presence of an earthly rather than a heavenly "Lord"). The metaphor of the cell suggests that exile, despite seeming to stem from rejection and to result in imprisonment and deprivation, can in fact be a means of learning to live "inclosed" with (and within) one's self.

The creative possibilities of this experience of exile for the writing of autobiography are plain to see. So, too, are the implications of Cavendish's experience for Said's idea of the "rift" in exile "between the self and its true home." She did not have one true home: it had once been her mother's house, but later it became England itself or the queen's court or her husband's chosen place of retirement; yet ultimately it became the metaphorical isolated hermitage within which her imagination performed in absolute freedom, fleshing out her identity and that of the imaginary company she kept. In this self-sufficiency, there was no rift between self and home, since her self *was* her home.

In mid-seventeenth-century Britain, there were large numbers of individuals who experienced a very different kind of exile from that of Margaret Cavendish. These were the victims of the tensions of the Civil War and Commonwealth who did not leave the country but found themselves alienated within their own land: the phenomenon of individuals in exile even when at "home." This is not unusual in a time of revolution and counterrevolution, where division and exclusion become common features of life inside (or outside) families and communities. The Welsh writer and Royalist Henry Vaughan was typical of many who were excluded by the Civil War from the intellectual and liturgical communities in which they had established their identities. For Vaughan, this meant enforced retreat from Oxford and London to his original home, Breconshire in Wales, and deprivation of the Anglican worship that had framed his spirituality. His twin brother, Thomas, was evicted from his living at the parish church of Llansantf-fraed in 1650, and life in the Usk Valley—the place of their birth—became for both of them, with cruel irony, a state of exile. In 1652, Henry Vaughan published his prose meditations, *The Mount of Olives*, prefacing them with two epistles that use the language of scripture to convey this experience of profound isolation. The first letter is addressed to Sir Charles Egerton.

> I know, *Sir*, you will be pleased to accept of this poore *Olive-leafe* presented to you, so that I shall not be driven to put forth my hand to take in my *Dove* againe. And indeed (considering how *fast* and how *soone* men degenerate), It must be counted for a great *blessing*, that there is yet any left which dares to *look* upon, and *commiserate*

distressed Religion. *Good men* in *bad times* are very scarce; They are like the *standing eares of Corne escaped out of the Reapers hands,* or the *Vine-dressers last gleanings after the first ripe fruits have been gathered.* Such a *precious generation are the Just* in the *day of trouble,* and their *names* are like to *afflicted truth,* like the *shadow of a great rock in a weary land,* or a *wayfaring mans lodge in the waste and howling Wilder-nesse.* (138)[9]

Vaughan seems to assume here that his personal experience of affliction and distress is identical to that of the "distressed Religion" of the Church of England itself, and he is grateful for the attention given to both church and churchman by Sir Charles. He writes to his patron in a distressed but bold tone, deriving solidarity from representing himself as a seventeenth-century Noah, exiled by a flood of troubles from the safe dry land of his spiritual and political home. His sketch of the Royalists' situation suggests that exile can be a temporal as well as a spatial phenomenon, for "good men" can be exiled in "bad times" as well as in bad places. He wanders sadly and wearily through both dimensions, like a "wayfaring man" in an inhospitable "Wildernesse," where Sir Charles, to whom the book is dedicated, offers welcome shelter from the harshness of climate and topography. As in so many of his poems, Vaughan depicts himself as a lost and vulnerable figure in a vast and mysterious landscape, hoping for a glimpse of light in the darkness or "bright *shoots* of everlastingness" in the transitory barren world (173).

The real comfort for the exiled writer lies in the realization that Christ, too, was in exile on earth.

The *Sonne* of God himselfe (when *he* was *here*) had no place to put his head in; and his *Servants* must not think the *present measure* too hard, seeing their *Master* himself took up his *nights-lodging* in the cold *Mount* of Olives. (138)

The recognition of the homelessness of God's own Son puts the "present measure" of his followers in its proper context; to experience exile is thus part of the vocation to imitate Christ. But Vaughan's piety is political, too. The frontispiece of the *Eikon Basilike,* the anonymous 1649 volume mourning and celebrating the executed Charles I, depicts the king praying like Christ on the Mount of Olives. Vaughan constructs himself simultaneously as a servant of both Christ and the martyred earthly king; loyalty to both these lords has led to his exiled condition.

Although we may equate exile with separation and isolation, it is important to remember that this does not necessarily mean a private or individual condition. It is, after all, possible for a whole group of people, such as the Jews of the Old Testament, to be seen as outcasts from their promised land. In the second epistle prefacing *The Mount of Olives*, addressed to "the Peaceful, humble, and pious Reader," Vaughan draws strongly on this idea of a community of the excluded.

> *Think not that thou art alone upon this Hill, there is an innumerable company both before and behinde thee. Those with their Palms in their hands, and these expecting them. If therefore the dust of this world chance to prick thine eyes, suffer it not to blinde them; but* running thy race with patience, look to JESUS the Authour and finisher of thy faith, who when he was reviled, reviled not againe. Presse thou towards the mark, *and let the people and their Seducers rage;* be faithful unto the death, and he will give thee a Crowne of life. (141)

Here Vaughan spurs on his readers by urging them to recollect that he and they are part of an invisible, timeless, and infinite "company": "thou art not alone." Echoing the Book of Revelation, as well as the epistles of Saint Paul, the mid-seventeenth-century political and spiritual exile claims kinship with Christ and all the other patient sufferers of the past and the future—"both before and behinde thee." This enormous and empowering sense of community merges, paradoxically, with references to distinctive individuals in exile. For in the end he exhorts his readers to

> *choose the better part, yea, that part with Saint* Hierome, *who preferred the poore Coate of* Paul *the Hermite to the purple and pride of the world. Thus with my simple Advise unto thee, I bid thee farewell.* (141)

The writer, speaking from the experience of lonely exile, exhorts his readers to choose, like him, the life of Saint Jerome, rejecting the attractions of the world for a hermit's "poore Coate" (recalling Margaret Cavendish's desire for the imaginary anchorite's gown). But in the very act of invoking the models of Jerome and Paul, Vaughan asserts that, even in their isolation on a seventeenth-century equivalent of the Mount of Olives, he and his fellow exiles are not "alone upon this Hill."

The state of exile, therefore, is a series of paradoxes. It signifies both rejection and affirmation and can be seen simultaneously as the devastation of a life and the opportunity to pursue a calling; as the poet

Joseph Brodsky commented, "Perhaps exile is the poet's natural condition. . . . I felt a certain privilege in the coincidence of my existential condition with my profession" (Brodsky 56). In a further paradox, exile is a punishment that, as in the case of Margaret Cavendish's early life, can also be sought and a banishment that, in the case of Henry Vaughan, can lead one home. The exiled condition is, in addition, associated with isolation, but at the same time it may involve a strong sense of mutual company. This last paradox applies to autobiography, too, particularly in the early modern period. We tend to think of selfhood as a unique individual phenomenon, and the use of the autobiographical "I" encourages the impression of identity as a distinctive subjectivity in charge of a personal narrative. But, as we have already seen, early modern writers tended to understand their lives—and, in the case of this particular study, their experience of exile—through the models and patterns of those who preceded them. Margaret Cavendish likened herself as an autobiographer to Julius Caesar but envisaged herself in exile as a modern-day anchorite;[10] Henry Vaughan sought the hermit's cave, too, but specified the examples of Saints Paul and Jerome, while the location of his meditations on the Mount of Olives evoked parallels with two kings, Charles I and Christ. Early modern identities may thus be said to have emerged in the interaction of particular lives with established precedents of personality, language, and behavior.

Another salutary constraint on our easy assumption that identity means individuality is the existence of the shared autobiography. My third example of midcentury exile is taken from the joint account of the lives of Katherine Evans and Sarah Cheevers, two Quaker missionaries whose *Cruel Sufferings, for the Truth's Sake* were recorded in a *Short Relation* published in 1662. In this fascinating text, the identities of the protagonists flow in and out of one another, sometimes distinctive and named, at other times merging in their shared experience. The autobiography was further removed from any straightforward notion of individuality by the fact that it was edited and published by their friend and fellow Quaker, Daniel Baker, who would have shaped their narrative to fit the needs of the Quaker readership for whom it was intended. As the title page states, the publication was for all who "have a feeling and fellowship with them in their sufferings, that they might see and know how it is with them" (Evans and Cheevers 56).[11] What mattered in the case of the *Short Relation* was not so much the distinctive or unique characters of Evans and Cheevers as the example they set, and the inspiration they gave, to their readers. At a time when

Quakers were repressed at home and imprisoned abroad, Evans and Cheevers were depicted as willing respondents to a calling from God to evangelize the world. Their individualities merged into their joint identity as missionaries and "sisters in Jesus Christ" (124), who accepted suffering in positive obedience to God's command. In this autobiography, identity is communal and exile is a vocation.

Evans and Cheevers's account focuses on their desperate experiences while imprisoned in Malta in the early 1660s at the hands of the Inquisition; indeed, it was published while they were still there, apparently "to be detained till they die" (117). The narrative is a notable mixture of passive and active identities, suggesting some of the tensions inherent in both the nature of exile and the process of autobiographical writing. The women interpret their own actions as Christ's interventions in their lives but come across as bold and assertive in their dealings with the friars of the Inquisition. They inscribe a personal narrative, complete with the material details and human perspectives of their story, yet the chief "voice" in it is often that of God. In the following passage, they recount a period of hunger strike.

> We did eat but little for three or four weeks. And then the Lord called us to fasting for eleven days together, but it was so little that the friars came and said it was impossible that creatures could live with so little meat as they did see we did, for so long time together, and asked what we would do, and said their Lord Inquisitor said we might have anything we would. We said we must wait to know the mind of God, what he would have us do. We did not fast in our own wills, but in obedience to the Lord. They were much troubled and sent us meat and said the English Consul sent it. We would not take anything till the Lord's time was come. We were weak, so that Sarah did dress her head as she would lie in her grave, poor lamb. I lay looking for the Lord to put an end to the sad trial, which way it seemed good in his sight. (128)

Here Evans and Cheevers have reached the most extreme point of human life: physically weakened by lack of food, the women prepare for their own deaths and anticipate their interment, even in the manner in which Cheevers "did dress her head." There is no going back; they are about to be exiled from life itself. Their behavior appears to be the ultimate in passivity: they accept the "call" of God to fast, and they lie and wait for death. Yet it is clear that this commitment takes enormous willpower, despite the fact that they declare they "did not fast in our own wills." When confronted by the friars, their captors, with the offer of "anything we would," there is defiance in the reply, "we must wait to know the mind of God." They cannot be sure of the outcome but remain determined in any case. Even the temptation of more neutral refreshment, the meat offered by the "English Consul," is calmly resisted; there is strength of character in this resilient passivity. Later they claim that the friars "could not tell whether we were dead or alive" (128); paradoxically, there is a genuine presence of personality in this declared absence of selfhood.

The difficulty of establishing a spiritual identity that is expressive enough to narrate an autobiography while submissive enough to reflect God's glory becomes apparent at this point in Evans and Cheevers's account. The "I" and "we" cease to be the speakers and become (briefly) listeners.

> Then I heard a voice saying, "Ye shall not die." I believed the Lord and his glory did appear much in our fast. He was very gracious to us and did refresh us with his living presence continually, and we did behold his beauty, to our great joy and comfort. . . . And they were made to bring many good things and laid them down by us, so that scripture we witnessed fulfilled: "Our enemies treated us kindly in a strange land," said I. (128)

The chief and determining speaker here is at first unidentified—it is simply "a voice"—but it would have been quickly recognized by Quaker readers as divine: the word of the Lord, a reassuring inner truth echoing the words of the Bible.[12] Later in the passage this scriptural context is overtly acknowledged, as the women specify the parallel between the experience of the Old Testament exiles and their own situation among adversaries "in a strange land." But despite the fact that the passage implies the presence of these other, divine voices—one heard, one read—which confirm the women's providential circumstances, Evans also remains prominent in the account as an active speaking subject: "I heard," "I believed," and, most striking of all, "said I." This last phrase seems superfluous, since the citation that precedes it is apparently biblical and to quote it ought to be sufficient, but in fact the sentence is a reinterpretation and reformulation of the scriptural echo to fit their own circumstances (Exodus 2:22). By declaring that she herself said this, Evans reminds the reader that the women have inserted their own perspective into the generality of the scriptural mode ("*our* enemies treated *us* kindly"). In addition, the phrase's inverted syntax—"said I"—results in the sentence ending with a focus not on the scriptural voice but on her status as speaker and thus on her subjectivity. This may have been "the Lord's song in a strange land" (Psalm 137:4), but Evans and Cheevers were very much the singers.

At this triumphant moment in the narrative, when they have remained obedient to the Lord, refused their captors' offers of food, passed through a kind of death, and survived "till the time that the Lord had appointed we should eat"(128), suddenly the women's understandable human doubts and fears emerge.

> But we were afraid to eat and cried to the Lord and said we had rather die than eat anything that is polluted and unclean. The Lord said unto me, "Thou mayest as freely eat as if thou hadst wrought it with thy hands. I will sanctify it to thee through the cross." And he said to Sarah, "Thou shalt eat the fruit of thy hands and be blessed." We did eat and were refreshed, to the praise and glory of our God forever. (128)

The episode is thus completed in a direct dialogue with "the Lord," whose words to this point had been hidden in those of the unnamed "voice" or the pages of scripture. After these reassuring personal encounters with God, Evans and Cheevers are able to "eat" and be "refreshed." The climax recalls George Herbert's "Love (III)," in which the speaker, hesitating and drawing back from God's loving offer of spiritual nourishment, is finally persuaded to "sit and eat" (192). In their physical exile, the Quaker missionaries endured "cruel sufferings," but the most profound exile of all would have been exclusion from the banquet of God.

In three very different autobiographical extracts—a secular memoir, the dedicatory epistles to a work of devout meditation, and a report of trials for the sake of faith—we have so far seen mid-seventeenth-century exiles driven by social, political, or religious loyalties to Antwerp, the Usk Valley, and a Maltese prison. Despite the record of these travels, however, it would be fair to say that the greater distances traveled by those in exile were internal rather than geographical. The texts, particularly that of Evans and Cheevers, demonstrate that the landscape of the excluded is often a mental or metaphorical place, an inner wilderness or psychological "strange land." To be deprived of family, community, security, freedom, and almost of life itself is a metaphysical trauma that is only partially mirrored in the actual physical experience of rejection and separation.[13] John Bunyan, for example, knew all too well what it was like to be imprisoned for preaching his Baptist faith when it was decreed illegal in the 1660s and to be exiled as a result from home and family. In his conversion narrative, *Grace Abounding*, he confesses that "parting with my Wife and poor children" was like "the pulling the flesh from my bones" (100).[14] However, this graphically painful separation is as nothing when compared with Bunyan's repeated sense of being cut off from God by his own sinfulness. In the midst of times when he felt secure in his relationship with God and "pretty well and savoury in my spirit," Bunyan would suddenly and inexplicably lose sight of the home of his spirit, as when he writes that

> there fell upon me a great cloud of darkness, which did so hide from
> me the things of God and Christ, that I was as if I had never seen or
> known them in my life; I was also so over-run in my Soul, with a
> senceless heartless frame of spirit, that I could not feel my soul to
> move or stir after grace and life by Christ; I was as if my loyns were
> broken, or as if my hands and feet had been tied or bound with
> chains. . . . After I had been in this condition some three or four
> days, as I was sitting by the fire, I suddenly felt this word to sound
> in my heart, *I must go to Jesus;* at this my former darkness and athe-
> ism fled away, and the blessed things of heaven were set within my
> view. (83–84)

In this account, as on so many of the pages of *Grace Abounding*, Bunyan's state of sin is represented as a form of exile by means of a series of physical metaphors expressing his intensely experienced spiritual condition. He finds himself under a "great cloud of darkness," cut off from the light of salvation and banished from "the things of God and Christ." In this exile from the divine presence, bereft even of the memory of knowing God, he is utterly helpless, without motion both spiritually and physically. His soul seems unable to "move or stir after grace," and his loins are as if "broken," in a disturbing image of impotence. Everything that defines him as a Christian and a man has been taken away with the removal of the sustaining assurance of God's love. Despair, the "sin against the Holy Spirit,"[15] deprives him not only of heaven but also of his autonomous self. In this state, Bunyan is depicted as one cut off from the world, bound hand and foot "with chains" like a prisoner. His inner state may, indeed, be compared with the outer circumstances of Evans and Cheevers: immobilized and imprisoned far from home.

Both situations—the actual incarceration of the Quaker women and the psychological exile of Bunyan—are transformed by a heavenly voice speaking and urging action. Evans and Cheevers feel that they are urged by Christ to "freely eat," returning from the self-imposed fasting that has led almost to death. In Bunyan's account, the restoration of his relationship with God from near extinction is achieved by a new conversion—a spiritual turning or voyage, *"I must go to Jesus"*— but it is experienced even before the homeward journey can begin. His assurance of salvation comes with the sight of the place toward which he must travel: "the blessed things of heaven were set within my view." After the terror of being in the wilderness, his recovery is expressed in sensual and topographical terms; the promise of redemption is again visible to him, seen as a distant city on the horizon of a landscape, quickening the heart of the wanderer. This is the language of exile applied vividly to the early modern dread of damnation. The parallels between rejection by God experienced as banishment and the physical experience of imprisonment or exile are not, however, confined to the seventeenth century. In the late twentieth century, when the British religious envoy Terry Waite was kidnaped and held hostage in Beirut, he was spiritually sustained in his ordeal by a postcard sent to him from England, bearing the image of the imprisoned John Bunyan as depicted in a stained glass window of Bedford parish church (Waite 326). Across the centuries and continents, there was community even in the torment of spiritual and material exile.

To examine a more secular form of psychological exile in early modern autobiographical writing, we turn to the diaries of Lady Anne Clifford. This strong-willed and intrepid figure, daughter of the earl and countess of Cumberland, was no stranger to physical exile throughout her life, having been denied the extensive lands and houses in Westmorland and Craven (in the north of England) to which she should have been the heir.[16] She spent nearly four decades banished to the south of England while fighting to regain her northern inheritance; once she had achieved this (after the further delay and exclusion caused by the Civil War), she devoted the rest of her long life, as Nancy E. Wright examines in chapter 13 of this collection, to reclaiming her lands while rebuilding and residing in her castles. However, long before she was able to return to her family's northern lands, Clifford had also experienced her married life as a kind of exile. Her years as the wife of Richard Sackville, earl of Dorset, living at Knole, and subsequently as the wife of Philip Herbert, earl of Pembroke, at Wilton, were comparable (her diaries suggest) to those of the Chosen People in the wilderness. While at Knole, when her husband opposed her claim on the Clifford family lands and was frequently absent in

London, she was left in Kent feeling, as she records in 1616, "like an Owl in the Desert" (Clifford 33).[17] This phrase is an echo of Psalm 102:6, a psalm introduced in the biblical text as "a Prayer of the afflicted"; it bewails the "reproach" of enemies, the bitter sorrow of eating "ashes like bread," and the speaker's heart "smitten, and withered like grass."[18] The biblical connection evoked in her diary suggests the kind of misery, as well as its precedents, that Clifford perceived as her lot while she was banished into marriage in the south of England. Later, in a notebook entry for 1635, Clifford refers to her life in both the great houses into which she married as a time of isolation and sorrow: "the marble pillars of Knole and Wilton were to mee oftentimes but the gay arbours of Anguish," from which she claims to have retreated as frequently as possible into "Retyredness," with "good bookes and virtuous thoughts" as her only companions (94).

Clifford's autobiographical account of her married life highlights the particular forms of exile experienced by early modern women. Not only were they vulnerable to the patriarchal legal structures that excluded them from any independent identity or rights—in this case, Anne Clifford being the only child and yet prohibited from inheriting her father's estates, the place that she knew as home and, even more fundamentally, with which her sense of being was bound up. Women were also vulnerable to the physical exile resulting from marriage, since even those partnerships that were happier than those of Clifford inevitably separated women from their own homes and families, taking them into a world ordered according to men's needs and vocations. Add to this the emotional and mental anguish experienced by Clifford and many other wives and the picture of marriage as a psychological (as well as bodily) exile, or an enforced "Retyredness," as Clifford calls it, becomes all too vivid. There is undoubtedly a gendering of selfhood in the early modern period; the nature and experience of exile, too, are shaped and sharpened according to gender.

Ironically, in her later life Clifford seems to have chosen what might be termed a voluntary exile in her "Inheritance in the North" (135), the homeland of her ancestors, which she had regained after much prolonged legal and emotional struggles. She refused to return to London and relished her role as a kind of alternative monarch in the north, making Elizabethan-style royal progresses from one estate to the next. On 27 January 1664, for example, she went "out of Pendraggon Castle in Westmoreland in my Coach drawn by 6 Horses, and most of my familie with me on Horsback into Applebie Castle" (169). She was perfectly aware of what was occurring in the south of the country, but saw it as a gloss on her own way of life, not as a challenge to it. In 1662, she notes that "a little before I removed from Brougham Castle, did our Queen Marie the Frenchwoman, Mother to our now King Charles, land at Greenwich in Kent, being newly come from her journie from Calais" (159). The sequence is fascinating: her own "removal" from one castle to another is mentioned first, followed by that of Queen Henrietta Maria, which acts as a kind of echo or supporting parallel to her own life. While the queen (with whom Margaret Cavendish had left England in the early 1640s) is returning from enforced exile, Clifford exults in her own freedom of movement and the "contentments and innocent pleasures of a Country Life" (112). As a defiant landowner, builder, widow, mother, grandmother, and great-grandmother, she regards with disdain those who question or criticize her distance from southern society.[19] There is an extent to which exile is determined by the perceptions of those who experience it. In the case of Clifford, she knew the latter part of her life not as exile but as the satisfying and largely benevolent exercise of power.[20]

There is, however, a further layer of self-definition through (or in defiance of) exile to be discerned in Anne Clifford's diaries. For most of her eighty-six years, Clifford took pleasure in recording her life and that of her extended family (past, present, and anticipated in "Posteritie" [112]) in a series of diaries and "great books." She was evidently obsessed by perceiving and inscribing the patterns of history, both personal and communal. As the diaries proceed, the entries that observe that something happened on the anniversary of a comparable event, or in the same room or castle, become more frequent. The reader of her diaries begins to realize that the process of autobiographical writing itself can be a form of psychological exile, offering as it does a means of dwelling in the lands and moods of the past. The following extract from Clifford's diary, written on what turned out to be her last birthday, highlights the way in which her identity in the final months of her life has come to be constructed entirely out of memories linked to the present through parallel dates and locations.

> I considered how this day [30 January 1676] was 86 years & then Friday about 7 a clock in the evening was my blessed Mother with very hard labor brought to bed of mee in hier owne chamber in Skipton Castle in Craven, where she then lay; my Brother Robert, Lord Clifford then also lying in the Castle. But my noble father than lay in Bedford House in the Strand in London, as also my Aunt of Warwick & her husband Ambrose, Earle of Warwick, who dyed the

21st of the month following. And about 6 years before my birth was my blessed Mother in the same place delivered of my eldest Brother, Francis Lord Clifford, but hee dyed before I was borne. (244)

This is the diary entry of a willing exile in the realms of memory, who understands and inscribes her present self through the coincidences of time and place. The crucial moments of individual and family life—birth and death—along with the places where individuals are when they "lye" or "dye," fill up her actual life. The only verbs of which she is the subject in this paragraph are those that frame it: "I considered" and "I was borne." Life for her, begun so long ago, is now completely focused on "considering": thinking, remembering, connecting. Of all the autobiographies we have considered so far in this discussion, Clifford's is the only one not published in her lifetime and probably not intended for publication. The manuscript diary is for her own satisfaction, and by the end the place it conjures up for her, into which she recedes in voluntary psychological exile, is the past.

It would be wrong, however, to suggest that the last pages of Anne Clifford's diary concerned only a private past with no reference to public history. The entry for 30 January 1676 continues.

And this day was 27 years [since] our then King Charles (who was borne in Scotland) was beheaded on a Scaffold in the open aire near the Banqueting house at Whitehall & his dead body afterwards buried in the Chappel at Windsor in Berkshire. And when this Tragedy was performed did I lye in Baynards Castle in London and my second Lord was in his lodgings by the Cockpit at Whitehall where he dyed about a year after.

And tho' it was Sunday yet I went not to church nor out of my Chamber today. (244)

By a striking coincidence, King Charles I was executed on Clifford's birthday, thus providing an annual reminder, particularly painful to a Royalist such as she, of the vulnerability of even God's anointed monarch. Once again, however, just as in her reference to the return of Henrietta Maria, Clifford records this "Tragedy" of national history only after she has noted her personal and family history in the earlier part of the entry. She and her "second Lord" may well have been in London when the execution was "performed" (to quote Clifford's theatrical vocabulary), but in the sequence of the diary they are the foreground, not the backdrop, to such events. Her own life, and not that of the official histories, provides the structure for this perspective on the remembered past.

Since Clifford was eighty-six years old on the day whose record we are reading, it is understandable that she did not leave her chamber that day. But, although her world had shrunk to "one little roome" (Donne 49), there was nothing passive or pathetic about her existence.[21] She goes on to note the many people who came to her during the day—gentlewomen, menservants, laundry maids, tenant farmers, and the parson—and she specifies that she kissed the women and took the men by the hand, as well as hearing psalms and prayers with them all. This might be a form of exile—in the far north of England in one room of an ancient, cold castle—but if her chamber is a small social and religious world, and her diary a record of the living past that has composed her own microcosm, then who is to describe it as undesirable or a banishment? The only threat to this existence was the danger lying in wait for any mortal being. Anne Clifford died less than two months after dictating this diary entry. However, her remarkable self-sufficiency remains, composed through memories inscribed in the surviving diary texts. She knew how powerful "Tyme" could be in bringing to "forgettfullness any memorable thing in this world, bee they never soe carefully preserved" (139), but her written defiance of transitoriness took her through a kind of exile in the past as a way of resisting the greater banishment of oblivion.

My final example in this exploration of early modern autobiographers and their multiple experiences of exile is a nonconformist preacher and writer of the Restoration period, Oliver Heywood. Like Anne Clifford, Heywood was an impressive keeper of diaries, records, accounts, lists, and other "alms against oblivion" (Shakespeare, *Troilus and Cressida* 3.3.146). Like John Bunyan, Heywood was frequently imprisoned for preaching without a license or calling together a congregation. Like Katherine Evans and Sarah Cheevers, he experienced the world as an arena in which his own actions and those of people around him bore the weight of providence. Like Henry Vaughan, though in a later period and from the other side of the political and religious divide, Heywood was an exile in his own land on account of his faith. Like Margaret Cavendish, though for profoundly different reasons, he was obsessed with understanding his own life.

The clearest evidence of this self-preoccupation is the following poem, which appears in one of his many notebooks, the "Little Black Book with Two Clasps" (Heywood 3.17), and seems to commemorate

his perplexity when he was arrested on a Sunday for preaching ille-
gally.[22] More metaphysically, it contemplates the mystery of identity
when the speaker faces what we might term the ultimate exile, that is,
separation from or within one's own self.

Selfe	Reflection
I am a Riddle to my selfe, I find	two partyes combating within my mind: *Rom 7 23*
my left hand saith that justice is unjust	my Right hand saith it may be & it must: *Eccl 5 16*
my left hand saith why should a record ly	my Right hand saith my record is on high: *job 16 16*
why was not Argent staind wth sable oaths	Darknes fears light & yt light darkness loaths: *job 3 20*
I would be poring upon injurys	I should cast out the beams fro mine own eyes: *luk 6 42*
why was I taken on a Sabbath-day?	t'was Sabboth work men to thy charge did lay : *luk 4 16*
why was I taken on that Sabbath-day?	Satan knew wt I wrote & meant to say *1 the 2 18*
why was I taken coming forth the church?	fowls of the air were lying at the lurch *mark 4 4*
why might I not the second sermon hear?	that I might pity those that have none near *Heb 4 16*
why did the roaring bull rant it so high?	to make the jaile a goal-delivery *2 pet 2 8:*
you took on you to preach thats an offence,	with dispensation paul could not dispence, *1 cor 9 16*
you suffered others in your house to hear	christ suffered more for such, & souls are dear *act 20 28*
why walkt you not with those yt are more wise	because I saw not with my betters eyes : *phi 3 15 16*
why kept you not within the limitation?	inclosures suit not with common salvation *jud 3*
why were you not to plead your own cause free?	my meaning was my cause should plead for me *gen 30 33*
why would you not part with a little clay?	because I durst not give my caus away *job 27 6*
was it not for a charitable use?	faith knows not charity for an excuse : *cor 13 3*
why made you not a promise to forbear?	a promise not a prison I did fear! *Rev 2 10*
why is your prison stricter then before?	because the judg is nearer to the door : *Jam. 5 8*
what wil you do in case of transportation?	Leave that to him that rules in every nation : *1 cor 10 13*

So let men curse for their curse thou wilt blesse
their hate to me, thy loue thou dost expresse
communion with thee is happines
I need no more & I shal haue no lesse:[23]

This unusual poem constructs, psychologically and visibly, a divided and yet whole self. The "two parties combating within my mind," referred to in the second "half" of the first line, are united in the one poem, as demonstrated by the fact that the second half of each of these double pentameter lines rhymes with the first. They are, however, separated, each on the opposite side of facing pages of the manuscript, and addressing one another in two, if not more, different voices. The left-hand side appears to be worldly, using the vocabulary of heraldry and the law, disputing justice and truth, and asking awkward questions—in short, arguing with the right-hand side of himself. It is surely no accident that this troublesome voice is on the left, recalling the disturbing and alienating associations of the Latin word for *left, sinister.* On the right-hand side, associated with correctness and sanity (being in one's right mind) and the place of favor in the Bible, is a reassuring voice.[24] This part of the self knows the answers and can cite the biblical evidence, as indicated in the right-hand margin. The language used is full of biblical echoes and deals in archetypes, such as light and darkness, rather than the material specificity of earthly places and events referred to on the left. The startlingly split being who is represented here is not just a "stranger in a strange land," like all exiles, but seems to be a stranger even to himself. Or, rather, it is not clear where his "self" is located; the pronouns *I* and *you* are both used, and there appears to be no simple answer to this "Riddle" of identity.

One of the disturbing effects of this poem, which seems to be a testimony to the experience of being exiled from a coherent self, is the uncertainty of who is looking at whom. There is a speaker with a "mind," "hands," and a "selfe," but who, then, is doing the reflecting? At the beginning, the speaker identifies a mystery or puzzle, apparently looking at himself from outside, but the subject ("I am") immediately becomes an object ("a Riddle") with a third party, "my selfe," which is also quickly brought into the picture. This is an intense case of fragmented identity—what we might informally call the "me, myself, and I" syndrome—and in his distress we can see the historical subject (the preacher arrested when leaving church) becoming literally beside himself, split apart down the fold of the facing pages. Is the identity that is projected by the left-hand side of the poem, then, an image of exile? The speaker there has no access to the right side, the norm, apparently the home where heavenly reassurance is given. At the end of the poem, curiously, there are four extra lines on the left, unanswered on the right-hand side. The left or earthly side prevails, for the time being at least, and the speaker remains in worldly exile, though with the promise of "communion" with Christ as hinted at in the words and punctuation of the final line. Perhaps, had the poem ended on the right, there would have been no need to write it; the imbalanced text Heywood gave us is a more accurate image of the self in exile, awaiting the return to the "right" place.

The idea of a self divided between experience and the thoughtful reflection on it is suggested by the title of Heywood's poem, with the words *Selfe* and *Reflection* carefully placed above the two halves of the work. During the course of the poem, there is a suggestion that the "reflection" is not only the meditation on selfhood that the whole poem represents but also the reflected image of the self, as in water or a mirror, or, more specifically, in the incarnate Christ and his words. At the end of the poem, or when reading ceases, the book is closed and the facing pages meet: the left-hand side collapses into the right, and the self is merged with its reflection. In this way, not in the writing of the poem but in its afterlife, is exile overcome and the divided self reunited. If in this context we return to Said's idea of the exiled self being taken from its "true home," then Oliver Heywood may help us to redefine that home. In the light of his poem and the temporary sojourn of his self in exile on the left-hand side of the page, can we see home, then, as a place not to return to, in the sense of turning back, but to go on to? This certainly seems to be suggested by the anticipatory colon with which the poem ends. Release from exile is achieved with acceptance and wholeness as the book closes and the divided lines meet each other face to face, as created and creator merge—that is, at home in heaven.

This consideration of exile and autobiography began with the fundamental premodern sense of the human condition as exile from heaven, and through a variety of mid-seventeenth-century texts we have returned to our starting point. Oliver Heywood's unique portrayal of the "selfe" shows an identity in dispute with itself, on the move (just as we read his lines) from left to right, and thus, the poem seems to suggest, from exile to spiritual home, from mortality to eternity. On our way to this final instance of early modern exile, we have encountered a female exile writing from outside her native land, a male writer deprived of his community, two women missionaries sacrificing their freedom, a preacher exiled from the light of forgiveness, and a mature woman voluntarily exiled in the past. The equivalents or

aspects of home that our autobiographical writers appear to lack—
mother country and language, religious and political groups, liberty
and choice, spiritual security, a place in the present, and a coherent
sense of self—are the very factors that might seem necessary to confer
or frame identity. These are the physical or emotional environs for the
habit of being, the contexts in and by which to know oneself.[25] The
poet Eavan Boland has recently taken this idea one step further, writing of her unhappy removal from Ireland as a child. In her retrospective adult account of this absence from the land of her birth, she puts
forward a sense of exile not simply as being deprived of a particular
place but as the loss of the means to relate self to place at all.

> What I had lost
> was not land
> but the habit of land:
> whether of growing out of
> or settling back on,
> or being
> defined by.
>   (96, 11.22–28)

Boland movingly suggests that the person in exile is removed from the
"habit" of forming an identity by association with a place through all
its natural, social, historical, and linguistic structures. This identity
may well develop through opposition or rejection ("growing out of")
but in the end it is a vital means of "being / defined." Her lines sum up
the idea that exile threatens the integrity or understanding of selfhood—in other words, that it would seem to be in conflict with the
autobiographical process.

    However, as we have seen in all six early modern examples, the
stress of exile, including the loss of those structures that almost automatically confer identity, can lead to an exploration and discovery of
selfhood outside the normal systems and comforts of life at home. In
addition, the knowledge that others have been in exile before one, as
examples and models, can fuel an intense preoccupation with autobiographical issues. In fact, it is quite possible to lose everything but find
a self, the one possession that remains or can be reconstructed when all
else has disintegrated. Perhaps the dislocation of exile, whether literal
or metaphorical, enables a clearer glimpse of a life, so that instead of
the autobiographical process being, as it is conventionally, to explore
the gap between the self now and the self then it becomes the juxtaposition of the self here (in exile of whatever kind) and the self there (at

home, whether actual or metaphorical). Exile, called by Said the "rift forced between a human being and a native place," is the space of auto-biography. It may be an "unhealable" rift in Said's view, but it is not an unwritable one.

Before leaving our six mid-seventeenth-century exiles, we should briefly consider what happened to them; was their separation from home ultimately unhealable? In most cases, their physical exile came to an end but the habit of mind that they had learned as a result of it remained with them. Margaret Cavendish and her husband returned to England after the Restoration, but her chief contentedness contin-ued to be in her writing, produced with great self-sufficiency in her aristocratic equivalent of the anchorite's cell for which she had yearned.[26] Vaughan remained in a state of exclusion from the church but found inspiration as a poet through the natural world and the com-munity of books, particularly the work of George Herbert; retreat became for him the way forward to an almost mystical spiritual life. Evans and Cheevers were released from the Maltese prison after three and a half years, but their vocation ensured that they continued to lead the nomadic life of wandering Quaker preachers, even if they were geographically closer to home. Bunyan left Bedford gaol convinced of God's abundant grace and went on to the successful authorship of, among other allegorical works, *Pilgrim's Progress*, itself essentially an account of an exile's journey through the Slough of Despond and the Valleys of Humiliation to the Celestial City. Meanwhile, Anne Clifford died just a few weeks after her eighty-sixth birthday, but her wish to live through her diary, and to inscribe her life in terms of its earlier history even to the very end, is poignantly confirmed by the fact that, after the entry for the day before her death, she had already filled in the next day's date in anticipation of the subsequent diary entry that never came (268). Oliver Heywood continued to preach, minister, and to leave his autobiographical traces until after the turn of the eighteenth century, achieving hopefulness in his strangely self-reflective condi-tion. Exile had produced reflection, and reflection had given back an image of the self. The "strange land" of exile could indeed be what Clif-ford referred to as a "place of Selfe fruition" (112).

NOTES

1. Fortunately, this essay did not take shape in exile but in quite the opposite setting, a community of generous scholars. I am grateful to col-leagues in Groningen, Newcastle-upon-Tyne, and Canberra, as well as to the editors of this collection, for their constructive contributions to the develop-ment of my essay.

2. To demonstrate this fact, the statement by Euripides stands at the entrance of the migration exhibition at the new Australian National Museum (Canberra) as a reminder of the layers of exile in Australia's relatively recent history.

3. These are said to have been the last words of Pope Gregory VII (1020–85); see Cowdrey 680.

4. *OED exile* (verb) 4.

5. In view of limitations of space here, I have not included the *transatlantic* "exiles" of the early and mid–seventeenth century.

6. For a discussion of the rise of autobiographical writing in England in this period, see Mascuch; and Sawday.

7. All further references are to this first edition and will be given by page number in the main text.

8. In "A True Relation," she describes her writing as more like a "ragged rout" than a "well armed body" marching on the "ground of white paper" (384), referring to her handwriting but also to the speed and relative chaos of her creative process.

9. All further references are to the edition of *The Mount of Olives* (1652), in Vaughan's *Works*, ed. L. C. Martin.

10. *Nature's Pictures* 390.

11. All further references are taken from Evans and Cheevers, *A Short Relation of Some of the Cruel Sufferings, for the Truth's Sake* (1662), reprinted in *Her Own Life: Autobiographical Writings by Seventeenth-Century Englishwomen*, ed. Graham et al.

12. See, for example, John 3:16: "God so loved the world, that he gave his only begotten Son, that whosoever believeth in him should not perish, but have everlasting life."

13. This phenomenon of psychological or "inner immigration" is found in the work of many modern autobiographers in exile, such as the late W. G. Sebald.

14. All further references are to the 1966 edition edited by Roger Sharrock and published by Oxford University Press.

15. See Mark 3:29, identifying what Baptists understood to be the one unpardonable sin.

16. Clifford (1590–1676) should have inherited the family estates on the death of her father in 1605, but they were willed to her uncle instead. For details of her biography, see Richard T. Spence, *Lady Anne Clifford, Countess of Pembroke, Dorset, and Montgomery*.

17. All further references are to this edition.

18. Psalm 102:8,9,4.

19. One of the clearest signs of her self-confidence is the Great Picture that Clifford commissioned as early as 1646, soon after she had come into her inheritance. It depicts her parents and brothers in the central panel and herself in youth and maturity in the two side panels. Her husbands appear only in the form of small portraits hanging behind the older Lady Anne, and the focus of the entire painting is the Clifford family and its northern pedigree.

20. For an account of Anne Clifford's autobiographical self-determination

in old age, see Helen Wilcox, "'A Wife and Lady Oneself': Maturity and Memory in the Diaries of Lady Anne Clifford."

21. See John Donne, "The good-morrow," l.11, in which just such a "little roome" is said to become "an every where."

22. The book is thus referred to in the printed edition of Heywood's works, *Autobiographies, Diaries, Anecdote and Event Books*.

23. Oliver Heywood, British Library MS 45,965, ff.69v–70r. The printed version—erroneously transcribed as two separate poems one after the other, "Selfe" and "Reflection"—appears in *Autobiographies* 3.29–30.

24. See, for example, Colossians 3:1: "Christ sitteth on the right hand of God."

25. This was the humanist maxim with which the seventeenth century began: "Nosce Teipsum" [Know Thyself], the title of the 1599 poetical work by Sir John Davies.

26. In a typically idiosyncratic simile, Cavendish likens the process of writing to the work of silkworms in making silk—they produce it with no assistance from outside but spin "from their own bowels" (386).

WORKS CITED

Boland, Eavan. "After a Childhood away from Ireland." *Collected Poems*. Manchester: Carcanet, 1995. 96.

Bornholdt, Jenny. "Home." *Waiting Shelter*. Wellington, NZ: Victoria UP, 1991. 47.

Brodsky, Joseph. *Brodsky's Poetics and Aesthetics*. Ed. Lev Loseff and Valentina Polukhina. Basingstoke: Macmillan, 1990.

Bunyan, John. *Grace Abounding to the Chief of Sinners* (1666). Ed. Roger Sharrock Oxford: Oxford UP, 1966.

Cavendish, Margaret. *CCXI Sociable Letters*. London, 1664.

———. *Nature's Pictures*. London, 1656.

———. *Poems and Fancies*. London, 1653.

Claassen, Jo-Marie. *Displaced Persons: The Literature of Exile from Cicero to Boethius*. London: Duckworth, 1999.

Clifford, Lady Anne. *Diaries*. Ed. D. J. H. Clifford. Stroud: Sutton, 1990.

Cowdrey, H. E. J. *Pope Gregory VII, 1073–1085*. Oxford: Clarendon, 1998.

Donne, John. *Complete English Poems*. Ed. C. A. Patrides. London: Dent, 1985.

Evans, Katherine, and Sarah Cheevers. *A Short Relation of Some of the Cruel Sufferings, for the Truth's Sake* (1662). *Her Own Life: Autobiographical Writings by Seventeenth-Century Englishwomen*. Ed. Elspeth Graham, Hillary Hinds, Elaine Hobby, and Helen Wilcox. London: Routledge, 1989. 116–30.

Friedman, Susan Stanford. "Exile in the American Grain: H. D.'s Diaspora." *Women's Writing in Exile*. Ed. Mary Lynn Broe and Angela Ingram. Chapel Hill: U of North Carolina P, 1989. 87–112.

Herbert, George. *The English Poems*. Ed. C. A. Patrides. London: Dent, 1974.

Heywood, Oliver. *Autobiographies, Diaries, Anecdote and Event Books*. Ed. J. Horsfall Turner. 4 vols. Privately published in Brighouse and Bingley, 1882–85.

Mascuch, Michael. *Origins of the Individualist Self: Autobiography and Self-Identity in England, 1591–1791*. Cambridge: Polity, 1997.

Milton, John. *Paradise Lost*. Ed. Christopher Ricks. Harmondsworth: Penguin, 1968.

Petrarch, Francesco. *Letters from Petrarch*. Trans. Morris Bishop. Bloomington: Indiana UP, 1966.

Said, Edward. *Reflections on Exile*. London: Granta, 2001.

Sawday, Jonathan. "Self and Selfhood in the Seventeenth Century." *Rewriting the Self: Histories from the Renaissance to the Present*. London: Routledge, 1997. 29–48.

Sebald, W. G. *On the Natural History of Destruction*. New York: Random House, 2003.

Seidel, Michael. *Exile and the Narrative Imagination*. New Haven: Yale UP, 1986.

Shakespeare, William. *The Riverside Shakespeare*. Gen. ed. G. Blakemore Evans. Boston: Houghton Mifflin, 1974.

Spence, Richard T. *Lady Anne Clifford, Countess of Pembroke, Dorset, and Montgomery*. Stroud: Sutton, 1997.

Vaughan, Henry. *The Complete Poems*. Ed. Alan Rudrum. Harmondsworth: Penguin, 1976.

———. *Works*. Ed. L. C. Martin. Oxford: Clarendon, 1957.

Waite, Terry. *Taken on Trust: An Autobiography*. London: Coronet, 1994.

Wilcox, Helen. "A Wife and Lady Oneself: Maturity and Memory in the Diaries of Lady Anne Clifford." *The Prime of Their Lives: Wise Old Women of Medieval and Early Modern Europe*. Ed. A. Mulder-Bakker and R. Nip. Leuven: Peters, 2005. 65–86.

Fig. 8.1. Frontispiece to Margaret Cavendish,
Nature's Pictures (1656)

Chapter 9

The Visual Autobiographic
Van Dyck's Portrait of Sir John Suckling

Belinda Tiffen

*L*ike most of the cognoscenti of the Caroline court, the poet and dramatist Sir John Suckling chose to have his portrait painted by Anthony Van Dyck. The act in itself seems to offer a small autobiographical clue. In the England of the 1630s, Van Dyck was a fashionable painter, sought after by the social elite for his ability to capture their wealth and achievements in flatteringly glamorous images. Simply to have sat for Van Dyck was a status symbol, an expression of belonging to an aristocratic social group with access to the privileges and values that class bestowed. The languid serene expressions, the elegant expressive hands, the lavish fabrics and exquisite jewels, and the idealized landscapes, which are all hallmarks of a Van Dyck portrait, act in a similar manner to the emblems of the highly symbolic Elizabethan portraits and Hilliard miniatures of a previous generation, providing signs that allow the audience to "read" the sitter's wealth, education, virtue, and nobility of station and character. As Kevin Sharpe notes of these depictions of the Stuart court: "Power belonged to those endowed with nature's riches—to the wealthy and beautiful whose outward qualities announced their inner virtues" (105). Suckling's decision to have his portrait painted by Van Dyck therefore appears to offer an insight into his personality, indicating his social aspirations and his vision of how he fit into his cultural and social environment. It signals an apparent attempt to align himself with the fashionable elite and an acceptance of the social, aesthetic, and political values of Caroline court culture represented by the Van Dyckian image.

A brief analysis of the portrait bears this impression out: as painted by Van Dyck, Suckling appears fully to belong to the platonically ordered world of the court. Clad in an elaborate costume of expensive fabric and leaning with customary Van Dyckian elegance against a rock, Suckling looks the cavalier par excellence. He is consciously presenting himself to the viewer as an aristocratic courtier. The elegance of his pose and the romanticized landscape that forms the background proclaim Suckling's nobility, his separation from sordid worldly concerns by means of the elevation of birth, position, and wealth.

This reading of the portrait accords with traditional views of both Van Dyck's and Suckling's professional and personal reputations. Although they were admired in their own time, a predominantly Whig historiography has led subsequent art historians and literary critics to devalue both men's artistic achievements because of a close association with, and apparently uncritical acceptance of, Caroline court culture. Van Dyck, for example, has been called the chief apologist in paint for the absolutist policies of Charles I (Waterhouse 70). Consequently, while he is acknowledged as a flawless technician and brilliant colorist, his work, especially that of his English period, has generally been regarded as somewhat empty and devoid of the genius that sparks the art of the truly great masters. Suckling has fared even worse at the hands of critics. While readily anthologized as one of the better lyrical poets of the Civil War period for a few of his better-known poems, a double negative of perceived allegiance to Stuart absolutism and self-declared frivolity in verse, a refusal to take his own art seriously, has seen him largely dismissed as a poetic amateur (Squier 98).

What is significant about this critical response to both artists' work is the close intertwining of artistic and literary criticism with character assessment. This effect comes into play despite the fact that, for much of the twentieth century at least, such an ad hominem approach to art history and literary criticism has usually been questioned or rejected. Images and texts are consistently separated from authorial intent and character. New historicist critical approaches have rarely attempted to engage with personality and individual psychology, choosing instead to look at the broader sociopolitical, geographical, and temporal contexts of a work, while remaining aware that these factors and conditions do affect artists in determinate ways.

It is perhaps the marked flamboyance of personalities hinted at in their works—and clearly suggested in this portrait, with its high-tonal values and saturation of color—that makes Suckling's poems and Van Dyck's paintings irresistible subjects for certain kinds of personal,

even psychological reading. A desire to respond to their works biographically has to some extent informed almost all critical analysis.
Yet the conflation of personality and aesthetic achievement has been to
the detriment of both Van Dyck's and Suckling's reputations, as artists
and historical personalities. Drawing on a few well-repeated, but often
unsubstantiated, biographical anecdotes—generally revolving around
drinking and womanizing—this style of criticism has foregrounded
apparent character flaws of immorality, frivolity, and unsound Royalist politics. Failings of personality have then been read into the works
to locate their literary and artistic equivalents in technical inadequacy,
amateurism, and mediocrity. The twin pillars of personal immorality
and artistic limitation can then be used indiscriminately to reinforce
one another; the apparent failure of the art supposedly proves its creator's shortcomings. The most notable example of this approach is
S. R. Gardiner's dismissal of Suckling as "a fribble" (9.312), based on
the licentious nature of his verse and his political support for the Royalist cause. There is no attempt to separate literary criticism from
assessment of the historical person.

A few more recent studies, however, have used biographically
focused criticism to reassess the canon of both artists in a more positive light. Van Dyck's most recent biographer, Robin Blake, proclaims
his intention to rehabilitate Van Dyck's reputation and affirms the
necessity of reconsidering an artist's personality as a component of
reassessing the paintings. "[T]he object of this study," Blake begins,
"is to show that we have before us a much more complex and vital personality" than previous critics have allowed (2). Following Blake's
lead, it is possible to impute much about Van Dyck's personality from
his portrait of Suckling. His interaction with a fellow court figure and
artist should, at the least, be suggestive of his attitude toward the
court and other forms of Caroline art, which Van Dyck undoubtedly
influenced and which in all likelihood also influenced him.

The sitter of any portrait, however, is not a passive recipient of the
painter's interpretation, a mere prop that the artist can use to articulate his or her own cultural attitudes and creative and psychological
impulses. Not infrequently, the sitter is also a highly active participant: he or she commissions the portrait, makes suggestions about
pose and costume, or may demand a particular setting. In Suckling's
portrait, such involvement is apparent in the choice of costume—borrowed from one of his own plays—a highly personal choice, made at
the sitter's rather than the painter's initiative. Given such evidence of
Suckling's input into conceiving the painting, it does not seem unrea-

sonable to search for other signs suggestive of his personality and to consider the portrait as an act of autobiography, taking that term less as a literary genre alone and more, as Mascuch terms it, as a "cultural practice," a means of conceptualizing and expressing self-identity (8).

A cursory viewing might suggest that what Suckling's portrait reveals of his "real" character is negligible. It appears to be a fairly standard midcentury pose of a courtier of some wealth and standing, recording his appearance for the purposes of posterity in the accepted visual idiom of the day. As autobiography—an act of self-revelation— it is predictable if not disappointing. Yet one of the marks of success- ful portraiture is a psychological acuity, the realization of insight into the sitter's inner world. In these terms and by all assessments, Van Dyck's painting is very effective. Its artistic success and penetration of the subject's personality—closely linked phenomena—lie beneath the conventional surface. It is only where the confident, monolithic image of untroubled aristocratic serenity begins to break down that Suck- ling's portrait begins to reveal its subject and become a work of visual autobiography.

Several commentators have noticed unique qualities in this paint- ing, points of divergence from conventional seventeenth-century por- traiture that also differentiate it from much of Van Dyck's other work. Blake describes it as one of Van Dyck's "more unusual productions" (316), and Malcolm Rogers has pinpointed this uniqueness in the prominent depiction of a book ("Meaning" 742). The work Suckling holds is a folio of Shakespeare—possibly the second folio of 1632— opened at *Hamlet*; the title is barely visible on the upper margin of the open pages. Rogers argues this is the only time Van Dyck portrayed one of his sitters with a book in his English portraits, and it is one of only a few examples from the period of a portrait showing a secular work. Usually, if a book appeared in a portrait it was the Bible or a devotional work, symbolizing the sitter's piety. The symbolism of the Shakespeare folio is less conventional and less clear, yet it provides a key insight into Suckling's public and private personae in the painting. It would seem that, at least on some levels, this insight is intentional on Suckling's part and so makes the portrait a type of autobiographi- cal act, a conscious public display of self-identity (Mascuch 9).

Most directly, the reference to *Hamlet* appears to be a piece of self- promotion for Suckling's own play, *Aglaura*. This play, quite popular in its own time, is a turgid revenge tragedy set in Persia. Rogers posits that the occasion of the portrait may have been the work's perfor- mance, and there are several clues in the painting to support his supposition. First, there is the faintly Eastern costume Suckling wears, which clearly refers to the Eastern setting of *Aglaura* and may well have been one of the costumes for the play. We know from Aubrey that Suckling had spent extravagantly on the dramatic production, paying particular attention to the costumes. In his *Brief Lives*, Aubrey writes that Suckling "bought all the cloathes himselfe, which were very rich; no tinsell, all the laces pure gold and silver" (244). The account is supported by a letter from George Garrard to the earl of Strafford in which he records that "Sutlin's play cost three or four hundred pounds setting out, eight or ten suits of new cloathes, he gave the Players, an unheard of prodigality" (qtd. Knowler 2.150).

Second, the date suggests a fundamental relationship between the portrait and the play. *Aglaura* was first performed before the king and queen at the Blackfriars Theatre in February 1638; it was revived in April with a newly written fifth act, which altered the play to a tragicomedy. Although undated, the most probable date for the Van Dyck portrait, based on internal and external evidence, is 1638. Third, and the most convincing evidence for a connection between the performance of *Aglaura* and the Van Dyck portrait, is the copy of Shakespeare that Suckling holds open at *Hamlet*. Suckling was a professed admirer of Shakespeare, and *Hamlet* had an obvious influence on *Aglaura*. There are frequent thematic and verbal echoes of the tragedy in Suckling's play—in fact, he was not above lifting whole lines of dialogue directly.

The psychological picture that begins to emerge of Suckling does not seem particularly attractive. Vanity and self-absorption are the overriding traits of someone who has chosen to commemorate his or her own achievements so elaborately. The impression is heightened for modern viewers because of the disparity between Suckling's apparent pride and the actuality of his achievement. To modern eyes, *Aglaura* is almost unreadable, let alone performable. Turgid and derivative, it is flawed by stilted dialogue and a fantastical plot, whose improbability and lack of inner logic are highlighted by the fact that Suckling altered the fifth act from a tragic to romantic ending without causing any significant damage to the work's coherence.

Van Dyck readily captures this degree of vanity. Despite his reputation as a sycophant who idealized his subjects to the detriment of his art, Van Dyck remains the most penetrating of portraitists. While never unsympathetic, he depicts the flaws and insecurities of his sitters as easily and candidly as he celebrates their achievements and virtues. Suckling's pride is apparent in his dandified air, the studied gracefulness of his pose, the artfully arranged hair, and the fashionable beard, which Aubrey also remarked on as an index of character (242). Against this vanity, the portrait communicates a serious pride about the sitter's artistic skill, which is rather appealing and acts as a corrective to the long-standing view of Suckling as a gifted amateur whose poetry suffers from technical slackness and inconsequential thematic content. As ever in Van Dyck, it is the hands that convey the important psychological detail. Sensitively rendered, the elegant, long-fingered hands draw attention to the book Suckling holds. The grasp is firm but almost reverent in the delicate manner in which he prepares to turn the page. It suggests a deep, thoughtful connection between the folio and the man.

Did Suckling seek to present this reflective persona in the portrait or is it a construct of modern viewers? In answering this question, boundaries between autobiography and biography blur. Undoubtedly Suckling chose the props and costume, and he clearly intended the image to express pride and seriousness about his own work, as well as conveying a debt to Shakespeare. More elusive is the identity of the intended recipient(s) of this message: it is difficult to say if Suckling had a particular audience in mind when he conceived the idea for his portrait. Also problematic are the discernible traces of vanity in the painting. It is unlikely that Suckling chose to reveal his own vanity; its significance seems rather to suggest the discreet intervention of the portraitist and/or viewer. The ideal transparency of autobiography is always muddied by the interaction between subjects and their audience in this manner. Understanding is hampered by the limitation of language and the impossibility of a writer conveying meaning that will not be colored by readers' interpretations. In the case of visual autobiography—unless we are dealing with a self-portrait—these connections are further clouded by the mediation of the portraitist, who takes cues from the subject but filters them through his or her own interpretation.

Some of these issues could perhaps be clarified if we knew more about the circumstances in which the portrait was conceived and who its intended recipients were. Did Suckling intend to keep it for himself? If so, where would it have hung, in a public or private space? Or was it commissioned as a gift for someone else? We do know that after Suckling's death the portrait belonged to his favorite sister, Lady Southwell, and it remained in the possession of her descendants until 1918, when it was sold to the Frick collection in New York, where it still hangs today (Clayton 108–10). Rogers has suggested that the painting may have been commissioned for Lady Southwell, which would soften some of the vanity that is apparent in the piece ("Meaning" 741). Playing a role for a fond sister is quite different from celebrating oneself simply for the sake of self-aggrandizement.

I think Rogers's suggestion is unlikely, however, as there is a defiance in the picture, a deliberateness about its self-display, that suggests a broader and perhaps less sympathetic audience was envisaged. Given the context within which the portrait was painted, it is almost impossible to conceive that Suckling was unaware that the painting and its celebration of his own work could be viewed as a vanity piece. And on closer examination it is possible to see that the arrogance of the portrait is not an unconscious slip, an unintended insight into a less attractive or acceptable facet of his personality, but is instead a motivated expression of self-identity.

Aglaura and the care Suckling lavished on it was broadly satirized by his contemporaries. There are at least three extant poems lampooning both the play and, in particular, the magnificent folio edition Suckling had printed as a presentation copy for the court. The best known of these attacks is by the dramatist Richard Brome, who was facetiously moved to fear that "If this new fashion should last but one yeare, / Poets, as Clerks, would make our paper dear"; he likens the disproportionate balance of margin to text on each page "To be like one that hath more haire than head / More excrement than body" ("Upon *Aglaura* Printed in Folio" 23–24, 14–15). The portrait can be seen as a response to this kind of derision: a defiant assertion of the self against opposition, which is perhaps the most significant aspect of the portrait as a visual autobiography. The defiance is highlighted by the motto printed in majuscules on the rock: NE TE QVAESIVERIS, or "Do not seek outside yourself." The assertion of self-sufficient individuality provides a sharp rebuke to Suckling's detractors and expresses his intention to assert his own will against the expectations of his literary and social milieu.

The motto's significance goes beyond a mere thumbing of the nose at critics. It points to Suckling's stance on one of the chief literary debates of the day—that is, the rivalry between devotees of Shakespeare and admirers of Ben Jonson's classicism. The portrait itself, which compositionally and thematically centers Shakespeare's work, is the strongest proof of Suckling's alignment in this debate. But the source of the motto and its context provide a further subtle clue. The Latin quotation is taken from Persius's *First Satire*, which takes the form of a dialogue between the poet and a friend, who mourn the debased literary taste of Rome, where precious and effete poetry is admired. They yearn for a more robust, vernacular poetic. Persius illustrates the point with some of his own muscular verse, which his friend is astonished to learn will be unappreciated in Rome. Persius's reply is that "If Rome disparages anything, do not go and put right the tongue in that false balance, nor seek outside yourself."

The motto is, therefore, not merely a rebuke to critics of Suckling's own drama: it is a statement of his aesthetic and poetic vision. On this point, Rogers suggests that the implications of the motto are threefold and almost amount to a personal and artistic manifesto. Suckling must, first, ignore those who criticize his love of Shakespeare; second, he must remain free of servile classical imitation in his own work; and, finally, he must ignore those who attack his writing ("Meaning" 742). It is ironic that Suckling chose to make the clearest statement of his literary values in a visual, rather than a textual, medium.

There is a certain incongruence between the serious artist whom Suckling embodies in the portrait and the elegant courtier of popular repute, whose shadow is clearly visible in the portrait and whose presence is simultaneously evoked by his negligent pose and the costume's expensive fabric. While artists such as Rubens and Van Dyck had elevated artists to a social status almost equal to that of their patrons, and it was perfectly acceptable for courtiers such as Suckling to make displays of wit and learning in verse, there was still in the period an incompatibility between the stance of gentleman and the display of professionalism in any field, especially when one strayed from the realm of coterie poetry into that of publicly performed drama, as Suckling had done in *Aglaura*. Part of the satire of Brome and other lampoonists can be traced to a certain disgruntlement at a court amateur impinging on the territory of the professional dramatist (Kaufmann 151–68).

Suckling himself would have been acutely aware of these class lines through the example of his uncle, Lionel Cranfield, the earl of Middlesex, who had risen from the rank of merchant to earl through his brilliant business acumen but whose court career had been blighted by his lowly birth and his merchantlike professional attitude to his post as chief financial minister to James I (Prestwich; Tawney). Suckling's family itself had only recently risen to privilege through his father's and grandfather's services to the crown. Although today we are inclined to think of Suckling as belonging comfortably to the nobility, his position in relation to the court and the aristocracy was not in fact entirely secure (Berry 1–23). Something of the anxiety engendered by his slightly uncertain social position is apparent in the complex self-image that Suckling is trying to project in Van Dyck's portrait as both elegant courtier and professional writer. The revelation of anxiety is apparently unintentional, but this illumination of an inner self, often in counterpoint to the projected image, can be one of the most striking aspects of an autobiography. The social anxiety manifest in the portrait is similarly betrayed in the insistent aristocratic disdain of Suckling's poetry, where the speaker is frequently at pains to depict himself in words as the elegant indifferent, cultivating the air of detachment that was the mark of the fashionable courtier. In one of Suckling's best-known poems, "A Sessions of the Poets," the poet declines to compete for the laurel because "He loved not the muses so well as his sport. / And prized black eyes, or a lucky hit / At bowls, above all the trophies of wit" (77–79, Clayton and Beaurline, 1.74).

The tensions among conflicting personal, social, and artistic imperatives apparent in the Van Dyck portrait are intensified by a simultaneous adoption and mockery of the tropes of the prevailing court culture. As has been frequently noted, Platonism was one of the planks of the personal rule of Charles I; it was the language whereby royal policies were disseminated, and its iconography was used to legitimize the philosophies and governmental and legislative actions of the 1630s. Suckling's portrait reveals a conflicted response to this politicized Platonism. The subject's pose is reminiscent of the romantic swain: his abstracted gaze into the distance is a universal symbol of the lover lost in contemplation of his mistress's killing eyes. He appears the perfect platonic lover, but the book in his hand, to return to that central symbol of the painting, signals that his thoughts are actually on the loftier subject of art. The clue results in an almost hidden joke within the picture. Just as Suckling's poems often appear to conform to platonic convention, but in fact mock its excesses and impossibilities, so his portrait seems to conform to devoted platonic love, but is in fact focused solely on the subject and his art.

An unmistakable political statement resides in this chosen representation: a negative response to the king's Platonism and the absolutist policies it supports. In his portrait, Suckling draws together the elements of art, Platonism, and power in a similar way to Van Dyck's famous equestrian portraits of Charles I, but the result is notably different. While the portraits of the monarch embrace Platonism and use it to elevate the king and locate the source of his majesty in a spiritual and platonic virtue (Strong), Suckling's portrait mocks Platonism as deftly as his poems do.

The same complex response to the Caroline aestheticization of politics can be found in other examples of Van Dyck's court art, where fissures crack the surface glamour of an elite and united, if effete and servile, ruling class. As David Howarth has noted, "Recent scholarship concerned with the English work of Van Dyck suggests that his portraits are much more than they used to seem. The imagery of Van Dyck has tended to be taken as the most visually alluring proof of the world of fantasy to which courtiers were supposed to have escaped prior to the civil war, an abnegation of responsibility which destined a doomed and decadent cause . . . but Van Dyck painted men who had a firm and competitive hold in society" (230). In the light of Howarth's comments it is interesting to note that, despite his reputation as an escapist ignoring political realities, at the time Suckling's portrait was painted he was taking an active part in the public life of the nation and was seeking to increase this role. In this period, his private letters are full of news of domestic and international affairs; he was appointed to the position of gentleman of the bedchamber, placing him at the heart of court life, and, most significantly, he wrote and distributed several political and religious tracts that express an often surprising divergence from the official policies of the Stuart rule, including "An Account of Religion by Reason" and "To Mr. Henry German, in the Beginning of Parliament, 1640." *Aglaura*, which the Van Dyck portrait commemorates, was also a highly political piece, its depiction of court affairs in distant Persia providing some acute commentary on English politics. While it fails as a piece of drama, the play is of great interest to the modern reader as a historical and political document. Perhaps the most interesting aspect of it in this regard is the prologue, addressed to the king.

> And here your powers more great
> And absolute, than in the royall Seat.
> There men dispute, and but by law obey,
> Here is no Law at all, but what you say.
> ("Aglaura" 25–28)

The compliment to the king's powers of artistic judgment in this address affords a very thin disguise to Suckling's references to contemporary political unrest. The "Prologue to the King" draws a clear division between "here," the fantastical world of the theater, where the king's powers are unquestioningly obeyed, and "there," the royal seat, with its metonymic association of the throne, and the seat of power, where the king's powers are less effective and "men dispute." The geopolitical distance between here and there emphasizes the difference between the worlds of art and the realities of power and government. It suggests impatience with a king who devotes himself passionately to the arts but appears ineffective in the world of realpolitik. The play proper returns to this theme, questioning the efficiency of Platonism as both a personal philosophy and a political tool and advocating a more active, robust mode of government. The portrait complements the dramatic viewpoint, first by drawing attention to the play and then by reinforcing the theme through repetition of the same ironically antiplatonic tropes in the sly mockery of Suckling's pose.

It is interesting in this context to speculate on the similarity between Suckling's portrait and that of another of Van Dyck's English subjects, Lord Stuart. In costume and pose, this painting bears a strong resemblance to the portrait of Suckling. Both figures appear wrapped dramatically in a shawl, leaning against a rock, while behind shimmers a romanticized landscape. In both portraits, an inscription on the rock is central to an understanding of the painting and the sitter's personality. The portrait of the king's cousin was painted by way of an apology after Lord Stuart had married Lady Katherine Howard against royal wishes (Rogers, "Van Dyck's Portrait" 264). In his languid, romantic pose against a faintly mythologized background, Stuart seems to appeal to the king to understand the irresistible promptings of the heart. The painting carries the motto ME FIRMIOR AMOR, or "Love is stronger than me." Yet the apology is couched in defiance: the rock is a symbol of steadfastness, and Lord Stuart will not budge from his chosen course. At his feet sprouts a thistle plant. It may appeal to the ties of blood and family, as well as nationality, binding the sitter to the king; yet it is also a reminder of Lord Stuart's own claims to nobility. Under the pose of the pale romantic resides a steely individuality, refusing to bow before the royal will and challenging its absolute authority. Although the intense, immediate biographical narrative that informs Lord Stuart's painting is absent from Suckling's portrait, something of the same desire to assert the individual will in defiance of the dictates of convention can be felt. It would be interesting to know if Suckling was aware of the Lord Stuart portrait and sought to borrow its pose and composition. Certainly both portraits use the same visual vocabulary to make a personal statement of individuality in defiance of society's prevailing norms.

In his writing, Suckling is an elusive figure, delighting in playing roles and hiding behind dramatic masks. In Van Dyck's portrait, too, he tries on different masks, but they are enacted on his own face and body, providing an immediate and unavoidable association between the persona and the poet in a manner that dramatic and poetic texts are able to elide. Suckling, a consummate consumer of court culture, must have been aware of the effect of choosing to represent himself in a performative manner. The resulting portrait provides a window onto Suckling's life and works, illuminating a surprisingly complex individual and revealing interesting, often contradictory and competing facets of the subject's self. Social, artistic, political, and aesthetic values are all communicated in the portrait, along with a perhaps less intentional insight into the insecurities and anxieties of Suckling's psychology—vanity, an uneasy relationship with society, and conflicting aspirational and disparaging attitudes toward court culture.

In a review of a book on Rembrandt's self-portraits written some years ago, Harry Berger took issue with the author's confusion of the terms *self-representation* and *self-fashioning*, pointing out that the first of these is an external action, involving the careful revelation of a selected and therefore static image of the self or a facet of the self, usually for some public purpose. Self-fashioning, on the other hand, is an internal action, a transitional act that involves the process of selecting and shaping a self-image that may be displayed (286). Both, I would argue, are autobiographical acts that either consciously or unconsciously reveal something about the personality of the subject. Self-representation, however, suggests an older type of autobiography: the careful depiction of a public face for a selected purpose. Self-fashioning accords with a later, relativistic sensibility and fulfils something of the not infrequent purpose of modern autobiography: to reveal the subjective self informed by an awareness of selfhood's multiplicity and mutability.

The seventeenth century has been suggested as the time of transition between these two modes, when a modern awareness of selfhood and an interest in depicting that kind of identity first arose (Mascuch 8). Suckling's portrait is significant in this regard, as it illustrates both earlier and later forms of conceptualizing the self, perhaps portraying a moment of historical change. The picture is an act of self-representation—a glamorous, confident image depicting the poet as a courtier and man of letters in a crafted public self-image; and it is equally an act of self-fashioning, recording the fissures in the public self and revealing the contradictory psychological and cultural imperatives that operate beneath but also penetrate and shape the surface image.

WORKS CITED

Aubrey, John. *Brief Lives*. Ed. Andrew Clark. Oxford: Clarendon, 1898.

Berger, Harry. Rev. of *Rembrandt's Self-Portraits: A Study in Seventeenth-Century Writing*, by H. Perry Chapman. *Clio* 23 (1994): 285–95.

Berry, Herbert. "A Life of Sir John Suckling." Diss. U of Nebraska, 1953.

Blake, Robin. *Anthony Van Dyck: A Life, 1599–1641*. London: Constable, 1999.

Brome, Richard. *The Weeding of Covent-Garden* in *Five New Plays*. London: 1659.

Clayton, Thomas. "An Historical Study of the Portraits of Sir John Suckling." *Journal of the Warburg and Courtauld Institutes* 23 (1978): 105–26.

Clayton, Thomas, and L. A. Beaurline, eds. *The Complete Works of Sir John Suckling*. 2 vols. Oxford: Clarendon, 1971.

Howarth, David. *Images of Rule: Art and Politics in the English Renaissance, 1485–1649*. London: Macmillan, 1997.

Gardiner, S. R. *History of England: From the Accession of James I to the Outbreak of the Civil War, 1603–1642*. 10 vols. London: Longmans, 1883–84.

Kaufmann, R. J. *Richard Brome: Caroline Playwright*. New York: Columbia UP, 1961.

Knowler, William, ed. *The Earl of Strafforde's Letters and Dispatches*. 2 vols. London, 1739.

Mascuch, Michael. *Origins of the Individualist Self: Autobiography and Self-Identity in England, 1591–1791*. Cambridge: Polity, 1997.

Prestwich, Menna. *Cranfield: Politics and Profit under the Early Stuarts*. Oxford: Clarendon, 1966.

Rogers, Malcolm. "The Meaning of Van Dyck's Portrait of Sir John Suckling." *Burlington Magazine* 120 (1978): 241–44.

———. "Van Dyck's Portrait of Lord George Stuart, Seigneur d'Aubigny, and Some Related Works." *Van Dyck 350*. Ed. Susan Barnes and Arthur K. Wheelock. Washington: National Gallery of Art, 1994.

Sharpe, Kevin. *Criticism and Compliment: The Politics of Literature in the England of Charles I*. Cambridge: Cambridge UP, 1987.

Squier, Charles L. *Sir John Suckling*. Boston: Twayne, 1978.

Strong, Roy. *Charles I on Horseback*. London: Allen Lane, 1972.

Suckling, John. "An Account of Religion by Reason." *Works of Sir John Suckling in Two Volumes*. Ed. Clayton and Beaurline. 169–80.

———. "Aglaura." *Works of Sir John Suckling*. Ed. Clayton and Beaurline. Vol. 1. 33–119.

———. "To Mr. Henry German, in the beginning of Parliament, 1640." *Works of Sir John Suckling*. Ed. Clayton and Beaurline. Vol. 1. 163–67.

Tawney, R. H. *Business and Politics under James I: Lionel Cranfield as Merchant and Minister*. Cambridge: Cambridge UP, 1958.

Waterhouse, Ellis. *Painting in Britain, 1530 to 1790*. 5th ed. Harmondsworth: Penguin, 1994.

Fig. 9.1. Anthony Van Dyck's Portrait of Sir John Suckling.
(The Frick Collection, New York.)

Chapter 10

Where Is Shakespeare's Autobiography?

R. S. White

*L*ike its great parody, *Tristram Shandy*, autobiography can rapidly tie us up in knots. It is assumed to be a literary genre that exists independently and can be defined and analyzed. But, the closer we look, problems seem to outweigh clarity until we can legitimately begin to doubt the very existence of autobiography. Alternatively, the doubts might lead us to reconceptualize the genre to include a wider range of accounts of the self and even to embrace the metaphysical notion of the "unwritten" autobiography, a version of the self's development that can be pieced together from multiple levels of records. In other words, we may, as third-party observers, be able to piece together the autobiography of somebody who has not written one. It is this whimsical speculation that I wish to pursue through the example of one of the most famous people who never wrote an autobiography, William Shakespeare.

Most people assume that autobiography presupposes a claim to substantial truthfulness. The emphasis may fall on the word *claim*, but it seems reasonable to assume that a person who buys an autobiography in a bookshop will be expecting to find at least a reasonably factual account of that person's life from his or her privileged knowledge. Of course, even gullible readers are capable of tolerating some leeway in the degree of truth that is told. Political memoirs will be expected not only to be slanted to present the subject's views in an act of self-justification but also to omit inconvenient personal details in the service of political interest. If, however, the subject is notorious for some scandal, we will be looking keenly for the very personal details that might illuminate the motivation for the blight on an illustrious career. When we read a film star's "kiss and tell" memoirs, surely we have at least an expectation of a lurid account of "the true story"? We may expect to find dietary preferences in the autobiography of a sports personality but not (necessarily) in that of an accountant. More generally, who, even with the best will in the world, can be unerringly accurate when memory of the past is involved? Truth to one's present situation and feelings is one thing, but truth to the long-gone past is quite another. One person's memory may be false to another's, and one person's truth may be another person's fallible and limited interpretation or even opinion. Carolyn Polizzotto's book, *Approaching Elise*, demonstrates the problems implicit in any form of memorially reconstructed life writing, whether it be autobiography, ghosted autobiography, or "authorized" biography. While her subject is an elderly artist with a fitful memory who changes her story every day, Polizzotto's analysis strongly implies that the vagaries and selectivity of memory are not confined to the old but are endemic, making "true" autobiography impossible.

The doubts pile up the more we think about the truth-claim basis for assuming the self-evidence of autobiography's status as a genre. If we are all made up of authentic actions in which we are "true to ourselves" and inauthentic moments when we are "not ourselves," should autobiography represent both or just the former? What about the deathbed conversion or deathbed confession—are they automatically more "true" than the lives we have led? How about the "born again," such as Saint Augustine or John Stuart Mill, who in hindsight read their former lives as in some way untrue and in need of suppression, or peculiar, hybrid cases like that of Hardy, who ghostwrote his own attempt at autobiography in the third person and published it under the name of his wife? Another question among many others left unasked is: how do we place a work that claims truth to the self when it unashamedly appropriates the words of poets to describe personal feelings and ideas? Is this some kind of "secondhand" autobiography, or a facet of all autobiography, pointing to its inevitable, intertextually constructed nature (cf. Johnston 28)? These questions can each be fruitfully debated and may have answers, but as a whole they problematize the very nature and function of autobiography.

Most of the answers to these questions will boil down to some invocation of authorial intention (truth telling), but, as we all know, to speculate on intention behind a written work itself is a fallacy (Anderson 2–3). Some theorists neatly step aside and argue that the appropriate level of referentiality or truth claim lies not in accurate recollection but in the very act of writing the autobiography, not in its recollections of the past.

> Thus, if autobiographical texts do not tell us as much about the autobiographer's past history as earlier students of the genre wished to believe, they may neverthelesss have a good deal to tell us about the autobiographer in the moment of his engagement in the act of composition. (Eakin, *Fictions* 22)

This would at least take care of the case of the elderly artist, Elise Blumann, and of the "road to Damascus" enlightenment narratives. Other kinds of doubts present themselves, even when we find documents written by the author that must have been composed more or less contemporaneously with the activity described, such as diaries, journals, letters, e-mail messages, the fabled laundry or shopping list, and so on. What degree of seriousness should be accorded these details of daily life? Many of us consign to ephemeral writing or print only inconsequential trivia or reminders about other people's situations rather than what is central to our own thinking or actions at the moment. For others, however, documenting such things is part of an attempt to leave footprints in the sand, to create a "true" record of their lives. Finally, to speak of "writing the self" presupposes that there *is* a self, something that these days is considered contentious, existing, perhaps, only in the realm of the fictional.

Such challenges are by no means my own alone. Many were raised, for example, by Paul de Man in an essay, "Autobiography as De-Facement," which has been regarded as spelling the end of autobiography and Romantic subjectivity and selfhood (Anderson 12–17). All modes of writing are simply language, and language is always figurative and arbitrary. Once we accord a truth status to any linguistic act, we can just as easily move right across a spectrum linking autobiography, biography, and fictional autobiography to fiction pure and simple. Many theorists today concede that in every autobiography there is some sort of buried grand narrative, a "plot" in the purely literary sense, almost certainly acquired unconsciously *from* literature. It is just as possible to defend the position that autobiography is always fiction as to argue more or less the opposite, that *all* writing, however apparently fictional or impersonal, is autobiographical. It is the last of these possibilities that I want to explore, the "immanent" autobiography that exists in the writing even when it makes no truth claims at all. This "hard case" provides the intriguing possibility that writers who leave no self-proclaimed autobiography are, in fact, giving us one. If this is possible, then Shakespeare is the obvious writer to turn to, since he left such a vast and diverse corpus.

The other important dimension is, of course, the historical. Early modern England emerged from a time when hagiography and demonisation could pass for biography and from a time when direct revelation or expression of the self was not a recognized mode of writing. Some claim the Montaigne of the *Essays* (1580s) as the inventor of distinctively modern self-writing, while others, such as Joel Fineman, credit Shakespeare's *Sonnets* (1590s) with that honor (Fineman). In such a time, it would be no surprise to find the lines even more blurred or nonexistent between what we would now call a set of distinctions that mark out autobiography, biography, and fiction. One of the more supple and plausible suggestions came in Stephen Greenblatt's ever-fresh study, *Renaissance Self-Fashioning: From More to Shakespeare.* Greenblatt writes, "Perhaps the simplest observation we can make is that in the sixteenth century there appears to be an increased self-consciousness about the fashioning of human identity as a manipulable, artful process" (2), a self-consciousness, which, we might in this context add, led eventually to the recognized genre of autobiography. "Self-fashioning" becomes "the achievement of a less tangible shape [than physical appearance]: a distinctive personality, a characteristic address to the world, a consistent mode of perceiving and behaving," in short, an articulated self. The expression of self-fashioning can come through a revealing gesture, such as Drake playing bowls before the Armada arrived or Raleigh laying down his cloak on a puddle before the queen; through verbal rumors artfully spread in a Spenserian court rife with blatant beasts; or through the category Greenblatt claims as "always, though not exclusively" applying, language. (Iago uses all three techniques in his fashioning of Othello and himself.) Out of this melting pot emerges Shakespeare. The "factual" marks he left on the world may be ones he found irrelevant and irksome, such as a will and various legal documents, all of which portray him in an unsympathetic light, while the self that he wished to leave for us—his own self-fashioning—resides in his plays, sonnets, and narrative poems. If, as Conal Condren suggests elsewhere in this book, the early moderns thought not in terms of selves but of personae, and no authentic, personal voice is left after the roles and offices have been fashioned, then it may be legitimate to think of the "self" of a theatrical practitioner like Shakespeare as the composite sum total of all the personae he invented through language. Liberated to externalize all his fleeting thoughts and observations in this fictional guise, we might surmise that if autobiography had existed it would have made Shakespeare inhibited and wary and paradoxically less forthcoming about himself. If he realized his own life would come under scrutiny, he may have chosen not to be so candid, as he in fact is, about the light and shade of the experiences gleaned from his multifarious roles as author, actor, father, son, husband, landowner, and so on.

Fortunately for Shakespeare, and for us, the author left no autobiography, diary, or memoirs, fortunate for him because it spared him the time and trouble of doing so and thus left him time to write plays instead, and fortunate for us because it has given centuries of writers the opportunity to write them for him. It is even more surprising that, as far as I can find, there has never been a forged or fake autobiography. Even J. Payne Collier did not leave us with Shakespeare's authentic memoirs or autobiography, which would have been a much more sensational find than the odd "lost" lines from plays that he did find. Mrs. Sarah Taylor Shatford of New York missed a golden opportunity to write the first posthumous autobiography of anyone ever written when in 1916 and 1917 she spoke to Shakespeare using the Ouija board. She did extract three new poems from him, but apart from that he seemed preoccupied with wanting to undo the mischief he had sown in the world with his words "enflaming the lusts of the craven for the flesh" instead of stirring the love of God. Unfortunately, Mrs. Shatford did not even ask him such perfectly straightforward questions as why he left Anne Hathaway his second-best bed or what was *Love's Labour's Won*, although she claimed that he advanced some opinions on the subjects of death, sex, the Vast Beyond, reincarnation, and other matters that revealed his purgatorial suffering (Schoenbaum 492–93). If indeed autobiography lies in truthfulness to the moment of composition, in fact this might be his latest version of a life story. If Stephen Greenblatt had been able to consult Mrs. Shatford, he might have considered the material for his *Hamlet in Purgatory* in a different light.

Anthony Burgess, in *Nothing Like the Sun: A Story of Shakespeare's Love Life*, does not supply first-person narration, but at least he does claim to know the innermost thoughts and feelings of WS.

Oh, the shame, the shame. I have married beneath me. I was taken unawares by a rogue's eye. I was ruined. Tears came to the eyes of

WS. It was, he claimed, the spring wind freshening. They had best get home to their dinner, greasy Joan and the great lady their mother, and their anxious smiling father. (63)

We shall hear more of that anxious smiling father later. There have been films that give Shakespeare a first-person voice, as if we are watching and hearing him in action—notably John Mortimer's six-part *The Life of Shakespeare* and more recently *Shakespeare in Love.* Both mingle fiction and fact in a very self-reflexive way, and, alas, they do not claim to be autobiographies. My task of making Shakespeare somehow relevant to a book on autobiography is becoming hopeless.

Surely it helps a little that we may have unearthed a portrait of him, the glamorous discovery documented in *Shakespeare's Face*, introduced on the front cover with the words "Is this the face of a genius?"(Nolan). But what are we to make of this face? The slightly curled, sardonic lip and the eyes shiftily not quite meeting ours are instantly recognizable to a schoolteacher as the sly boy always sitting at the back, plotting mischief. This might confirm the persistent mythologies about Shakespeare's early penchant for practical joking and petty theft, his later penchant for plagiarism, and the occasional impressions of mischief making and time serving; but, even if the portrait is contemporary and of Shakespeare, it does not tell us much. How could it, when we know from family snapshots and press photographs that serial killers can look like professors of theology while mild librarians can have an appearance of satanic evil? "There's no art to find the mind's construction in the face" (*Macbeth* 1.4.12–13). To answer the book's question, no, this is not (necessarily) the face of a genius, nor is the face of the "self-satisfied pork-butcher" of the Janssen bust.

There are at least two other potential catchments if we are looking for Shakespeare's autobiography. One, his own works, I shall return to; the other is the large group of his biographers. Added to the doubt, expressed earlier, that autobiography *is* biography *is* fiction, there is another disquieting complication. One of the most distinguished and apparently reliable biographers of all, Samuel Schoenbaum, came up against a dismaying realization.

Desmond McCarthy . . . said somewhere that trying to work out Shakespeare's personality was like looking at a very dark glazed picture in the National Portrait Gallery: at first you see nothing, then you begin to recognize features, and then you realize that they are your own. (vii)

Schoenbaum himself more or less acknowledges such a phenomenon, and certainly demonstrates it, in his indispensable and very readable *Shakespeare's Lives*. But presumably he succeeded in putting this doubt behind him before it undermined his own life's work. Given my assumed skepticism, I would have to rephrase his words to "you realize that they are *what you want to be* your own" because it is possible without too much effort to find in the works of all Shakespeare's biographers a revelation of the biographer's fantasy self-image, which may be unsustainable for his family and friends. Like everybody else, academics have dreams and secret personalities just waiting to get out, and biographers can surreptitiously and without detection live out these self-lives. When I read Schoenbaum, for example, I find reflected the image of Master William Shakespeare, known to his friends as Will, not as mischief maker but as urbane, witty skeptic, speaking in an unmistakably American accent—in fact, as none other than the lightly patrician Professor Samuel Schoenbaum, known to friends as Sam.

By far the most influential of the constructed Shakespeare self-writings has been Edward Dowden's. His very headings in a four-stage life story denote a reassuringly sequential and optimistic reading of the playwright's inner life.

> *In the workshop* (learning his craft)
> *In the world* (politics and commerce)
> *Out of the depths* (recognition of evil, unhappiness, and disillusionment)
> *On the heights* (detachment, mellow inner peace)

This might be so effective because it taps into the hopes of a Western collective unconscious—the life we would like to write of ourselves or at least the life Dowden would like told of himself. It also has a kind of pattern that has suited the psyche of the Western professional man, and particularly the academic scholar—getting a qualification, getting a job, midlife crisis, productive retirement. Indeed, in looking at Dowden's own biography, we find statements such as, "He was dedicated to his work: he was . . . immensely conscientious and hardworking" (Serafin 77). He spent virtually all of his days in Trinity College, Dublin, having been given a chair of English at the age of twenty-six, so his eventual retirement phase was no such thing, but instead an emeritus chair, like the one he seemed to envisage Shakespeare holding when he wrote the last plays. He was seen by his friends as a poet manqué, being described by Yeats (as reported by J. B. Yeats) as one who "looked the poet and was primarily the poet" (413–14), and,

indeed, he did write closet poetry. The midlife crisis, concealed sto-
ically beneath his routine existence, coincided, as always in the myth,
with the loss of his wife, through death in his case, but more often
through divorce today. His life of Shakespeare is remarkably close to a
veiled life of Edward Dowden, and when he left directions that no life
of him should be written it may have been because he had written it
already in this book.

E. A. J. Honigmann is a more recent biographer, whose particular
contribution has been to imaginatively reconstruct Shakespeare's
early career, his "lost years," hypothesizing that he was a tutor in a
Lancashire home before becoming a dramatist in London. Elsewhere
Honigmann has spoken of his own impression of Shakespeare's personality, the self that would emerge from an autobiography.

> We must learn to live with two images of Shakespeare. He could
> have been easy and unconstrained with his friends ("of an open and
> free nature," as Jonson put it), and at the same time more forbidding
> to the world at large. (17)

Without pressing the point, what fascinates me about this statement,
having been a close colleague of Ernst Honigmann, is that it applies
perfectly to himself—an amusing, loyal, and human friend who turned
to the world outside a more critical and even "forbidding" scholarly
face. He says that Shakespeare was "an essentially reserved and private
man . . . [with] a convivial temperament," and I can think of no better
description of Ernst himself. Perhaps in a more wishful way, he praises
Shakespeare as a businessman who exercised the hardheaded acumen
that made his fortune in theater in a way that mere academics never
can. In fact, it is interesting that many of the biographers present similar paradoxes and contradictions in Shakespeare's life, and it is possible that in both his works and his life he more or less created for the
modern world a paradigm of the "divided" rather than "unitary" self, a
notion embraced by some recent theorists of autobiography (Anderson
60–61).

Before elevating to the status of a rule Schoenbaum's perception
that in writing a biography of Shakespeare each scholar is in effect
writing an autobiography of himself or herself, I should mention the
latest to enter the field, where this cannot possibly apply. Katherine
Duncan-Jones, in *Ungentle Shakespeare*, holds the view that Shakespeare was mean, petty, and vindictive. She claims to present nothing
more definitive than "scenes from his life," and by snapping up uncon-
sidered trifles (some of them not so trifling) she draws her own vivid

picture. She focuses on areas that others have either considered taboo, such as "social class, sex and money," or glided over in reticence. Her aim is to make Shakespeare emerge as a "man among men, a writer among writers," and she is fearlessly happy to speculate, perhaps liberated by her gender from the temptation for self-identification. Shakespeare emerges as something between an adaptable chameleon and a strategic sycophant: a generally disagreeable and even unpleasant man, eventually "gentle" in status but "ungentle" in character. He was ruthlessly ambitious in his social aspirations, fussing about getting his coat of arms, vain, and vindictive. He did not make proper provision for his wife and family, being positively rude to the former in his will by ensuring she could not enjoy his possessions after his death. The notorious second-best bed is just that. Neither the Stratford nor London parish had reason to be swayed by his reputation as a writer nor his financial success, since he consistently evaded taxes and parish dues, hoarded food during shortages, was mean-minded to the poor, and left no generous public legacies. He was probably homosexual, contemptuous of women, and had, or thought he had, syphilis, which may have been the long-term cause of his death. During the course of the book, he gently swells from plumpish to corpulent to a "mountain belly" rivaling Ben Jonson in size. None of this rings true of Duncan-Jones herself. She is the exception to the self-reflecting Schoenbaum principle of the biographer as autobiographer, although the exception may highlight the rule for all the others, and particularly the males.

I have confidently asserted that Shakespeare left no autobiography, but is this correct? Might it not be contained—though not in a literal sense—in the posthumously published First Folio, put together by his friends, together with the quartos, the sonnets, and the narrative poems? The sonnets are among the most famously self-revealing poems ever written in any language, yet as autobiography they reveal little or nothing and are shrouded in complete mystery. They were printed in 1609 by a publisher called Thomas Thorpe. That is all we know about them. Was the publication authorized by Shakespeare? We don't know. When were they written? We don't know, although the consensus is the 1590s, more than a decade before they were published. Who were the people whose portraits are so indelibly and memorably etched in a sonnet sequence that seems inescapably autobiographical and biographical? We don't know. When Shakespeare wrote, so knowingly and with teasing hints at tumescent arousal, "flesh stays no farther reason, / But rising at thy name doth point out thee, / As his triumphant prize" (Sonnet 151), the one crucial thing he neglects to tell us is this woman's "name." Was the order of sonnets one that Shakespeare chose, designed to tell a sequential story, a narrative? We don't know. But, most maddening of all, there *is* a name, and just one name, in a dedication set with even more casual and gnomic enigma than "The Phoenix and the Turtle," in a sentence that defies untangling and sometimes seems like the emanation of an illiterate.

To the onlie begetter of these insuing sonnets Mr. W.H. all happinesse and that eternitie promised by our ever-living poet wisheth the well-wishing adventurer in setting forth. T.T.

The most celebrated and insoluble mystery in literary scholarship lies in these words. Who was Mr. W.H.? The young man of the sonnets, whether W. H. or not, is indeed immortalized, but no factual detail of any kind about even his appearance, let alone his identity, is offered in the sonnets. Stephen Booth wittily summarizes what the sonnets tell us of their writer's sexual preferences: "William Shakespeare was almost certainly homosexual, bisexual, or heterosexual. The sonnets provide no evidence on the matter" (548). Stephen Greenblatt sensibly reminds us not to ask inappropriately lifelike questions of art.

Swept or unswept, stones have the names of the dead indelibly carved in them—that is the whole point of using stone—but Shakespeare's powerful rhymes name no names. We know next to nothing about the young man—sluttish time has taken care of that—though the lines in which he is praised continue, as the poet hoped, to possess an eerie and intense life. (*Hamlet in Purgatory*, 313)

However, there may be another way in which writing reveals the writer. John Keats said, "A man's life of any worth is a continual Allegory—and very few eyes can see the mystery of his life—a life like the Scriptures, figurative—a Lord Byron cuts a figure, but he is not figurative. Shakespeare led a life of allegory: his works are the comments on it" (67). Perhaps Shakespeare's life story is contained in his complete works, if we are able to read the allegory correctly. After all, it has been said—more cruelly than Keats says it—that the only interesting thing about the lives of many writers is their works. Certainly not only Dowden but a whole tribe of psychological critics have decided that within those thirty-eight or so plays, and the handful of poems, there is more than enough material to construct the kind of person Shakespeare was, and how his life evolved, just as effectively as if he had left a candid record of his daily doings. Maybe the works never lie. If so, then the people we should turn to for some insight into the autobiography Shakespeare never wrote are the psychoanalysts.

And there is no shortage of them, from Freud, who constructed many of his most famous concepts directly from Shakespearean sources, down to more recent Freudian studies such as C. L. Barber and Richard P. Wheeler's *The Whole Journey: Shakespeare's Power of Development*. Most agree that the autobiography would give plenty of evidence of the dramatist having had a weak father-figure and that many of Shakespeare's achievements and aspirations were pursued as a compensation for his father's deficiencies, possibly as a defense against his resentment of father or brother (14–15). After all, he literally killed off a succession of father figures—Henry IV, Duncan, old Hamlet, Brabantio, and Lear, not to mention Falstaff, who is as hapless and impecunious as John Shakespeare seems to have been—and he didn't seem to like brothers, as witness Edmund (his own brother's name; he may even have written this unsympathetic part for his actor brother, as Duncan-Jones suggests), Duke Frederick, Oliver, and others. Insecurities about sex would loom large, focused on the binaries of male and female.

> He found sexuality between man and woman a far more troubling subject—dark, soiling, frightening—a feeling he overcame only at the end of his career. He constructed his world as split between male and female, parent and child, private and public, love and war, word and deed, theater and polity, play and reality. These differences, deeply felt, harbored deep dangers. . . . Throughout, however, his verbal wit provided him a way of equivocating, even disappearing, amid the profound dualities of his mind. He could deal with the dangers and the differences by flowing easily from one side of the chasm to the other, by being, as occasion admitted, male or female, parent or child, private man or public figure, lover or soldier, talker or doer, skeptic or idealist, rebel or conservative, presence or absence. (Holland 14–15)

However, rather disconcertingly, the psychoanalysts return us, in their different specialist terminology, to what I have called the Schoenbaum principle.

> All this recapitulates the *méconnaissance* of Jacques Lacan's version of psychoanalysis. The plays express the fictionalities by which the ego is constructed and maintained. "Shakespeare's personality" in this sense, is just one more of the phantoms erected by our own

desire, which itself is necessarily displaced and dislocated from our deepest selves. (Holland 14–15)

Thus, searching for Shakespeare's lost autobiography, we find the self-writing of countless psychoanalysts, and eventually we are tolled back even to our "sole selves."

A different, less psychoanalytically inclined form of autobiography might be read through Shakespeare's works in an act of ficto-autobiography. Even harmless literary critics without psychiatric training can be let loose on such an enterprise, even if the results may, like Caroline Spurgeon's, dwell on things we may not want to know, such as his eating preferences. If we assume that he wrote with something more than a cynical regard for theatrical fashion, then we might assume that his choice of plots, characters, and language reflects at least something of his own experiences. The fact that he and Anne Hathaway had twins in 1585, and that Shakespeare wrote a play about two sets of identical twins at the time when they were young children, may hint at the problems a parent of twins can have and what speculations on individual identity they might stimulate. Or, leapfrogging to his last plays, *The Winter's Tale*, so full of references to time, to youth and old age, may provide a sardonic "allegory" of his thoughts in middle age on sexuality in marriage. Sixteen years of a child's life is approximately the period when the mother can be said to be primarily involved in bearing and rearing that child. Do we have a glimpse, through Hermione's fate, of Anne Hathaway's self-immolation during her absentee husband's years of employment in the London theaters? There is plenty of evidence in the sonnets and several plays that Shakespeare, if not a jealous man himself, was clearly very interested in the state of sexual jealousy that afflicts Leontes as strongly as Othello. Such an approach would allow us to see what interested and engaged him without requiring us to impute to him motives, opinions, or psychological traits. It also cannot help but open up the mind-boggling plurality of Shakespeare's autobiographers.

Stephen Greenblatt, in his infectiously written *Will in the World: How Shakespeare Became Shakespeare*, perhaps takes "the works as the life" about as far as it can go, with some glorious consequences. Here we feel we are made privy to Shakespeare's secret life, guided by somebody as shrewdly self-effacing and empathetic as the enigmatic dramatist himself and certainly one who equally reveres the magic of words. Greenblatt defies our attempts to apply the Schoenbaum principle of seeing the biography reflected in the subject, since he is as adroit at covering his traces as his continually conjuring and evasive subject. Greenblatt also uniquely probes what Shakespeare did *not* say, returning hypnotically to the subject of his love life and finding a persistent opacity in "Shakespeare's reluctance or inability to represent marriage, as it were, from the inside" (129), one who goes only so far as to express a "frustrated longing for spousal intimacy" but no fulfillment. Macbeth and his lady are, it seems, the best he can do by way of a close couple, and the best advice he can give lies in Prospero's warning that premarital sex will plague the marriage. Greenblatt suggests that this "was precisely the circumstance of the marriage of Will and Anne" (142). Shakespeare's only solace was the product of a loveless marriage, his favorite daughter, Susanna, who married so respectably, and the possibility of an inner narrative of this life story haunted Shakespeare to the end of his life and haunts Greenblatt to the last words of his book.

Some readers, if they have persevered with this chapter up till now, will find it perverse and disagreeable in a volume on early modern autobiography, like a cuckoo in the nest. However, I think some serious questions are raised, if not answered, in its apparent meanderings. At the least, a set of paradoxes emerges. One suggestion is that autobiography can never exist as a discrete genre and all we have are biographies written by the "author as living person" observed and written about in hindsight by the "author as author." Furthermore, even if a reasonably prolific author does not leave to posterity an authorized autobiography, in some ways the self-writing can still be said to exist in a metasense. The works never lie about the writer, since they are the product of his or her own unique imagination, intellect, and language. On the other hand, the plays and poems congenitally and always lie, in the sense meant by Plato in Book X of *The Republic:* their truth value is figurative rather than literal. But the extra paradox is that the genre of autobiography itself may attain only figurative truth, since we can see only a very small portion of our lives at any one time. Shakespeare can use his plays and sonnets as self-revealing or self-effacing—through them he can be totally visible and yet totally invisible. They can be read as notes toward an autobiography of an identity, a self, but simultaneously as an evasion of the self. We cannot tell whether Shakespeare wrote to explore his own reality or avoid it in escapism. Another possibility that has emerged is that his works write our own autobiographies. They are the ultimate reflectors, allowing us to see only ourselves, giving us a language, imagery, and a set of narratives to construct our own lives. And yet, as

I suggested at the outset, the mirrors are always distorting, proving that even our most soulful attempts at self-truth are scripts written for us by another, a mishmash of partial truth and total fiction. Or, alternatively, to what extent is he just exercising the skill of a competent playwright constructing different characters, nothing to do with his own self-image and nothing to do with ours? Whichever way I look, I find myself returned to the surprisingly simple, opening words of a play, *Hamlet,* which has been turned into one of the most culturally significant works ever written and was regarded by Coleridge, at least, as his own autobiography and probably Shakespeare's: "Who's there?" Shakespeare, that preeminent early modern writer, never provides the answers, but his questions can open up other fascinating inquiries that allow us to acknowledge the complexity of autobiography in any age.

WORKS CITED

Anderson, Linda. *Autobiography.* New York: Routledge, 2001. New Critical Idiom Series.

Barber, C. L., and Richard P. Wheeler. *The Whole Journey: Shakespeare's Power of Development.* Berkeley: U of California P, 1986.

Booth, Stephen. *Shakespeare's Sonnets.* New Haven: Yale University Press. 1977.

Burgess, Anthony. *Nothing like the Sun: A Story of Shakespeare's Love Life.* London: Heinemann, 1972.

de Man, Paul. "Autobiography as De-Facement." *Modern Language Notes* 94 (1979): 919–30.

Duncan-Jones, Katherine. *Ungentle Shakespeare: Scenes from His Life.* London: Arden Shakespeare, 2001.

Eakin, Paul John. *Fictions in Autobiograaphy: Studies in the Art of Self-Invention.* Princeton: Princeton UP, 1985.

Fineman, Joel. *Shakespeare's Perjured Eye: The Invention of Poetic Subjectivity in the Sonnets.* Berkeley: U of California P, 1986.

Greenblatt, Stephen. *Hamlet in Purgatory.* Princeton: Princeton University Press. 2001.

———. *Renaissance Self-Fashioning: From More to Shakespeare.* Chicago: U of Chicago P, 1980.

———. *Will in the World: How Shakespeare Became Shakespeare.* London: Jonathan Cape, 2004.

Greenblatt, Stephen, Walter Cohen, Jean E. Howard, and Katherine Eisaman Maus. *The Norton Shakespeare.* New York: Norton, 1997.

Holland, Norman N. Introduction. *Shakespeare's Personality.* Ed. Norman N. Holland, Sidney Homan, and Bernard J. Paris. Berkeley: U of California P, 1989. 1–15.

Honigmann, E. A. J. *Myriad-Minded Shakespeare.* Basingstoke: Macmillan, 1989.

Johnston, Judith. "Anna Jameson's Girlhood." *Biography* 22 (1999): 517–32.

Keats, John. Letter to George and Georgiana Keats, 1819. *The Letters of John Keats, 1814–1821*. Ed. Hyder Edward Rollins. 2 vols. Cambridge: Harvard UP, 1958.

Nolan, Stephanie. *Shakespeare's Face*. Melbourne: Text Publishing, 2002.

Polizzotto, Carolyn. *Approaching Elise*. Fremantle: Fremantle Arts Centre Press, 1988.

Serafin, Steven, ed. *Late Nineteenth and Early Twentieth-Century British Literary Biographers*. Detroit: Gale Research, 1995.

Schoenbaum, Samuel. *Shakespeare's Lives*. New ed. Oxford: Clarendon, 1991.

Spurgeon, Caroline F. *Shakespeare's Imagery and What It Tells Us*. Cambridge: Cambridge UP, 1935.

Yeats, J. B. "Edward Dowden." *Nation* 24 April 1913: 413–14.

PART III

Self Practices

✳

Chapter 11

Autobiography & the Discourse
of Urban Subjectivity
The Paston Letters

Helen Fulton

*T*he fifteenth-century Paston letters were written mainly between 1425 and 1495 by members of four generations of the Paston family, which owned manors and properties in Norfolk. Although the family traced its genealogy back to the Norman Conquest, there is little documentary evidence of this particular family line until the middle of the fourteenth century, and it was only during the lifetime of the earliest letter writer, William Paston I (1378–1444) that the family fortunes significantly improved.[1] Having inherited some modest landholdings in and around the village of Paston, on the coast of Norfolk not far from Cromer, William used the proceeds from his successful career as a lawyer and judge to purchase many other properties throughout the county.

In the course of the century, the family's economic position fluctuated, and the letters constantly remind us that armed raids on contested properties were not uncommon in the troubled period of the Wars of the Roses. The bulk of the letters are between John Paston I, William's son (1421–66) and his wife Margaret (ca. 1422–84), who sent regular news bulletins about business affairs and family and local matters to her husband and later her adult sons, John Paston II (Sir John, 1442–79) and John III (1444–1504). It was Margaret who suffered a dramatic eviction from one of the Paston manors at Gresham in 1450, orchestrated by a rival claimant to the manor, Lord Molynes, and who had to endure two other major sieges on Paston properties at Hellesdon and Caister.[2]

With her husband and sons often absent in London, Margaret proved a formidable matriarch, running the family estates, collecting rents, and presiding over her children's education and marital prospects. The mother of seven children, she outlived three of them as well as her husband. Her eldest son, Sir John, never married, and the Paston line was continued through her second son, John III, who married Margery Brews in 1477. Through the letters exchanged between Margaret and her family, as well as others written to them by a wide range of contemporary nobility, gentry, and ecclesiastics, we are given a rare insight into fifteenth-century social history in southern England, from the rituals of daily life to the impact of the Wars of the Roses on county families such as the Pastons. How this insight relates to "autobiographical" concerns is the question here, and to this end I will begin by discussing autobiographical self-expression in its generic, expository, and social and cultural dimensions.

Letter Writing and Autobiography

Structuralist analyses of letter writing as a genre—its linear structure, lack of closure, feminized style of self-revelation, implied third-person reader, representation of reality, and absent narrator—suggest it should be set apart from the commonsense understanding of autobiography as a genre. Autobiography is something shaped to represent oneself and one's experience, a form of realist narrative, whereas epistolary communication appears to be spontaneous and unpremeditated. For Gerald MacLean, "Letters are never an entirely private exchange involving only two people. They position a third person, to whom they simultaneously are and are not addressed" (177–78), whereas autobiography seems to be open in its acknowledgment of a reading audience. Elizabeth MacArthur distinguishes between the metonymic, linear structure of epistolary writing, which moves by juxtaposition of events and avoids closure, and the metaphorical, paradigmatic structure of narrative fiction by which reality is [autobiographically] transformed into a symbolic world (3–10, 22–28). By implication, the latter style is evaluated as richer, more complex, and more rewarding of interpretation than the former.

In reading autobiography as narrative, then, modern structuralist interpretations privilege it as a form of creative and symbolic self-construction as opposed to the spontaneous self-revelation of letter writing. It is a narrative form, consciously structured by an authoritative presence, synonymous with a real person who is telling the story. The third-person reader, an implied presence in personal letters, is elided in autobiography, which is directed outward to an external second-person readership. Far from being metonymic and syntagmatic, the autobiography is metaphoric and paradigmatic, like a fictional work: the writer, as authorized narrator, deliberately selects events and outcomes from what is available and creates metaphorical images that lead to a preferred interpretation of those events.

Most important, an autobiography, unlike a correspondence, is structured as a narrative rather than a segmented sequence. It has closure. It is "masculine," in contrast to the "femininity" of letter writing (Gilroy and Verhoeven 1–7). As Aldo Scaglione says, "autobiography must have a plot, tell a story—the story of a life in the world, hence be dramatic and relate an individual personality, seen from within, to its social outside world" (456). In accepting its narrative logic, its metaphorical premises, the reader cannot be naive enough to imagine that this is unmediated reality. On the contrary, the quality of autobiography is evaluated by how consciously and delicately its author draws attention to his or her own role as focalizer, the necessarily positioned viewpoint from which truth and reality are retrospectively constructed.

This relationship with time and truth is what, according to Scaglione, distinguishes autobiography from the diary or personal chronicle: "In this respect autobiography is a review of a life from a particular moment in time, with a coherent, retrospective, ex post facto design," whereas "the diary or journal . . . moves through a prolonged chain of moments in time. This latter's message as to the meaning of life cannot, therefore, be planned coherently and intentionally beforehand, as in the autobiography" (456–57). Here autobiography is still theorized as mediated reality, implying that letters are somehow closer to unmediated reality, with all of its incoherence and contradiction.

Such views of letter writing and autobiography as related but discrete genres are based ultimately on a structuralist reading of texts and a structuralist understanding of genre. In its emphasis on the text as *parole*, exemplifying a generic *langue*, structuralism ignored the self and merely maintained unquestioningly a humanist view of the individual. Both genres—letter writing and autobiography—are defined according to a commonsense view of the self as a coherent being separate from and preexisting its social and cultural formation. It is no coincidence that this concept of the individual—one that by and large continues to dominate the ideologies of the contemporary world, having been successfully appropriated by commodity consumerism—developed early in the eighteenth century, simultaneous with the flowering of literary biography, autobiography, and the epistolary novel. The first biography of Shakespeare did not appear until 1707, while Samuel Johnson's *Lives of the Most Eminent English Poets*, published between 1779 and 1781, was a response to a growing interest in authors as individuals separate from their works.[3] With the rise of liberal-humanist philosophy in the eighteenth century and the development of a scientific method based on external objects of study, the individual was theorized as external to its context, as self-contained and freely choosing.[4] According to this essentialist view, individuals have "singular, integral, altogether harmonious and unproblematic identities" that preexist both texts and the social order (Calhoun 13). The modern view of autobiography, then, is that it is a basically truthful account of such an individual, presented according to dominant historical and psychological models based on evidence, chronology, causation, and self-knowledge. The function of this type of autobiography—and of biography itself as a broader generic category—is primarily to explain achievements in terms of a coherent and preexistent selfhood.

This concept of autobiography, like those of many other literary genres, has become so naturalized that it is often difficult to remember that it is a cultural construct that survives only as long as there is economic support for it. Michel Foucault has argued that the idea of the "author" arose in conjunction with the economic transaction of copyright in the eighteenth century and that the author, constructed as an individual, was allowed to have privileged access to meaning.

> The author explains the presence of certain events within a text, as well as their transformations, distortions, and their various modifications (and this through an author's biography or by reference to his particular point of view, in the analysis of his social preferences and his position within a class or by delineating his fundamental objectives). The author also constitutes a principle of unity in writing where any unevenness of production is ascribed to changes caused by evolution, maturation, or outside influence. (Foucault 128)

Foucault goes on, of course, to critique this view of the author from a poststructuralist perspective, arguing that the concept of "author" is in fact a generic distinction, a function of discourse that works to group texts together for economic advantage.

Like other genres, the post-eighteenth-century genre of autobiography, which has become naturalized as the only possible type of auto-biography, is a product of discourse. There is no external category of "autobiography" waiting to be applied to texts; rather, it is a category brought into being, culturally and ideologically positioned, by texts themselves. Where writers such as Scaglione see a distinction between the mediated reality of autobiography and the unmediated improvisa-tional reality conveyed through letters, we might suggest instead that autobiography typically draws on discourses of realism while letters and journals typically draw on discourses of naturalism. Generic dif-ference can therefore be defined in terms of discourse, in isolation from issues relating to authorial intention, authority, or reality.

This essentially poststructuralist view of autobiography as a genre, that is, as a discursive formation, can be used to explain the apparent absence of autobiography in the medieval period. This absence or lack is not a lack of autobiography in any absolute sense but rather a lack of the discourse of post-eighteenth-century autobiography, a discourse of realism that constructs and naturalizes a coherent single subject external to its historical and social context. In the medieval period, such theorizing of the self was not discursively possible, so that in ret-rospect there seems to be a gap in the Middle Ages where autobiogra-phy ought to have been.

Medieval Autobiography

What evidence is there, in fact, for a genre of medieval autobiography, and what were its discursive strategies? If we retheorize biography and autobiography as constructions of subjectivity rather than indi-viduality, using Foucault's understanding of individuals as subjects of discourse, it is clear that the medieval period was as closely engaged with that activity as later periods. From the evidence of biographical and autobiographical genres such as confessions, penitentials, dream visions, allegories, and saints' lives, we can see that medieval writers, in both Latin and the vernaculars, regularly presented themselves as consciously constructed personae, that is, as social subjects, rather than as the apparently unmediated individuals of modern autobiogra-phy.

This project of self-construction and self-representation took place primarily within a Christian context, and the self that was to be repre-sented was, first and foremost, a Christian self. Modern biography is theorized as a chronological journey from birth to death (or some other, less final point of closure), and the meaning of life is to be found in an individual's achievements in relation to early life experiences. Medieval biography, on the other hand, is theorized as the struggle for salvation, and life events consist of those *gesta* or deeds that either secure or threaten our hopes of salvation. The meaning of life is simply to prepare for the afterlife, and, rather than making a division between childhood and adult experiences, medieval biographers allegorize earthly events as foreshadowings of the eternal life to come.

These different theories of biography, medieval and modern, are predicated on different theories of the individual. Far from being the freely choosing subject of liberal humanist philosophy, the medieval self was a creature of God. But the medieval self was also theorized as a social subject, that is, as someone actively produced by social and discursive contexts, not as a preexistent individual outside of the social order. Whereas modern subjects of capitalism might believe that they operate independent of the symbolic order of language and authority—that they are "free" insofar as they see, and can reflect on, its operations—medieval subjects knew that they were totally bound by the symbolic order as ordained by God and articulated by the church.

In the medieval discursive formation, individuals are positioned as collective subjects of God's will on the one hand and of feudalism on the other. The subjects of these discourses are located spiritually and economically in a social fabric that had few discourses for the kind of freely choosing individualism normalized in modern Western societies. In the ideology of Western Christendom, where the self was mediated through God via the institution of the church, the kind of self-reflection and self-construction required for autobiography took place most visibly in the confessional literature of the church. The *Confessions* of Saint Augustine, written between A.D. 397 and 400, are among the earliest examples of the confessional genre, which inspired later writers, such as Julian of Norwich in the fourteenth century, to construct their subjectivity entirely through the discourses of Christian revelation. *De Vita Sua*, the autobiography of Guibert, abbot of Nogent in Picardy, composed in the early twelfth century, focuses on political and administrative events of the abbot's life, but these are explicitly located within the boundaries of his Christian belief, defined by confessions of sin, accounts of visions, and the virtues of scriptural study.[5]

Confessional and penitential writing also found expression in autobiographical genres such as the pilgrimage journal and the allegorical journey of life. One of the earliest accounts of a Christian pilgrimage comes from Egeria, a woman traveler from Gaul or Spain who was part of a pilgrim group to the Holy Land in the late fourth century A.D.[6] Egeria's account of her travels is written as a first-person narrative in the form of a diary or journal and provides detailed topographical descriptions of the towns and cities that were visited on the pilgrimage, as well as references to Egeria's deep spiritual inspiration during the journey. In many ways, the much later account by Margery Kempe in the fifteenth century of her various travels, not to mention those of Chaucer's Wife of Bath recounted in her prologue, are the direct descendants of a type of confessional writing couched in the form of travelers' tales.[7]

Other first-person narratives recounting spiritual and confessional awakenings appear in the form of dream visions and allegorical pilgrimages describing the sinner's journey through life and his or her attempts to reach the heavenly Jerusalem. One of the most famous of these allegories is *Le Pélérinage de la Vie Humaine*, composed by Guillaume de Deguileville, a monk in the Cistercian abbey of Chaalis, in 1330–31 and translated into English in the fifteenth century as *The Pilgrimage of the Lyfe of the Manhode* (Henry; Hagen). In this text, the dreamer is a pilgrim who learns about church doctrine, sails in the ship of religion, battles with the vices, and is saved by the virtues before ending up at the gates of Jerusalem, where he began his journey. Another fourteenth-century dream vision, the *Peregrinarius*, composed by Hugues de Liège in 1342–43, frames a political exhortation to the kings of France and England to make peace at the beginning of the Hundred Years' War within an imagined pilgrimage to Rome (Pastre). The "I" of such narratives is clearly represented as a generic sinner, an everyman, rather than as a specific individual identical with the author.

In terms of biography, the most common medieval forms were saints' lives and *gesta*, catalogs of deeds by famous personages such as bishops, abbots, popes, or secular rulers. These subjects of biography are defined by their public roles and evaluated according to their performance of Christian duties rather than as individuals. As Charles Haskins said, "Much of mediaeval biography, like mediaeval portraiture, deals with types, and the edge of personal characterization is usually blunt" (244). This bluntness is particularly evident in the prologues attached to the works of the Latin *auctoritates*, which often contain a biographical or autobiographical element.[8] In their commentaries on the works of these ancient authorities, monastic writers implicitly position them as products of their own and their commentators' discourses. In medieval textual theory, the Christian subject was the product of texts, starting from the one true text of the Bible.

For the subjects of feudalism, self-revelation found a platform in the secular vernacular literatures of courtly love. Such discourses themselves borrowed heavily from those of Christianity, invoking similar ideals of the sublimation of self into the worship of a higher being in order to achieve identity. Lyrics and romances addressed to courtly audiences, though far from being autobiographical in the modern sense of truthful accounts of individual lives, construct the "self" of the poet as mediator of communal experiences. In particular, the poet mediates the social phenomena of devotional love on the one hand and the business of marriage among the property-owning classes on the other. Dante's commentary on his love for Beatrice, composed in the late thirteenth century, and Abelard's letters to Héloïse construct poetic personae of the unrequited courtly lover that were to become templates of idealized devotion and self-sublimation for the next two centuries.

Lacking both the *auctoritas* of writers in Latin and the religious pre-eminence of those saints whose lives were exemplary subjects for biography, vernacular writers were literally self-effacing, eliding their names and lives from their texts.[9] Within a worldview that privileged Latin writing and classical authors above the vernaculars, poets writing secular material either effaced their own selves as writers or allegorized themselves as representatives of the human condition on earth. Chaucer and Gower deliberately represented themselves as compiler, translator, or pilgrim, while apparently self-revelatory pieces such as Chaucer's "Retraction" or Petrarch's "Letter to Posterity" were stylized examples of generic writing.[10]

Identity, therefore, resided in the surrender of self to God, a lover, or, more practically, one's duty on earth, preordained and class controlled. The discourse of medieval autobiography was essentially a public discourse, and the self that was represented was a public self defined through Christian and feudal expectations of normative behavior. The authorial personae of religious and feudal texts, positioned as first-person representatives of the social order, were rarely offset by biographies that attempted to recuperate the "real" authors in any sense of the private individuals behind the texts. While literary biographies of classical writers, such as Ovid and Virgil, remained popular from antiquity to the Renaissance and beyond, similar biographies of major English writers such as Chaucer did not begin to appear until the sixteenth century, with the rise of humanism. In Europe, prose biographies, or *vidas,* of some of the Provençal troubadours, produced mainly in the thirteenth century, functioned less as life narratives than as assertions that the poems themselves were authentic records inspired by real events in the poet's life.[11] Even in Latin, discourses of self-revelation or self-reflection approximating anything comparable to autobiography in the modern sense were unavailable beyond a devoutly Christian context.

The Paston Letters and the Construction of Subjectivity

From the brief discussion above we might conclude that the discourse of medieval autobiography is Christian, feudal, and public and that it was not until the eighteenth century, with its theoretical split between the public communal self and the private individualized self, that autobiography developed into the self-revelatory genre that is now its naturalized form.[12] Before then, first-person narration had other, culturally specific functions in medieval literature, to "authorize" the text as truthful and authentic, to suggest universal truths arising out of individual experience, and to position the narrator metonymically as a pilgrim on the journey of life. The construction of the first person, the "I" of the narrative, was a self-consciously public self whose identity was invested in communal patterns of behavior that characterized the world of Christendom. The mode of realism developed in the modern novel and adapted to modern autobiography was prefigured by the medieval modes of naturalism and allegory in which the self had a symbolic and metonymic function.

One might claim that whether one speaks from a position of unself-conscious social formation and obligation or from the most skeptically self-conscious point of view, all autobiographies are in some sense self-revelatory and therefore "autobiographical." But such a reading position elides the specifically historical awareness that can position the Paston letters in the context of the "meaning" of their concerns, their rhetorical strategies and gestures, and the (constantly shifting) meaning of *autobiography* itself. In constantly eliding coherent individual presences and reiterating the structured public roles through which the identities of the Pastons are continually being invented, the letters speak from a highly encoded position.

If we were to move seamlessly from the Paston letters as text to the historical reality and the historical individuals that they seem to reflect and reveal, we would implicitly apply all sorts of notions about autonomy and individual skepticism that were simply not culturally specific to the society in which the Pastons lived and wrote. The authenticity of the letters as historical documents can only be judged by comparison with other textual constructions of a fifteenth-century reality, so that, indeed, we can never move beyond a discursively produced world that exists only in text.

Nevertheless, the textual world of the Paston letters is in itself a valuable creation since it tells us something about the discursive choices that were available to bring the letters and their writers into being. In his canonical edition of the letters, Norman Davis emphasizes their linguistic value "as specimens of the English language at an important stage in its history" (*PL* xxi), an emphasis that disappointed some reviewers of his edition, who were hoping for more of the "mirror of history" approach favored by many editors of primary documents.[13] Davis was right, in my view, to take a fairly empirical view of what the letters can tell us in the way of contemporary evidence of the period, but I would add to his linguistic and paleographic commentary some consideration of the subjectivities encoded by the text of the letters.

In the Paston letters, we can see in full relief a type of subjectivity— a discursively produced social identity—that was beginning to come into focus in the latter half of the fourteenth century. The feudal Christian subject of the medieval period, grounded in a natural landscape of courtly garden and untamed wilderness, was competing with an increasingly secularized subject, whose identity was inevitably shaped by towns and urban culture. One effect of the rapid urbanization of medieval Europe from the twelfth century onward was the development of new discourses to provide subject positions for individuals beyond those of devotional Christianity and economic feudalism. From the fourteenth century, we can clearly discern, in both vernacular and Latin texts, the emergence of characters and identities whose histories are located in an urban commercial context.

As cultural production became centralized within the larger cities of England, particularly in London, and as royal power also became entrenched in London, writers not only identified themselves with the city and its commercial products but also addressed their work increasingly to urban audiences. The sense of self, however public, symbolic, and allegorical it remained in written texts, became inseparably attached to urban locations or at least to the expectation of access to such a location and its attendant materialisms. One consequence of this was that individual selves could now be read as signifiers of commercial materialism, subjects of consumption, expressed through the externals of image and appearance rather than merely as symbols of Christian moral evaluation.

The new urban locations in literary and historical texts constructed new kinds of discursive subjects. Whereas the characters of courtly lyric and romance were broadly categorized according to social status and moral worth, the individuals of urban writing—such as Chaucer's pilgrims—required more finely tuned classifications of status, occupation, and material display, which marked urban society off from the older, land-based feudal hierarchy. In the same way, the identity of the poet or writer was redefined in an urban context, constructing an autobiography that wrote the self in terms of the city. Chaucer's work is intensely preoccupied with the rituals of London life seen from the perspective of the upper echelons of the royal administration. Gower's hortatory moralizing and exempla could only have been produced within the context of late-fourteenth-century London life, where royal privilege competed with mercantile ambition.

A number of modern critics have commented on the close connections between the Paston family and the world of business. Making a broad generalization, Malcolm Richardson claims that: "When medieval people wrote, they did not relate events to each other. Their proto-capitalist culture demanded that they narrate the circulation of commodities. They sent each other bills" (Richardson 225). He was referring here not so much to the Paston letters themselves, which as "sprawling newsy bulletins" were obviously of a different order, as to the regular kinds of correspondence among the gentry of the fourteenth and fifteenth centuries. However, as suggested earlier, these business formats supplied the models for personal letters and provided at the same time a discourse of commercial transaction that we see replicated throughout the Paston letters.

The Pastons' involvement with the business world is sometimes interpreted as an unfortunate blot on their otherwise chivalric and romantic fifteenth-century Wars of the Roses world. Roger Dalrymple, for example, refers to their "notorious concern for worldly goods" (21). Commercial activity, however, was central to their self-identity. As landowners and lawyers who worked in London, as well as maintaining estates and doing business with their neighbors in Norfolk, the Pastons construct themselves as subjects of an urban discourse, one that inevitably shapes their sense of self and defines the borders of their self-revelation. The competing discourses that we see in the Paston letters, those of manorial feudalism in decline and those of urban commerce and administration, exactly articulate the contemporary economic context of England on the cusp of feudalism and capitalism.

I would define the urban discourse that shapes the Paston identities, and the subjectivity it constructs, as having four main areas of reference. Most obviously, the Pastons are subjects of commodification. In an economy in which an unregulated market was beginning to have a significant impact on an older system of inherited landownership, the language of commodification was being naturalized in every area of life. Drawing on the Marxist theory of commodity fetishism, where objects acquire an exchange value that is separate from and often far greater than their actual use value, we can see that consumer goods, agricultural surpluses, and even people themselves are routinely constructed as commodities in the Paston letters.[14]

Margaret Paston was clearly an inveterate shopper, both in person and by proxy through her husband or sons, who lived mainly in London and therefore had access to a superior range and quality of goods. This was not simply the frivolous pastime of someone with too much leisure on her hands: on the contrary, we know from the letters the extent to which Margaret was fully engaged with all aspects of running the farming estates. Her interest in consumer goods is as much social as personal, since domestic commodities were a crucial marker of status in a society in which the prestige of landownership was being both challenged and supplemented by the fortunes made in trade.

Writing from Norwich in 1449 to her husband, John Paston I, Margaret asks him "to bey a pese of blak bukram for to lyn wyth a gown for me. I xuld bey me a murrey gown to gon in this somer, and leyn in the kolere the satyn pat ge geve me for an hodde, and I kan gettyn non gode bokeram jn pis town to lyn it with" (to buy a piece of black buckram to line a gown for me. I would like to buy myself a murrey gown to wear this summer, and face the collar with the satin that you gave me for a hood; and I cannot get any good buckram in this town to line it with) (*PL* 135). Margaret's appearance, as the wife of an important landowner who socialized with the local aristocracy, was as significant to her husband as to herself, not just a matter of personal taste or vanity but a visible semiotic of social location.

John Paston, in his turn, represented the emerging class of landowners who profited from the urban mercantile economy, keeping close track of the goods produced on his land and their market value. The economic dominance of London and its impact on regional producers such as the Pastons is a common theme of the letters. John writes to his wife in 1465:

> Also I woll pat ye warne both Daubeney and Richard Calle pat thei disclose nat what malt I haue, ne what I shalle selle, ne pat on marchaunt knowe nat what an other hath; for ther is gret spies leid here

at London for ingrosers of malt to heyghne the prise, hough be it myne is not but of myn owne growyng and my tenauntes. (*PL* 71)

[I would like you to warn both Dawbeney and Richard Calle (his stewards) not to disclose what malt I have, nor what I shall sell, nor that one merchant does not know what another has, for there are great spies laid here at London so that engrossers of malt can raise the price; even though mine is entirely grown by myself and my tenants.]

The growth of a property market for both land and houses in fifteenth-century England is an obvious example of commodification encouraged by urban wealth.[15] The Pastons and their neighbors bought and sold land and houses, as well as inheriting them, so that the two systems, consumerist and feudal, operated side by side. The matriarch of the family, Agnes Paston, wrote to her son, John Paston I, in 1452:

Sere John Fastolf hath sold Heylysdon to Boleyn of London, and if it be so it semeth he will selle more; wherfore I preye you, as ye will haue my loue and my blissyng, pat ye will helpe and do youre deuer that sumthyng were purchased for youre ii bretheren. I suppose pat Ser John Fastolf, and he were spoke to, wolde be gladere to lete his kensemen han parte that straunge men. (*PL* 25)

[Sir John Fastolf has sold Hellesdon to Boleyn of London; and if that's true, it is likely he will sell more. So I pray you, if you want my love and my blessing, that you will help and do your duty so that something might be purchased for your two brothers. I suppose that Sir John Fastolf, if he were spoken to, would be happier to let his relatives have a share than strangers.]

Marriage was a major area of commodification, since it was an opportunity for money, land, and property to change hands. Many of the letters are preoccupied with the business of arranging marriages for one or another of the Paston children, with many plans foundering on the rocks of a shaky income, while the children sometimes defied their parents' wishes and took matters into their own hands. Following her marriage to Robert Poynings, Agnes's daughter Elizabeth was forced to write to her mother in 1459, asking her to produce the dowry that had been promised on her marriage.

Wherfore I beseke you, gode moder, as oure most syngler trost is yn youre gode moderhode, that my maystre, my best beloved, fayle not of the c marc at the begynnyng of this terme the which ye promysed hym to his mariage, wyth the remanent of the money of my faders wille. (*PL* 121)

[So I beseech you, good mother, as our most particular trust is in your good motherhood, that my master, my best beloved, does not fail to receive the hundred marks at the beginning of this term, which you promised him on his marriage, with the rest of the money from my father's will.]

Women themselves were often constructed as the commodity that was changing hands, preferably to the advantage of both parties. Among a range of local gossip sent to her husband in 1448, Margaret Paston comments on a forthcoming wedding in which the bride is positioned as one among a number of commodities that are to be exchanged.

Kateryn Walsam xal be weddyd on þe Munday nexst after Trinyté Sonday, as it is told me, to þe galawnte wyth þe grete chene; and þer js purvayd fore here meche gode aray of gwnys, gyrdelys, and atyrys, and meche oper gode aray. And he hathe purcheysyd a gret purcheys of v mark be gere to gevyn here to here joynture. (*PL* 128)

[Katharine Walsham shall be married on the Monday next after Trinity Sunday, as I have been told, to the gallant (suitor) with the great chain. And there has been purchased for her a great array of gowns, girdles, and outfits, and many other excellent accessories; and he has made a great outlay of five marks per year to give her as her settlement.]

In a second area of urban discourse, the Pastons are constructed as the subjects of bureaucracy. English towns of any size at all, including Norwich, the nearest large town to the Paston estates, were repositories of paperwork relating to administration, municipal regulations, guilds, and local courts. London was a powerhouse of bureaucracy, containing the royal administration at Westminster, home of the centralized English government and Parliament, as well as the central legal system and city archives, located in the City of London.[16] The discourse of urban bureaucracy, emanating like a fog from the major source of power in England, infiltrated every part of the country, from London itself to the most isolated hamlet.

Not surprisingly in a legal family like that of the Pastons, their letters often resort to the language of the law, recounting petitions and legal cases with a positively Dickensian flavor. John Paston III writes to his brother, Sir John, in 1470:

It is so pat on Wednysday last past ye and J. Pampyng and Edmund Broom wer endytted of felonye at the sessyons her in Norwyche for shotyng of a gonne at Caster in August last past, whyche goone slowghe two men: J. Pampyng and Broom as pryncypall and ye as accessary. Notwythstandyng Townysend and Lomnor hold an oppynyon that the verdytt is voyd, for ther wer ii of th'enqwest that wold not agré to th'endyttment, and in as myche as they ii wer agreyd in othyr maters and not in that, and that they two wer not dyschargyd fro the remnant at syche tym as that verdyth of yowyr endytment was gouyn, ther oppynyon is that all the verdyght is voyde, as well of all othyr maters as of yowyr. Whedyr ther opynyon be good or not I can not determyne, nor them-sylf neythyr. (*PL* 342)

[It happens that on Wednesday last you and J. Pampyng and Edmund Broom were indicted for felony at the sessions here in Norwich, for shooting off a gun at Caister last August, which killed two men—J. Pampyng and Broom as principal, and you as accessory. Nevertheless, Townsend and Lomnor are of the opinion that the verdict is void, for there were two members of the inquest who would not agree to the indictment. And since those two agreed on other matters, but not on that, and since those two were not discharged from the rest at the time when that verdict of your indictment was given, their opinion is that the whole verdict is void, both in relation to you and to all other matters. Whether their opinion is right or not I cannot determine, and neither can they.]

Their mother, Margaret Paston, entered into accounts of legal disputes with equal enthusiasm. Writing to her husband in 1464, she describes a dispute between two vicars, Master Constantine and the vicar of Dereham.

Master Constantyn sewyd hym fore feyth and trowth brekyng, and he sewyd Master Constantyn in the temporal curte vppon an oblygacion of x li.; and there was made appoyntment betwen hem by the aduyce of bothe there conceylis be-fore Master Robert Popy pat eche of hem shuld relece othyre, and so they dede and the sewtys were wythdrawyn on both partyes and jche of hem aquytauncyd othyre; and as fore any copy of the plee he had neuer non, nere he nere Master John Estegate, pat was hys aturnay, remembryth nat pat it was regestryd. And Master John Estegate seythe if it schuld be scergyd in the regester it wold take a fortenyght werk and yit parauenture neuer be the nere. (*PL* 177)

[Master Constantine sued him for faith and troth breaking, and he sued Master Constantine in the temporal court over a debt of ten pounds. And on the advice of their lawyers they made an agreement before Master Robert Popy that each of them should release the other; and so they did, and the suits were withdrawn from both parties, and each of them acquittanced the other. But as for any copy of the plea, he never had one; neither he nor Master John Eastgate, his attorney, could remember whether it was registered. And Master John Eastgate said, even if the register were searched for it, it would take a fortnight's work and they would probably be no nearer to finding it.]

In the Paston letters, the most common context of this discourse of bureaucracy is the management of estates, including the collection of rents and other obligations. Financial matters, particularly debts, were a major preoccupation of the family, whose fortunes fluctuated in a century of civil unrest. Following the death of her husband, William, Agnes Paston continued to organize the family finances, including a complex network of debts. She sent these instructions to her son, John Paston I, in 1452.

Item, as for Horwellbury I sende you a bill of all the reseytes syn the deth of youre fadere, and a copy wrete on the bak how youre fader lete it to ferme to the seide Gurnay. I wulde ye shulde write Gurnay and charge him to mete wyth you fro London warde, and at the lest weye lete him purveye x li., for owyth be my reknyng at Myhelmesse last passed, be-syde youre faderes dette, xviii li. xiiii s. viii d. If ye wolde write to him to brynge suerté bope for youre faderys dette and myn, and pay be dayes so pat the man myte leven and paye vs, I wolde for-yeve him of the olde arrerages x li., and he myte be mad to paye xx marc. be yere. On that condicion I wolde for-yeven him x li . . . (*PL* 25)

[Item, as for Orwellbury (manor), I send you a bill of all the receipts since the death of your father, and a copy written on the back saying that your father let it to the said Gurney to farm. I want you to write to Gurney and tell him to meet with you on the way from London and at the very least he must hand over ten pounds; for he owes, by my reckoning at Michaelmas last, besides your father's debt, 18 pounds 14 shillings and 8 pence. If you would write to him to bring surety for both your father's debt and mine, and pay on fixed days, so that the man can still live and pay us as well, I would release him from the old arrears of ten pounds. If he can be made to

pay 20 marks per year, on that condition I would release him from
ten pounds . . .]

Bureaucracy was sustained not only by written documents but also by
the spoken word of those who daily petitioned the powerful and well
placed, from court officials to the king himself. Not long after Edward
IV seized the throne in 1461, John Paston II reports to his father of his
attempts to petition the king to recognize the Pastons' claim to the
manor of Dedham, a delicate process of negotiation that had to be
filtered through an influential third party.

> I laboryd dayly my lord of Estsexe, treserere of Ynglond, to haue
> meuyd the Kyng bothe of the manere [of] Deddham and of the byll
> copye of the corte rolle euerye mornyng ore he went to the Kyng,
> and often tymys jnquieryd of hym and he had meuyd the Kyng in
> these materys. He answeryd me naye, seyying it was no tyme, and
> seyd he wold it ware osse fayne spedd os I my-selfe; so offte tymys
> de-layeng me that jn trowthe I thowt ta haue send yowe word that
> I felyd by hym that he was not wyllyng to meue the Kyng there-in.
> (*PL* 231)

> [I have daily urged my Lord Essex, Treasurer of England, to peti-
> tion the King regarding both the manor of Dedham and the bill
> copy of the court roll, every morning before he went to the King,
> and many times I have asked him if he had petitioned the King in
> these matters. He answered me "no," saying it was not the time, and
> that he wished it were over with as much as I do myself, putting me
> off all the time so that in truth I considered sending you word that
> he gave me the impression he was not willing to petition the King
> on the matter.]

The concentration of power in London contributes to a third aspect
of urban discourse in the Paston letters, the claim to centrality. Just as
historians naturally refer to towns as "urban centers," as if the center
of any activity must be located where there is a density of population,
so medieval towns claimed a preeminence in terms of economic and
cultural power. Those Paston letters that are written from Norfolk
encode an awareness of marginalization, of writing back to the center
from a less empowered place, a regional area that has its own rhythms
and demands but lacks the centralized power and economic diversity
of the cities, especially London.

As well as being a source of superior consumer goods, London was
perceived to be the place where hard news could be gathered, where

people knew what was really going on. Following the restoration of Henry VI to the throne in 1470, John Paston III writes to his mother, Margaret, in July of the following year, regretting that he is out of touch with the London news.

> As for tydyngys, her be non but þat the Scottys and Walyshe men be besy. What they meane I can not seye. My cosyn John Loueday can tell yow and ther be eny odyr flyeyng talys, for he hathe walkyd in London, and so do not I. (*PL 347*)

> [As for news, there is none except that the Scots and Welsh are busy; what they intend I cannot say. My cousin John Loveday can tell you if there are any other flying tales, for he has walked in London, while I do not.]

London was the center of social and political life among the ruling classes, the place where reputations were made or lost and where the king's favor had to be constantly sought and maintained. Which nobleman was in or out of favor was a matter of intense interest for those in the provinces, like the Pastons, whose local standing depended on their alignments with the neighboring nobility. Margaret Paston is invariably a fount of knowledge about London life, as in this comment to her husband in March 1450.

> Wyllyam Butt, the whiche is wyth Sere Jon Hevenyngham, kom hom from London gesterday, and he syd pleynly to his mayster and to many othere folkys þat the Duke of Suffolk is pardonyd and hath his men agen waytyng up-on hym, and is rytg wel at ese and mery, and is in the Kyngys godegrase and in þe gode conseyt of all þe lordys as well as ever he was. (*PL 136*)

> [William Butt, who works for Sir John Heveningham, came home from London yesterday, and he said plainly to his master, and to many other folks, that the Duke of Suffolk has been pardoned, and has his men waiting on him again, and is very well at ease and merry, and is in the King's good grace, and in the good favor of all the lords, as well as he ever was.]

More significantly, London is positioned as the center of the military activity that dominated the century. Many letters refer to men being summoned to London on the king's service and then being sent back to their homes when the alarm died down. Immediately after Edward IV took the throne in 1461, John Paston III wrote from Norfolk a graphic account of the unstable temperature of the times.

I recomawnde me to yow, and lete yow wete þat notwythstandyng tydingges come downe, os ye knowe, þat pepill shuld not come vp tyll thei were sent fore, but to be redy at all tymes, this notwith-standyng mech pepill owt of the cuntré have take wages, sying thei woll goo vp to London. But thei have no capteyn ner rewler assigned be the comissioneres to awayte vp-on, and so thei stragyll abowte be them-self and be lyklynes arn not leke to come at Lon-don, half of them. (*PL* 317)

[I recommend me to you, and let you know that despite the news that comes down (to Norfolk), as you know, that people should not come up (to London) until they are sent for, but should be ready at all times; despite this, most people outside the county have taken wages (as soldiers), saying they will go up to London. But they have no captain nor leader assigned by the commissioners to report to; and so they straggle about by themselves, and are very likely not to come to London, half of them.]

The use of the deictic prepositions *down* to Norfolk and *up* to London, a usage that persisted into the twentieth century despite the fact that Norfolk is a hundred miles north of London, testifies to the perceived centrality of London on the basis of its economic, political, and military power concentrated on the king, his court, and the royal administration.

Finally, the discourse of status is another aspect of urban subjectiv-ity, since it was the rise of the urban gentry, especially the merchant class, that most threatened the stability of the landowning gentry such as the Pastons. Even the distinction between wealth based on trade and wealth based on land was being undermined by the growth of the land market and the ability of merchants to buy or marry into their own family estates. Amid this social mobility generated by the urban economy, the Pastons identify themselves through a language of socioeconomic status that continues to privilege birth and inherited wealth over trade and the annual salary, while simultaneously endors-ing bourgeois values of hard work and commodity exchange. In terms of the old dichotomy between the feudal nobility, characterized by "careless generosity that paid no heed to expenditure, theatrical behaviour and a demonstrative performance of a particular social role," and the merchants, characterized by "frugality, financial prudence and attention to detail," we can see the Pastons as representatives of a third group, which invented itself by adapting feudal habits to a mercantile economy (Gurevich 184).

The feudal aspects of the Pastons' social positioning is clear from their references to members of the neighboring aristocracy, with whom they consider themselves to be in a relationship of client and patron, and with their own tenants, whom they patronize in turn. While Margaret Paston keeps up with all the local gossip about the nobility, her husband and sons take care to sustain a respectful relationship, bordering on the sycophantic, with those whose elevated position determines their own status. Following a violent assault in 1452, John Paston I made an appeal to the sheriff of Norfolk on the grounds that he was in service to the duke of Norfolk and therefore should not be on the receiving end of violence from another of the duke's men—especially one of more recent clientship. His appeal has little to do with the law and everything to do with the bonds of class-based obligations, both financial and moral.

> Plese yow to wete þat Charlis Nowell, with odir, hath in þis cuntré mad many riot and savtis, and among othir he and v of his felachip set vp-on me and to of my seruantis at þe Chathedrall chirch of Norwich, he smyting at me whilis on of his felaws held myn armis at my bak as the berer herof shall more playnly inform yow; whech was to me strawnge cas, thinking in my conseyth þat I was my lordis man and his homagere or Charlis knew hys lordschipe and þat my lord was my god lord, þat I had be with my lord at London within viii days be-for Lent, at which tyme he grantyd me his godlordship so largely þat it must cause me euer to be his trew seruant to myn power. (*PL* 43)

> [Please note that Charles Nowell, with others, has in this country made many riots and assaults; and, among other things, he and five of his fellowship set upon me and two of my servants at the Cathedral church of Norwich, he striking me whilse one of his fellows held my arms at my back, as the bearer of this letter shall inform you in more detail. This was to me a strange situation, thinking in my conceit that I was my Lord's man and his homager before Charles knew his Lordship, and that my Lord was my good lord, that I had been with my Lord in London within eight days before Lent, at which time he granted me his good lordship so generously that it must cause me ever to be his true servant to the best of my ability.]

With regard to their own tenants, the Pastons display both concern—comforting them when their manors are under threat from the duke of Norfolk, for example—and a rapacious desire to extract every penny that is owed to them. Margaret Paston's comment, in November 1455, about finding suitable material for her husband's liveries, indicates the importance of these outward displays of status.

> As towchyng for your leveryes, ther can noon be gete heere of that coloure that ye wolde haue of nouther murrey nor blwe nor goode russettys undrenethe iii s. the yerde at the lowest price, and yet is ther not j-nough of on clothe and coloure to serue you. (*PL* 156)

> [With regard to your liveries, there is none to be had here of that color which you want, neither murrey nor blue nor good russets, for less than 3 shillings a yard at the lowest price; and also there is not enough of one cloth and color to provide for you.]

Awareness of the social hierarchy was finely tuned, even as the urban economy was producing merchants and administrators whose wealth, in the one case, and education, in the other, were challenging the older feudal privileges based on birth. The marriage of Margery Paston to Richard Calle, the family bailiff, was a severe blow to family pride and caused Margery to be disowned by her entire family. In London, the center of class-based privilege, anomalies of upward social mobility achieved through marriage or patronage were both accepted and ruthlessly exposed, as this piece of gossip from William Paston to his brother John reveals.

> As for tydyngys, my Lord Ryuers was brougth to Caleys and by-for the lordys wyth viii xx torches, and there my lord of Salesbury reheted hym, callyng hym knaves son that he schuld be so rude to calle hym and these oper lordys traytours, for they schull be found the Kyngys treue liege men whan he schuld be found a traytour, &c. And my lord of Warrewyk reheted hym and seyd that his fader was but a squyer and broute vp wyth Kyng Herry the v, and sethen hym-self made by maryage and also made lord, and that it was not his parte to have swyche langage of lordys beyng of the Kyngys blood. (*PL* 88)

> [As for tidings, my Lord Rivers was brought to Calais and before the lords with eight score torches, and there my Lord of Salisbury berated him, calling him a knave's son because he was so rude as to call him and these other lords traitors, for they would prove to be the King's true liege men when he should be found a traitor, and so on. And my Lord of Warwick berated him, and said that his father was only a squire, brought up with King Henry V, and had since made himself by marriage, and had also been made a lord, and that

he was not entitled to use such language about lords who were of the King's blood.]

The king's household was the pinnacle of social ambition and the place where the social hierarchy was most clearly defined and reproduced. One of the Pastons, John II, spent some time in the household of Edward IV shortly after his succession in 1461, a service that was fraught with social dangers, as his uncle, Clement, suggested in a letter to John's father, John Paston I, in August 1461.

> I fele by W. Pekok þat my nevew is not get verily aqweyntyd in þe Kyngys howse, nore wyth þe officerys of þe Kyngys howse. He is not takyn as non of þat howse, fore þe cokys be not charged to serue hym nore þe sewere to gue hym no dyche, fore þe sewere wyll not tak no men no dischys till þey be comawndyd by þe cownterrollere. Also, he is not aqueynted wyth no body but wyth Wekys, and Wekys ad told hym þat he wold bryng hym to þe Kyng; but he hathe not get do soo. Were-fore it were best fore hym to tak hiis leve and cum hom, till ge hadd spok wyth swm body to helpe hym forthe, fore he is not bold y-now to put forthe hym-selfe. (*PL* 116)

> [I gather from W. Peacock that my nephew is not yet fully acquainted with the king's house, nor with the officers of the king's house. He is not taken as one of that house, for the cooks are not ordered to serve him, nor the server to give him a dish, for the server will not take any man a dish until they are ordered to do so by the comptroller. Also, he is not acquainted with anyone but Weeks; and Weeks has told him that he would bring him to the king, but he has not yet done so. For these reasons, it would be best for him to take his leave and come home until you have spoken with someone who can help him forward, for he is not bold enough to put himself forward.]

Such accounts in the letters convey something of the range of social and discursive practices that marked out the finely graded partitions between different status groups. The discourse of status, particularly in relation to the royal administration and household, was characteristic of the urban subjectivity within which the Pastons located and "recognized" themselves.

My argument, then, is that the Paston letters are not autobiographical if by that term we expect to retrieve coherent and historically authentic individuals from a self-consciously produced first-person narrative. But they clearly are autobiographical in that they present self-constructed accounts of particular subjectivities, positioned historically, culturally, and discursively. As the subjects of epistolary discourse, the "I" of the letters is no more authentic, singular, or coherent than any other "I" positioned in discourse; nor are the events of the letters any less complex, symbolic, or metaphorical than those of autobiographical or fictional narratives.

The significance of the Paston letters lies not so much in their value as historical evidence as in the evidence they provide for an emerging subjectivity produced by the secular discourses of urban exchange. This urban subjectivity had already achieved hegemonic status well before the fifteenth century in the great city-states of Renaissance Italy, but it was not to triumph in England until the Industrial Revolution. In the Paston letters, we see the beginnings of its challenge to the prevailing subjectivities of medieval Christianity and land-based feudalism. Through the discourses of commodification, bureaucracy, urban centrality, and socioeconomic status, and in the significant absence of the discourse of Christian devotion, the Paston letters bring into being the increasingly secularized and urbanized individuals of the fifteenth-century English gentry.

NOTES

1. The genealogical evidence is discussed by Davis in his authoritative edition of the letters (1.xl–xlii). All references to the letters are taken from this edition, subsequently abbreviated to *PL*. It should be noted that the fifteenth-century Paston letters are merely the earliest and most chronologically cohesive section of a much larger collection of letters and papers related to the Paston family from the fifteenth to eighteenth centuries. See *PL* 1.xxiv–xxvii; also Stoker.

2. Details of these attacks are provided in Bennett.

3. The first published biography of Shakespeare appeared in Nicholas Rowe's edition of the plays in 1709.

4. I have discussed this point in more detail in my article, "Individual and Society in *Owein/Yvain* and *Gereint/Erec*."

5. Guibert's vita clearly has a confessional aspect as well, in that it uses contemporary events of his life as moral exempla; see Batany.

6. Egeria's journal has been edited and translated by Gingrass; see also Wilkinson.

7. On Margery Kempe, see Staley, *Margery Kempe's Dissenting Fictions* and *The Book of Margery Kempe*.

8. For examples of such prologues, in Middle English, see Wogan-Browne, Nicholas Watson, Andrew Taylor, and Ruth Evans.

9. Pask has observed that "the vernacular writers of Chaucer's time characteristically made obeisance to their own marginalization" (10).

10. Minnis argues that, whereas Gower claimed the role of "author," Chaucer preferred to represent himself as a compiler. He also suggests that Chaucer's retractions "were added to the Canterbury Tales—probably by Chaucer but possibly by someone else—in keeping with the usual practice of *compilation*" (208). For an English translation of Petrarch's "Letter to Posterity," which was written to conclude his *Epistolae Seniles* (ca.1367–71), see Thompson 1–13.

11. According to Topsfield, "the *vidas* or 'lives' appear to give reliable information about the place of birth and death and social status of a troubadour. In other matters they are probably fictitious except occasionally" (259).

12. Habermas associates the institutionalization of the public identity of individuals with eighteenth-century European culture (2–30).

13. See, for example, the review by Charles Ross.

14. See, for example, Hadden, especially 46–50, "Commodity Fetishism and the Representation of Science and Nature."

15. See, for example, Keene.

16. The standard survey of medieval administrative systems is Jewell. For a comparative view of medieval French administration, see Kittell.

WORKS CITED

Batany, Jean. "L'autobiographie de Guibert de Nogent (vers 1115): Mémoire, identité sociale, et identité langagière." *Die Autobiographie im Mittelalter. Autobiographie et References Autobiographiques au Moyen Age.* Ed. Danielle Buschinger and Wolfgang Spiewok. Greifswald: Reineke-Verlag, 1995. 1–10.

Bennett, H. S. *The Pastons and Their England.* Cambridge: Cambridge UP, 1968.

Calhoun, C. "Social Theory and the Politics of Identity." *Social Theory and the Politics of Identity.* Ed. C. Calhoun. Oxford: Blackwell, 1994. 9–36.

Dalrymple, Roger. "Reaction, Consolation, and Redress in the Letters of the Paston Women." *Early Modern Women's Letter Writing, 1450–1700.* Ed. James Daybell. Basingstoke: Palgrave, 2001. 16–28.

Davis, Norman. *Paston Letters and Papers of the Fifteenth Century.* 2 vols. 1971; Oxford: Clarendon, 1976.

Foucault, M. "What Is an Author?" *Language, Counter-memory, Practice.* Trans. Donald F. Bourchard and Sherry Simon. Oxford: Blackwell, 1977. 113–38.

Fulton, Helen. "Individual and Society in *Owein/Yvain* and *Gereint/Erec*." *The Individual in Celtic Literatures.* Ed. Joseph Falaky Nagy. Dublin: Four Courts Press, 2001. 15–50.

Gilroy, Amanda, and W. M. Verhoeven, eds. *Epistolary Histories: Letters, Fiction, Culture.* Charlottesville: UP of Virginia, 2000.

Gingrass, George E. *Egeria: Diary of a Pilgrimage.* New York: Newman, 1970.

Gurevich, Aaron. *The Origins of European Feudalism.* Trans. Katharine Judelson. Oxford: Blackwell, 1995.

Habermas, Jürgen. *The Structural Transformation of the Public Sphere: An Inquiry into a Category of Bourgeois Society.* Cambridge: Harvard UP, 1989.

Hadden, Richard W. *On the Shoulders of Merchants: Exchange and the Mathematical Conception of Nature in Early Modern Europe.* Albany: State U of New York P, 1994.

Hagen, Susan K. *Allegorical Remembrance: A Study of the* Pilgrimage of the Life of Man *as a Medieval Treatise on Seeing and Remembering.* Athens: U of Georgia P, 1990.

Haskins, Charles Homer. *The Renaissance of the Twelfth Century.* Cambridge: Harvard UP, 1927.

Henry, Avril, ed. *The Pilgrimage of the Lyfe of the Manhode.* Vol. 1. London: Oxford UP, 1985. Early English Text Society No. 288.

Jewell, Helen M. *English Local Administration in the Middle Ages.* New York: Barnes and Noble, 1972.

Keene, Derek. "Landlords, the Property Market and Urban Development in Medieval England." *Power, Profit, and Urban Land Ownership in Medieval and Early Modern Northern European Towns.* Ed. Finn-Einar Eliassen and Geir Atle Ersland. Aldershot: Scolar, 1996. 93–119.

Kittell, Ellen. *From Ad Hoc to Routine: A Case Study in Medieval Bureaucracy.* Philadelphia: U of Pennsylvania P, 1991.

MacArthur, Elizabeth J. *Extravagant Narratives: Closure and Dynamics in the Epistolary Form.* Princeton: Princeton UP, 1990.

MacLean, Gerald. "Re-siting the Subject." *Epistolary Histories: Letters, Fiction, Culture.* Ed. Amanda Gilroy and W. M. Verhoeven. Charlottesville: UP of Virginia, 2000. 176–97.

Minnis, Alastair. *Medieval Theory of Authorship. Scholastic Literary Attitudes in the Later Middle Ages.* 2nd ed. Aldershot: Scolar, 1988.

Pask, Kevin. *The Emergence of the English Author.* Cambridge: Cambridge UP, 1996.

Pastre, J. M. "Un Pélérinage Autobiographique: Le *Peregrinarius* d'Hugues de Liège." *Die Autobiographie im Mittelalter: Autobiographie et References Autobiographiques au Moyen Age.* Ed. Danielle Buschinger and Wolfgang Spiewok. Greifswald: Reineke-Verlag, 1995. 53–63.

Richardson, Malcolm. "The Fading Art of the Medieval *Ars Dictaminis* in England after 1400." *Rhetorica* 19 (2001): 225–47.

Ross, Charles. *Times Literary Supplement* 3927 (1977).

Rowe, Nicholas. *The Works of Mr. William Shakespear: In Six Volumes / Adorn'd with Cuts, Revis'd and Corrected, with an Account of the Life and Writings of the Author.* London, 1709.

Scaglione, Aldo. "The Mediterranean's Three Spiritual Shores: Images of the Self between Christianity and Islam in the Later Middle Ages." *The Craft of Fiction: Essays in Medieval Poetics.* Ed. Leigh A. Arrathoon. Rochester, MI: Solaris, 1984. 453–74.

Staley, Lynn. *Margery Kempe's Dissenting Fictions.* Philadelphia: Pennsylvania State UP, 1994.

Staley, Lynn, ed. *The Book of Margery Kempe.* Kalamazoo, MI: The Consortium for the Teaching of the Middle Ages, Medieval Institute, 1996. Middle English Texts Series.

Stoker, David. "'Innumerable Letters of Good Consequence in History': The

Discovery and First Publication of the Paston Letters." *The Library*, 6th ser., 17.2 (1995): 107–55.

Thompson, David, ed. *Petrarch: A Humanist among Princes*. New York: Harper and Row, 1971.

Topsfield, L. T. *Troubadours and Love*. Cambridge: Cambridge UP, 1975.

Wilkinson, John. *Jerusalem Pilgrims before the Crusades*. Warminster: Aris and Phillips, 1977.

Wogan-Browne, Jocelyn, Nicholas Watson, Andrew Taylor, and Ruth Evans, eds. *The Idea of the Vernacular: An Anthology of Middle English Literary Theory, 1280–1520*. Exeter: U of Exeter P, 1999.

Chapter 12

Textualizing an Urban Life
The Case of Isabella Whitney

Jean E. Howard

As other chapters in this volume have demonstrated, imposing nine-teenth- and twentieth-century concepts of autobiography onto early modern texts is problematic.[1] Not only were modern concepts of indi-vidualism historically unavailable to pre-Enlightenment writers, but identity was understood in terms of externally formulated social roles and duties to a degree unimaginable to most twenty-first-century westerners.[2] That is, to be a wife, a servant, a member of the gentry, a Christian, a Protestant—these were social identities that constructed those designated by them more forcefully than any sense of an inner essence that eluded or preexisted the social sphere. That, of course, does not mean that people never changed their social positions or lived out their allotted social roles without contradiction and struggle. As spiritual autobiographies attest, it was not, for example, an easy thing to be a good Christian, and it is surely a mistake to think that early modern lives were less complex than modern ones. The difference between now and then lies, rather, in the degree to which earlier times saw the self first and foremost in what I am calling social terms, that is, in terms of ascribed roles. These were often externally signified by the clothing, such as livery, one wore and materialized through regimes of diet, labor (or nonlabor), and deference (or authority).[3]

When early modern people wrote about their lives, they often did so in religious terms, modeling their accounts on the genres of the con-fession or the spiritual psychomachia. The goal, broadly speaking, was to record an exemplary struggle to attain salvation and conform to valorized spiritual norms (Ebner 1971). Some writers textualized their lives in more secular terms but seldom without a strong sense of the social roles, whether it be the good housewife or the good counselor, that defined the primary coordinates of their existence. And almost invariably they relied on preexisting genres of writing—the epistle, the complaint, the vision—to fashion an account of an irredeemably social self.

Isabella Whitney is, in this regard, an interesting and important example of an early modern subject who composed in verse an "auto-biographical" account of a female life in primarily secular terms. Important not only as the first published female poet in English, Whitney also commands attention for the complex way she utilizes established poetic genres to create a sense of what it meant to occupy the social role of maidservant, and eventually that of writer, in London just as that city began to experience the spectacular demographic and commercial growth that was to make it a cosmopolitan capital and the center of England's global commercial expansion. Closely examining her second book of published poems, *The Sweet Nosegay* of 1573, and especially her final poem, her "Wyll and Testament," I will argue that the urban milieu in which Whitney was immersed enabled her to imagine a female life in which one could relinquish the overdetermined social roles of maidservant and prospective wife and tentatively assume the position, typically gendered male, of social critic and urban writer. London and its increasingly capitalist marketplace were thus the crucial factors in Whitney's innovative representation of a work-ingwoman's life.

The facts about the historical Isabella Whitney are sparse, and much of what people take for truth about her derives directly from her seemingly autobiographical verse. She does not appear in court or parish records, no marriage is documented, and no death date is recorded. Perhaps she was the sister of Geoffrey Whitney, the creator of *The Choice of Emblems*. An epistle in her second book of poetry is addressed to a brother, G. W., and she dedicates the whole volume to George Mainwaring, the man to whom Geoffrey Whitney also dedicated one of his emblems (Travitsky, "'Wyll'" 77–78). And yet in her poem, the "Wyll and Testament," Whitney claims to have been London bred and says that "To Smithfeelde I must something leave / my Parents there did dwell" (267–68).[4] Geoffrey Whitney's family came from the minor gentry in Cheshire. There are ways to explain the discrepancy (that her parents moved to London for a time, she was not Geoffrey's sister but a more distant relative, or the poem's reference to her Smithfield parents is a convenient fiction), but the fact remains that Isabella's link to the more famous emblem poet remains in part speculation.[5] The connection, however, would help to explain the learning evident in Whitney's verse. Some of her early poems in *Copy of a Letter* (1567) are modeled on Ovid's *Heroides* and refer to the stories of Dido, Theseus, Cassandra, and Jason.[6] Her second collection, *A Sweet Nosegay* (1573), participates in the vogue for printed poetic miscellanies such as George Gascoigne's *A Hundreth Sundrie Flowres* and uses Hugh Plat's *The Flours of Philosophie* as the basis for Whitney's own poetic renderings of his sententious and moralizing pieties. Whitney could have become familiar with these elements of London literary culture simply by living in the city and frequenting its booksellers' stalls, but her accomplished participation in this culture may suggest either an educated family or service in the house of a lady where her duties could have included participating in the reading aloud of learned, pious, and popular books while household tasks, such as needlework, were performed.

From her verse, we can guess at other aspects of Whitney's life: that she had a least five siblings, to whom she addressed verse epistles; and that she herself lived for a time in London as a domestic servant. At least, this is the fiction the speaker creates in *The Sweet Nosegay*, in which she laments her lost position in the household of a "virtuous Lady," whom "till death I honor will: / The loss I had of service hers, / I languish for it still" ("To her Brother. G. W." 29–32). This, then, is the sum of what we probably know about Isabella Whitney the historical person. She may have come from a minor gentry family in Cheshire but have spent a good portion of her life in service in London. There she fell on hard times but managed to publish two books of poetry, in 1567 and 1573, before bidding farewell to London and disappearing from view.

While an elite woman might have circulated her poems in manuscript, Lynette McGrath has recently suggested the route by which the less socially exalted Whitney found her way into print. Both of her books were published by Richard Jones, who seems to have developed a minor specialization in books by, about, and geared toward women (McGrath, *Subjectivity* 125). Besides Whitney, for example, he published the pamphlet attributed to Jane Anger, and with Whitney's *Copy of a Letter* he appears to have been cashing in on the fashion for female complaint poems such as the extremely popular complaint of Jane Shore, which had been added to *The Mirror for Magistrates* in 1563, just four years before Whitney's book appeared (125). McGrath speculates

that Jones felt it was worth taking the chance that the novelty of a gentlewoman writing "in metre" could attract a readership (131–32).

If the London publishing industry afforded Whitney her opportunity for print immortality, the city also was central to the particular
life narrative constructed in Whitney's most substantive collection of
verse, *The Sweet Nosegay.* My intent in examining aspects of the autobiographical persona created in this volume of Whitney's verse is not
to make claims about "the real" Isabella Whitney, the historical person
often indicated simply by the initials Is. W. Rather, I want to examine
how the collection creates an incipient autobiographical effect by
drawing on extant literary genres to tell the story of its first-person
speaker as an unfortunate but virtuous maidservant. Moreover, Whitney's structuring of these materials within a decisively urban frame is
crucial to her fashioning of a persona who exceeds the expected social
positions afforded someone of her gender. Immersion in the life of
England's capital city thus provides the conditions of possibility for
Whitney to textualize a female life in a particular way. In making this
case, I will focus primarily on Whitney's longest poem, a "Wyll and
Testament," which concludes *A Sweet Nosegay,* though I will also discuss its place in the implied narrative of the entire volume. I will focus
on three things: first, the insistently urban frame of this collection of
verse; second, the speaker's use of the will as a textual mode that
grants her a certain position of control and status within her urban
environment and a means both to capitalize on her social position as
urban maidservant and also to begin to rewrite it; and, third, the
poem's utilization, as well, of the genres of urban complaint and
chorography, a conjunction that allows the delineation of a particular
kind of subject position for the speaker, one associated with masculine
authority, which accounts for the poem's arresting mixture of satirical
commentary on and affirmation of urban life.

A Sweet Nosegay is, first, an interesting departure from the much
shorter *Copy of a Letter,* which contains only four poems, two of them
female complaints, modeled on Ovid's *Heroides,* about the inconstancy
of men, and two by men upbraiding women for similar failings.[7] The
title page describes the writer as "a yonge Gentilwoman," who has
written her letters "in meeter" and who is intent on admonishing
young gentlewomen to beware the flattery of men (Travitsky and
Cullen). The speaker introduces the theme of abandonment, which is
to permeate both collections, but the female speaker of the first two
poems is careful to present herself as more than an injured party. She
is also a moral tutor, who draws from the examples of antiquity (the

stories of Dido, Medea, and other abandoned women), as well as from her own experience, in order to instruct other women about the necessity of exercising caution when dealing with the duplicities of men (Foster 32–39). Drawing attention to the conventional nature of the speaker's advice, Elizabeth Heale argues that Whitney, like other mid-century poets, is drawing on a common set of tropes to create an autobiographical effect. In Heale's succinct summary, "Is.W.'s implied presence is a rhetorical device to stabilize a conventional discourse as true speech" (37). Moreover, in this first collection Whitney creates her autobiographical effect from nowhere, that is, from a resolutely unlocalized setting, the land of books and stories, not of London life.

The second collection is very different: longer, more varied, more localized in its setting, and more insistently autobiographical in effect, as Whitney's persona experiments with claiming new subject positions even as she constantly references her primary social position as a down-at-heel London maidservant who begins to write. Perhaps the most innovative aspect of the sequence is its insistent localization. Whitney repeatedly calls attention to the fact that the poems have been written and published in London, and they depict a vividly realized maidservant's experience within the city. The first poem, "The Author to the Reader," opens in a cityscape. The speaker, in harvest time, finds herself "harvestless" and "serviceless" (ll.1–2), that is, unemployed, sick and with time on her hands. Not unlike those of us who, when ill, read Jane Austen for solace, Whitney's speaker turns in her illness to books, first to the Scriptures, then to history, and finally to the poets Virgil and Ovid. None suffices. She then goes into the streets of the city to see if her "limbs / had got their strength again" (ll.27–28). There she meets a friend, who urges her for her health's sake to get out of the dirty lane: "shift you to some better air, / for fear to be infect: / With noisome smell and savors ill" (ll.33–35). The city seems a place of infection and ill smells, perhaps even of plague, so intent is the friend on a quick departure. The speaker, however, stays where she is, finally going home "all sole alone" (l.51), a phrase that refers to the speaker's intense isolation, certainly, but also to her status as a *feme sole*, someone not yet "covered" by marriage. It is a state of extreme precariousness for a young woman, one suggesting that she has not yet made the crucial social transformation to wife, and yet one that allows her certain freedoms and control over the disposition of her property—if, that is, she is lucky enough to have any property. In the immediate context of the first poem, the speaker's solitary urban condition yields at least one benefit. Fortune has brought her to "Plat his Plot," the anthology from which Whitney "gathers" the raw materials she will put into verse for her own *Sweet Nosegay.* The wholesome smell of Plat's flowers, the speaker insists, "prevents each harm, / if yet yourself be sound" (ll.59–60).

In this account, the city is at once the source of offensive smells and deadly infection and, simultaneously, of healing in the form of the book. In a volume in which Whitney often details her sickness, loss of employment, and separation from relatives, her acquisition of Plat's work, she avers, "made me pleasures feele" (l.56). She describes reading it as like reposing in a bed of goodly flowers, and even though business calls her away she returns to the book obsessively, carrying poems from it about the city with her to be her defense "In stinking streetes, or loathsome Lanes" (l.73). One must not, of course, discount the degree to which Whitney's account of Plat's rather tedious book is tactically enhanced in order to invite the reader into the pages of her own, rather better, florilegium. Nonetheless, apparent in this opening poem is the outline of a narrative in which the urban speaker, "all sole alone," finds amid the stink, sickness, and busyness of the city a source, in books, of both pleasure and creativity, as she eventually "translates" some of Plat's "flowers" into verse of her own devising. It is by this route that she can reassume the novel position of female author, though with much greater self-consciousness about the material conditions of that possibility within London print culture than she displayed in her first collection.

At first, in *The Sweet Nosegay,* Whitney seemingly subordinates herself and her poems to the authority of Hugh Plat, insisting that she is simply making his work available to others, even though she is selecting from, arranging, and versifying the flowers in what she eventually characterizes as his "maze" (l.179).[8] But the translation of Plat forms only part of Whitney's volume. It is followed by a series of poetic epistles to and from Whitney's friends and relatives. Not translations, many of these epistles are nonetheless based on the popular genre of the female complaint, and they assume her serviceless position in the city. Many detail her distressed state and attempt to establish or reestablish a connection with those who might give her material or psychological help. Collectively, they mark out the speaker's attempts to find an alternative to or to come to terms with the urban life lived "all sole alone" that the speaker described in her initial poem to the reader. In articulating the speaker's longing to make contact with those whose whereabouts she does not know or who have been too busy to reply to her letters, the epistles attempt to weave Whitney into

a familial and communal network, and they even hint at her possible
assumption of the social role of wife.

As Patricia Phillippy has discussed, young women who left the
country for service in London typically worked for several years,
"earning their dowries and gaining experience in the art of 'housewifery,' which would be of use in their subsequent careers as wives"
(445). Service was not imagined as a permanent state but a transition
between maidenhood and the status of wife. By presenting an unemployed speaker, Whitney shows what could go wrong with this sce-
nario. Presumably, this young woman is not stockpiling money for a
dowry. In other cases, one partner or the other could abandon a
planned marriage arrangement and wed someone else or an unwanted
or unplanned pregnancy could put an abrupt end to a servant woman's
career.[9] In an epistle to two of her younger unmarried sisters, who
have also entered London service, the epistle writer offers them advice
about how to thrive in their jobs. Though herself "serviceless," she
presents herself as a mistress of housewifery and a moral tutor to the
young, concerned with protecting their virtue. One can read this epistle as Whitney's public proclamation of her own credentials for assuming the position of married housewife.

Yet there is one other epistle, this one addressed to an older married
sister, that reveals deep ambivalence about the life of domesticity her
sister has achieved and to which the speaker herself might be assumed
to be heading (Phillippy 450). In the poem, Whitney appears to mull
over a sort of pleasure quite different from that obtained by reading
and writing, namely, the pleasure to be had with a husband and her sister's "pretty Boys" (l.17). The speaker even tries to imagine such a life
for herself before returning to what she actually has: her writing
implements. "Had I a Husband, or a house, / and all that 'longs thereto
/ Myself could frame about to rouse, / as other women do: / But till
some household cares me tie, / My books and Pen I will apply"
(ll.37–42). The speaker's stance in these lines is complicated: she recognizes her anomalous status vis-à-vis other women and half seems to
desire their lives; yet household cares—probably the nearly endless
demands of bake house, dairy, and child rearing—Whitney can only
imagine as constraints that would "tie" her, probably at the expense of
her alternative pleasures, those of her books and her pen.

Importantly, the last epistle in this section of her book, "Is.W. being
weary of writing, sendeth this for Answer," bids a decisive farewell to
the exchange of familiar letters. Proclaiming again her extreme
poverty, Whitney tells her cousin to send her no more letters and to

expect no more replies. "For now I will my writing clean forsake / till of my griefs, my stomack I discharge: / and tyll I row, in Lady Fortune's barge. / Good Cousin write not nor any more reply, / But give me leave, more quietness to try" (ll.10–14). To me, this epistle marks the moment when Whitney turns away from the domestic networks in which her married sister, for example, is so thoroughly enmeshed and in which Whitney can participate only through the exchange of familiar letters. Instead, the speaker moves toward "quietness," the quietness of a woman "all sole alone." Were the collection to stop at this point, it might seem a grim ending to Whitney's fictionalized life story. However, she does not stop writing; she simply stops writing epistles. Paradoxically, from her quietness issues Whitney's most remarkable, original, and insistently urban poem, the "Wyll and Testament."

As the final poem in *The Sweet Nosegay*, the "Wyll and Testament" has a position of special prominence in the collection. It is the way Whitney chose to conclude the implicit narrative of the life and choices of her textualized self, and it is a remarkably complex, dense, and multilayered production. Part of its complexity stems from its generic intermixtures (Beilin 252–53). First of all, the poem takes the form of a poetic will, and it is the speaker's status as *feme sole* that legitimates her composition of it. As Amy Erickson's *Women and Property in Early Modern England* has shown, most *married* women could not make wills without special arrangements with the husbands (204). However, widows and single women could make wills if they had enough property to make it worthwhile to do so. In fact, single women such as Isabella Whitney made 20 percent of all wills written by women in England between 1550 and 1750. In general, as Erickson has shown, women tended to have distinctive ways of distributing wealth. More than men, they tended to leave bequests to a wide range of people and to personalize their gifts, that is, leaving different kinds of things to different people. Household furnishings and items of clothing were often carefully parceled out to friends, kin, and servants with an eye to both their use and their sentimental value. Women tended to leave bequests to women more frequently than men did, and their charitable bequests tended to designate widows and the poor in general as beneficiaries, while men were more likely to leave money for municipal improvements or public buildings.

Whitney's poetic will, of course, is a fictive and highly fanciful document, but it takes some care to draw on the actual language of legal bequests and both mimics and departs from the usual concerns of historical women's wills. The speaker insists, for example, that she is "whole in body, and in minde" (l.51), she enumerates her many bequests, she makes provision for her own burial, and she dates the document within the poem: "This xx of October I, / in ANNO DOMINI: / A Thousand: v. hundred seventy three / as Alminacks descry. / Did write this Wyll with mine owne hand / And it to London gave" (ll.362–68). But Whitney mimics the language of actual wills only to play fast and loose with their basic assumptions. Most strikingly, the speaker is so poor that she has nothing of her own to give to anyone. At first blush, as an unemployed maidservant, the speaker seems to have all the vulnerabilities of a *feme sole* and none of the benefits. The only thing she can distribute to London is what London already possesses: its shops, streets, prisons, foodstuffs, cloth, luxury items, and places of physic and entertainment (Hutson 127).

A high-spirited irony thus pervades Whitney's will. Miserably poor and fearing things will get even worse, the speaker munificently gives away not only the content of whole shops but what might be counted the common property of the entire city: its municipal infrastructure of streets and buildings and common meeting places. Precisely because of its counterfactual outrageousness, Whitney's is a vigorously empowered speaking position. The poem is long, the bequests roll on and on, and in enumerating them Whitney appears transcendently generous to a city that, as she claims at both the beginning and end of the poem, has not given her specific kinds of material sustenance: "Thou never yet, woldst credit geve / to boord me for a yeare: / Nor with Apparell me releve / except thou payed weare" (ll.32–35). Specifically, she is calling attention to the benefits traditionally allowed servants, who would receive an allotment of apparel and food, as well as wages, during their time of employment. These benefits her unemployment has denied her. Whitney thus showers gifts on a metropolis imagined in the opening lines as a lover who has treated her cruelly. There is little sentimental self-pity in this poem, however. This is partly because it is written in alternating tetrameter and rhyming trimeter lines that thump along like a sturdy pony trotting to market.[10] Moreover, even when enjoining the city to give her a pauper's burial utterly devoid of ceremony, Whitney does not plead for charity so much as warn about the stink of unburied bodies in city space: "And though I nothing named have, / to bury mee withall: / Consider that above the ground, / annoyance bee I shall" (ll.311–14). Contemplating a pauper's death, she frames a request for burial as advice about the city's best interest in getting rotting carcasses underground.

Wendy Wall has suggested that, in making her poetic will, Whitney draws on the moral authority of mothers' legacies to their children. Clearly Whitney does use the occasion of her imagined death to authorize the creation of a last will and testament, but it is striking how unmaternal a persona she creates. The speaker not only fails to mention children, but her advice to the city and its inhabitants is resolutely social rather than personal. She addresses economic inequities in the city, and in this she echoes concerns Amy Erickson connects with female will makers, but she steadfastly refrains from making personal legacies to friends or kinfolk, even those to whom she addressed her epistles. Her gifts are to a city, imagined in all its multiplicity, and not to a family network. When she summons witnesses to make her will legally binding, she does not choose her family or friends as witnesses but rather her "Paper, Pen, and Standish," or inkpot (l.371), the tools of her writing trade. She also summons Time, "who promised to reveale / so fast as she could hye / The same: least of my nearer kyn, / for any thing should vary" (ll.373–76). In other words, her writing tools and the time that brings their productions to light are the best witnesses to Whitney's intentions and will stand as guarantors lest her kinfolk, here imagined as potential meddlers, attempt to change the least particular of her will. In appropriating the legal form of the will to lend authority to her final poetic pronouncements in *The Sweet Nosegay*, Whitney thus turns decisively away from domestic ties to address the city and her own position as observer and writer within it. Moreover, in doing so she creates the one thing that is uniquely her own to bestow—her poems. As a writer, Whitney creates a legacy in print rather than through the passage of goods and property to children and friends. Although she says she bears her poems as a gift to the virtuous lady she once served, they are nonetheless primarily a commodity to be bought and sold along with London's other commodities. Whitney carefully indicates where one can buy the book in the shops surrounding Saint Paul's Cathedral. Her poem is thus less a mother's legacy than an advertisement for a product in which Londoners can read about the city in which they live and in which novel kinds of female self-fashioning are possible.

Yet the poem is more than a poetic will. It is also an urban chorography and complaint, and as such it allows Whitney to assume an authoritative position as an anatomist of urban ills and the proponent of a cure. No longer focusing on abandonment by a male lover, as in *Copy of a Letter*, and no longer "curing" the reader by rehashing Plat's pious platitudes, the female speaker instead forges a public voice of authoritative description and critique (Beilin 249). Again, her social position as urban maidservant provides the foundation for her textual performance. "The Wyll and Testament" is in part a description of city space, and authoritative knowledge of such space is exactly what a female servant would acquire in her daily activities within the London cityscape. As Richard Helgerson has shown, the sixteenth and seventeenth centuries were the age of both rural and urban chorographies, that is, a mode of writing attentive to the physical landmarks, streets, fields, and local histories of particular regions (105–47). He connects chorography to forms of national identity that implicitly tie subjects to the land—to place broadly conceived—as much as to the monarch. Whitney's poem sutures urban subjects to the city of London, inviting complex forms of recognition and identification. Whitney's is a very particular mapping of city space. The places she names are mostly clustered within the walls in the southwestern quadrants of the city, and they include such well-known sites as Saint Paul's Cathedral, the Mint, and the shops in the Pawn at the Royal Exchange (Brace 279–82). She also lists street upon street and the particular kinds of goods and services that could be obtained at each. At the Stilyard, one can buy wine from the German merchants who congregate there; at Watling Street, one can purchase wool, gold in Cheapside, hose in Birchin Lane, shoes at Saint Martin's, books in the yard of Saint Paul's, and legal services at the Inns of Court.

Whitney's mapping of urban space is thus not just a random naming of places but a carefully selected textualization of the city. It displays places in a purposeful order and focuses on some kinds of urban institutions and not others. Several decades later John Stow would produce his masterful *Survey of London,* a chorography focused primarily on the public monuments of London, particularly its churches and public buildings, and the many charitable endowments with which it was studded. Whitney, by contrast, says relatively little about the churches of London, other than Saint Paul's, and little about the great monuments. About the court, she is silent. Instead, she focuses on the more mundane aspects of city life, such as where one goes to buy shoes or bread or where one might be imprisoned for debt. Only glancingly does she record more upscale places of entertainment or consumption. Her small book, cheap and poorly printed (McGrath, "Isabella" 286), clearly is aimed at Londoners who possessed no great social standing or wealth but could take pleasure in their own recognition of the urban landscape Whitney describes.

The persona Whitney fashions for herself in *The Sweet Nosegay,* that of an unemployed urban female servant, authorizes her to write London from this particular vantage point. As a household servant, Whitney would almost certainly have been sent to the shops to buy from the stalls of butchers and linen makers, or she would have accompanied a mistress who visited those stalls. Books such as *Hugh Alley's Caveat* (1598) contain pictures of women moving freely through the markets and streets of London with shopping baskets on their arms. Her social role would thus have given her some freedom to be a legitimate "walker in the city," while her times of unemployment would have cast her into a more dangerous position, one that, for example, could have led her to the inside of London's debtors' prisons.

These details lead me to suggest that at its most complex level Whitney's "Wyll and Testament" fashions her description of urban life into a powerful piece of social critique. As Lawrence Manley reminds us in *Literature and Culture in Early Modern England*, the midcentury was a time of enormous political, social, and cultural upheaval. The Reformation, the rapid change of monarchs, changes in market practice, the spectacular growth of the city of London—all of these things caused the midcentury to be a time when a literature of complaint flourished, full of anxious laments about indifferent rulers, economic dislocation, greedy upstart crows, and the suffering of the poor (63–122). Increasingly, as Manley outlines, London became a major target in Tudor complaint. It was seen, for example, as eroding traditional social hierarchies by means of its relentless commercialization of life and the introduction of every sort of newfangledness in dress, diet, and manners into the Commonwealth. Growing incredibly rapidly between 1550 and 1600 (the population quadrupled in those years), the city became a magnet for people, like Whitney, seeking employment and a target, as well, of satirical invective and serious social commentary.

Manley does not list Whitney among those who wrote complaints about London, and yet she did. As Ann Rosalind Jones argued early on, the "Wyll and Testament" is fundamentally concerned with oppositions of abundance and dearth, with retailing the riches of London and documenting the consequences of exclusion from the charmed circle of those who can partake of its abundance (Jones 157). It thus shares with the genre of Tudor complaint an underlying awareness of the forms of inequality, both new and old, that deform the social whole. The speaker herself, of course, has lived the irony of immersion in streets lined with shops full of things to eat and clothes to wear, while failing to attain or to retain a toehold in service that would bring her both board and apparel. Yet, positioned at a fault line in the city's rapidly changing economy, Whitney also benefits as well as suffers from it, since her writings can become a novelty in an expanding print market. The city thus offers her the immortality of print as well as the subject matter for her best poem. Poverty amid plenty is the underlying theme of the "Wyll and Testament," marked out most starkly in the contrast between the first 130 lines of verse, which are concerned primarily with the shops of London, where the bakers, butchers, fishmongers, tailors, apothecaries, and goldsmiths offer their wares, and the following 60 lines, in which the speaker searingly catalogs the prisons of London: the Counter, Newgate, the Fleet, Ludgate, and later Bridewell and Bedlam, workhouse and insane asylum. These are the places where London's castoffs are sent, those who are unable to pay for the things they need to live.

The juxtaposition of these two sections of the poem—commercial London and carceral London—implies, without direct statement, that there is something fundamentally wrong with the economic hydraulics of the city. Some people are rising, buying more and more linens and plate and purgatives, while others are sinking deeper and deeper into the stinking corners of Newgate Prison. As I have said before, the sturdy thump of Whitney's verse and the underlying gaiety of tone prevent the poem from being either maudlin or histrionic. Whitney's own plight is folded quietly into the plight of many others. She, too, has either been in Ludgate or contemplated going there to escape her creditors. But her sprightly tone is also, I would argue, a calculated tactic for unmasking what could only seem reasonable to those who do not have to worry about being lodged in Ludgate. For example, toward the end of the section on the city's shops, Whitney says that if the people of London to whom she is bequeathing its riches realize that the shopkeepers actually ask them for money they can find all the money they need at the Mint: "At Mint, there is such store, it is / unpossible to tell it" (161–62). Of course, the money in the Mint is not just there for the taking, but Whitney's calculatedly naive assumption that it should be unsettles fixed notions of property and ownership. On a larger scale, by bequeathing all the things of London to London, that is, to its inhabitants, Whitney is counterfactually trying to refigure the logic of the capitalist marketplace and make acquisition, especially of food and clothing, her first two preoccupations, a matter of course rather than a tortured process of monetary exchange. At other points, she explicitly fantasizes actions that will equalize imbalances of abundance and dearth. For example, she imagines bequeathing rich widowers to poor maidens and rich widows to poor young gentlemen so as not to let the wealthy's "Bags too long be full, / for feare that they doo burst" (ll.261–62). Such redistribution, Whitney cheekily implies, does the rich a favor, for otherwise their plate and jewels would go rusty from disuse and their moneybags burst from excess.

Part of the public persona Whitney establishes for herself in this poem, then, is as an implicit participant in the urban complaint genre, typically written by men, a form of writing anatomizing the ills of the city and suggesting an alternative. Unlike most complaint writers, Whitney does not posit a golden age of past perfection (usually imagined as preexisting the heating up of the commercial market with its corrosive social consequences); instead, she gestures toward a regime of redistribution in which urban plenty is more equitably spread across the social spectrum and where use, not display, determines the social function of urban goods. Whitney does not seem at all adverse to the multiplication of things in the marketplace. In fact, she seems to regard the well-stocked shops of London as one of the city's most attractive features. Material well-being is thus not bad in itself; in fact, it appears very attractive. What Whitney critiques are the searing inequities of access to these material goods such that the basic needs of many go unfulfilled.

This is a poem, then, in which Whitney makes full and creative use of the position she probably half chose and half had thrust upon her: that of a London maidservant who, perhaps quite unexpectedly, turned writer. From these circumstances, she created a highly innovative and accomplished poem, a work that anatomizes the city from a perspective that could not be shared by the likes of John Stow: the position of a literate serving woman who could take a special delight in the material and intellectual pleasures of urban life while sharply delineating its devastating inequalities. The poem is also the endpoint of the implicit autobiography that Whitney created in *The Sweet Nosegay.* The collection is decisively bookended by poems underscoring the urban context in which the speaker lived and wrote. Both poems record the speaker's sickness and poverty; both record her fundamental "aloneness." Yet each also connects these states to the intense pleasures of reading and writing; and both can imagine an audience much broader than that of the domestic circle. In the first, she enjoins many to read her translations of Plat's "plot"; in the second, she sends readers to her bookseller's in Saint Paul's churchyard.

But between these two poems is an implicit record of the speaker's growth and her increasing confidence in iconoclastic choices. At first subordinating her voice to Plat's, and then in the epistles still toying with the possibility of domestic life, toward the end of the sequence she seems more purposefully to turn away from domestic pleasures and networks to embrace the perilous challenges of a life lived "sole alone" in London. While the city is a place of foul smells and sickness, poverty and incarceration, it is also where she finds deep and abiding pleasure through dwelling in the company of "Paper, Pen, and Standish." It is the place where Whitney finds an alternative to the typical trajectory from female servant to married housewife in the unstable position of urban writer. The final pages of *The Sweet Nosegay* present what may be necessity as choice: the speaker chooses to stay in London's smelly streets, to leave off the writing of epistles to her family, and to turn from the poetic translation of Plat to the creation of her own master-piece, her poem on London. We do not know what happened to the historical Isabella Whitney. Perhaps she left London eventually or made a marriage. On that point, there is silence. But the life in verse she has left us imagines another end, a death in London after the mak-ing of a will that expresses the poet's "will," her desire to live "sole alone" and have only her writing instruments about her as witnesses to the productivity and dangers of that choice. And it is London, I have been arguing, that made such an imagined life possible.

NOTES

1. See, for a discussion of the difficult matter of terminology and the dan-gers of anachronism, the introduction to this volume. I am grateful to all the members of the "Theory and Practice of Early Modern Autobiography" sym-posium for their stimulating contributions to the evolving conversation about pre-Enlightenment forms of life writing.

2. In this regard, I take as exemplary the work of Conal Condren on the degree to which a sense of "office" and "duties," rather than authentic self-hood, shaped lives in the early modern period. See his essay in chapter 2 of this volume.

3. For an important study of the role of clothing in demarcating identity in the early modern period, see Ann Rosalind Jones and Peter Stallybrass (2000). They argue strongly against the notion that identity in this culture was understood as either inwardness or individuality; rather, it was a matter of social inscription, often on the surface of the body.

4. For copy text of the "Wyll and Testament," I use the edition prepared by Betty Travitsky and printed in *English Literary Renaissance* (1980). For the rest of Whitney's poetry, I consult *The Early Modern Englishwoman: A Fac-simile Library of Essential Works* (edited by Travitsky and Cullen), but for *The Sweet Nosegay* I cite the modernized edition of that volume prepared by the students of Sarah Jayne Steen (1995).

5. See Betty Travitsky's entry on Whitney in the *New Oxford Dictionary of National Biography* (746).

6. Elizabeth Heale has convincingly argued that this short collection also draws on the language of George Turbervile's *Epitaphes, Epigrams, Songs, and Sonets* (36).

7. McGrath suggests that Richard Jones may have had a hand in organizing the structure of this volume so that it would appear as part of the formal debate about women's worth (*Subjectivity* 128).

8. The degree of conscious one-upmanship in Whitney's "translation" of Plat is an open question. Seeming to defer to his authority, she nonetheless casts his prose as poetry and imposes an order and selective process on his work that constitute a substantial transformation of the original. I find it significant, however, that she begins her collection with this act of supposed translation before moving to more obviously original works.

9. I am grateful to the work of two of my former graduate students, Fiona McNeill and Michelle Dowd, who in their dissertations have shown the gap between the idealized life narratives of early modern women, particularly those at the bottom of the social scale, and the actualities of their frequently makeshift and troubled existences.

10. I therefore disagree with Lynette McGrath's emphasis in her very fine reading of the poem on Whitney's posture of abjection (*Subjectivity* 153–63). Although the speaker clearly records her destitution, the poem rather stringently eschews self-pity and seems aimed as much at celebration of a reimagined city as at personal lament.

WORKS CITED

Beilin, Elaine V. "Writing Public Poetry: Humanism and the Woman Writer." *Modern Language Quarterly* 51 (1990): 249–71.

Brace, Patricia. "Teaching Class: Whitney's 'Wyll and Testament' and Nashe's 'Litany in Time of Plague.'" *Teaching Tudor and Stuart Women Writers*. Ed. Susanne Woods and Margaret Hannay. New York: Modern Language Association, 2000. 279–82.

Ebner, Dean. *Autobiography in Seventeenth-Century England*. The Hague: Mouton, 1971.

Erickson, Amy. *Women and Property in Early Modern England*. London: Routledge, 1993.

Foster, Gwendolyn Audrey. *Troping the Body: Gender, Etiquette, and Performance*. Carbondale: Southern Illinois UP, 2000.

Heale, Elizabeth. *Autobiography and Authorship in Renaissance Verse*. Houndmills, Basingstoke: Palgrave Macmillan, 2003.

Helgerson, Richard. *Forms of Nationhood: The Elizabethan Writing of England*. Chicago: U of Chicago P, 1992.

Hutson, Lorna. *The Usurer's Daughter: Male Friendship and Fictions of Woman in Sixteenth-Century England*. London: Routledge, 1994.

Jones, Ann Rosalind. "Apostrophes to Cities: Urban Rhetorics in Isabella Whitney and Moderata Fonte." *Attending to Early Modern Women*. Ed. Susan D. Amussen and Adele Seeff. Newark: U of Delaware P, 1998. 155–75.

Jones, Ann Rosalind, and Peter Stallybrass. *Renaissance Clothing and the Materials of Memory.* Cambridge: Cambridge UP, 2000.

Manley, Lawrence. *Literature and Culture in Early Modern England.* Cambridge: Cambridge UP, 1995.

McGrath, Lynette. "Isabella Whitney and the Ideologies of Writing and Publication." *Teaching Tudor and Stuart Women Writers.* Ed. Susanne Woods and Margaret Hannay. New York: Modern Language Association, 2000. 283–88.

————. *Subjectivity and Women's Poetry in Early Modern England.* Aldershot: Ashgate, 2002.

New Oxford Dictionary of National Biography. Oxford: Oxford UP, 2004.

Phillippy, Patricia. "The Maid's Lawful Liberty: Service, the Household, and 'Mother B' in Isabella Whitney's *A Sweet Nosegay.*" *Modern Philology* 95 (1998): 439–62.

Steen, Sara Jayne. *A Sweet Nosegay.* Edition prepared by students in her senior seminar at Montana State University at Bozeman. 1995. <http://www.montana.edu/wwwwhitn/whitney.html> (accessed 16 December 2003).

Travitsky, Betty S. "The 'Wyll and Testament' of Isabella Whitney." *English Literary Renaissance* 10 (1980): 76–95.

Travitsky, Betty S., and Patrick Cullen. *The Early Modern Englishwoman: A Facsimile Library of Essential Works.* Ser. 1, vol. 10. Aldershot: Ashgate, 2001.

Wall, Wendy. "Isabella Whitney and the Female Legacy." *English Literary History* 58 (1991): 35–62.

Chapter 13

Accounting for a Life
The Household Accounts of Lady Anne Clifford

Nancy E. Wright

The autobiographical writings of Anne, Lady Clifford, Countess of
Dorset, Pembroke, and Montgomery, are a substantial corpus that
includes her diaries, personal letters, and family chronicles, the three-
volume *Great Books of Record* (Lewalski 125–51). Studies of the autobiographical writings usually focus on their representation of the period
of her life when she and her mother "waged law" in an unsuccessful
effort to assert her status as heir general, according to common law
rules of succession, and thereby succeed to her father's estate rather
than the collateral male relatives to whom he transferred it in his will.
This essay, in contrast, focuses on Anne's later life, particularly the
period of her widowhood (ca. 1650–76) after the death of her second
husband, when, as one of England's great landowners, she engaged in
textual practices associated with the management of vast estates. Her
substantial books of household accounts are examples of a genre commonly produced by clerks of great households in the medieval and
early modern period (Mertes, 194–215; *Household Accounts from
Medieval England* 2.691–726). Like many other aristocratic widows,
such as Mary, duchess of Richmond (Harris 145), Anne did not merely
rely on clerks to write household accounts but in addition reviewed,
annotated, and signed them herself. These books were documents
intended accurately to record revenues, expenditures, and disbursements. They served the purpose of enabling heads of aristocratic
households to survey the management of their households, estates,
and finances.

In the case of Anne, however, these books are also autobiographical accounts that provide an important opportunity to evaluate the textual representation of her life as a woman of property. As I will explain, a series of her account books titled *The Expenses of My House* and *The Expenses of My Private Purse*, in particular, modulate the genre of household accounts with the genre of the diary because both the clerk's entries as well as Anne's marginalia use first-person pronouns, identified with her voice and her role as the head of a great aristocratic household. Consequently, it is not surprising that her books of household accounts, along with her will, circulated posthumously as part of an archive of muniments that she bequeathed to her heirs. The muniments—that is, documents about her family and family properties— were initially collected in order to wage her legal battle to succeed to her father's estate. That archive of deeds, court rolls, and so forth was maintained and augmented by her, after she succeeded to the family property, with the assistance of antiquarian scholars and clerks, whom she employed in order to secure her property and record her family's history. Both the production and circulation of her will and household accounts represent her life as a woman of property.

The dichotomy of being a subject or object of property—as used by political theorists such as Donna Dickenson and Carole Pateman— provides a means to map women's property relationships.[1] Because a married woman, according to the early modern English common law doctrine of coverture, transferred absolute ownership of her personal property and the use rights of her real property or land to her husband, it is customary to describe a married woman as an "object of property." The term *object of property* means that she lacks not only legal agency but also political subjectivity bestowed in the period by property ownership. The majority of "singlewomen," a category that included both widows and women who never married, could own property but rarely owned the substantial property necessary in early modern England to gain the franchise and thereby wield political agency.[2]

Anne, Lady Clifford, dowager Countess of Dorset, Pembroke, and Montgomery, however, was an exception to these generalizations. As a widow, she was a substantial property owner, who commanded both political and legal agency. She nominated the burgesses of Appleby, who were the political representatives for her locality. Because she was sheriff of her barony, manorial courts were held in her name and provided a venue in which she could wage law against her tenants and others in order to enforce and augment her seignorial rights to land.

Evidence of her agency appears in her autobiographical writings in her diaries and household accounts. For example, on 29 December 1651, she records in her *Kendal Diary* (1650–75) that she signed and sealed "a Pattent to Mr Thomas Gabetis to be my Deputy Sheriff for ye county of Westmerland for the execution of which Office he had ye Counsell of States order for his approbacon bearing date 21st November before" (113). This statement records her success in having her nomination of Gabetis, a trusted servant and tenant, confirmed by the Council of State.[3] As a great landlord, Anne commanded the loyalty and service of men such as Gabetis because of her ability to lease to him valuable land within her Skipton estate and to pay him a substantial salary. In April 1675, her clerk records in *The Expenses of My House* that she "Payed then to mr Thomas Gabetis my Sheriffe as hee is my Auditr: his halfe years wages due to him as aforesaid Tenn Pounds" (13).[4] This kind of statement suggests that her household accounts not only represented but also contributed to her agency as a "subject of property," that is, her textual practice of household accounting enabled her to maintain her property and assert her own and her family's status. The instrumentality of her textual practice directs attention to the following kinds of questions. How do these practices and texts account for her life? What kind of life writing do they represent? How do they relate to other genres, such as wills that women of middling and elite status in early modern England wrote as "subjects" rather than "objects" of property?

The early modern household is customarily the subject of studies focusing on the material practices and traces of a life (Mertes; Friedman; Woolgar). The etymology of *hold*, as described by Natasha Korda, reveals ideas associated with both the household and the gendered role of the "housewife" in early modern England: "The proliferation of status objects," Korda explains, "lent increasing importance to the household's function as a 'hold,' a place where goods of value were held, kept safe, watched over, and maintained. The term 'hold' derives from the Gothic *haldan*, which carries the senses of 'to watch over, guard, defend; to keep possession of, contain.' This constellation of terms precisely defined the housewife's managerial function in a nascent consumer society: to watch over, or vigilantly *behold*, her household stuff" (87). In the case of Anne, Lady Clifford, dowager Countess of Dorset, Pembroke, and Montgomery, her status as a property owner involved textual practices that enabled her to "oversee" her complex household and its relationship to her jointure properties in

Sussex and Kent, which were far removed from her large estates in Craven and Westmorland, where she lived alternately.[5]

Most conduct books, which provided advice on household management, are addressed to women of middling and elite status, who are told how to supervise and visually survey aspects of their household (e.g., maintaining linens, preserving foods, and supervising servants).[6] As an aristocratic property owner, Anne's surveillance of her estates and buildings, as well as the household within which she resided, was mediated by staff persons responsible for fulfilling specific functions according to the household orders established by her. Yet her textual practice of supervising and annotating her household accounts bears a similarity to the conduct described in household advice books. For example, she records carefully the purchase of fruit and sugar for preserves, tobacco, and new linens, as well as "my Payment of wages for my Servants for this Year" (*Expenses of My House* 1). She used books of household accounting to maintain surveillance over all her properties (in this case, lands as well as personal property such as consumer goods) and to supervise the activities of members of her household.

Clifford's method of household accounting, as Richard T. Spence has explained, involved a series of texts produced by her clerks, including her annual *Book of Receipts, Book of Disbursement,* and *Book of Weekly Household Expenditure.* In them, she had her clerks record the net income, derived from her estates in Westmorland, Craven, Kent, and Sussex, that she received from her estate managers three or four times a year. Upon its receipt, she checked the money, recorded in her annual *Book of Receipts* from which estate it came, and placed it in a marked bag in a strongbox in her chamber (Spence 209). The annual *Books of Receipts* name four sources: Westmorland, Craven, Returned Moneys, and Borrowed Moneys. She recorded in the *Books of Disbursements* how she (through her officers) spent the cash. Her system was carefully cross-referenced, and she marked the *Books of Disbursement* with marginal notes in her hand stating where each sum of money originated. Her practice of accounting for the receipt of money and her expenditures may be described as "idiosyncratic"; it does, however, bear similarity to the accounting systems of other great households: "Although merchants at this time adopted new, Italian-style methods of accounting, Anne's bailiffs and receivers followed the older 'charge' and 'discharge' system. By this, an officer 'charged' himself with the receipt of moneys and 'discharged' himself of that spent or passed on to other officers or Anne herself" (Spence 211).[7] She kept two other kinds of accounts, which were audited in a similar manner. Allan Strickland, the clerk of the kitchen, kept *Books of Weekly Household Expenditure*, in which he recorded daily and weekly expenses for food and drink consumed in the household. His entries and those in the *Books of Disbursements* were duplicated in a separate series of accounts, books of household expenses that were her personal record of all payments. Her copy of the household accounts comprises books that record the expenses for one calendar year. Each book begins with *The Expenses of My House* and at the reverse includes *The Expenses of my Private Purse*, including her lawsuits. Each book included her servants' wages and board, as well as money disbursed by her servants, such as the clerk of the kitchen. In *The Expenses of My Private Purse*, her clerk recorded payments, such as gifts and alms as well as food, signed by the recipients and marked with annotations in Anne's own hand. From her personal copy of the accounts, "Anne could quickly tell the amounts which had been disbursed and for what purposes. . . . Both the individual entries and the summaries at the close of the accounts allowed cross-checking" with the *Books of Receipts, Books of Disbursements*, and *Books of Weekly Household Expenditure* (Spence 211). In addition, these books functioned as a means for her to maintain rigorous surveillance over her household and all her properties—a textual practice that parallels the physical conduct that housewives of middling status were advised to practice in order to manage their households.

As a widow, Anne, Lady Clifford, dowager Countess of Dorset, Pembroke, and Montgomery, kept accounts in order to manage not only the extensive real and personal property that she inherited from her father but also her jointure properties. The latter were properties, including land and the buildings on them, settled on Anne for the duration of her widowhood, as part of her marriage settlements or by means of a subsequent agreement with her two husbands. She held only a life interest in the use rights to these properties; after her death, they were transferred to her husbands' heirs. Consequently, she did not own and could not sell the jointure properties, but she was able to reside on them and to gain an income from the rents accrued by leasing them to tenants. She managed the jointure properties carefully in order to profit from their rents during her own lifetime and so that her husbands' heirs could benefit from them after her death. She chose the tenants of these properties, invested in the maintenance of the tenements and other fixtures, such as walls and gates, and determined the rents during her long widowhood. Her *Books of Receipts* record the expenditures and profits necessary for her to manage her jointure properties in Sussex and Kent.[8] Her personal copy of the household accounts contains records of how she supervised the accounting and collection of jointure rents, which were due twice a year. In the *Expenses of My Private Purse*, she entered marginal notes acknowledging the role of Thomas Gabetis, "my Shreeve," who was responsible for auditing the jointure rents returned to her by employees in Sussex. A marginal note glosses the entry for May 1675, recording that she "Payed the :21st: day to Mr Thomas Gabetis my Sheriffe and Auditr: when hee now examined mr Edges and mr Lanes accompts for Sussex for halfe a year ending at our lady day in 1674. . . ." The responsibilities delegated to employees such as Gabetis, however, were in turn supervised by Anne, whose accounts specify that on this and other occasions her jointure rents were only accepted when she had examined them, after which she recorded, "I gave my allowance too by signing them both with my hand" (*Private Purse* 19). This assertion of agency, particularly the assertion of her own signature to authorize household accounts, attests to her vigilance in performing her role as a woman of property.

According to Barbara J. Harris, from 1450 to 1550, "the majority of aristocratic widows managed their jointures and the land they held on behalf of their husbands. . . . As estate managers, the widows concentrated on maximising and collecting their rents; finding tenants for vacant tenements . . . and keeping their property in good repair. Although, like men of their class aristocratic widows hired dozens of estate officials to assist them, most of them directed their employees personally" (145). Anne, like the aristocratic widows discussed by Harris, depended on estate officials to maintain her accounts but nevertheless diligently checked these records for errors and money owed (146). Unlike the stereotype of "a step-dame or a dowager / Long withering out a young man's revenues" (*A Midsummer Night's Dream* 1.1.5–6), Anne maintained and protected the integrity of her jointure properties during the fifty-two years that she survived after the death of her first husband, Richard Sackville, Earl of Dorset, and the twenty-five years that she survived after the death of her second husband, Philip Herbert, Earl of Pembroke and Montgomery. In this manner, her household accounts confirm Harris's conclusion that "overall, long widowhoods were a benefit, not a danger, to their husbands' patrilineages." Anne typifies aristocratic widows who "contributed to the survival and continued prosperity of their families and, collectively, of their class" (Harris 151–52).

Anne's textual practice of keeping accounts is similar to that of her father and other men who were great landowners. However, the first-person pronouns used in entries by her clerk and in her own annotations in her personal copies of her household accounts—*The Expenses of My House* and *The Expenses of My Private Purse*—differ from most other extant household records that men, as heads of great households, marked with marginal annotations and signed. The *Disbursement Book* for Robert Dudley, earl of Leicester, for example, contains entries for 12 September 1585 recording the alms distributed on his behalf: "Geyvin in reward to a poore woman the same day by your lordship's commandment . . . Geyvin in reward to a poore woman for presenting a Holand chese to your lordship at Nonsuch the same daye" (*Household Accounts and Disbursement Books* 309). In contrast to the entries made by one of the earl's clerks, who refers to Robert Dudley, earl of Leicester, in the second person, the records written by Anne's clerk in 1675 in her copy of the household accounts use the first person to refer to her disbursements; for example, her copy of *The Expenses of My House* records the payment of twenty shillings on "the: 25th day to mr Christopher Harison our Parson of Brough for saying the common prayers upon Sundayes and Wednesdayes to mee and my ffamilie in the next chamber to mine at this Brough Castle for a month last past ending yesterday" (2). The entry is annotated in her own writing in a marginal note that states "payed the parson Christo: Harison for saying of Comone prayers to mee and my Family for months last past" (2). Both the entries written in the clerk's hand and in her own record Anne's use of money to pay servants acting on her own and her family's behalf. This style of expression is characteristic of the account of her life that she dictated to her scribes in her final months; in February 1676, while at Brougham Castle, one of her scribes records: "And then Mr Grasty said Common Prayres and read a Chapter (as usuall upon Wednesdayes and Sundayes) to mee and them and my family" (*Diaries* 249).

Her personal copy of the household accounts has more than simply a documentary value for recording information about the daily lives of Anne and her family. Reading these texts provides insight into her understanding of herself as a woman of property, particularly her role in relation to her family and her household servants. The administration of the sacrament to Anne and her family was an occasion marked not only by religious observance but also by gifts and mementos to household servants. Anne pays £2 18s. 2d. for "30 bookes of devotion of severall sorts and different rates which I intend to give away to my servants against my receiving the blessed Sacrament" (*Private Purse*

22). This entry in her household accounts reveals how Anne represented her life as head of an aristocratic household to others, both her family and household staff. Other occasions recorded in her household accounts indicate that Anne organized ceremonies that enabled her to "perform" herself as a woman of property by confirming her identity as baroness and landlord to those residing on her lands. When she removed from one property to another, she disbursed money as wages, gratuities, and alms to those who attended. In May 1675, her accounts record the payment on "the :12th: day what was given and disburst at my removall yesterday from Brough Castle to this Appleby viz: to the poor at Brough : 6s: to the ringers there : 5d: to the poor by the way : 3s: 10d: and to the ringers by the way : 2s: 6d: to the poor at Appleby : 5d : to the ringers : 5d : to the piper 2s 6d: and to the prison there : 2s 6d. In all One Pound Twelve Shillings and ffour pence" (*Private Purse* 16). Anne annotates this passage with the terse comment, "payed for my Removen the 12th day of the month from Brough Ca[stel] into Appleby Castel" (*Private Purse* 16). These entries in her accounts indicate how processions marking her removal from one residence to another were occasions on which she represented and reinforced to residents of the area, including local gentry and her tenants, her status as a woman of property.

The modulation of the genres of the household account and diary is most evident in entries that refer to the commemoration of events in Anne's life, such as her final parting from her mother. In her *Knole Diary* during April 1616 she briefly noted the departure of her mother: "Upon the 2nd I went after my Folks in my lady's Coach, she bringing me a Quarter of a mile in the Way, where she & I had a grevious & heavy Parting. Most part of the way I rid behind mr Hodgson" (31). This was the last time that Anne saw her mother, an event that she commemorated thirty-eight years later by building a monument, known as the Countess's Pillar, on the location where they said farewell. Her household accounts, rather than her diary, record the construction of the pillar in 1654. The significance of the pillar in her accounts, however, is not simply recorded as an expense incurred in 1654, the year it was constructed, but instead as an annual ceremony of commemoration. An entry in her accounts for 2 April 1675, for example, records that four pounds were "Distributed the: 2d: day by mr Samuell Grasty the Parson of Brougham by my order mr Hassell, John Webster, Allan Strickland Rich: Lowis and Cuthbert Rowling (mr Hasells man) being by at the Pillar which I caused to bee erected near Brougham Castle in memory of my blessed mother's and my last parting the second of April as usuall to the poor people of the Parish there" (*Private Purse* 16). Similar entries recurring in her accounts for 2 April from 1655 to 1675 record the fulfilment of a pledge inscribed on the monument itself that announces the annual distribution of four pounds to the poor of Brougham parish at the pillar. The construction of the pillar, as Mihoko Suzuki suggests, typifies how Anne positions women as historical "subjects" using monuments as well as family chronicles to "gender history" (Suzuki). In addition, I suggest, references to the pillar in Anne's household accounts reveal that, as a woman of property, she represented the continuity of her roles as daughter, heiress, and landowner. Indeed, the household accounts for 1675 indicate her bonds of identity with both of her parents by recording her payments "for new binding an old bible that was my Mother's Margaret Countesse of Cumberland's" (*Private Purse* 20) and "for writing over a coppy of the book of my ffathers George Earle of Cumberland's Sea voyages" (*Private Purse* 13). Her detailed, annotated personal copy of household accounts for the year 1675, in fact, seems less a supplement to the few pages of retrospective autobiography in the *Kendal Diary* for that year than the primary written account of her life.[9]

Clifford's personal copy of the household accounts bears a great similarity to her *Knole Diary* (1603–1619); both use the past tense to record recent events in her life, both are annotated with her marginalia, and both refer to her as the primary intended reader. While the former represents the life of a young married woman dissociated from property rights, the latter represents the life of a woman of property, for whom the "business" of financial management and litigation is part of daily, household, and familial life. In her household accounts, she specifies the amounts paid to employees, such as George Goodgion, "for his charges yesterday to Appleby about my businesse" (*Private Purse* 1675, 14). The careful management of her estates, and particularly her finances, in her household accounts is striking to anyone who remembers her contemptuous attitude toward men who presumed to "manage" her financial affairs when she was a young married woman. She used the terms *business* and *businesses* pejoratively in her *Knole Diary* to describe her male relatives' negotiation of an award for her in lieu of succession to her father's property (31–37). As a widow and great landowner, she pursued business ventures and litigation so that she and her family would "profit" from her property rights. We need to understand, however, that the term *profit* in this usage does not mean simply benefiting financially but also socially by accruing the agency that arose from their status as property owners.

Whereas it is customary to valorize the determined conduct of the young Lady Anne Clifford, who struggled to assert a common law right of succession, it is more difficult to condone the litigious conduct of the Anne, Lady Clifford, dowager Countess of Dorset, Pembroke, and Montgomery. Spence's analysis of her protracted litigation with relatives, the earl and countess of Cork, for example, indicates the lengths to which she would go in order to improve her finances as well as her lands. Her household accounts and letters to legal counsel and estate managers show that to accrue profit she waged law against the Corks in order to assert seignorial rights to land for which she had no viable claim (Spence 114–15, 122–24). Her litigation to defend an economic project—a corn mill that she had built in 1653 in Silsden, a township within her Craven estates—provides another important example of how she used the law not only to secure but also to extend and enhance her existing property rights (see *Kendal Diary* 120). Because her tenants could be compelled by their leases to grind their crops at her mill, the project was both profitable and symbolic of the seignorial rights of a landowner. Her tenants, however, had previously used an existing mill owned by Hugh Currer, who held a monopoly for Silsden recognized by courts in 1641 and 1642. The construction of a new mill led to a series of lawsuits that had the greatest financial impact on her tenants in Silsden, against whom Currer brought litigation in the Exchequer Court in 1654 for taking their crops to her mill. Clifford provided funds for their defense, but in 1655 the court found for Currer and affirmed his monopoly. She initiated on her own behalf a series of countersuits in 1655, all of which she had lost by 1660. Clifford continued, however, to pursue the matter at law up to 1667.[10] Tenants in Silsden petitioned the Exchequer Court in 1663 to secure a final judgment in the matter because their livelihood and the economy of the town had been so adversely affected.[11] Indeed, they were repeatedly prosecuted at law either by her or Currer; the welfare of the lesser tenants of Silsden was jeopardized by her protracted litigation. In 1668, an Exchequer decree required her to pay £95 5s. 4d. to Currer, which represented the costs of his last suit against her.[12]

What is the significance of Clifford's use of litigation to enforce her agency as a woman of property? Her conduct of litigation at her own and her tenants' expense seems an obvious instance of inefficient management of financial affairs. There are, however, other implications of her use of the law that merit attention. The economic project of establishing a corn mill on the manorial property identifies her with the culture of agricultural improvement that flourished in seventeenth-century England. As Andrew McRae has explained, the word *improvement* in the early modern period drew "together legal, moral, and economic implications in order to justify radical processes of change in the English countryside" (35). From the sixteenth century on, the word *improvement* came to conflate ideas of "qualitative changes in land-use with increases in the financial returns of the landlord" (McRae 37). Husbandry manuals, such as Fitzherbert's *Boke of Husbandrye* (1523), discussed methods of land use and management to make agriculture more productive, with the assumption that "agrarian 'improvement' is bound to an essentially conservative model of 'good ordre,' focused around—and directed by—the manorial lord" (McRae 38). Although, as Laura Brace has explained, "improvement" was not an uncontested concept in seventeenth-century England, agrarian manuals provide insight into the ideas informing the economic projects and litigation pursued by Anne Clifford. Ideas about her role as a manorial landlord responsible for improving the productivity and profitability of her estates guided her determined efforts to establish a corn mill in Silsden. Her attitude toward her tenants, who served as pawns in her litigation with Hugh Currer, was also typical of the discourse of improvement. Seventeenth-century agrarian manuals, Brace explains, argued that the labor of tenants and the poor should be channeled into the projects of improvers in order to implement capital projects managed by improving landlords, whose efforts would contribute to the commonweal ("Husbanding" 13).[13] Like her economic project, Anne's use of litigation to accrue revenue seems clearly related to ideas of financial profit and a commodified understanding of real property. It cannot, however, be simply equated with them. Instead her manner of using the law to exercise agency as a property owner is informed by alternative concepts, including her duty of office as a baroness who used seignorial rights to order and protect her family's lands. In seventeenth-century England the social status of a landowner was understood as an "office," which, as Conal Condren has explained, did not imply the idea of individual liberty but instead the idea of duties and obligations requiring rights in order to fulfil the responsibilities of one's office (466–67). Her responsibilities as a landlord were to be exercised on behalf of her family, not only her own children but also those of subsequent generations, for whom she held and managed the property as a trust. Her office as a landowner was to manage, preserve, and improve landed property, of which she, like her contemporaries, had a complex understanding: it was the basis of the family's identity as members of the aristocracy, an elite social status based on a land-family bond (Bonfield); it was a source of income to maintain both the land itself and the buildings and family that resided on it; and it was a valuable commodity.

Clifford's will, which divided her real and personal property like her household accounts, effects the ends to be secured by the conduct and duties prescribed by marriage sermons and conduct books for women of middling and elite households, specifically their duty to safeguard their household goods. Anne in her will divides among her heirs, her only living daughter and grandchildren, her extensive estates, buildings, and muniments (i.e., records and deeds pertaining to those properties). In her will, she specifies her intention to distribute household goods and personal belongings with the estates in which they had been housed: "unto such issue of my said two daughters as shall inheritt my castles, etcs., in Westmorland, all my goods, household stuffe, and books which shall be remaineing in my castles of Appleby, Brougham, Brough, and Pendragon, willing and desireing my daughter, the Countesse of Thanett, that the goods (though they be of small vallue) may not bee removed out of my said castles, but may still remaine as heire-loomes, for the good of my posterity" (Clay 407). The "books" to which she referred included an archive of muniments that, after her death, came to include copies of her diaries, will, and household accounts. Although she specifies that her "wearing appareell and linnens" are to be distributed among her serving ladies, she excepts her "household linnen, which I give to my daughter, the Countesse of Thanett" (410). In addition, the will specifies her desire that, as was customary, her "household and family may bee kept together as it was in my life time for the space of one moneth after my death" (410).

The will extends Clifford's textual practice of household accounting by specifying how outstanding debts should be paid to her daughter, the executrix of her will, "for the better enabling her to pay all legacies, and whatsoever surplusage to remain to my daughter" (Clay 411). Her will specifies that these include: "all rents and arrears of rents out of my joynture lands in Sussex and in the Isle of Sheppey or elsewhere; and two thousand pounds in the hands of Sr Robert Vyner, knight, and alderman of London, for which I have two bonds; and three thousand pounds in the hands of my daughter, for which I have her bond; and two hundred pounds owing by my grandson, Mr. John Tufton; and one thousand four hundred pounds in the hands of Mrs Covell, widdow to Mr. Covell, late cittizen and goldsmith of London, per two bonds" (Clay 411). The will concludes with a "cheque roll of my household servants," indicating money to be given to each. This list is similar to those recurring in her household accounts whenever Clifford removed from one property to another; on her removal from Brougham to Appleby in May 1675, for example, *The Expenses of My Private Purse* lists gifts of money that range from four pounds to ten shillings given, "as I usually doe when I remove," to each of the servants (16).

The will is similar to her mother's, which is, however, less extensive. Anne's will is more detailed than her father's, which focuses on the transmission of his estate to collateral male heirs and his daughter's portion (Clay 387–96). In her will, Anne modulates that genre by using it as a means of reiterating her genealogy, as she does in her diaries (Lamb 354–56), in order to consecrate her claim to her inheritance of real property. The will begins, according to convention, with pious sentiments.

> [A]s for my bodie, I desire that it may be buried decently, and with as little charge as may be, being sensible of the folly and vanity of superfluous pompes and solemnityes; and I desire that my bodie may be unopened, wrapt onely in seare cloath and leade, with an inscription on the breast whose body it is, and soe to bee interred in the vault in Appleby Church, in Westmorland, which I caused to bee made there, with a tombe over it, for my self; in which Church of Appleby my deare and blessed mother, Margarett Russell, Countesse of Cumberland, lyes alsoe interred, by whose prudence, goodnesse, and industrie the right and inheritance to the lands both in Westmorland and in Craven was discovered to the courts of judicature in this nation to appertaine unto mee as right and lawfull heire to my noble father, George, Earle of Cumberland, and other noble progenitors, the Veteriponts, Cliffords, and Veseyes, wch otherwise had been posest by others who had no right thereunto . . .
> (Clay 401)

Although this passage accurately describes her family lineage, it inaccurately represents the circumstances of her "inheritance" of her father's estate. The courts, in fact, had not recognized her common law right of succession as heir general but instead the right of her father, according to the 1540 Statute of Wills, to transfer his property to his brother by will. She only succeeded to the property when her cousin, the fifth earl, died without a male heir. Contrary to the conventions of wills, which usually include assertions not only of piety but also of truth telling, Anne's will tacitly eschews factual accuracy in order to represent and assert the rightfulness of her office of heiress. In a similar manner, her will invokes her genealogy when stating that her granddaughter, Lady Aletheia, should have properties "though they be now and have been for some yeares last past in the tenure of the Earle and Countesse of Burlington and Corke, yet undoubtedly and of right due belong and appertaine unto mee as parte of the lands and possessions of my noble father, George, Earle of Cumberland, deceased, and which castle and honnor of Skipton and Tower of Barden, forests, chaces, etc., were granted by King Edward the Second, King of England, unto Robert, Lord Clifford, my ancestor (to whom I am lineall heire), in the firth yeare of the said King's reigne" (Clay 405). In addition, her will bequeaths properties to which her claim was contested as if to extend and determine litigation. According to the will, her granddaughter was to inherit, among other substantial landholdings, "those that are still depending in controversy betweene mee and my cozen, the Countesse of Burlington and Corke, and her husband, wherof the right undoubtedly belongs to mee" (Clay 405). Although protracted litigation, recorded in her household accounts and diaries, had failed to prove her "rights" to these properties, Anne attempts both to assert and validate them in her will, a kind of text associated with legal agency, particularly the ability to effect the transfer of property between generations.

In her *Kendal Diary*, written from 1650 to 1675, while living on her family estates, Anne reflected on the experience of being a property owner. In 1651, while the effects of the Civil War disrupted the countryside near Appleby Castle, where she lived, she wrote:

> And in this settled aboad of mine in theis three ancient Houses of mine Inheritance, Apleby Castle and Brougham Castle in Westmerland, and Skipton castle or House of Craven, I doe more and more fall in love with the contentments and innocent pleasures of a Country Life. Which humour of mine I do [wish] with all my heart (if it bee the Will of Almightie God) may be conferred on my Posteritie that are to succeed mee in these places, for a Wife and Lady oneself, to make their owne houses the place of Selfe fruition and bee comfortably parte of this Life. (112)

The concept of being a "subject of property," I suggest, is well described by her wish for her daughters to make "their owne houses the place of Selfe fruition." *Fruition*, deriving from Old French, in the seventeenth century meant "pleasurable possession" or "the pleasure or enjoyment of possession" (*Oxford English Dictionary*). Anne's compound term *selfe Fruition* suggests ideas of self-ownership or self-possession bestowed on a woman by property ownership. The concept of self-ownership—of property in the person—is well explained in a later seventeenth-century text, John Locke's *An Essay concerning Human Understanding*. Indeed, Anne exercises her role as a woman of property in a manner that anticipates Locke's concept of "property in the person," which, as Jeremy Waldron explains, concerns "property in the *moral* person, in one's self, one's power of agency" (177). The term *person* in Locke's usage is to be understood, James Tully argues, as "a technical term" or, in Locke's own words as a "Forensick Term appropriating actions and their merit" (*Essay* 2.27.16). It implies concepts of agency and propriety. Locke defines his understanding of "property" not simply with the legal categories of real property or land and chattels or personal property but instead with the phrase "lives, liberties and estates" (*Second Treatise* 173). I would emphasize that his complex understanding of the relationship of "persons" not only to their own "lives, liberties and estates" but also to those of their children is of significance when evaluating Anne's textual practices of household accounting and producing a will. Locke evokes a complex relationship of persons (or parents) to property when he discusses a parent's management of his or her children's property during their minority. Locke explains, "By property I must be understood here, as in other places, to mean that property which men have in their persons as well as goods" (*Second Treatise* 173). It is a particular duty to manage family property and preserve it for her children and their heirs that Anne relates to her own financial and textual practice of "selfe Fruition" during her widowhood.

Anne associates the experience of selfe Fruition with the role of both a property owner and a "wife," who orders and benefits her household and family. Many scholars emphasize the irony of the position of the wife of elite or middling status, who is assigned the role of caring for consumer goods within the household that comprise personal property that she does not own. This situation often leads to questions about whether married women do belong to the category of the person understood by Locke as a "Forensick Term appropriating actions and their merit." It is not a simple equation that I would want to make here: when she produces her household accounts and her will, Anne is a widow and a member of the elite class and, because of the extent of her landholdings, an exception even among the landed aristocracy. However, her varied genres of life writing make us aware that her conception of the role of the wife is similar to that of the housewife prescribed for women of middling status: it involves obligations and duties to account for the use and management of property undertaken on behalf of the welfare of her family and household. Reading her household accounts and her will provides a means to evaluate Charles Taylor's suggestion that in the early modern period self-identity is "oriented in moral space" (28), which he defines as "a space of concerns" for oneself and others (51). The ethical or moral dimensions of the "space" or settings in which Anne's writings position her inform the ways in which she exercises her agency as a woman of property. This role or office is meaningful only to the extent that she uses it on behalf of her family (comprised of past and future generations) and her household (comprised of her family, servants, and neighbors, particularly the poor)—two vast and complex settings that define her "self."

NOTES

1. This dichotomy often leads to sharp but imprecise differentiations between married women, who, according to the doctrine of coverture, could not own property, and single women, both never married and widows, who could. As Churches has explained, coverture did not apply uniformly to married women because property regimes varied across regions of England throughout the early modern period (165–80).

2. See Froide on the use of the compound term *singlewomen* to designate women who have never married as well as widows.

3. See Spence (117) on Gabetis's leasehold in Craven and his nomination by Anne, which is recorded in the *Calendar of State Papers, 1651–1652* (29).

4. Anne secured the loyalty of Thomas Gabetis and other servants by giving gifts and gratuities to them and members of their families. For example, in February 1675, she records in *The Expenses of my Private Purse* a payment of ten pounds to "mr William Norton who is lately married to mrs Margaret Gabetis daughter mr Thomas Gabetis my Sheriffe to buy him and his wife a peice of plate." This entry written by her clerk is annotated in her writing with the comment "Given to mr William Norton to buy him and his wife a peice of plate" (6).

5. Her "jointure" included land and buildings to which she held only a life's interest. Subsequently in this chapter, I discuss her jointure properties in greater detail. On jointures, see Staves (95–96, 126–30) and Spring (49–52).

6. Korda studies domestic manuals and marriage sermons, which described household duties and conduct appropriate to a wife (86–88).

7. See Woolgar (44, 85–86) and Mertes (76–120).

8. Spence lists her annual income from her jointure properties (83, 212).

9. Paul Salzman differentiates the *Knole Diary* and *Kendal Diary* by noting that the latter bears greater similarity to the *Great Books of Record* produced by Anne as family chronicles directed to readers other than herself.

10. PRO, Exchequer, Deposition, E134, 12 Chas II, Mich.27.

11. Yorkshire Archaeological Society, MS.1325, 46.

12. This cost is recorded in her *Books of Weekly Household Expenditure* KRO, JAC 495/7, 53 1668; see Spence 122.

13. In *The Idea of Property in Seventeenth-Century England,* Brace documents the fact that many writers contested the discourse of improvement. Improvement was not uniformly seen as a positive good to the social order of the commonweal by writers who criticized the pursuit of economic gain at the cost of customary relationships of the commons to the land and their customary use rights.

WORKS CITED

Bonfield, Lloyd. "Debate: The Land-Family Bond in England." *Past and Present* 146 (1995): 151–73.

Brace, Laura. "Husbanding the Earth and Hedging out the Poor." *Land and Freedom: Law, Property Rights, and the British Diaspora.* Ed. A. R. Buck, J. McLaren, and Nancy E. Wright. Aldershot: Ashgate/Dartmouth, 2001. 5–18.

———. *The Idea of Property in Seventeenth-Century England.* Manchester: Manchester UP, 1998.

Churches, Christine. "Women and Property in Early Modern England: A Case Study." *Social History* 23 (1998): 65–80.

Clay, J. W. "The Clifford Family." *Yorkshire Archaeological Journal* 18 (1905): 354–411.

Clifford, Anne. "*The Expenses of My House* (1675)" and "*The Expenses of My Private Purse* (1675)." University of Sydney, Supplementary MS.074.

———. "*The Knole Diary* (1603–1619)" and "*The Kendal Diary* (1650–1675)." *The Diaries of Lady Anne Clifford.* Ed. D. J. H. Clifford. Stroud: Sutton, 1990. 19–81, 103–227.

Condren, Conal. "Liberty of Office and Its Defence in Seventeenth-Century Political Argument." *History of Political Thought* 18.3 (1997): 460–82.

Dickenson, Donna. *Property, Women, and Politics: Subjects or Objects?* Cambridge: Polity, 1997.

Friedman, Alice T. *House and Household in Elizabethan England: Wollaton Hall and the Willoughby Family.* Chicago: U of Chicago P, 1989.

Froide, Amy M. "Marital Status as a Category of Difference: Singlewomen and Widows in Early Modern England." *Singlewomen in the European Past.* Ed. Judith M. Bennett and Amy M. Froide. Philadelphia: U of Pennsylvania P, 1999. 236–69.

Harris, Barbara J. *English Aristocratic Women, 1450–1550: Marriage, Property, and Careers.* Oxford: Oxford UP, 2002.

Household Accounts and Disbursement Books of Robert Dudley, Earl of Leicester, 1558–1561, 1584–1586. Ed. Simon Adams. Cambridge: Cambridge UP, 1995.

Household Accounts from Medieval England. Ed. C. M. Woolgar. 2 vols. Oxford: Oxford UP, 1992–93.

Korda, Natasha. "'Judicious oeillades': Supervising Marital Property in *The Merry Wives of Windsor.*" *Marxist Shakespeares.* Ed. Jean E. Howard and Scott Cutler Shershow. London: Routledge, 2001. 82–103.

Lamb, Mary Ellen. "The Agency of the Split Subject: Lady Anne Clifford and the Uses of Reading." *English Literary Renaissance* 22 (1992): 346–68.

Lewalski, Barbara Kiefer. *Writing Women in Jacobean England.* Cambridge: Harvard UP, 1993.

Locke, John. *An Essay concerning Human Understanding.* Ed. John W. Yolton. 2 vols. London: Dent, 1961.

———. *The Second Treatise of Government.* Ed. Thomas P. Peardon. New York: Liberal Arts, 1952.

McRae, Andrew. *God Speed the Plough: The Representation of Agrarian England, 1500–1660.* Cambridge: Cambridge UP, 1996.

Mertes, Kate. *The English Noble Household, 1250–1600: Good Governance and Politic Rule.* Oxford: Blackwell, 1988.

Pateman, Carole. *The Sexual Contract.* Cambridge: Polity, 1988.

Public Record Office, Exchequer.

Salzman, Paul. "Early Modern (Aristocratic) Women and Textual Property." *Women, Property, and the Letters of the Law in Early Modern England.* Ed. Nancy E. Wright, Margaret W. Ferguson, and A. R. Buck. Toronto: U of Toronto P, 2004.

Shakespeare, William. *A Midsummer Night's Dream.* Ed. Harold F. Brooks. London: Methuen, 1966.

Spence, Richard T. *Lady Anne Clifford, Countess of Pembroke, Dorset, and Montgomery (1590–1676).* Stroud: Sutton, 1997.

Spring, Eileen. *Law, Land, and Family: Aristocratic Inheritance, 1300 to 1800.* Chapel Hill: U of North Carolina P, 1993.

Staves, Susan. *Married Women's Separate Property in England, 1660–1883.* Cambridge: Harvard UP, 1990.

Suzuki, Mihoko. "Anne Clifford and the Gendering of History." *Clio* 30.2 (2001): 195–210.

Taylor, Charles. *Sources of the Self: The Making of the Modern Identity.* Cambridge: Harvard UP, 1989.

Tully, James. *A Discourse on Property: John Locke and His Adversaries.* Cambridge: Cambridge UP, 1980.

Waldron, Jeremy. *The Right to Private Property.* Oxford: Clarendon, 1988.

Woolgar, C. M. *The Great Household in Elizabethan England.* New Haven: Yale UP, 1999.

Yorkshire Archaeological Society, MS. 1325.

Chapter 14

Designs on the Self
Inigo Jones, Marginal Writing,
& Renaissance Self-Assembly

Liam E. Semler

Read seriously whatever is before you, and reduce and digest it to
practice and observation. . . . Trust not to your Memory, but put all
remarkable, notable things you shall meet with in your Books *sub
salva custodia* [under the sound care] of Pen and Ink, but so alter
the property by your own Scholia and Annotations on it, that your
memory may speedily recur to the place it was committed to.
Review frequently such memorandums, and you will find you have
made a signal progress and proficiency, in whatever sort of
Learning you studied.
(Archibald Campbell, Eighth Earl of Argyll, 1661)[1]

*I*nigo Jones began his career as an inconsequential joiner's apprentice,
passed through a stage as a "picture-maker" for the earl of Rutland
(1603), consolidated as a designer of royal masques, and climaxed as
surveyor of the king's works and dominator of royal entertainments
from 1615 to 1641 under James I and Charles I. He was England's first
truly classical architect, whose grasp of classical principles of style was
never matched by his coevals, his subordinates in the Works Office, or
even his pupil, John Webb.

Although he never wrote an art treatise to codify his accumulated
wisdom in a form accessible to his countrymen and he wrote almost
nothing intended for wide circulation, Inigo Jones was a prolific writer
of a particular sort.[2] He kept at least three sets of notes (quite probably more) in which he jotted ideas, sketched designs (many of them
copied from prints of works by Italian masters), and translated passages from continental art treatises.[3] He annotated printed books in
his possession with everything from underlining to difference of opinion, from summary remarks and translations to personally taken
architectural measurements and medicinal remedies. He even added

his own pen sketch of an artist to fill an empty printed cartouche accompanying the "Life of Correggio" in his copy of Vasari (Wood fig. 3).[4] The marginal realm is a highly attractive and active space for Jones—one in which he invests not only much ink but also much mental effort.[5] The blank spaces in the margins of great printed works by established continental writers on art cry out to Jones to be filled, to be inhabited with his script and his opinions, alongside and in contradistinction to theirs. Chief among his extant annotated books are important architectural treatises by Sebastiano Serlio and Andrea Palladio,[6] the first volume of the third part of Giorgio Vasari's celebrated *Vite* (1568), and Daniele Barbaro's widely used Italian critical edition of Vitruvius's *Libri decem* (1567).

Not only does Jones enter into scrawled dialogue with the printed authors' opinions, but he often casts his additions explicitly as notes to himself or, more accurately, as notes to a conceived future version of his self, one that he imagines will return to reread a text that then bears the traces of that future self's past opinions. When he does indeed return to his books, he reads his old opinions along with the printed text they surround, and various aspects of either side of the crystallized debate are further adjusted by the living self, who wields the pen.[7] In some cases, distinct layers of increasingly educated comment (often separated by many years and physically displaced by lack of space) may be determined by analysis of handwriting, location on the page, and sense.

Autobiography does not seem to be the right word for Jones's activity, nor its textual, or indeed its corporeal, result. "Self-writing" is an improvement, but in this particular instance its generality can be greatly improved upon. My suggestion is that the term *self-design* cannot be bettered as a describer for the sort of operation I want to suggest is occurring in Jones's marginal praxis. Its peculiar aptness will be clarified later: suffice to say for the moment that the word *design* is to be taken in the expansive Italian sense, signifying the essence of all visual arts and encompassing both mental conception and manual graphic activity. Jones introduces the term to England in his marginalia and conversation, and this essay, while acknowledging the long critical tradition detailing Jones's Vitruvian classicism, explores the peculiarly textual way in which Jones assembles his desired self.

Jones's habit of writing is governed by desire, a sense of personal lack, and a faith in the possibility of strenuous (and humanistic) becoming. This becoming is really a self-conscious process of entering into a specific, predefined type or genre of social being.[8] His marginalia fabricate, as well as navigate toward the inhabitation of, a triple office of humanist-courtier-architect as modeled by contemporary Italians.

This ubiquitous desire pervades the ink-filled marginal space of Jones's books and notebooks and suggests the existence of an intensely focused consciousness at work. The gap between the "am" and the "would be" is bridged by the desiring-I, a figure who in writing gradually models and adopts the attributes of the desired future self as present habits, reflexes, and knowledges until the characters of the prior self are overwritten and finally (it is hoped) put out of sight. The desiring-I is reaching for significant social visibility via the incarnation of a significant office. The present self, in contrast, is conceived by Jones as possessing an essential social invisibility deriving from its incoherence or insignificance of office. The desiring-I posited here is therefore the singular affective voice, which dominates the Jonesian marginalia; it is the engine driving the pen. Its textual praxis is really an energetic changing of clothes within the personal space of Jones's book margins. The mirror in this private change room, in which Jones's desiring eye may, and does, judge his transforming appearance, is his own drying ink.

This textual matrix of being, desire, and becoming may be illustrated by reference to one page of Inigo Jones's celebrated Roman Sketchbook, the page dated 19 January 1614 (new style, 1615).[9] Jones has just returned from his invaluable tour of Italy with Arundel: they have brought back a wealth of experience and a cache of artifacts, prints, drawings, and books. The trip was preceded by a crucial couple of years spent as surveyor to Prince Henry and many years of preparatory reading and note making, during which Jones, in the privacy of his Barbaro margins, "was engaged in mastering the basic terms and concepts on which Vitruvian discourse depended" (Johnson, *Three Volumes* xxiv). In a similar manner, he had been absorbing and turning into English key art-theoretical concepts from Vasari and elsewhere, *disegno* being one of particular relevance (Cast). By the time of his return home, Jones was absolutely ready to take up the post of surveyor of His Majesty's works and buildings (the reversion of which had been promised him on 27 April 1613), which at last fell vacant at the death of its old incumbent, Simon Basil, in September 1615 (Lees-Milne 32–35, 63). Jones stepped into office on 1 October 1615 and immediately began an astonishing revolution in English architectural design. Over this page and the next (also dated, in the old style, 20 January 1614), Jones writes a few generalizations about art, generalizations that would not count for too much in the sophisticated art-theoretical environment of Italy (out of which they are culled) but count for everything in England in January 1615.

In a mixed hand that is predominantly italic, the page affirms the Cinquecento commonplace that the art of architecture is one of the arts of design.[10] More specifically, it argues that the process of architectural invention, composition, and ornamentation is akin to the art of drawing the human figure and composing narrative paintings.[11] As John Peacock has pointed out, Jones's focus on composition followed by ornamentation is basically Albertian, with the exception that he has imported the word *dessigne* from Vasari and the method of repeatedly sketching individual body parts from early-seventeenth-century drawing manuals (*Stage Designs* 122–23, 232–33; "Figurative Drawings").[12]

Jones's first paragraph explains how in the art of design one should initially become competent in the representation of parts of the human body and only then begin to assemble them into a whole figure, which is subsequently clothed and disposed with other figures into "a hoole Storry" or narrative (*istoria*), with all its attendant graces or "ornamentes." His second paragraph effects the parallel with architecture by saying that one must likewise study the basic components of buildings, such as entrances, halls, chambers, stairs, and windows, and then adorn them with decorative ingredients, which he goes on to list copiously, beginning with basic architectural features associated with the orders and then moving to an indiscriminate listing of every form of architectural ornamentation that springs to mind.[13] Jones disposes his bipartite idea in two rhetorically linked paragraphs: "As in dessigne," the first begins; "So in Architecture" completes the second. The tone of voice is formal and pedagogical. It is a voice of public authority, which employs circumlocutory expressions and logical connectors conducive to a sense of abstract truth: "As in dessigne first on[e] Sttudies . . . and so of the rest . . . and consequently . . ."; "So in Architecture on[e] must studdy . . ."; and so forth. He appears very much in control of his idea and his expression of it on the page; no wonder if critics suspect him of making notes here for a future architectural treatise.[14] My suggestion is therefore that here lies an example of the future self—the self that speaks with a sort of theoretically informed cultural authority that is new in England. This self speaks formally and authoritatively to others who would follow in the art. It is the voice of the continental Vitruvian architect (as practitioner and theoretician and as reconceived by Alberti and subsequent Italians) that Inigo Jones desires to become. It is consequent on this intention that Jones overtly jettisons the secretary hand in favor of the more gentlemanly italic used by his patron,

the earl of Arundel, and that his language consciously resists employing terminology left over from his youthful apprenticeship as a joiner
in Saint Paul's churchyard and outlines instead a proposed artistic
method that carries a genealogy stretching back through Italian,
French, and Latin vocabularies of the continental arts of design.[15] An
aspect of this adopted heritage is Jones's employment in the Roman
Sketchbook of the Italian art academies' method of teaching students
"the alphabet of *disegno*" (wherein students relentlessly perfect drafts
of individual body parts). This strategy is affirmed in drawing manuals by Odoardo Fialetti, Agostino Carracci, Giovanni Luigi Valesio,
and Guido Reni (a number of which Jones had access to), which provide pages of carefully modeled body parts as an anatomical ABC.[16]
From one viewpoint, we could say that Jones is merely articulating an
elevated (i.e., theorized) form of graphic "joinery," but it is fundamentally important that his style of voice is that of Albertian *compositio*
(grounded in Vitruvius and ancient oratory), mannerist *imitatio*, and
humanist *rhetorica*.[17]

Since this desired future voice is presented as arising out of the continental humanistic tradition, not the English heritage of manual arts,
we may conclude that the origin of the proposed future self is therefore
not—or, rather, not to be—identical with the origin of the present
writing self. The intention is to render unnecessary the present self
and its insignificant origin and simultaneously to present as essential
and innate the prosthetic continental origin of the new self. Jones
knows that to change oneself one must change one's voice, and to
change one's voice is to change one's parents. It is this strategy that
Ben Jonson bitterly resents and exposes: "Are you grown rich and
proud? / Your trappings will not change you" ("An Expostulacion
with Inigo Jones" ll.24–25). For Jonson, Jones remains "a Joyner"
regardless of his pretentious murdering of Latin, his bandying of continental art terms such as *designe*, his rising through civic office, and
his intolerable vainglory (*A Tale of a Tub* 5.2.35–37; "An Expostulacion"). Jonson, who was well aware of Vitruvian doctrine, acutely
deconstructs the dichotomous Jonesian self in *Love's Welcome at
Bolsover* (1634), wherein Coronell Iniquo Vitruvius employs a self-
deflating mock "Oration" to introduce the antimasque "Dance of the
Mechanickes" (Jonson 7.809).[18] In short: "Be what beast you will, /
you'l be . . . an Inigo still" ("An Expostulacion" ll.21–22).

It is perhaps to be expected, therefore, that the projected public
voice one finds on this page of the Roman Sketchbook is far from pure.
For a start, Jones's bipartite arrangement of his idea of artistic compo-

sition promises and fails to deliver structural parallelism. What was intended as a rhetorical period employing protasis and apodosis in hypotactic arrangement ("As in dessigne . . . So in Architecture") actually disintegrates in practice into a nonsyntactic chaos by the end. The second paragraph is overlong and annihilates its own grammatical structure and that of the whole period. It collapses into a messy, breathless, and eventually random list of architectural components (including "stattues, paintings"), which does not distinguish categories of ornament, media employed, or locations suitable. The polished public voice of the orator has become the rant of an obsessive name-dropper, the dexterity of good rhetorical *copia* has tended toward the verbosity of bad, and the sense the reader received of the voice as something that *is* now decays toward a sense of the voice as something that pretends to be.

In reading this page, we are witness to the strain of office—the labor of holding together in some sort of coherence the not yet fully cohered attributes of a desired role. Jones's struggle in the first paragraph to present a regularly spaced, neat, and justified textual trace of his orderly and learned mind becomes all too clear as struggle when the second paragraph cramps, crowds, corrects, and fails to justify. An increasing upward drift of lines shows that the writer is so preoccupied with listing all the architectural components he knows that he begins to forget his sense of direction both grammatically and graphically. The final line looks very like he suddenly realized this tendency and desperately sought to bring things back to level.

This reading is confirmed by the note at the bottom of the page. With a neatly centered heading and in lines absolutely level with the lower edge of the sheet, Jones writes:

nooate

I must euer remember to Curbe the deffette [that is, defect] of
    wrighting and drauinge awrye upwards to ye right hande and
    rather sinn in the contrary[19]

This coda reveals that Jones has stopped to reflect on the page as a graphic expression of the self. He finds it wanting: it is visually indecorous and asymmetrical—a flaw the note itself is anxious to avoid. The look of the page is, to put it curtly, counterproductive, for the script appears to the desiring-I to be a symptom of the present self, not the projected future self. The indecorous mechanic's hand gives the lie to the authoritative voice of the liberal artist. In the view of the desiring-I, this graphic mirror, resembling truth-telling steel rather than idealizing glass, needs some adjustment. To the twenty-first-century eye familiar with early-seventeenth-century manuscripts made for the recording of personal thoughts, Jones's page is actually not all that illegible or scrappy. This fact, and the impression one gets that the words on the page betray *varying* levels of self-conscious neatness or graphic alertness, together suggest that Jones's project of self-design is always toward the front of his mind and that he is aiming for a deep imprinting of a high degree of polish.

In contrast to the public voice of the first two paragraphs, which projects imperious formal assertions ("on[e] Sttudies," "ear on[e] comm[es]," "on[e] must") the first-person intimacy of the note ("I must euer remember") feels superbly grounded in a real body living and writing in the present. Here speaks the underside of the self of desire, not in glory but in shame, not in public pronouncement but in private self-rebuke. We see here merely another part of Jones's wide-ranging project of self-fabrication, which displays continental architectural terms and rhetorical modes while burying old English craft terms, attempts to drive out residual secretary letter forms from an increasingly italic hand, and subjects its own graphic image to scrutiny. Alongside this is Jones's strenuous self-education in classical philosophy, history, and the sciences. The three paragraphs on this page map one on top of another. They are all concerned with the art of design for public consumption: of a narrative painting, of a classical building, of a self. This private text records the desiring-I's pursuit of public identity: a continental triplex of offices conceived as the humanistically learned courtier-architect. Jones is his own one-man private Italian academy.

However, the rhetorical and graphical breakdown of his instruction on architectural design is also the breakdown of his desired self-image. The attention to detail required in the composition of an ultimately unified artistic design is matched by the attention to detail required in the composition of a particular sort of self. In both cases, what is required is a continental sense of *disegno* (rare in England) that carries simultaneously the burdens of mental invention of a coherent idea and the physical drafting of form(s).[20] In the Sketchbook and his other marginalia, we see Jones at work on this Italianate program of self-design: he is in possession of a mental ideation of his future self; he is intellectually scheming its attainment; and he is, via painstaking efforts of personal adjustment and graphic expression, becoming "practicke" (as he advises one should be in the drawing of body parts) in its attributes. We see him at work on self-design. That Jones considered the Italianate concept of *disegno* an essential component of his role as architect may be seen from Jonson's frequent ridiculing of his use of the word as "a specious fyne / Terme of ye Architects" ("An Expostulacion" ll.55–56). Jonson is aware that Jones employs the term *disegno* as a social, not merely an aesthetic, enabler: "that vnbounded lyne / Aymd at in thy omnipotent Designe!" (ll.95–96).

Jonson's rhetorical horror should not obscure the fact that the Jonesian rise had respectable precedents. In Vasari's *Vite*, Jones read the "Life of Baccio d'Agnolo," which is essentially the story of a wood-carver who "went to Rome, where he carefully studied architecture" and finally won grand architectural commissions in Florence, thereby proving that "carvers in the process of time become architects by constant practice" (3.55–56). If this story of a determined and talented father inspired the joiner Jones, he had the example of the son, Giuliano, as a complementary negative exemplar. Giuliano, like his father, rose from carving and joinery to architecture but failed to consolidate his position because, Vasari concludes (in Jones's marginal translation), "he who hath not desine and great Inuention of himsealfe shal euer be Poore of graace[,] perfection and Iudgment In great Compositions of archetetture" (Johnson, *Three Volumes* 19). This negative proverb arising from Giuliano—and supplying Jones with the indispensable concepts of "desine and great Inuention"—is matched by a positive one arising from the life of his father, which Jones also translates.

> Architeture must be Masculine fearme (Sollid) Simpell and Inriched with ye grace of desine and of a varried subiecte in the Compossition that with nether too littell nor to[o] much alterithe ye Order of architecture nor ye sight of ye Iuditious. (Johnson, *Three Volumes* 18)

Thus, in this Vasarian "Life," which Jones read and annotated around 1610, he had all he needed to inspire him, to teach and warn him, in regard to a path that had been trodden before and, while passable, possessed many pitfalls.[21] There were, however, no adequate precedents in England, and therefore Jones had to grasp every clue to perfect a very special art of design: that of being a courtier à la Castiglione and an architect à la Alberti.

The panoply of prerogatives, skills, and behaviors characteristic of each role is equivalent to the smorgasbord of gracefully represented body parts available for imitation in early-seventeenth-century drawing manuals for those who would master *disegno*. *Disegno* in this period signifies a complex mixture of close imitation of nature and graceful beautification of nature by *grazia* and *maniera*. The results testify to art's power to triumph over nature, perfecting and (we would say) artificializing her to an extraordinary degree. Consequently, the narrative painting and the graceful human figures extravagantly posturing within it together possess a blend of art and nature that may also be found in the daily enactment of a public role such as architect, courtier, or humanist.

Only one thing remained needful to complete this textual assumption of office: a suitable English container for such a personality or, more accurately, an already culturally situated office that might be simultaneously inhabited and renovated. This is the office of surveyor of the king's works, an office that for nearly one hundred years was rather unremarkably held and was typically burdened not so much with creative work as with "an unremitting stream of crude business" (Summerson, *Inigo Jones* 40). Sir John Summerson identifies three of Jones's subordinates in the Works Office as capable of sustaining the title "architect": Francis Carter, chief clerk from 1614; Nicholas Stone, master mason from 1632; and Robert Stickles, a talented clerk who was recommended for the surveyorship of works in 1595 but failed to gain it. All had done design work as well as construction; Carter possessed a library of "bookes of Architeckter"; and Stickles had read Vitruvius and Serlio, as well as writing two minitreatises himself ("The Surveyorship" and "Three Elizabethan Architects"). However, Summerson concludes that the architectural views of these men were either old-fashioned or caught up on "the picturesquely mannered style of [Hans Vredeman] De Vries" ("The Surveyorship" 137).[22] In short, Surveyor Jones was on his own in an office that would have appeared to him "almost ludicrously provincial and out-moded." It is not without justice, or charity, then, that Jones is called the "Supream Officer" by John Webb and "the autocrat of the Works" by Summerson ("The Surveyorship" 131, 138).

It may be more precise, then, to say that this English office, which Jones was to inhabit from 1615 on, was not transformed by the inserted presence of so powerful an individual as Inigo Jones so much as by the inserted presence of so powerful a formulation of office as the modern continental architect.[23] The only significant alteration in the office before Jones appears to have been James Nedeham's promotion from master carpenter to clerk of the king's works in 1532, a promotion that for the first time elevated a trained craftsman (rather than a clerk) to the chief administrative post. With this came a transformation of the title from clerk of the king's works to clerk and surveyor and finally just surveyor of the king's works. This evolution was important, and Nedeham did add design work to his job description, but the administrative responsibilities and the organization of the Works Office barely changed (Ransome). Retrospectively, we might observe that the ground had been prepared for an English "rise of the artist." A precedent had been set for a triple master of theory, administration, and craft, and the title of office had been altered accordingly. All that was required was a convincing redefinition of the English surveyor as someone more nearly approaching the continental architect. It was Jones who effected this transvaluation of office.

This refiguring of the office of surveyor draws Jonson's ire. The poet tries to reverse the effect by deconstructing the Vitruvian Jones and recuperating the joiner Jones so as to represent the English surveyorship as essentially mechanical, blandly supervisorial, or usurped by an intolerably vain laborer who pretends to be a polymath (rather than renovated by knowledgeable importation of new socioaesthetic principles).[24] The Inigo Jones that we know—the person history records as England's first great classical architect—is very much a product of the book. The office of architect as defined initially by Vitruvius and subsequently reconstituted by Cinquecento Italian architectural writers is a textually understood and possessable genre of social being. Jones begins as a marginal artist from a continentally marginal nation and succeeds in building himself into the abstraction of this high office and then embedding it concretely in his culture via what is essentially a process of increasing cultural leverage driven by relentless marginal notation. Without the Jonesian praxis of marginal writing, there would be no Inigo Jones as we have him, for without the relentless, self-conscious, and messy scrawl that stains so many of his books he would not have achieved the thorough, personal redefinition that was essential for him to design some of England's most lasting architectural monuments. Structures such as the Queen's House, Greenwich (1616–18), and Whitehall Banqueting Hall (1619–22) are the product not of the old office of English surveyor but of the office of the modern continental Vitruvian architect. The Inigo Jones of history is more precisely a figure of *istoria*, a figure self-consciously designed and displayed but no less real for that.

NOTES

1. Archibald Campbell, *Instructions to a Son* (Edinburgh, 1661), 102–4, qtd. Zwicker 101. Zwicker makes the important point that by 1661 Camp-

bell's humanistic advice would seem somewhat old-fashioned to his son, who would be more familiar with the intensely partisan and acerbic style of pen book notation during the Civil Wars and Interregnum. Campbell's words evoke the first quarter of the century with which this essay is concerned. I would like to thank the Australian Research Council for funding my research for this essay.

2. Jones probably composed the proscenium description for *Tempe Restor'd* (1632) and possibly for other masques, wrote a poetic riposte to Jonson's attacks, and jotted some rough notes on Stonehenge that John Webb fabricated into *The Most Notable Antiquity of Great Britain Called Stone-Heng* (1655). See Gordon 152n1, 164; Gotch 254–55; and Summerson, *Inigo Jones* 71–73.

3. These included the so-called Roman Sketchbook, now held at Chatsworth, and the unidentifiable and probably lost "My Papars" and "My Noat Book Marked A." See Newman, "Inigo Jones's Architectural Education" 21, 50n15. Also John Webb says the first Stonehenge book relies on "some few indigested notes" left by Jones (Colvin, Ransome, and Summerson 122).

4. Hans Holbein the younger is a significant precursor to Jones in the turning of marginal space to significant ends. Both artists make the margins a space in which to formulate a powerful social self. Holbein and his brother Ambrosius marginally illustrated their Latin teacher Oswald Myconius's copy of Erasmus's *Encomium moriae* (1515). Erasmus's good opinion of Holbein's talents was bolstered by these marginal sketches, with the result that he recommended the artist to Thomas More and thereby fast-tracked Holbein's rise in England. Thus, Holbein successfully merges a humanist education with artistic demonstration and self-promotion. He goes on to become England's foremost exponent of the marginally located and yet centrally significant art of grotesque-work. On the *Encomium moriae* sketches, see Roskill and Hand 45 fig. 11, 72 fig. 1, 73, 228 figs. 1–2; and Bätschmann and Greiner 36, 90 fig. 115.

5. Handwritten marginal annotation is a growing field of study for early modern scholars interested in self-revelation in Renaissance writing. See, for example, Orgel; Zwicker; Lewalski; Evans; Riddell and Stewart; Johnson, *Ben Jonson* 9–19, 41–42; Barney; Jardine and Grafton; Newman, "Italian Treatises"; and Stern.

6. Serlio's *Architettura* (1560–62, folio) and *Tutte l'Opere d'Architettura* (1601, quarto); and Palladio's *I Quattro Libri dell' Architettura* (1601, folio).

7. Jones's acts of underlining, summary, or notation also serve as present-tense reinforcements of a mental idea. He cross-references his notes (as does Gabriel Harvey), presumably for his own aid.

8. My account of Jones as annotator strengthens Lisa Jardine and Anthony Grafton's claim that humanistic "scholarly reading . . . was always goal oriented—an active rather than a passive pursuit. It was conducted under conditions of strenuous attentiveness" (30). Harvey's prolific annotative praxis—as discussed in Stern; and Jardine and Grafton—makes a fascinating comparison with Jones's.

9. This page and the following page in the Roman Sketchbook have been

discussed in a number of recent studies: Semler (including a transcription of both pages); Higgott, "Varying with Reason" 55–58; Higgott, "The Making of an Architect"; Wood; Cast; Peacock, *Stage Designs* 53, 122–25, 140–51, 227–35; and Anderson, "Masculinity."

10. The ascenders and descenders characteristic of secretary are quite contained, and most letterforms are italic or simplified secretary. The most obvious secretary residues, appearing intermittently, include the reverse final *e* (second-last line: "drawinge awrye") and the final *es* (third line: "noses" but not "Eyees").

11. On the Italian arts of design, see Roman.

12. See also Smith; and Wood. Peacock, Smith, and Wood have indicated the relevance to the Roman Sketchbook of images collected in Oliviero Gatti's manual (1619) and also manuals by Odoardo Fialetti (1608) and Giovanni Luigi Valesio and others, many of which rely on engravings by the Caracci School and Guercino. Most of Jones's drawings in the Sketchbook date from the 1630s. Wood discusses why this might be so, given that Jones must have learned to draw initially before 1605. On the drawing manuals, see note 16.

13. Higgott writes that Jones's failure to distinguish "between architectural features associated with the orders . . . and purely decorative motifs . . . suggests he considered all ornaments, whether architectural or fanciful, to be subject to the same compositional rules" ("Varying with Reason" 55). I would be wary of this conclusion. More probable is Peacock's not unrelated argument that Jones belongs "in the tradition which tended to view grotesques, in their controversial complexity, as paradigmatic of all ornament, rather than among those Vitruvian purists who dismissed them as perverse and eccentric" (*Stage Designs* 249). For a detailed discussion of Jones, ornament, and the grotesque, see Semler.

14. See Cast 188. Compare Sir Henry Wotton, who made notes in his copy of Philibert Delorme's *l'Architecture* (1603), which then appeared in final form in his own treatise, *The Elements of Architecture* (1624) (Mitchell).

15. Newman notes how some old English craft terms are visible in Jones's early notes ("Architectural Education" 18, 40). On Jones's development of a continental language of architecture, see Cast. On the English response to continental architecture, including a discussion of Jones and marginal notation, see Anderson "Learning."

16. See Alberti 92–93; Fialetti in Buffa 315–37; Carracci in Bohlin 294–368; and Valesio and Reni in Birke 47–66, 184–95. On the Italian drawing manuals, see Rosand; Amornpichetkul; Tonelli 97–101; and Bury 198–201; see also Bolten.

17. On Alberti and the humanist rhetorical forms of art theory and practice, see Berry; Westfall; Gilbert; Wittkower; and Lee.

18. On Jonson and Vitruvius, see Johnson, *Ben Jonson* 1–35. On the dispute between Jonson and Jones, see Gordon; and Semler 134–41.

19. Transcript in Semler 142.

20. See Baxandall's discussion, which gives special attention to the place of *disegno* in the Jonson-Jones quarrel.

21. On the importance of the Baccio note to Jones's developing theory of

design, see Higgott, "Varying" 57–58. Higgott says the word *Sollid* was added around 1614–15.

22. Peacock explains how Jones, contrary to his coevals' wholesale acceptance of de Vries's fantastical architecture, "corrects" the Flemish architect's designs by application of Vitruvian consistency, particularly in regard to the orders (*Stage Designs* 93–96).

23. I note here with gratitude the influence of Conal Condren's refreshing theory of early modern offices.

24. See Jonson's bitter responses to Jones's new rendition of "Surveyor" in "An Expostulation with Inigo Jones" and *Love's Welcome at Bolsover* (7.809).

WORKS CITED

Alberti, Leon Battista. *On Painting.* Trans. John R. Spencer. New Haven: Yale UP, 1966.

Amornpichetkul, Chittima. "Seventeenth-Century Italian Drawing Books: Their Origin and Development." *Children of Mercury: The Education of Artists in the Sixteenth and Seventeenth Centuries.* Ed. Jeffrey Muller. Providence: Bell Gallery, List Art Center, Brown University, 1984. 109–18.

Anderson, Christy. "Learning to Read Architecture in the English Renaissance." *Albion's Classicism: The Visual Arts in Britain, 1550–1660.* Ed. Lucy Gent. New Haven: Yale UP, 1995. 239–86.

———. "Masculinity and English Architectural Classicism." *Gender and Art.* Ed. Gill Perry. New Haven: Yale UP, 1999. 130–53.

Barney, Stephen, ed. *Annotation and Its Texts.* Oxford: Oxford UP, 1991.

Bätschmann, Oskar, and Pascal Greiner. *Hans Holbein.* London: Reaktion, 1997.

Baxandall, Michael. "English *Disegno.*" *England and the Continental Renaissance: Essays in Honour of J. B. Trapp.* Ed. Edward Chaney and Peter Mack. Woodbridge: Boydell, 1990. 203–14.

Berry, J. Duncan. "Imagination into Image: On Visual Literacy." *Children of Mercury: The Education of Artists in the Sixteenth and Seventeenth Centuries.* Ed. Jeffrey Muller. Providence: Bell Gallery, List Art Center, Brown University, 1984. 70–80.

Birke, Veronika, ed. *The Illustrated Bartsch 40 (Formerly Volume 18 [Part 2]): Italian Masters of the Sixteenth and Seventeenth Centuries.* New York: Abaris, 1982.

Bohlin, Diane DeGrazia, ed. *The Illustrated Bartsch 39 (Formerly Volume 18 [Part 1]): Italian Masters of the Sixteenth Century.* New York: Abaris, 1980.

Bolten, Jaap. *Method and Practice: Dutch and Flemish Drawing Books, 1600–1750.* Landau: PVA, 1985.

Buffa, Sebastian, ed. *The Illustrated Bartsch 38 (Formerly Volume 17 [Part 5]): Italian Artists of the Sixteenth Century.* New York: Abaris, 1983.

Bury, Michael. *The Print in Italy, 1550–1620.* London: British Museum Press, 2001.

Campbell, Archibald. *Instructions to a Son.* Edinburgh, 1661. 102–4.

Cast, David. "Speaking of Architecture: The Evolution of a Vocabulary in

Vasari, Jones, and Sir John Vanbrugh." *Journal of the Society of Architectural Historians* 52 (June 1993): 179–88.

Colvin, H. M., D. R. Ransome, and John Summerson, eds. *The History of the King's Works*. Vol. 3: *1485–1660 (Part I)*. London: Her Majesty's Stationery Office, 1975.

Condren, Conal. "Historicism and the Problem of Renaissance 'Self-Fashioning.'" *The Touch of the Real: Essays in Early Modern Culture*. Ed. Philippa Kelly. Crawley: U of Western Australia P, 2002. 105–24.

Evans, Robert C. *Habits of Mind: Evidence and Effects of Ben Jonson's Reading*. Lewisburg: Bucknell UP, 1995.

Gilbert, Creighton E. "Antique Frameworks for Renaissance Art Theory: Alberti and Pino." *Marsyas* 3 (1945): 87–106.

Gordon, D. J. "Poet and Architect: The Intellectual Setting of the Quarrel between Ben Jonson and Inigo Jones." *Journal of the Warburg and Courtauld Institutes* 12 (1949): 152–78.

Gotch, J. A. *Inigo Jones*. London: Methuen, 1928.

Higgott, Gordon. "The Making of an Architect: Inigo Jones's Second Tour of Italy, 1613–14." *Inigo Jones: Complete Architectural Drawings*. Ed. John Harris and Gordon Higgott. New York: Drawing Center, 1989. 52–57.

———. "'Varying with Reason': Inigo Jones' Theory of Design." *Architectural History* 35 (1992): 51–77.

Jardine, Lisa, and Anthony Grafton. "'Studied for Action': How Gabriel Harvey Read His Livy." *Past and Present* 129 (1990): 30–78.

Johnson, A. W. *Ben Jonson: Poetry and Architecture*. Oxford: Clarendon, 1994.

Johnson, A. W., ed. *Three Volumes Annotated by Inigo Jones: Vasari's* Lives *(1568), Plutarch's* Moralia *(1614), and Plato's* Republic *(1554)*. Abo: Abo Akademi UP, 1997.

Jonson, Ben. *Ben Jonson*. Ed. C. H. Herford, Percy Simpson, and Evelyn Simpson. 11 vols. Oxford: Clarendon, 1925–52.

Lee, Rensselaer W. "*Ut pictura poesis:* The Humanistic Theory of Painting." *Art Bulletin* 22 (1940): 197–269.

Lees-Milne, James. *The Age of Inigo Jones*. London: Batsford, 1953.

Lewalski, Barbara K. "Female Text, Male Reader Response: Contemporary Marginalia in Rachel Speght's *A Mouzell for Melastomus*." *Representing Women in Renaissance England*. Ed. Claude J. Summers and Ted-Larry Pebworth. Columbia: U of Missouri P, 1997. 136–62.

Mitchell, Herbert. "An Unrecorded Issue of Philibert Delorme's *Le premier tome de l'architecture* Annotated by Sir Henry Wotton." *Journal of the Society of Architectural Historians* 53 (1994): 20–29.

Newman, John. "Inigo Jones's Architectural Education before 1614." *Architectural History* 35 (1992): 18–50.

———. "Italian Treatises in Use: The Significance of Inigo Jones's Annotations." *Les Traites d'Architecture de la Renaissance*. Ed. Jean Guillaume. Paris: Picard, 1988. 435–41.

Orgel, Stephen. "Margins of Truth." *The Renaissance Text: Theory, Editing, Textuality*. Ed. Andrew Murphy. Manchester: Manchester UP, 2000. 91–107.

Peacock, John. "Figurative Drawings." *Inigo Jones: Complete Architectural Drawings.* Ed. John Harris and Gordon Higgott. New York: Drawing Center, 1989. 284–97.

———. *The Stage Designs of Inigo Jones: The European Context.* Cambridge: Cambridge UP, 1995.

Ransome, D. R. "The Administrators." *The History of the King's Works.* Vol. 3: *1485–1660 (Part I).* Ed. H. M. Colvin, D. R. Ransome, and John Summerson. London: Her Majesty's Stationery Office, 1975. 10–13.

Riddell, James A., and Stanley Stewart. *Jonson's Spenser: Evidence and Historical Criticism.* Pittsburgh: Duquesne UP, 1995.

Roman, Cynthia E. "Academic Ideals of Art Education." *Children of Mercury: The Education of Artists in the Sixteenth and Seventeenth Centuries.* Ed. Jeffrey Muller. Providence: Bell Gallery, List Art Center, Brown University, 1984. 81–95.

Rosand, David. "The Crisis of the Venetian Renaissance Tradition." *L'arte: Rivista di storia dell'arte medievale e modernae d'arte decorativa* 3.11–12 (1970): 5–53.

Roskill, Mark, and John Oliver Hand, eds. *Hans Holbein: Paintings, Prints, and Reception.* New Haven: National Gallery of Art, 2001.

Semler, L. E. "Inigo Jones, Capricious Ornament, and Plutarch's Wise Man." *Journal of the Warburg and Courtauld Institutes* 66 (2003): 123–42.

Smith, Joan Sumner. "The Italian Sources of Inigo Jones' Style." *Burlington Magazine* 94 (1952): 200–207.

Stern, Virginia F. *Gabriel Harvey: His Life, Marginalia, and Library.* Oxford: Clarendon, 1979.

Summerson, Sir John. *Inigo Jones.* Harmondsworth: Penguin, 1966.

———. "The Surveyorship of Inigo Jones, 1615–43." *The History of the King's Works.* Vol. 3: *1485–1660 (Part I).* Ed. H. M. Colvin, D. R. Ransome, and John Summerson. London: Her Majesty's Stationery Office, 1975. 132–37.

———. "Three Elizabethan Architects." *Bulletin of the John Rylands Library* 40 (1957–58): 202–28.

Tonelli, Laura Olmstead. "Academic Practice in the Sixteenth and Seventeenth Centuries." *Children of Mercury: The Education of Artists in the Sixteenth and Seventeenth Centuries.* Ed. Jeffrey Muller. Providence: Bell Gallery, List Art Center, Brown University, 1984. 96–108.

Vasari, Giorgio. *The Lives of the Painters, Sculptors, and Architects.* Trans. A. B. Hinds. 4 vols. London: Dent, 1963.

Westfall, Carroll W. "Painting and the Liberal Arts: Alberti's View." *Journal of the History of Ideas* 30 (1969): 487–506.

Wittkower, Rudolf. *Architectural Principles in the Age of Humanism.* Rev. ed. London: Academy, 1974.

Wood, Jeremy. "Inigo Jones, Italian Art, and the Practice of Drawing." *Art Bulletin* 74.2 (June 1992): 247–70.

Zwicker, Steven. "Reading the Margins: Politics and the Habits of Appropriation." *Refiguring Revolutions: Aesthetics and Politics from the English Revolution to the Romantic Revolution.* Ed. Kevin Sharpe and Steven Zwicker. Berkeley: U of California P, 1998. 101–16.

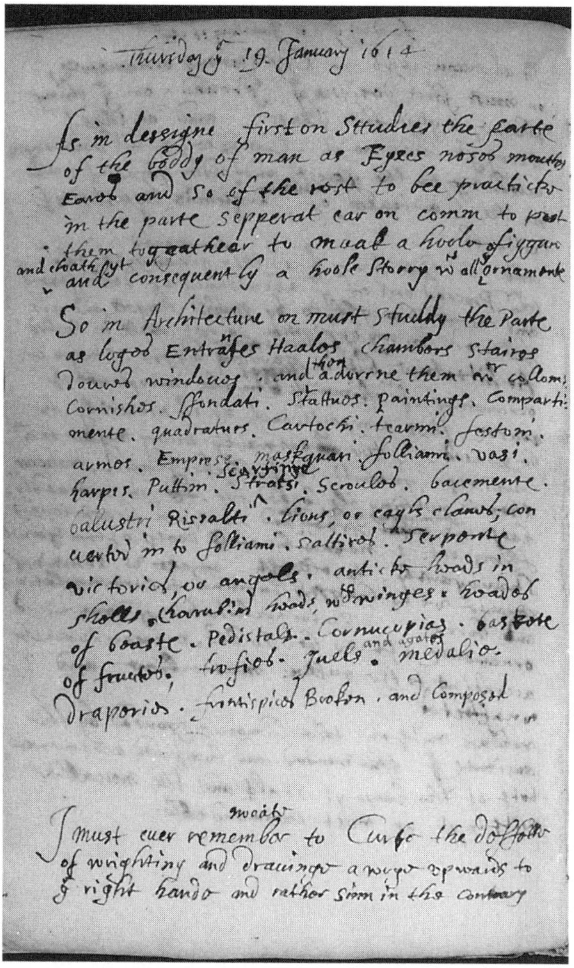
Thursday ye 19 January 1614

As in dessigne first on Studies the parte
of the boddy of man as Eyes noses mouths
Eares and so of the rest to bee practicke
in the parte sepperat car on comm to put
them toggeathear to maak a hoole figgure
and cloathe yt and consequently a hoole Storry wth all ornaments

So in Architecture on must studdy the Parte
as loges Entrances Haalls chambers staires
doures windoues and then adorne them wth colloms
cornishes. sfondati. stattues. paintings. Compartimente. quadratures. Cartochi. tearmi. festoni.
armes. Empreses. maskerari. folliami. vasi.
harpis. Puttini. Scartocci. Strossi. Scroules. bacemente.
balustri Risalti . Lions, or cayls clawes; con
certed in to folliami. saltires. serpente
victories, or angels. antick heads in
shells. Charubin heads wth winges. heades
of beaste. Pedistals. Cornucupias. bascete
of fruetes. trofies. Juels and agates. medalio.
draperies. frontispices Booken. and Composed

I must ever remember to Curbe the doffollo
of wrighting and drawinge a waye upwards to
ye right hande and rather sinn in the contrary

Fig. 14.1. Inigo Jones, Roman Sketchbook, for. 100.
(The Devonshire Collection, Chatsworth. Reproduced by
permission of the Chatsworth Settlement of Trustees.
Photograph: Photographic Survey, Courtauld Institute of Art.)

Chapter 15

William Dampier's Unaccepted Life

Adrian Mitchell

Books are not absolutely dead things, wrote Milton in *Areopagitica* (1644), but contain a potency of life in them to be as active as that soul whose progeny they are. In more modern or perhaps late modern terms, we might prefer to argue that we give books life; and in autobiography we give them our own. Well and good, but, just as with talkback radio these days, so for the seventeenth century there is a question about whether just anyone's life and opinions are interesting. Increasingly, scholarship is acknowledging the voices of those who had no prominent or official position, but the interest for cultural and social history of these mainly unheard lives still needs to be tested. The aim of this essay is to test one such life, that of an explorer and privateer, William Dampier.

What the seventeenth century did interest itself in was a self-accounting, in the newfangled commercial idiom of an age of share investments, the foundation of the Bank of England, and John Locke's retrieval of the word *change*, for our little bits and pieces. The practice was something more sophisticated than the biblical "weighing in the balance," a casting up of spiritual accounts, as though Saint Peter had a double-entry ledger book like that of Samuel Pepys, where everything must be reconciled and all debts paid before proceeding any further. The age was growing increasingly interested in the internal constitution of things—Harvey looking for the master pump of human circulation, Descartes for some primary cog. Painters of the era moved on from portraiture to self-portraiture, sometimes through literal self-reflection, as in Vermeer; or through anatomy, literally seeing for one-self, as in Caravaggio's portrait of doubting Thomas, *The Incredulity of Saint Thomas* (1601–2), or Rembrandt's *The Anatomy Lesson of Dr. Nicolaes Tulp* (1632). These paintings do reveal a preoccupation with physical display, but they also have a more seriously considered pur-pose. However we might choose to entertain or respond to the ques-tion of self-representation in the seventeenth century, in these works we see as a kind of Newtonian constant: individuals stand increasingly in their own right, independent, separate from some containing or even sustaining institution. The seventeenth century gives us the woman or the man, warts and all.

In his recent essay on selfhood in the 1600s, Jonathan Sawday reminds us of the differentiations among individuality, autonomy, sub-jectivity, selfhood, and personality and calls attention to the number of *self*-compounds being used and introduced in the middle of the cen-tury, particularly in theological and philosophical writing. For Milton, self is a state of spiritual isolation, even though many of the Protestant movements were inclined to emphasize much more than did his major poem the experience of inwardness. This milieu, it is worth remem-bering, is also that of Dampier, an old pirating dog, buccaneer, cir-cumnavigator, would-be projector, scam merchant and meticulous observer, Lemuel Gulliver's cousin, and Daniel Defoe's unacknowl-edged archive. The early modern literary fascination with the self and autobiography, which is raised so strikingly in Montaigne's preface to his *Essais* (1580), when he proposes that "I am myself the subject of my book," remains in force for this very different kind of subject, who announces, "I am only to answer for myself" (Sloane f.233v; 424).

Dampier's three volumes of published *Voyages* were consumed not only by those narrative appropriators, and others, such as Coleridge, still later, but were carefully and respectfully consulted by Cook and Nelson and Flinders and Darwin. He was not, we might observe, an insignificant writer. He was not an insignificant navigator either. As far as we know, he was the first European to travel around the world three times, admittedly with breaks in between. Yet it is all too appar-ent that we learn almost nothing about him from those wonderful accounts of parts of a world relatively or totally unknown to the Euro-pean reading public. He was not predisposed to give voice to his own private reflections or to position himself in overt ways in his own nar-rative. Not that the latter was a noticeable lapse, for which readers would want to travel around the inside of a Somerset farm boy's hat-band when there was a whole exotic world to discover? His was just the kind of writing that the Royal Society had hoped to encourage, a steady and uncolored record of empirical observation. Dampier not only avoided the marvelous, he conscientiously disavowed it. For example (and to contradict myself momentarily), he speaks strongly if briefly of his disbelief in the practice of cannibalism, but in giving reasons for that disbelief he is proposing probability (or rather improbability), not a personal point of view.[1] He does from time to time remark on his own presence close to some natural wonder (a volcano, a waterspout, a band of blinking aborigines) but rarely with any acknowledgment or measure of his own experience of that event. There is in the printed version of Dampier's travels one, and one only, admission of the workings of providence, which we might assume says as much about a psychological as a theological frame of mind.[2] However, in the marginal annotations and also in the running text of the manuscript journal, there is a rather more recognizably seventeenth-century awareness of the self in relation to providence. He acknowledges "being tired with this Crosse of life" (Sloane fol. 209r; 375) and later recounts how "as soone as my freinds were gone I kneeled down and gave thanks to god allmighty for this deliverance" from having been marooned (Sloane fol. 226v; 410).

The difficulty with coming to terms with writing such as Dampier's is as much modern as contemporary. Those who recorded meeting and dining with him, John Evelyn, Samuel Pepys, and Charles Hatton, for example,[3] were more interested than they expected to be by what he had to say, for he did not impress them as an animated conversationalist and he lacked the social graces common to such high tables. Nor was he particularly lively. He did not, one speculates, have much sense of his own social consequence, certainly not as those other master essayists and stylists insistently displayed. His adventures had to speak for themselves. Or so it would seem, looking at the published voyages.

Problems in knowing how best to respond to these texts derive not so much from the insufficiency of detailed evidence, I suggest, as from a difficulty of our own making. We tend to be overly determined on a notion of the unified self and overly ready to impose our own reading on the seventeenth century, not letting it account for itself in its own terms. We know of those celebrated figures from literary history through what their books and letters say, but we do not know who or what they were in themselves. Pope told us this quite explicitly in setting out his theory of character and telling us just what persona he was going to adopt, unlikely choice as that may have seemed to some of his contemporaries. Dock-eared Defoe is invisible behind his eponymous heroes, distanced as they are from us by the intervening, unconvincing, and anonymous Editor of their narrated lives. The pretense, of course, is highly visible. The actuality is not there at all. The effect is, if we read the small print carefully, merely verisimilitude.

So what about Dampier? The surviving manuscript of his first volume is freely peppered with reference to his own opinion, but that personal assertion is for the most part edited out of the printed text. Such personal detail as does survive in print form is pretty much corralled into a subsequent volume of side trips (assuming, as one probably should not, that there had been a main itinerary in the first place) or, to think in terms more recognizably of book production, analects. In other words, Dampier himself does not belong in the *opus magnum*. The work by which he was known, and on which his literary reputation rests, is in the spirit of the Royal Society recommendations: plain, honest, matter of fact.[4] Those who have looked into the manuscript BL Sloane 3236 know that the draft copy of William Dampier's *New Voyage Round the World* (eventually published in 1697) has a series of running annotations in his own hand. The Sloane manuscript is evidently a fair copy of the journals that Dampier so carefully carried with him from ship to ship, or on his various buccaneer raids in Central America, rolled up in a length of bamboo and sealed at each end with wax. These are the manuscripts he carefully dried out when marooned in the Nicobar Islands.

What the manuscript provides is evidence of incrementing layers of composition. Dampier's annotations are, interestingly, heavily in the first person—in effect an incipient autobiography largely repressed in the published *Voyage*. And, it goes without saying, it is supplementary to the carefully written out manuscript journal, a journal draft not in Dampier's own hand. This marginal commentary forms something of an intermittent, companion autobiographical narrative to the account of Dampier's travels in the main body of the manuscript and the published version; it is also virtually a critical assessment of the buccaneering life. One way to read this suppressed "life" might be as rogue (auto)biography rather than buccaneer adventure. Dampier presents himself in this commentary as an informed participating witness rather than the more customary view of him, as we read in the *New Voyage*, as the prototype of a new scientific traveler. The running marginal annotations to Sloane 3236 are much more specific about events and personalities, more precise about such matters as slavery, and more technical about the ethos of privateering, than is the main narrative. They supply both expert and increased detail. Through such elaboration, they confirm, in the manner of travelers' tales, that "indeed, I must have been there." Yet, of course, as we know from Mandeville to Defoe, the detail does not prove any such thing. What it does demonstrate is that Dampier has an attitude toward his subject matter; he knows he is expert in what he witnesses. We are familiar with one kind of testimony he is making, one addressed to the new science; we are not so familiar with the other, a more intriguing autobiographical commentary. Is he expert about himself?

Dampier was not religious, and he was not preoccupied with his identity; he was not given to the egotistical sublime. He had, however, a new kind of individuality to reflect and express. He was, I suggest, an early version of a recognizably modern type: he was a professional. By this, I mean he recognized himself for what he was, and he measured himself against that model, just as he also measured his companions against it. And what the commentary shows again and again is that he found them wanting.

The self he expresses is not the inner man; it is the professional man, a man who is contemptuous of his fellows, who have fallen away from the old ways. He is a *privateer*. He is speaking for the kind of professionalism that was embedded in Cromwell's model army, not in such an apparently *religiose* way but in terms of control and self-management. He is dismayed by stupidity, especially when it is inspired by unthinking selfishness. At one point, Dampier comments acerbically in the margin: "all their armes were wet & some their ammunition for some men are soe careless that they will not wax their Cadure boxes tite though theyr Lives Depend on it" (Sloane fol. 136v; 241).

In writing of his perceptions and offering his criticism from the basis of professionalism, writing his life in that sense, Dampier is writing of "how it used to be." The modern generation is a degeneration, and pirate lives would in the near future become an Errol Flynn–like buckling of swashes, the colorful brag comparable to the declamations of notorious rogues in the Newgate Calendar. Dampier is not like that, nor is his close colleague Lionel Wafer. He is eventually almost as contemptuous of his shipmates as he is of the Spanish. They do not know their business, and they certainly do not know their own interest. They are a mad crew, thoughtless and spendthrift; they are a stubborn rabble. Dampier did indeed join with them as they made their raids on various towns and villages along the Central Americas. But it is apparent that he did not regard himself as one of them; he was as disdainful of their military strategy as he was of their disorderliness at sea. They were at best buccaneers, and he regarded himself as a privateer. When he and his fellows joined forces with another ship, he comments, "we . . . did not well agree on ye voyage for Eaton's men were but young beginners to the trade and Davis his men old privateers valued themselves on that score and would not agree on equal terms" (Sloane fol. 44r; 61). Bit by bit, the joined forces fell out; the old hands were mistrustful and, as in Dampier's case, apparently dissociated themselves from "our destructive crew" (*New Voyage* 228). For example, he amplifies a comment in the running text with a long marginal note: "I relate this and other passages of the like kind that the reader may know how bloody minded some men are & oft times it does not lie in the power of the commander nor any other men to hinder them yet these bloody mad swearing flashy fellows are commonly but ordinary fellows in the face of their enemies but I always observed in the greatest straits the more sober men most stout & undaunted" (Sloane fol. 128v; 280). These men are of course dangerous, not least to themselves. For Dampier, privateers are self-accountable, independent; as he recounts them, buccaneers exist only as a corporate entity.

A Bunyanesque climax to the buccaneering/privateering venture comes after the attempted sacking of Panama City. It was the last great buccaneering raid, though Dampier could not have had much sense of that as a historically significant event when there was a further and even more abortive raid to follow, on Guayaquil on the coast of Ecuador, and another greater disaster just nearby on the Santiago River. Everything goes wrong, and mostly because of the bungling and cowardice of the raiders. Dampier was both sickened and disgusted at the incompetence and folly of his countrymen. A whole squad is killed because they did not practice the proven strategies of the privateers and exposed themselves to ambush by riding in single file.

The distinction between privateer and buccaneer is more than semantic. I suggest that it gives us the key to Dampier's self-imaging and self-valuing. At his court-martial in 1702, witnesses attested to his anger at being called an old pirate. That had been an insult from the Admiralty's man, and the trading of insults, which went both ways between the cantankerous parties, would certainly support a reading about the potency of bad language aboard the *Roebuck*. Dampier's chief accuser at that trial, Lieutenant Fisher, evidently misunderstood the crucial distinction, or possibly willfully and insultingly misunderstood the distinction, in identifying Dampier with piracy: "I being in my Capt. Mess after Dinner we was Drinking a Boule of Punch in Company . . . wee happened into Discourse Conserning a Pirats Life which my Capt. Called Privateers and he sayed thear Life was the Best of Lives" (qtd. Baer 109). Dampier's estimation of privateering was not disputed by other witnesses.

What the marginal notes begin to unpack for us is crucial in our understanding of the curious situation of a man who associated with both admirals and drifters, a man who held to an older way of seafaring life not so much in terms of acquired skills—significant as these indisputably were in his case—as in terms of the set of values associated with it. The privateers made their decisions in common; they held equal shares in plunder (but not, interestingly, in whatever they could provide for themselves by hunting); they signed agreed articles and demanded certain privileges; and they acknowledged no hierarchy but elected such officers as the all important quartermaster, who could expect to be given command of the next prize.[5] But such authority was only lent, and it could be withdrawn at the whim of the men. From the navy's point of view, this was no way to run a ship, and Fisher was right to be alarmed. As it turned out, Dampier showed on his second voyage that he was not much good at running a ship, once given that office. But any comment about that is, if it exists, in a journal no one has ever seen.

The point about privateering is not in some possible continuance of Leveler sympathies and communal values (though at least one of Dampier's shipmates had fought with Oliver Cromwell, probably as part of the Western Design, Cromwell's Caribbean strategy).[6] On the contrary, what privateering tacitly conceded was a substantial degree of autonomy within that collective framework. Those two complementary directions are what the late Christopher Hill, for example, finds entrenched in the seventeenth century. The word *privateering* itself signals independence of activity, and one should not be surprised to learn that privateering continued extensively off the Americas throughout the nineteenth century, until the United States invented both its own navy and the gob hat. Dampier did not fit in well with regulation, yet his whole inquiry was into identifying and so underpinning the scientific regulation of the world (though he was not, it appears, much interested in cataloging or categorizing).

The marginalia are, of course, more expansive than the fair copy of the journal on every point of detail; indeed, that is why they are there, as additional commentary. The printed text is much more selective about all sorts of matters of opinion, about slavery, for example, and ethnography; about interest in the exotic and erotic customs of the Philippines; and about the reciprocal interest of the sailors there and thereabouts. The published text likewise reduces the extent of Dampier's antipathy toward the Spanish. There may have been good political reasons for such censorship at this time, if that is what it was, but one consequence is that the excisions increase the distance between Dampier and his role model, Francis Drake. In so doing, they reduce any claim that Dampier could make that he was advancing the national and Protestant interest. To be more precise, Dampier patterned, rather than modeled, himself on Sir Francis Drake. Drake had the formula, we might say, of success—the West Country nobody who forced a knighthood out of the system—and Dampier was an early modern in the "Hamlet sense" of trying on available roles and so in his own way affirmed that early modern sense that identity is a complex structure and practice.

So the question arises how and why this more immediately autobiographical side of Dampier's activities, these insights into his life, were largely suppressed in the published work. There are references to editorial assistance both by Dampier himself and in Swift's jeers.[7] In the preface to *A Voyage to New Holland*, Dampier concedes, "I think it so far from being a Diminution to one of my Education and Employment, to have what I write, Revised and Corrected by Friends; that on the contrary, the best and most eminent Authors are not ashamed to own the same Thing, and look upon it as an Advantage" (lxviii). We can also speculate on the interference of the publisher, James Knapton. In the history of publishing, Knapton has received good press. He was acknowledged as a leading publisher of travel journals, and he included in these the maps of Hermann Moll. But in fact it can be readily seen that Dampier made him rather than that he made Dampier. Dampier was his trademark success. In the decade before he took up Dampier's journal, he had published mainly the last works of the unfairly notorious poet laureate, Thomas Shadwell, some of Aphra Behn's plays, and one of John Crowne's less successful comedies. Like Moll and Pitt and others, he frequented Jonathan's Coffee House in Change Alley, a Tory stronghold where subscriptions were taken for the formation of the National Bank and where subsequently much of the activity that led to the foundation of the Stock Exchange and also to the South Sea Bubble occurred. Jonathan's was by reputation a meeting place for merchants, seafarers, and traders; it is supposed that Dampier, Wafer, and other would-be projectors found their contacts there. Certainly Knapton did. The publisher and bookseller John Dunton commented of him: "Mr. Knapton—He is a very accomplisht Person, not that thin sort of Animal, that flutters from Tavern to Playhouse, and back again, all his Life made up with Wig and Cravat, without one Dram of Thought in his Composition; but a person made up with Solid Worth, Brave, and Generous; and shews by his purchasing Dampier's Voyages, he knows how to value a good Copy" (*Life*). He also knew the value of advertising, placing advertisements of forthcoming publications in the *Spectator*.[8] A decade later, however, he was chasing after a more sensationalist kind of publication, in choosing to publish Dampier's nemesis, William Funnell, for example.[9] The earlier determination to celebrate respectability became compromised, just as was Dampier himself. There is a correlation here that has still to be unraveled. What Knapton did, it may be supposed, was cancel the evidence of Dampier himself from the manuscript that was offered him and had it replaced with much more sustained and detailed descriptions of strange parts of the world. Dampier, that is, was precluded from speaking for himself. Knapton, it could be argued, erased the liveliness of Dampier's life to present a more respectable author and therefore a more credible work. We do not in fact know. What we can measure is the degree of the suppression of Dampier's own opinion, if not his life. Paradoxically, the extent of the erasure can be perceived.

There is one other piece of evidence about William Dampier, the portrait of 1697.[10] This, too, displays the marginalized Dampier, even though he is the subject of the painting. The fact that it was commissioned means that a particular version of him is being commemorated. He is found to be respectable, and for once sober, with his book between viewer and subject, a book modestly lowered, offered rather than claimed. The facial image is not modest, though, but guarded, self-contained. What self is to be expressed? The title of the portrait gives us a choice of two—William Dampier, pirate and hydrographer. More choices are on offer: he is the acquaintance and in some sense protégé of the respectable world, of the senior officers and social leaders of the Royal Society (through Sir Hans Sloane in the first instance). Yet his leather jacket reminds us of Cromwell and then of the Leveler sympathies identifiable among the privateers and buccaneers, the "brotherhood of the coast." Is the orange of his waistcoat a hint of or appeal to a royal favor? He was, several years later, invited to kiss the queen's hand. And as we look more carefully we can see that he is, as it were, standing back from his own portrait. The light falls on his forehead, his mind let us say, but more emphatically on the spine of the book. In terms of the painting, the book carries the imaginative color; the rest is plain speaking and homespun. It is possible to read the gold lettering, "Dampier's Voyage," and something inscrutable on the third line. There is always something more to dig out of the text. What we chiefly see is the golden blaze along the spine, the gold of all Dampier's aspirations, the gold of his dreaming, and the gold that, apart from this one instance, he seemed unable to hold on to. Dampier himself is already receding into a plain and unspeaking background. That is to say, the portrait is the very emblem of the autobiographical project. Dampier is his book, and that is what autobiographies do: they turn people into books of themselves.

Dampier, then, has given us more than we recognize, if we only knew it. And it is particularly apt, given the way his life turned out, that we should discover him literally in the margins. When we reinstitute the marginal, in this as in the greater generality, we reconstitute the man Dampier could claim to be. Yet there is a certain poignancy in seeing him as one who continues to inhabit the margin, off to one side, as though historically speaking that is not only his inevitable but also his proper stance. That is where we find him drawing his own self-portrait. It is a life that Knapton, for one, chose not to read, and chose for us not to read, the life of an old piratical dog, whom time had left behind. Yet, as we can see when we can see it, Dampier's is also an exemplary life; a life unaccepted, but in his own view not altogether unacceptable.

NOTES

1. "As for the common Opinion of Authropophagi [*sic*], or Man-eaters, I did never meet with any such People: All Nations or Families in the World, that I have seen or heard of, having some sort of Food to live on, either Fruit, Grain, Pulse or Rootes, which grow naturally, or else planted by them; if not Fish and Land-Animals besides; (yea, even the People of New-Holland had Fish amidst all their Penury) and would scarce kill a Man purposely to eat him. I know not what barbarous Customs may formerly have been in the World; and to sacrifice their Enemies to their Gods, is a thing hath been much talked of, with Relation to the Savages of America. I am a Stranger to that also, if it be, or have been customary in any Nation there; and yet, if they sacrifice their Enemies, it is not necessary they should eat them too. After all, I will not be peremptory in the Negative; but I speak as to the Compass of my own Knowledge, and know some of these Cannibal Stories to be false, and many of them have been disproved since I first went to the West-Indies" (*New Voyage* 325).

2. "I had long before this repented me of that roving Course of Life, but never with such Concern as now. I did also call to mind the miraculous Acts of God's Providence towards me in the whole Course of my Life, of which kind I believe few Men have met with the like. For all these I returned Thanks in a peculiar Manner. . . . Submitting our selves therefore to God's

good Providence, and taking all the Care we could to preserve our Lives, Mr. Hall and I took turns to steer" (*New Voyage* 333).

3. "I have discoursed with Dampier. He is a blunt fellow, but of better understanding then wou'd be exspected from one of his education. He is a very good navigator, kept his journall esactly, and set down every day what he thought remearkable; but, you must imagine, had assistance in dressing up his history, in which are many mistakes in naming of places" (Charles Hatton to Christopher Hatton, May 27, 1697, *Correspondence* 1.225).

4. The marginal comment to Sloane MS. fol. 128v reads: "I came into those seas this second time more to Endulge my curiosity then to gett wealth though I must confess at that time I did think the trade Lawfull yet had never followed it but in hopes to make such descoveryes as might in time conduce to the benefit of my nation" (228).

5. "The Companyes quartermaster is the next man to the Captain & yet servant to all the ships Company & is in many things beyond a lieutenant in a kings ship & they should understand navagation because the prise oft to be Commanded by him" (Sloane fol. 59r [marginal note]; 92).

6. "[O]ne John Swan a man of 84 year old whoe had ben a privateer Ever since Jamaica was taken" (Sloane fol. 26r [marginal note]; 224). In the printed version, it is precisely stated that he served under Cromwell (*New Voyage* 155). For the Leveler sympathies, see Linebaugh and Rediker, *Many-Headed Hydra*.

7. Jonathan Swift, "A Letter from Captain Gulliver to His Cousin Sympson," *Gulliver's Travels* (1726): "I hope you will be ready to own publicly, whenever you should be called to it, that by your great and frequent urgency you prevailed on me to publish a very loose and uncorrect account of my travels; with direction to hire some young gentlemen of either University to put them in order, and correct the style, as my Cousin Dampier did by my advice, in his book called *A Voyage round the World*." Dampier had died ten years previous to this.

8. For Knapton's advertising strategy, see Bonner, *Captain William Dampier:* "Addison quoted from him [Dampier] in the *Tatler* and the *Spectator* and Knapton advertised Dampier in the *Spectator*" (37).

9. Funnell was Dampier's mate on the *St. George* in 1703–4 and published his own account of some of their voyages.

10. The portrait is *William Dampier: Pirate and Hydrographer*, by Thomas Murray, ca.1697, commissioned by Sir Hans Sloane. It now hangs in the National Portrait Gallery, London.

WORKS CITED

Baer, Joel H. "William Dampier at the Crossroads: New Light on the 'Missing Years,' 1691–1697." *International Journal of Maritime History* 8 (1996): 97–117.

Bonner, William Hallam. *Captain William Dampier, Buccaneer-Author*. Stanford: Stanford UP, 1934.

Correspondence of the Family of Hatton. Vol. 1. Ed. Edward Maunde Thompson. London: Camden Society, 1878.

Dampier, William. Sloane MS. 3236. British Library, London.

———. *A New Voyage Round the World.* Ed. N. M. Penzer 1697; London: Argonaut Press, 1927; London: A. and C. Black, 1937.

———. *A Supplement to the Voyage Round the World.* London: James Knapton, 1698. Short title *Voyages and Descriptions.*

———. *A Voyage to New Holland.* Ed. James Williamson. 1703; 1708; London: Argonaut, 1939.

Dunton, John. *The Life and Errors of John Dunton.* London: Printed for S. Malthus, 1705.

Funnell, William. *A Voyage Round the World: Containing an Account of Captain Dampier's Expedition into the South-Sea in the Ship of St. George.* London: Printed by W. Botham for James Knapton, 1707.

Hill, Christopher. *Some Intellectual Consequences of the English Revolution.* Madison: U of Wisconsin P, 1980.

Linebaugh, Peter, and Marcus Rediker. *The Many-Headed Hydra: The Hidden History of the Revolutionary Atlantic.* Boston: Beacon, 2000.

Sawday, Jonathan. "Self and Selfhood in the Seventeenth Century." *Rewriting the Self: Histories from the Renaissance to the Present.* Ed. Roy Porter. London: Routledge, 1997. 29–48.

Chapter 16

Legal Autobiography in Early Modern England

Wilfrid Prest

The boundary fences between history, literature, and other human-istic disciplines have sagged a little over the past decade. Yet while some historians of early modern England are now busily exploring the cultural dimensions of the English Renaissance state, this "remap-ping," in Kevin Sharpe's phrase, seems somewhat narrowly conceived. The new cultural history's institutional focus is almost exclusively on the royal court and the church. Despite a considerable burgeoning of legal-historical studies since the 1970s, the secular law courts, together with the crowds of litigants and legal practitioners who—as it now appears—frequented them more intensively in this period than ever before or since in the course of English history, remain largely overlooked. Further elaboration of the labyrinthine complexities of a reified "common-law mind" is no adequate substitute for a systematic exploration of the ways in which resort to law and lawyers molded both popular and elite attitudes during the later sixteenth and seven-teenth centuries.

Alas, a single essay could hardly begin to fill that gap. But, having once attempted to use the memoirs of common lawyers and law stu-dents to illuminate the working conditions, mind-sets, and private and domestic lives of members of the English bar in the half century before the Long Parliament (Prest), I welcome the opportunity to reflect on this material as a cultural artifact in its own right. I use a rather con-ventional conception of autobiography, while by *lawyer* I refer primar-ily to members of the bar and bench, the "upper-branch" elite of the common-law profession. The chapter focuses particularly on Sir William Blackstone, whose influential *Commentaries on the Laws of England* (1765–69) appears in retrospect to mark a decisive turning point in the common law's long history. It commences with an overview of later sixteenth- and seventeenth-century legal autobiography, moving on to consider Blackstone's own unusual self-life, which in some respects represents a revival of what had once been a flourishing subgenre.

Casual perusal of some standard works on early modern English autobiography might leave the impression that there is no substance to the subject of legal autobiography in early modern England. From the dated literary scholarship of Margaret Bottrall's *Every Man a Phoenix* (1958) and Paul Delany's *British Autobiography in the Seventeenth Century* (1969) to the theoretically informed and methodologically sophisticated overview offered by Michael Mascuch's *Origins of the Individualist Self* (1997), lawyers barely figure as autobiographical subjects. Thus Delany's survey of "nearly two hundred autobiographies, published and unpublished" is organized around a simple binary division between religious and secular autobiography. The latter category includes traveler's tales, military and political memoirs, and the life histories of miscellaneous "individualists" in the form of courtiers, "declassé opportunists and adventurers," and "Gentlemen of Leisure" (Delany 3, 133, 142). Lawyers—whether civil, common, or ecclesiastical, attorneys, barristers, judges, law clerks, legal bureaucrats or officeholders, notaries and solicitors—simply pass unnoticed. Indeed, Delany wholly disregards even the "Liber Famelicus" of the Jacobean and Caroline judge Sir James Whitelocke, to which Bottrall had at least alluded, somewhat condescendingly, ten years earlier (Bottrall 144). The omission is compounded by an unfortunate categorization of the extensive autobiographical writings of Bulstrode, James Whitelocke's son, a practicing common lawyer before his career as parliamentarian politician, judge, and diplomat during the 1640s–50s, as "conventional. . . . *military* memoirs" (Delany 119; my italics).

These mis- (or perhaps non-) readings may result in part from the nature of Delany's sources, as well as his teleological focus on the development of the autobiographical genre. Writing more than a generation ago, Delany used very few original manuscripts, relying almost exclusively on printed texts. In the case of both Whitelockes, that meant two unsatisfactory nineteenth-century editions of seventeenth-century manuscripts, one of which reached the British Museum only in the late 1960s, while the other, still privately held, did not appear in a comprehensive scholarly edition until 1990 (Powell 11–12; Spalding, 27–37). Similar circumstances help explain his failure to notice some (if not quite all) of the other relevant early modern legal autobiographies. And yet, while Delany does devote several pages to the autobiography of the barrister Roger North (as reproduced in Augustus Jessopp's defective 1887 edition) as "a mature example of the dominant mode of seventeenth-century secular autobiography," he treats Clarendon's *History of His Own Life* entirely as "political memoir," the "testament of a great historian, statesman and observer," albeit one that "fails to satisfy our curiosity about the inner nature of the man who wrote it" (120–21, 148–51).[1]

Another reason why Bottrall and Delany largely ignore or elide early modern lawyer autobiographers is that their work was undertaken before the twin 1960s booms in social history and legal-historical studies, which saw growing attention paid to the culture, mind-set, and working lives of early modern English legal practitioners, both common lawyers and civilians. In this respect, Mascuch's neglect of early modern lawyers as autobiographers is all the more puzzling. By the same token, his claim that despite the long preexistence of "ship's logs, business ledgers, corporate chronicles and family estate and household account books" in pre-Reformation England "writing skills were indispensable only to persons engaged in trade"—or to monks— would have raised some eyebrows around fifteenth-century Chancery Lane, High Holborn, and Westminster Hall (Mascuch 74). Mascuch's further assertion that "the use of private notebooks by individual persons to record matter pertaining to their own experience was something new in 1600" (72) is also difficult to reconcile with the known prevalence of common placing and the compilation of diaries or journals by students at the Tudor Inns of Court, the ubiquity of case notes and reports of legal argument written down by students and practitioners for their own use, and what was possibly a widespread practice of keeping fee books, combining rudimentary financial accounts and work diaries, despite the low survival rate of these workaday records. Such vocational habits and techniques undoubtedly contributed, though to what extent may be debatable, to the tally of recorded late-sixteenth- and seventeenth-century legal autobiographies, which I list here in chronological order of composition.

Ralph Rokeby, *Oeconomia Rokebiorum* (1565–93)
John Savile, *Autobiography* [modern title] (ca.1607)
James Whitelocke, *Liber Famelicus* (1609–32)

John Lowther, *Autobiography* [modern title] (1612–35)
Richard Hutton, *Diary* [modern title] (1614–39)
Robert Ashley, *Vita R. A. ab ipso conscripta* (ca.1632)
Justinian Pagitt, *Journal* [modern title] (1633–35)
Simonds D'Ewes, *Book of My Life* (1635–50)
Edward Hyde, *The History of His Own Life* (1646–74)
Bulstrode Whitelocke, *Annales of His Own Life, History and Diary*
     [modern title] (before 1663–75)
John Bramston, *Memoires* (ca.1682–99)
Roger North, *Notes of Me* (ca.1693–98)

All twelve authors were qualified barristers, belonging to the voca-
tionally and socially privileged "upper branch" of the common-law
profession, although Simonds D'Ewes inherited his father's estate
before he had to earn his own living at the bar, while John Bramston
only practiced as a barrister for seven years following his call to the
bar in 1635, "untill, as I may say, the drums and trumpets blew my
gowne ouer my eares" (Bramston 103). Ralph Rokeby and John
Lowther both ended their professional careers with the Council of the
North in York, on which body Lowther sat as a judge; others who held
judicial office were Savile, both Whitelockes, Richard Hutton, and
Edward Hyde. Bulstrode Whitelocke shared a room with Hyde when
they were law students together at the Middle Temple, and both practiced at the bar in the 1630s, although they eventually achieved more
prominence as politicians than lawyers and acquired high politico-
judicial office, as commissioner of the Great Seal and lord chancellor,
respectively, for reasons other than their jurisprudential attainments.
Of the rest, the virtuoso Robert Ashley was a scholar; traveler; published translator of works from the French, Italian, and Spanish; and
de facto founder of the Middle Temple library, as well as an unsuccessful barrister. Justinian Pagitt became a legal bureaucrat, practicing counselor, and friend of Samuel Pepys, while Roger North practiced at the bar under the protection of his elder brother, Lord
Chancellor Francis North, before retiring to his country estate during
the Glorious Revolution.
     How far were these lawyers—by training and formal qualification,
and mostly by occupation—autobiographers? All the writings listed
earlier contain at least some autobiographical element in the form of
retrospective accounts of the author's life, though modes and proportions vary. In terms of autobiographical content, most are somewhat
prosaic and matter-of-fact, largely avoiding the introspective emo-

tional analysis characteristic of autobiography as it is usually categorized today. At the thinner and perhaps more tenuous end of the spectrum from this point of view are the occasional first-person authorial
reminiscences that punctuate Rokeby's family chronicle, the *Oeconomia
Rokebiourum*. One example is a paragraph recalling Ralph having
"richlye beautified" the window of his Lincoln's Inn chamber with his
own "coate armes" and those of his pious roommates Charles
Calthrope, John Tindall, and John Stubbes: "where me seemed then
the chamber, for the most part was well furnished . . . and for good Mr
Stubbs I highlye thanke God for him, for the correcting of many
unrulye humours in me, and trayneing me into the pathe to God"
(Whitaker 179). Richard Hutton's diary or journal is a public and professional account of the author's times rather than a personal memoir;
other than the bare mention of the death of his elder son in 1619,
domestic or family detail is entirely absent. Written largely in law-
French, the working shorthand of the bar, the two volumes now in the
Cambridge University Library may well have been extracted from the
working case notes or law reports that Hutton also compiled during
his working life. Yet personal references are not rigidly excluded. Hutton's text, like that of his fellow North countryman Rokeby, is frequently cast in the first person, with numerous accounts of events in
which the author was involved as participant-observer, for example
James I's ceremonial stopover in York on his journey to Edinburgh in
1617: as the city's recorder, Serjeant Hutton took a prominent role in
welcoming the royal guest and in turn was knighted by his monarch,
who "dit a moy ridendo que ceo fait forsque un additament a mon honour" (Hutton 18).

While Rokeby and Hutton provide only fleeting glimpses of their
own life histories, Justinian Pagitt's manuscript *Journal* or "Memorandum Book" is almost wholly introspective, if not an exercise in self-
exploration. This document includes notes of sermons and on theological issues, copies of letters, adages, maxims, self-examinations,
"meditacons and Resolues," and accounts of his stepmother's misdeeds
and his own dealings with friends, servants, and family, together with
a diary record of daily activities extending over nearly three months in
1633–34. Yet, while highly self-conscious, and self-regarding, since
the *Journal* involves little more than short-range retrospectivity and
lacks any coherent narrative structure, this text is perhaps best
regarded as potential rather than actual autobiography. Indeed, it
comprises what Francis Bacon might have termed "preparatives to
autobiography," that is to say, a collection of miscellaneous materials

from which a self-life or life history could have been constructed but apparently was not (Shapiro 38).

No such reservations apply to the other nine items listed earlier. Sir John Savile, elder brother of the scholar Sir Henry, wrote his brief autobiography in Latin and largely in the third person. It chronicles his Yorkshire parentage, education at Oxford and the Middle Temple, parliamentary service, and the offices held en route to the ranks of sergeant at law and baron of the Exchequer. The same flat, distant, impersonal tone is maintained throughout Savile's sparse recital of his successive marriages (four in all), the deaths of his wives, the births of two sons and three daughters, and the surviving girls' eventual marriages. Betraying little sense of authorial character or personal involvement, Savile's curt record of advancement through professional distinction, royal service, and connections both marital and legal might suggest that (rather like Hutton) he had internalized the North country adage to "See all and say nowt," if not (or perhaps more likely) the neo-Stoic emphasis on personal restraint and self-mastery often associated with the writings of Justus Lipsius (Clay and Lister 420–27).

With James Whitelocke's *Liber Famelicus*, we enter a distinctly more emotionally charged and individualized environment. Contrary to Bottrall's dismissal of this work as "the simplest type of chronicle autobiography" (144), his recent biographer maintains that careful contextualized reading of the holograph text "draws one ever deeper into James Whitelocke's changing perception of the world" (Powell 11). Whitelocke's purpose is openly avowed at the start of the small paper notebook in which he began, as he states, on 18 April 1609, "to set downe memorialls for my posterity of thinges most properly concerning myself and my familye" (Bruce 1). Besides predictable accounts of career and family milestones, these "thinges" include colorful and sometimes mordant vignettes of contemporary legal and political issues and personalities, as, for example, an extensive narrative of the court machinations that denied Whitelocke an appointment to the recordership of London in 1619 (Bruce 63–69). Thereafter promotion to the judicial bench, heightened national political polarization, and perhaps the weight of years produced what is generally a barer and blander account, essentially structured around the course of his professional life, even if still including details of family and personal interest, as well as public events.

As revealed in his autobiography, Whitelocke's personal identity, like that of Savile and Hutton, seems to grow out of his vocational involvement with the common law, both as barrister and judge. An equally pronounced sense of professional belonging and self-identification characterizes Sir John Lowther's lengthy autobiographical memoir, which occurs in a volume of estate accounts and memoranda dating from the mid-sixteenth to the later seventeenth century, part of the extensive Lonsdale archive now held by the Cumbria Record Office at Carlisle. This document also purports to have been prepared primarily for the benefit of the author's children. "[M]y principall Intention," wrote Lowther, "is to leave unto you my posteritie With the evidences of my lands allsoe these undigested notes as evidences of my heart and minde, which is the best purtraiture, and my owne observations and practise in my perticulars, and somewhat toutching other generall occurents in my time as occasion serveth" (Phillips 206). John Lowther (1581–1637) emphasized that what he had written was far from being "an exact and orderly composed treatise for that my time is otherwise employed and I am at this present exercised in the practice of the law which requireth an whole man and all his time and whatsoever I write now is [in] an hour of leisure, which will make it a disjointed word, having forgotten when I begin to write what I wrote last" (Phillips 202). Composed at various points over the long period 1612–35, Lowther's text is indeed discursive, even chatty in a ponderous fashion, mixing large slabs of self-history with accounts of current issues and problems confronting the author and his estate, pious ejaculations, philosophical observations, and prudential precepts for the future conduct of his readers. His personal tale is one of worldly advancement. In the words of Lowther's modern editor, he "chronicles the rise of a young man lacking wealth or influence . . . [and] self-effacing comments on his own progress serve really to magnify rather than to play down his achievements" (Phillips ix).

    In terms of the development of autobiography as a genre, perhaps the two most interesting texts are the picaresque Latin narrative of Robert Ashley, with its unusually detailed account of the author's childhood and multiple schooling experiences; his dreams, illnesses, studies, and travels (Ashley); and the expansive meditations and vivid reflections of the polymathic Roger North, whose *Notes of Me*, now available in an excellent modern edition, employs a narrative of life events as pegs on which to hang extended explorations of the author's own character, interests, and predilections (Millard). By contrast, Bramston, D'Ewes, Hyde, and Bulstrode Whitelocke wrote far more conventional and less personal memoirs of their eventful lives and times, influenced in D'Ewes's case by the Protestant spiritual diary tradition, but otherwise by more classical models.

Shortage of space prevents detailed discussion of each of these works, but it may be helpful to attempt a few generalizations about the whole dozen. First, and unsurprisingly, early modern legal autobiographers tended to start from the family origins of their subject, then to trace his progress in the (secular) world. With the obvious exception of North's introspective *Notes of Me*, and despite some partial counterindications in the cases of Ashley, Rokeby, D'Ewes, and Pagitt, they seldom focus explicitly on the development of the inner soul or consciousness. Accordingly, their readers, if any, seem to be envisaged as members of the next generation (although Savile and Hutton do not address a specific audience, while Pagitt and North are perhaps primarily interested in exploring their own reactions). Similarly, their main narrative principle, insofar as they have one, is success (or perhaps the lack of it in the case of Ashley) in making good or rising in the world. Second, autobiographical form and style vary no less widely than the language in which they were written: as we have seen, Hutton's *Diary* is penned mainly in law-French, while Savile and Ashley wrote in Latin and Hyde notoriously used a very Latinate English prose. By choosing the third person and avoiding the vernacular, these writers signaled their overt purpose as an objective account of public events, res gestae; the individual subject's involvement in or reaction to those events is not always explicitly indicated and rarely if ever the main overt focus of attention. Third, note taking at Inns of Court moots and readings, and other writing habits associated with the educational formation and working lives of barristers, may have helped mold the loosely organized, somewhat desultory format of the compilations by Hutton, Lowther, Pagitt, James Whitelocke, perhaps his son Bulstrode, and North. The latter's complex and wide-ranging text was also plainly influenced (as his modern editor suggests) by the fashionable post-Restoration interest in closely observed experiment, together with a more highly developed, post-Montaigne, self-referential "individualism" than is exhibited by any other early modern lawyer autobiographer (Millard 42–56). Last, a simply quantitative point: there was a good deal of autobiographical writing by early modern English common lawyers.

Yet, remarkably, from the end of the seventeenth century this tradition appears to have dried up and remained in abeyance for the best part of a hundred years. Indeed, I cannot identify a single barrister or judge autobiographer between Roger North in the 1690s and William Blackstone in the 1770s—and, as we shall shortly see, Blackstone's original autobiography can be only partially recovered. The remainder of this essay discusses the nature of that work and the circumstances of its creation. By looking at Blackstone's autobiography—which is preeminently the history of someone who rose in the world through diligence and virtuous self-application—in the context of his professional circumstances as well as his personal practice, I also aim to provide at least some partial explanation of his role in reviving an apparently defunct subgenre.

Sir William Blackstone, justice of the King's Bench and author of *Commentaries on the Laws of England,* the most widely studied lawbook—indeed one of the most influential books of any kind—ever written in the English language, died in February 1780 at the relatively early age of fifty-six years. His will directed that the case notes or law reports he had compiled for his own use since Michaelmas term 1746 should be published after his death. Preparing this material for the press fell to his brother-in-law, friend, and executor, James Clitherow, whose preface to the first volume of the *Reports* on their publication in 1781 claimed that he had been persuaded by many of Blackstone's friends "to pay a Tribute due to the Memory of so respectable a Person, by imparting at the same time to the Public a short Account of his Life and gradual Rise from a posthumous Orphan to the Dignity and high Station He at last attained" (Clitherow i). Clitherow goes on to explain that he had hoped to leave this responsibility to "an abler Pen." But, since these expectations were unfulfilled because of the illness and death of "the learned and ingenious Dr Buckler . . . one of Mr Justice Blackstone's oldest and most intimate Friends," he had "ventured, though totally unused to writing for the public Eye, to undertake the Task himself." Fortunately Clitherow could call on "An intimate Acquaintance with Mr Justice Blackstone for above thirty years," the assistance of others who had known him even longer, "and a short Abstract of every Circumstance of Consequence in his Life, written by himself with his accustomed Accuracy . . ."(Clitherow ii).

How much of that original "short Abstract" can now be extracted from the text of Clitherow's biographical "Memoirs"? Most of the material on its subject's family origins and education was probably derived from Blackstone's summary of his own career, including the account of the "affectionate, it may be said the parental, Care" given his young fatherless nephews by the London surgeon Thomas Bigg and the description of Blackstone's early schooldays at the Charterhouse, as "the favourite of his Masters, who encouraged and assisted him with the utmost Attention" (Clitherow iv). The same perhaps applies to the picture of his early days at Oxford, where "he prosecuted his Studies with unremitting Ardour . . . although the Classics, and especially the Greek and Roman Poets were his Favourites . . . Logick, Mathematicks, and the other Sciences were not neglected" (Clitherow v). There may also be a direct autobiographical note in the candid account of Blackstone's early difficulties at the bar, "not being happy in a graceful Delivery or a Flow of Elocution (both which he much wanted) nor having any powerful Friends or Connexions to recommend him" (Clitherow vii). Another place at which Blackstone's own voice seems to come through is in the paragraphs dealing with his resignation from Oxford's Vinerian chair in the Laws of England, "finding he could not discharge the personal Duties of the former, consistently with his professional Attendances in London, or the Delicacy of his Feelings as an honest Man," after the frustration of his plan to set up in Oxford a society for "Students of the Common Law, similar to that of *Trinity-Hall* in *Cambridge* for Civilians" (Clitherow xvii–xviii). Otherwise pure Blackstone can hardly be distinguished from Blackstone-cum-Clitherow.

Yet the broad theme of Clitherow's narrative must also reflect Blackstone's own view of his life and its meaning: "to the rising Generation a bright example of a Man, who without Fortune, Family Interest, or Connexions, raised himself by a diligent Attention to his Studies, even from his earliest Youth" (Clitherow ii). We have already seen that this story of upward mobility through virtuous effort is a pervasive motif of early modern legal autobiography. How are we to account for its revival by Blackstone and his posthumous editor, especially after the apparent drying up of legal autobiography from the end of the seventeenth century?

Of course, it may be that the seeming drought is really an optical illusion, due to my having overlooked relevant sources that once did or do still exist, perhaps because they remain in more or less inaccessible manuscript repositories. Yet, despite that theoretical possibility, which can never be entirely eliminated, later Stuart and Hanoverian barristers have recently attracted considerable attention from historians, whose labors have nevertheless failed to reveal any such sources (Duman; Lemmings *Gentlemen*). Nor does a search of the standard bibliographies and other works of reference prove any more productive (Pargellis and Medley; Greene; Stauffer). Instead it deepens the mystery, revealing that legal biography, whether the lives of individual lawyers or group portraits and collected lives, is also exceedingly thin on the ground for most of the eighteenth century, that "High Renaissance in the art of biography" according to one authority (Stauffer 457). Stauffer identifies physicians, scientists, painters, and admirals—but not lawyers—as among the various occupational groups that had "learned to take care of themselves very well biographically" in Hanoverian England (506–7). In literary terms, the law was represented less by lives of legal practitioners than by the purported true confessions and last dying speeches of those who may variously be regarded as its objects, or victims, since "Hanging was the most nearly direct way to immediate biographical fame" (Stauffer 199).

Thus we may be confronting a real bibliographical and cultural phenomenon, not merely an evidential mirage. But then why should barristers have both received less attention from biographers and also felt less inclined to write their own lives during the seventy-five years or so after 1700 than they had done in the previous century or more? Here are some possible answers. First, there were significantly fewer common lawyers in the later period. Admissions to the Inns of Court and calls to the bar (like matriculations at Oxford and Cambridge), showed a general downward trend from the 1680s to the 1760s; in the decade of George III's accession, fewer than twenty-five men were called to the bar each year, which is less than half the figure of calls for the peak decades of the early seventeenth century. This numerical shrinkage partly reflected broader national demographic trends. But it was also associated with an apparent slump in the volume of litigation, which saw the volume of noncriminal business handled by the superior courts of Westminster Hall contract very markedly during the first half of the eighteenth century (Brooks chaps. 3–4). This downturn had various effects on barristers' working lives. It probably became more difficult to establish a career at the bar; while a small number of leading counsels increasingly dominated each court, their workloads rose steeply in consequence. Together with other developments (notably the continued numerical expansion and vocational consolidation of the profession's "lower branch" of attorneys and solicitors), the litigation squeeze accentuated preexisting tendencies for barristers' practices to concentrate in London, to become more intensely focused on specialized professional functions, and to restrict contact with the general public, which found it increasingly difficult to consult members of the bar directly rather than via a solicitor (Lemmings *Gentlemen*). Hence in the eighteenth century there were fewer barristers either to write their own lives or to be written about, while those few possibly had less leisure to write and less diversely interesting—or indeed rewarding—lives as biographical subjects than had their seventeenth-century predecessors.

But, third, it was not merely a matter of smaller numbers and more restricted opportunities for literary pursuits. There were also significant changes in the public image and self-identification of lawyers. As William Bowsma has notably argued, throughout Renaissance and Reformation Europe the law and its practitioners held a position of unprecedented cultural, as well as political and administrative, salience. Contemporaries were well aware of this phenomenon: thus Edward Waterhouse, a writer who has been claimed as England's first sociologist, celebrated "those Behemoths of learning," Thomas More, Francis Bacon, and John Selden, "all lawyers by profession" (137). Indeed, it is not entirely misleading to characterize common lawyers as cultural heroes of the late sixteenth and early seventeenth centuries. Their occupation, office, trade, profession, or craft offered unequaled opportunities for rising in the world by means of the accumulation of office, power, rank, and wealth. Not surprisingly, practitioners of the law seem to have enjoyed a high collective morale and sense of self-worth. They saw or represented themselves, and were seen by at least a significant fraction of their contemporaries, as servants of the commonweal, defenders of the ancient constitution, denizens of the third university of England, mediators between continuity and change, and upholders of order in a world of turmoil and transition (Prest 258–61, 314–22; Bowsma 316–25).

A century later things were very different. The great constitutional and political upheavals in which the common lawyers had actively participated—unsurprisingly on both sides—achieved what turned out to be a lasting resolution by the time of the Glorious Revolution of 1688–89. That settlement has also been termed "the triumph of the lawyers" because it finally secured the common law's ascendancy over rival ecclesiastical and civil codes and jurisdictions, as well as the independence of its practitioners from direct monarchical intervention of the sort practiced by both Charles II and James II (Landon). But this triumph was qualified, doing nothing to diminish, and possibly even tending to exacerbate, long-standing dissatisfactions with the common law's costs, delays, irrationalities, and uncertainties. The grumblings of country squires and urban merchants were reinforced by the rationalized prejudices of mercantilist pamphleteers and pointed up by a diverse body of commentators, satirists, and wits, elaborating countless variations on the theme that "Law is a Bottomless Pit" (Arbuthnot 1712), which inverted reason and commonsense (Brooks 44–45, 60; Lemmings, *Professors* 9–23). The burgeoning cults of civility, politeness, and the fashionable new natural philosophy were neither particularly sympathetic to nor congruent with the Gothic complexities of a far from Enlightened common law. With the worldly prospects of its practitioners apparently contracting, English economic and geopolitical expansion simultaneously opened up a variety of other highly attractive career opportunities in the army and navy, the plantations, banking, insurance, and stockbroking, as well as domestic and international trade. Small wonder in these circumstances that the Inns of Court could no longer claim to be major centers of learning and cultural creativity, let alone to provide any formal instruction in the common law.

This conjunction of circumstances helps us understand why lawyers did not make particularly attractive subjects for biographers during the first half of the eighteenth century. But the lack of legal *autobiography* remains puzzling. Of course, we are dealing in very small numbers, and it is never easy to explain instances of individual creativity or the lack thereof. Before resorting to the invocation of blind chance, however, it is worth considering that the theme of individual socioeconomic betterment through service in the public office or vocation of the bar expounded by many earlier legal autobiographers was less readily available to their potential successors for seventy years or so after 1700. Perhaps one reason why William Blackstone, via James Clitherow, could break the autobiographical drought was that he was in a position to make a plausible claim to fit the previous pattern or stereotype, thanks to the unusual trajectory of his legal career.

For Blackstone's professional life and achievements were not confined to the uncouth and arcane technicalities of common-law advocacy and pleading. His outstanding humanistic credentials as classical scholar and man of letters, won at the Charterhouse, London, then at Pembroke College, Oxford (that "nest of singing birds," according to Samuel Johnson, another famous alumnus), and finally at All Souls, gave him a cultural standing that few of his contemporaries at the bar could have matched. Indeed, it is significant that Blackstone's auto/biography plays down his attainments in what he himself had once termed the "bustling practical part" of the law (Doolittle 47), highlighting rather his initial lack of success or impact at the bar, where he gained "little notice and less practice" (Clitherow vii). Hence his life story could be presented as one of individual achievement through virtuous diligence and "Great Genius," which finally had the effect of both transcending and transforming the common law, by the compilation of "a Work" (the *Commentaries*) that would "transmit his name to Posterity among the first Class of English Authors" (Clitherow vii, xvii).

NOTES

This chapter is dedicated to the memory of Christopher Hill (1912–2003), whose teaching and writing displayed exemplary interdisciplinarity, even if he might have bridled at that term.

1. Delany read this in the 1759 Oxford edition, apparently without benefit of C. H. Firth's unscrambling of the texts in his "Clarendon's 'History of the Rebellion.'"

WORKS CITED

Arbuthnot, John. *Law Is a Bottom-Less Pit*. London: John Morphew, 1712.

Ashley, Robert. "Vita R. A. ab ipso conscripta." British Library, MS Sloane 2131, fols. 16–20. Summarized in W. D. Macray. *Register of Members of St Mary Magdalen College, Oxford*. Oxford: Oxford Historical Society, 1901. 92–97.

Bottrall, Margaret. *Every Man a Phoenix: Studies in Seventeenth-Century Auto-biography*. London: John Murray, 1958.

Bowsma, William J. "Lawyers and Early Modern Culture." *American Histori-cal Review* 78 (1973): 303–27.

[Bramston, John]. *The Autobiography of Sir John Bramston, K.B., of Skreens, in the Hundred of Chelmsford*. Ed. P. Braybrooke. London: Camden Society, 1840.

Brooks, Christopher. *Lawyers, Litigation, and English Society since 1450*. Lon-don: Hambledon, 1998.

Bruce, John. *Liber Famelicus of Sir James Whitelocke, A Judge of the Court of King's Bench in the Reigns of James I, and Charles I, Now First Published from the Original Manuscript*. Ed. J. Bruce. London: Camden Society, 1858.

Clay, J. W., and J. Lister. "The Autobiography of Sir John Savile of Methley, Knight, Baron of the Exchequer, 1546–1607." *Yorkshire Archaeological Journal* 15 (1898–1900): 420–27.

[Clitherow, James]. *Reports of Cases Determined in the Several Courts of West-minster-Hall, from 1746 to 1779 . . . by the Honourable Sir William Blackstone . . .* Vol. 1. London: W. Strahan, T. Cadell, and D. Prince, 1781.

Delany, Paul. *British Autobiography in the Seventeenth Century*. London: Rout-ledge and Kegan Paul, 1969.

Doolittle, Ian. *William Blackstone: A Biography*. Haslemere: Privately printed, 2001.

Duman, Daniel. *The Judicial Bench in England, 1727–1875: The Reshaping of a Professional Elite*. London: Royal Historical Society, 1982.

Firth, Charles H. "Clarendon's History of the Rebellion." *English Historical Review* 19 (1904): 26–54, 246–62, 464–83.

Greene, Donald. "A Reading Course in Autobiography." *Essays in Eighteenth-Century Biography*. Ed. Philip B. Daghlian. Bloomington: Indiana UP, 1968.

Hutton, Richard. *The Diary of Sir Richard Hutton, 1614–1639, with Related Texts*. Ed. Wilfrid Prest. London: Selden Society, 1991.

Hyde, Edward, Earl of Clarendon. *The Life of Edward, Earl of Clarendon*. Oxford: Clarendon, 1759.

Landon, Michael. *The Triumph of the Lawyers: Their Role in English Politics, 1678–1689*. University: U of Alabama P, 1970.

Lemmings, David. *Gentlemen and Barristers: The Inns of Court and the English Bar, 1680–1730.* Oxford: Clarendon, 1990.

———. *Professors of the Law: Barristers and English Legal Culture in the Eighteenth Century.* Oxford: Clarendon, 2000.

Mascuch, Michael. *Origins of the Individualist Self: Autobiography and Self-Identity in England, 1591–1791.* Cambridge: Polity, 1997.

Millard, Peter. *Notes of Me: The Autobiography of Roger North.* Ed. P. Millard. Toronto: U of Toronto P, 2000.

North, Roger. *The Autobiography of Roger North.* Ed. Augustus Jessopp. London: Bohn's Standard Library, 1887.

Pagitt, Justinian. British Library, MS Harley 1026, "Memorandum Book of Justinian Pagitt."

Pargellis, Stanley, and D. J. Medley. *Bibliography of British History: The Eighteenth Century, 1714–1789.* Oxford: Oxford UP, 1951.

Phillips, Colin B. *Lowther Family Estate Books, 1617–1675.* Ed. C. B. Phillips. Durham: Surtees Society, 1979.

Powell, Damian X. *Sir James Whitelocke's Liber Famelicus, 1570–1632: Law and Politics in Early Stuart England.* New York: Lang, 2000.

Prest, Wilfrid. *The Rise of the Barristers: A Social History of the English Bar, 1590–1640.* Oxford: Clarendon, 1991.

Rokeby, Ralph. *Oeconomia Rokebeiorum.* British Library, MS Additional 24470, fols. 294–333. *A History of Richmondshire.* Vol. 1. Ed. Thomas Dunham Whitaker. London: Longman, 1823. 158–80.

Shapiro, Barbara J. *A Culture of Fact: England, 1550–1720.* Ithaca: Cornell UP, 2000.

Sharpe, Kevin. *Remapping Early Modern England: The Culture of Seventeenth-Century Politics.* Cambridge: Cambridge UP, 2000.

Spalding, Ruth. *The Diary of Bulstrode Whitelocke, 1605–1675.* London: British Academy, 1990.

Stauffer, Donald A. *The Art of Biography in the Eighteenth Century.* 2 vols. Princeton: Princeton UP, 1941.

Waterhouse, Edward. *A Discourse and Defence of Arms and Armory.* London: T. R. for Samuel Mearns, 1660.

Whitaker, Thomas Dunham. *A History of Richmondshire, in the North Riding of the County of York.* 2 vols. London: Longman, 1823.

Contributors

*

About the Editors

The editors will follow the publication of this collection with *Early Modern English Lives: Autobiography and Self-Representation, 1500–1660*, a jointly authored study of early modern autobiographical practice (Ashgate, 2006).

Individual Authors

RONALD BEDFORD teaches in the School of English, Communication and Theatre at the University of New England in Armidale, Australia. He studied at Cambridge University and has taught at the universities of Cambridge, Giessen (Germany), and Exeter (United Kingdom). In addition to many journal articles, reviews, and bibliographic works on sixteenth- and seventeenth-century literature and drama, especially on Milton, he is the author of *The Defence of Truth: Herbert of Cherbury and the Seventeenth Century* (1979) *and Dialogues with Convention: Readings in Renaissance Poetry* (1989).

CONAL CONDREN is Scientia Professor at the University of New South Wales. He has written several works on early modern political theory and the philosophy of historical interpretation, including *George Lawson's 'Politica' and the English Revolution* (1999/2002), *The Language of Politics in Seventeenth-Century England* (1994), and *Thomas Hobbes,* (2000). *Satire, Lies, and Politics: The Case of Dr. Arbuth-*

not was published in 1997. His study of officeholding in seventeenth-century England, *Argument and Authority in Early Modern England*, is forthcoming from Cambridge University Press.

LLOYD DAVIS, who died in August 2005, was Reader in the School of English at the University of Queensland in Brisbane. He studied at the University of Sydney and the City University of New York. He was the author of many essays and books on cultural studies and Victorian and early modern literature, including *Guise and Disguise: Rhetoric and Characterization in the English Renaissance* (1993). He was the editor *of Sexuality and Gender in the English Renaissance: An Annotated Edition of Contemporary Documents* (1998) and *Shakespeare Matters: History, Teaching, Performance* (2003). He was a past editor of *AUMLA*, the journal of the Australasian Universities' Languages and Literature Association.

HELEN FULTON was for many years based in the School of English at the University of Sydney and has recently taken up a Chair of English at the University of Wales, Swansea. Her research interests include medieval literatures and languages, as well as discourse, narrative, and other aspects of cultural theory. She teaches Middle Welsh and Old Irish, among other things, and has published widely on medieval English and Welsh texts. She is currently completing *The Medieval Town Imagined: Representations of Urban Culture in Medieval British Literature*, a book on the representation of towns in medieval literature, funded by an Australian Research Council Discovery Project grant.

PETER GOODALL is currently Acting Dean of Humanities at Macquarie University in Sydney and the editor of *AUMLA*, the journal of the Australasian Universities' Languages and Literature Association. His research interests are divided between medieval English literature, especially Chaucer, and twentieth-century British cultural history and literature, especially George Orwell. He is the author of articles in both areas and of the book *High Culture, Popular Culture: The Long Debate* (1995). His annotated bibliography of Chaucer's *Monks' Tale* and *Nun's Priest's Tale* is forthcoming in 2006. He has a long-term interest in the literary and cultural history of privacy and private life.

JEAN E. HOWARD is William E. Ransford Professor of English at Columbia University. She is the author of *Shakespeare's Art of Orchestration: Stagecraft and Audience Response* (1984), *The Stage and Social*

Struggle in Early Modern England (1994), and, with Phyllis Rackin, *Engendering a Nation: A Feminist Reading of Shakespeare's English Histories* (1997). She is also one of the four editors of *The Norton Shakespeare* (1997) and general editor of the Bedford Contextual editions of Shakespeare. She has just finished a new book entitled *Theater of a City,* about London comedies in the first half of the seventeenth century.

PHILIPPA KELLY is Senior Research Fellow at the University of New South Wales. She has published a monograph, *King Lear* (1993), and an edition of the play (2000) and was the Australian contributor for the Cambridge University Press's *King Lear* CD-ROM (2000). In 2002, she edited *The Touch of the Real: Essays in Early Modern Culture.* Besides early modern autobiography, her research interests include the teaching of Shakespeare in locked facilities, feminist performance theory, analyses of the mirror in early modern English texts, and Australian literature. Her most recent articles have been published in *Renaissance Drama* (2004), *Shakespeare Yearbook* (2004), and *Theatre Journal* (2005).

ADRIAN MITCHELL is Head of the School of English, Art History, Film and Media at the University of Sydney. He has published extensively on Australian literature, including editions, anthologies, monographs, and articles, and is coeditor *of The Oxford Anthology of Australian Literature* (1985) and *New Directions in Australian Studies* (2000). In recent years, his research interests have become increasingly directed toward the literature of travel as encounter. He is currently completing a book on the writings of William Dampier.

WILFRID PREST was born in Melbourne. He studied history at the University of Melbourne and wrote his Oxford doctoral thesis as a student of Christopher Hill. He is the author of *Albion Ascendant: English History, 1660–1815* (1998) and is an Australian Research Council Professorial Research Fellow at the University of Adelaide, where he is writing a biography of William Blackstone.

DOSIA REICHARDT studied at the University of York (United Kingdom); the University of New England, New South Wales; and James Cook University, Queensland. She teaches English literature at the Cairns campus of James Cook University. Her research interests and publications have focused on Richard Lovelace and the "grunge" poetry and culture of the seventeenth century. Her most recent publication is "Their Faces Are Not Their Own: Powders, Patches, and Paint in Seventeenth-Century Poetry," *Dalhousie Review* 82.4 (2004). She is also editor of the journal *LiNQ* (*Literature in North Queensland*).

ANNE M. SCOTT is Postdoctoral Research Fellow in English, Communication and Cultural Studies at the University of Western Australia. Her field of research is fourteenth-century English literature, and she has recently published a monograph entitled *Piers Plowman and the Poor* (2004). Current research topics include the iconography and representations of poverty in fourteenth-century literature and art.

LIAM. E. SEMLER teaches early modern literature and culture in the English Department, University of Sydney. He is author of *The English Mannerist Poets and the Visual Arts* (1998) and the editor of both critical and facsimile editions of *Eliza's Babes* (2001, 2003). He is currently working on a study of the grotesque in Tudor and Stuart times.

BELINDA TIFFEN graduated from the University of New England in 2002 with a Ph.D. on the work of Sir John Suckling. Since then, she has completed a graduate diploma in information studies at Curtin University and a masters degree in cultural heritage at Deakin University. She is currently working at the National Library of Australia.

R. S. WHITE is Professor of English, Communication and Cultural Studies at the University of Western Australia. He has published many books, articles, and essays on Shakespeare, including *Innocent Victims: Poetic Injustice in Shakespearean Tragedy* and *Keats as a Reader of Shakespeare*. His *Natural Law in English Renaissance Literature* (1996) has led to a sequel, *Natural Rights and the Birth of Romanticism in the 1790s* (2005). He is now writing a book on pacifism and literature.

HELEN WILCOX, after many years as Professor of English Literature at the University of Groningen, has moved to a chair at the University of Wales, Bangor. Professor Wilcox has published numerous books and papers on early modern texts, including devotional poetry, autobiography, women's writing, Shakespearian tragicomedy and literature and music. Her work on autobiography includes *Her Own Life: Autobiographical Writings by Seventeenth-Century English-women* (1989) and *Betraying Our Selves: Forms of Self-Representation in Early Modern English Texts* (2000), as well as an edited collection, *Women and Literature in Britain, 1500–1700* (1996). Her many chapters in books include "Literature and the Household," in *The Cambridge History of Early Modern Literature* (2003); and "A Wife and Lady Oneself: Maturity and Memory in the Diaries of Lady Anne Clifford," in *The Prime of Their Lives: Wise Old Women of Medieval and Early Modern Europe* (2005).

NANCY E. WRIGHT is Director of the Centre for the Interdisciplinary Study of Property Rights at the University of Newcastle, Australia. Her research focuses on the property rights of women in seventeenth-century England and nineteenth-century Australia. Her recent publications include *Women, Property, and the Letters of the Law in Early Modern England* (2004) and *Despotic Dominion: Property Rights in British Settler Societies* (2005).

Index

*